FEDERAL RULES OF EVIDENCE

and Excerpts from the California Evidence Code and Uniform Rules of Evidence

2026-2027

I0894923

FEDERAL RULES OF EVIDENCE

and Excerpts from the California Evidence Code and Uniform Rules of Evidence

2026-2027

LAURIE L. LEVENSON

Professor of Law and David W. Burcham Chair in Ethical Advocacy
Loyola Law School

HON. BRIAN M. HOFFSTADT

Presiding Justice, Division Five, Second Appellate District,
California Court of Appeal

ASPEN
PUBLISHING

To contact Customer Service, e-mail customer.service@aspenpublishing.com, call 1-800-950-5259, or mail correspondence to:

Aspen Publishing
Attn: Order Department
1 Wall Street
Burlington, MA 01803

1 2 3 4 5 6 7 8 9 0

ISBN 979-8-8996-3927-2

ABOUT ASPEN PUBLISHING

Aspen Publishing is a leading provider of legal education content and digital learning solutions in the United States and globally. Our innovative products and platforms—designed based on best practices in learning science—engage students and enhance outcomes. From textbooks and audiobooks authored by renowned experts to digital platforms and products like LEAF, Connected eBooks, Connected Quizzing, PracticePerfect, and JD-Next, we empower the next generation of legal professionals with innovative, trusted, and accessible resources.

The Aspen Casebook Series, affectionately known as the "red and black" casebooks among law faculty and students, includes hundreds of highly regarded textbooks across more than 80 disciplines. These range from foundational courses like Torts and Contracts to emerging electives such as Sustainability and the Law of Policing. Our study aids, including the popular *Examples & Explanations* series, help law students master complex topics with clarity and confidence.

Aspen's expertise extends to undergraduate education with our Paralegal, Criminal Justice, and Business Law series, offering the same hallmark quality to a broader audience. JD-Next, our groundbreaking online law school prep course and admissions test, provides a realistic preview of law school, equips students with essential skills for academic success, and evaluates their readiness for legal studies.

Aspen Publishing Is Proud to Be a UWorld Company

Since 2003, UWorld has been a global leader in developing high-quality learning tools for students preparing for high-stakes exams. With a commitment to excellence, UWorld has helped millions of students in undergraduate, graduate, and professional programs in fields such as medicine, nursing, finance, and law achieve their academic and career goals.

Founded by Chandra S. Pemmasani, M.D., during his medical residency, UWorld began focusing on medical education and has since expanded into various academic fields, including law. In 2020, UWorld launched its Legal vertical, starting with its comprehensive Multistate Bar Exam (MBE®) Question Bank, followed by the acquisition of Themis Bar Review, which integrated resources to provide a complete bar exam preparation experience. In 2024, UWorld expanded its offerings by acquiring Aspen Publishing, enhancing its suite of legal education products.

Today, UWorld offers an unparalleled range of study materials that blend active learning methods with expert content, ensuring students and educators can access the most effective resources. From bar preparation to law school success, UWorld is committed to supporting the next generation of legal professionals. Learn more at uworld.com.

SUMMARY OF CONTENTS

If amendments to the law of evidence are codified and take effect prior to the next edition of this supplement, the amendments will be available under "Professor Materials" and "Student Materials" on the product page at aspenpublishing.com.

CONTENTS

CONTENTS

Part 1

FEDERAL RULES OF EVIDENCE

ARTICLE I. GENERAL PROVISIONS

RULE 101. SCOPE; DEFINITIONS

(a) Scope. These rules apply to proceedings in United States courts. The specific courts and proceedings to which the rules apply, along with exceptions, are set out in Rule 1101.

(b) Definitions. In these rules:

(1) "civil case" means a civil action or proceeding;

(2) "criminal case" includes a criminal proceeding;

(3) "public office" includes a public agency;

(4) "record" includes a memorandum, report, or data compilation;

(5) a "rule prescribed by the Supreme Court" means a rule adopted by the Supreme Court under statutory authority; and

(6) a reference to any kind of written material or any other medium includes electronically stored information.

RULE 102. PURPOSE

These rules should be construed so as to administer every proceeding fairly, eliminate unjustifiable expense and delay, and promote the development of evidence law, to the end of ascertaining the truth and securing a just determination.

RULE 103. RULINGS ON EVIDENCE

(a) Preserving a Claim of Error. A party may claim error in a ruling to admit or exclude evidence only if the error affects a substantial right of the party and:

(1) if the ruling admits evidence, a party, on the record:

(A) timely objects or moves to strike; and

(B) states the specific ground, unless it was apparent from the context; or

(2) if the ruling excludes evidence, a party informs the court of its substance by an offer of proof, unless the substance was apparent from the context.

(b) Not Needing to Renew an Objection or Offer of Proof. Once the court rules definitively on the record—either before or at trial—a party need not renew an objection or offer of proof to preserve a claim of error for appeal.

(c) Court's Statement About the Ruling; Directing an Offer of Proof. The court may make any statement about the character or form of the evidence, the objection made, and the ruling. The court may direct that an offer of proof be made in question-and-answer form.

(d) Preventing the Jury from Hearing Inadmissible Evidence. To the extent practicable, the court must conduct a jury trial so that inadmissible evidence is not suggested to the jury by any means.

(e) Taking Notice of Plain Error. A court may take notice of a plain error affecting a substantial right, even if the claim of error was not properly preserved.

RULE 104. PRELIMINARY QUESTIONS

(a) In General. The court must decide any preliminary question about whether a witness is qualified, a privilege exists, or evidence is admissible. In so deciding, the court is not bound by evidence rules, except those on privilege.

(b) Relevance That Depends on a Fact. When the relevance of evidence depends on whether a fact exists, proof must be introduced sufficient to support a finding that the fact does exist. The court may admit the proposed evidence on the condition that the proof be introduced later.

(c) Conducting a Hearing So That the Jury Cannot Hear It. The court must conduct any hearing on a preliminary question so that the jury cannot hear it if:

(1) the hearing involves the admissibility of a confession;

(2) a defendant in a criminal case is a witness and so requests; or
(3) justice so requires.

(d) Cross-Examining a Defendant in a Criminal Case. By testifying on a preliminary question, a defendant in a criminal case does not become subject to cross-examination on other issues in the case.

(e) Evidence Relevant to Weight and Credibility. This rule does not limit a party's right to introduce before the jury evidence that is relevant to the weight or credibility of other evidence.

RULE 105. LIMITING EVIDENCE THAT IS NOT ADMISSIBLE AGAINST OTHER PARTIES OR FOR OTHER PURPOSES

If the court admits evidence that is admissible against a party or for a purpose—but not against another party or for another purpose—the court, on timely request, must restrict the evidence to its proper scope and instruct the jury accordingly.

RULE 106. REMAINDER OF OR RELATED WRITINGS OR RECORDED STATEMENTS

If a party introduces all or part of a statement, an adverse party may require the introduction, at that time, of any other part—or any other statement—that in fairness ought to be considered at the same time. The adverse party may do so over a hearsay objection.

Author's Note: *The main difference between the pre-2023 and the current version of FRE 106 is the forms of statement it covers. The current rule, effective December 1, 2023 and set forth above, was amended to cover all "statements," including unrecorded oral statements, and explicitly allows for the admission of necessary completing evidence over a hearsay objection. The pre-2023 rule was textually restricted to only writings and recorded statements. It did not, by its plain language, directly cover unrecorded oral statements.*

RULE 107. ILLUSTRATIVE AIDS

(a) Permitted Uses. The court may allow a party to present an illustrative aid to help the trier of fact understand the evidence or argument if the aid's utility in assisting comprehension is not substantially outweigh by the danger of unfair prejudice, confusing the issues, misleading the jury, undue delay, or wasting time.

(b) Use in Jury Deliberations. An illustrative aid is not evidence and must not be provided to the jury during deliberations unless:

(1) all parties consent; or

(2) the court, for good cause, orders otherwise.

(c) Record. When practicable, an illustrative aid used at trial must be entered into the record.

(d) Summaries of Voluminous Materials Admitted as Evidence. A summary, chart, or calculation admitted as evidence to prove the content of voluminous admissible evidence is governed by Rule 1006.

ARTICLE II. JUDICIAL NOTICE

RULE 201. JUDICIAL NOTICE OF ADJUDICATIVE FACTS

(a) Scope. This rule governs judicial notice of an adjudicative fact only, not a legislative fact.

(b) Kinds of Facts That May Be Judicially Noticed. The court may judicially notice a fact that is not subject to reasonable dispute because it:

(1) is generally known within the trial court's territorial jurisdiction; or

(2) can be accurately and readily determined from sources whose accuracy cannot reasonably be questioned.

(c) Taking Notice. The court:

(1) may take judicial notice on its own; or

(2) must take judicial notice if a party requests it and the court is supplied with the necessary information.

(d) Timing. The court may take judicial notice at any stage of the proceeding.

(e) Opportunity to Be Heard. On timely request, a party is entitled to be heard on the propriety of taking judicial notice and the nature of the fact to be noticed. If the court takes judicial notice before notifying a party, the party, on request, is still entitled to be heard.

(f) Instructing the Jury. In a civil case, the court must instruct the jury to accept the noticed fact as conclusive. In a criminal case, the court must instruct the jury that it may or may not accept the noticed fact as conclusive.

NOTES OF ADVISORY COMMITTEE ON PROPOSED RULES (1973)

Subdivision (a). This is the only evidence rule on the subject of judicial notice. It deals only with judicial notice of "adjudicative" facts. No rule deals with judicial notice of "legislative" facts. Judicial notice of matters of foreign law is treated in Rule 44.1 of the Federal Rules of Civil Procedure and Rule 26.1 of the Federal Rules of Criminal Procedure.

The omission of any treatment of legislative facts results from fundamental differences between adjudicative facts and legislative facts. Adjudicative facts are simply the facts of the particular case. Legislative facts, on the other hand, are those which have relevance to legal reasoning and the lawmaking process, whether in the formulation of a legal principle or ruling by a judge or court or in the enactment of a legislative body. The terminology was coined by Professor Kenneth Davis in his article An Approach to Problems of Evidence in the Administrative Process, 55 Harv. L. Rev. 364, 404–407 (1942). The following discussion draws extensively upon his writings. In addition, see the same author's Judicial Notice, 55 Colum. L. Rev. 945 (1955); Administrative Law Treatise, ch. 15 (1958); A System of Judicial Notice Based on Fairness and Convenience, in Perspectives of Law 69 (1964).

The usual method of establishing adjudicative facts i[s] through the introduction of evidence, ordinarily consisting of the testimony of witnesses. If particular facts are outside of reasonable controversy, this process is dispensed with as unnecessary. A high degree of indisputability is the essential prerequisite.

Legislative facts are quite different. As Professor Davis says:

"My opinion is that judge-made law would stop growing if judges, in thinking about questions of law and policy, were forbidden to take into account the facts they believe, as distinguished from facts which are 'clearly * * * within the domain of the indisputable.' Facts most needed in thinking about difficult problems of law and policy have a way of being outside the domain of the clearly indisputable." A System of Judicial Notice Based on Fairness and Convenience, *supra,* at 82.

An illustration is *Hawkins v. United States,* 358 U.S. 74, 79 S.Ct. 136, 3 L.Ed.2d 125 (1958), in which the Court refused to discard the common law rule that one spouse could not testify against the other, saying, "Adverse testimony given in criminal proceedings would, we think, be likely to destroy almost any marriage." This conclusion has a large intermixture of fact, but the factual aspect is scarcely "indisputable." See Hutchins and Slesinger,

Some Observations on the Law of Evidence—Family Relations, 13 Minn. L. Rev. 675 (1929). If the destructive effect of the giving of adverse testimony by a spouse is not indisputable, should the Court have refrained from considering it in the absence of supporting evidence?

"If the Model Code or the Uniform Rules had been applicable, the Court would have been barred from thinking about the essential factual ingredient of the problems before it, and such a result would be obviously intolerable. What the law needs as its growing points is more, not less, judicial thinking about the factual ingredients of problems of what the law ought to be, and the needed facts are seldom 'clearly' indisputable." Davis, *supra,* at 83.

Professor Morgan gave the following description of the methodology of determining domestic law:

"In determining the content or applicability of a rule of domestic law, the judge is unrestricted in his investigation and conclusion. He may reject the propositions of either party or of both parties. He may consult the sources of pertinent data to which they refer, or he may refuse to do so. He may make an independent search for persuasive data or rest content with what he has or what the parties present. * * * [T]he parties do no more than to assist; they control no part of the process." Morgan, Judicial Notice, 57 Harv.L.Rev. 269, 270–271 (1944).

This is the view which should govern judicial access to legislative facts. It renders inappropriate any limitation in the form of indisputability, any formal requirements of notice other than those already inherent in affording opportunity to hear and be heard and exchanging briefs, and any requirement of formal findings at any level. It should, however, leave open the possibility of introducing evidence through regular channels in appropriate situations. See *Borden's Farm Products Co. v. Baldwin,* 293 U.S. 194, 55 S.Ct. 187, 79 L.Ed. 281 (1934), where the cause was remanded for the taking of evidence as to the economic conditions and trade practices underlying the New York Milk Control Law.

Similar considerations govern the judicial use of nonadjudicative facts in ways other than formulating laws and rules. Thayer described them as a part of the judicial reasoning process.

"In conducting a process of judicial reasoning, as of other reasoning, not a step can be taken without assuming something which has not been proved; and the capacity to do this with competent judgement and efficiency, is imputed to judges and juries as part of their necessary mental outfit." Thayer, Preliminary Treatise on Evidence 279–280 (1898).

As Professor Davis points out, A System of Judicial Notice Based on Fairness and Convenience, in Perspectives of Law 69, 73 (1964), every case involves the use of hundreds or thousands of non-evidence facts. When a witness in an automobile accident case says "car," everyone, judge and jury included, furnishes, from non-evidence sources within himself, the supplementing information that the "car" is an automobile, not a railroad car, that it is self-propelled, probably by an internal combustion engine, that it may be assumed to have four wheels with pneumatic rubber tires, and so on. The judicial process cannot construct every case from scratch, like Descartes creating a world based on the postulate *Cogito, ergo sum.* These items could not possibly be introduced into evidence, and no one suggests that they be. Nor are they appropriate subjects for any formalized treatment of judicial notice of facts. See Levin and Levy, Persuading the Jury with Facts Not in Evidence: The Fiction-Science Spectrum, 105 U. Pa.L.Rev. 139 (1956).

Another aspect of what Thayer had in mind is the use of non-evidence facts to appraise or assess the adjudicative facts of the case. Pairs of cases from two jurisdictions illustrate this use and also the difference between non-evidence facts thus used and adjudicative facts. In *People v. Strook,* 347 Ill. 460, 179 N.E. 821 (1932), venue in Cook County had been held not established by testimony that the crime was committed at 7956 South Chicago Avenue, since judicial notice would not be taken that the address was in Chicago. However, the same court subsequently ruled that venue in Cook County was established by testimony that a crime occurred at 8900 South Anthony Avenue, since notice would be taken of the common practice of omitting the name of the city when speaking of local addresses, and the witness was testifying in Chicago. *People v. Pride,* 16 Ill.2d 82, 156 N.E.2d 551 (1951). And in *Hughes v. Vestal,* 264 N.C. 500, 142 S.E.2d 361 (1965), the Supreme Court of North Carolina disapproved the trial judge's admission in evidence of a state-published table of automobile stopping distances on the basis of judicial notice, though the court itself had referred to the same table in an earlier case in a "rhetorical and illustrative" way in determining that the defendant could not have stopped her car in time to avoid striking a child who suddenly appeared in the highway and that a non-suit was properly granted. *Ennis v. Dupree,* 262 N.C. 224, 136 S.E.2d 702 (1964). See also *Brown v. Hale,* 263 N.C. 176, 139 S.E.2d 210 (1964); *Clayton v. Rimmer,* 262 N.C. 302, 136 S.E.2d 562 (1964). It is apparent that this use of non-evidence facts in evaluating the adjudicative facts of the case is not an appropriate subject for a formalized judicial notice treatment.

In view of these considerations, the regulation of judicial notice of facts by the present rule extends only to adjudicative facts.

What, then, are "adjudicative" facts? Davis refers to them as those "which relate to the parties," or more fully:

"When a court or an agency finds facts concerning the immediate parties—who did what, where, when, how, and with what motive or intent—the court or agency is performing an adjudicative function, and the facts are conveniently called adjudicative facts. * * *

"Stated in other terms, the adjudicative facts are those to which the law is applied in the process of adjudication. They are the facts that normally go to the jury in a jury case. They relate to the parties, their activities, their properties, their businesses." 2 Administrative Law Treatise 353.

Subdivision (b). With respect to judicial notice of adjudicative facts, the tradition has been one of caution in requiring that the matter be beyond reasonable controversy. This tradition of circumspection appears to be soundly based, and no reason to depart from it is apparent. As Professor Davis says:

"The reason we use trial-type procedure, I think, is that we make the practical judgement, on the basis of experience, that taking evidence, subject to cross-examination and rebuttal, is the best way to resolve controversies involving disputes of adjudicative facts, that is, facts pertaining to the parties. The reason we require a determination on the record is that we think fair procedure in resolving disputes of adjudicative facts calls for giving each party a chance to meet in the appropriate fashion the facts that come to the tribunal's attention, and the appropriate fashion for meeting disputed adjudicative facts includes rebuttal evidence, cross-examination, usually confrontation, and argument (either written or oral or both). The key to a fair trial is opportunity to use the appropriate weapons (rebuttal evidence, cross-examination, and argument) to meet adverse materials that come to the tribunal's attention." A System of Judicial Notice Based on Fairness and Convenience, in Perspectives of Law 69, 93 (1964).

The rule proceeds upon the theory that these considerations call for dispensing with traditional methods of proof only in clear cases. Compare Professor Davis' conclusion that judicial notice should be a matter of convenience, subject to requirements of procedural fairness. *Id.*, 94.

This rule is consistent with Uniform Rule 9(1) and (2) which limit judicial notice of facts to those "so universally known that they cannot reasonably be the subject of dispute," those "so generally known or of such common notoriety within the territorial jurisdiction of the court that they cannot reasonably be the subject of dispute," and those "capable of immediate and accurate determination by resort to easily accessible sources of indisputable accuracy." The traditional textbook treatment has included these general categories (matters of common knowledge, facts capable of verification), McCormick §§324, 325, and then has passed on into detailed treatment of such specific topics as facts relating to the personnel and records of the court, *Id.* §327, and other governmental facts, *Id.* §328. The California draftsmen, with a background of detailed statutory regulation of judicial notice, followed a somewhat similar pattern. California Evidence Code §§451, 452. The Uniform Rules, however, were drafted on the theory that these particular matters are included within the general categories and need no specific mention. This approach is followed in the present rule.

The phrase "propositions of generalized knowledge," found in Uniform Rule 9(1) and (2) is not included in the present rule. It was, it is believed, originally included in Model Code Rules 801 and 802 primarily in order to afford some minimum recognition to the right of the judge in his "legislative" capacity (not acting as the trier of fact) to take judicial notice of very limited categories of generalized knowledge. The limitations thus imposed have been discarded herein as undesirable, unworkable, and contrary to existing practice. What is left, then, to be considered, is the status of a "proposition of generalized knowledge" as an "adjudicative" fact to be noticed judicially and communicated by the judge to the jury. Thus viewed, it is considered to be lacking practical significance. While judges use judicial notice of "propositions of generalized knowledge" in a variety of situations: determining the validity and meaning of statutes, formulating common law rules, deciding whether evidence should be admitted, assessing the sufficiency and effect of evidence, all are essentially nonadjudicative in nature. When judicial notice is seen as a significant vehicle for progress in the law, these are the areas involved, particularly in developing fields of scientific knowledge. See McCormick 712. It is not believed that judges now instruct juries as to "propositions of generalized knowledge" derived from encyclopedias or other sources, or that they are likely to do so, or, indeed, that it is desirable that they do so. There is a vast difference between ruling on the basis of judicial notice that radar evidence of speed is admissible and explaining to the jury its principles and degree of accuracy, or between using a table of stopping distances of automobiles at various speeds in a judicial evaluation of testimony and telling the jury its precise application in the case. For cases raising doubt as to the propriety of the use of medical texts by lay triers of fact in passing on disability claims in administrative proceedings, see *Sayers v. Gardner*, 380 F.2d 940 (6th Cir. 1967); *Ross v. Gardner*, 365 F.2d 554 (6th Cir. 1966); *Sosna v. Celebrezze*, 234 F. Supp. 289 (E.D.Pa. 1964); *Glendenning v. Ribicoff*, 213 F.Supp. 301 (W.D.Mo. 1962).

Subdivisions (c) and (d). Under subdivision (c) the judge has a discretionary authority to take judicial notice, regardless of whether he is so requested by a party. The taking of judicial notice is mandatory, under subdivision (d), only when a party requests it and the necessary information is supplied. This scheme is believed to reflect existing practice. It is simple and workable. It avoids troublesome distinctions in the many situations in which the process of taking judicial notice is not recognized as such.

Compare Uniform Rule 9 making judicial notice of facts universally known mandatory without request, and making judicial notice of facts generally known in the jurisdiction or capable of determination by resort to accurate sources discretionary in the absence of request but mandatory if request is made and the information furnished. But see Uniform Rule 10(3), which directs the judge to decline to take judicial notice if available information fails to convince him that the matter falls clearly within Uniform Rule 9 or is insufficient to enable him to notice it judicially.

Substantially the same approach is found in California Evidence Code §§451–453 and in New Jersey Evidence Rule 9. In contrast, the present rule treats alike all adjudicative facts which are subject to judicial notice.

Subdivision (e). Basic considerations of procedural fairness demand an opportunity to be heard on the propriety of taking judicial notice and the tenor of the matter noticed. The rule requires the granting of that opportunity upon request. No formal scheme of giving notice is provided. An adversely affected party may learn in advance that judicial notice is in contemplation, either by virtue of being served with a copy of a request by another party under subdivision (d) that judicial notice be taken, or through an advance indication by the judge. Or he may have no advance notice at all. The likelihood of the latter is enhanced by the frequent failure to recognize judicial notice as such. And in the absence of advance notice, a request made after the fact could not in fairness be considered untimely. See the provision for hearing on timely request in the Administrative Procedure Act, 5 U.S.C. §556(e). See also Revised Model State Administrative Procedure Act (1961), 9C U.L.A. §10(4) (Supp. 1967).

Subdivision (f). In accord with the usual view, judicial notice may be taken at any stage of the proceedings, whether in the trial court or on appeal. Uniform Rule 12; California Evidence Code §459; Kansas Rules of Evidence §60–412; New Jersey Evidence Rule 12; McCormick §330, p. 712.

Subdivision (g). Much of the controversy about judicial notice has centered upon the question whether evidence should be admitted in disproof of facts of which judicial notice is taken.

The writers have been divided. Favoring admissibility are Thayer, Preliminary Treatise on Evidence 308 (1898); 9 Wigmore §2567; Davis, A System of Judicial Notice Based on Fairness and Convenience, in Perspectives of Law, 69, 76–77 (1964). Opposing admissibility are Keeffe, Landis and Shaad, Sense and Nonsense about Judicial Notice, 2 Stan.L.Rev. 664, 668 (1950); McNaughton, Judicial Notice—Excerpts Relating to the Morgan-Whitmore Controversy, 14 Vand.L.Rev. 779 (1961); Morgan, Judicial Notice, 57 Harv.L.Rev. 269, 279 (1944); McCormick 710–711. The Model Code and the Uniform Rules are predicated upon [the] indisputability of judicially noticed facts.

The proponents of admitting evidence in disproof have concentrated largely upon legislative facts. Since the present rule deals only with judicial notice of adjudicative facts, arguments directed to legislative facts lose their relevancy.

Within its relatively narrow area of adjudicative facts, the rule contemplates there is to be no evidence before the jury in disproof. The judge instructs the jury to take judicially noticed facts as established. This position is justified by the undesirable effects of the opposite rule in limiting the rebutting party, though not his opponent, to admissible evidence, in defeating the reasons for judicial notice, and in affecting the substantive law to an extent and in ways largely unforeseeable. Ample protection and flexibility are afforded by the broad provision for opportunity to be heard on request, set forth in subdivision (e).

Authority upon the propriety of taking judicial notice against an accused in a criminal case with respect to matters other than venue is relatively meager. Proceeding upon the theory that the right of jury trial does not extend to matters which are beyond reasonable dispute, the rule does not distinguish between criminal and civil cases. *People v. Mayes,* 113 Cal. 618, 45 P. 860 (1896); *Ross v. United States,* 374 F.2d 97 (8th Cir. 1967). Cf. *State v. Main,* 94 R.I. 338, 180 A.2d 814 (1962); *State v. Lawrence,* 120 Utah 323, 234 P.2d 600 (1951).

Note on Judicial Notice of Law. By rules effective July 1, 1966, the method of invoking the law of a foreign country is covered elsewhere. Rule 44.1 of the Federal Rules of Civil Procedure; Rule 26.1 of the Federal Rules of Criminal Procedure. These two new admirably designed rules are founded upon the assumption that the manner in which law is fed into the judicial process is never a proper concern of the rules of evidence but rather of the rules of procedure. The Advisory Committee on Evidence, believing that this assumption is entirely correct, proposes no evidence rule with respect to judicial notice of law, and suggests that those matters of law which, in addition to foreign-country law, have traditionally been treated as requiring pleading and proof and more recently as the subject of judicial notice be left to the Rules of Civil and Criminal Procedure.

ARTICLE III. PRESUMPTIONS IN CIVIL CASES

RULE 301. PRESUMPTIONS IN CIVIL CASES GENERALLY

In a civil case, unless a federal statute or these rules provide otherwise, the party against whom a presumption is directed has the burden of producing evidence to rebut the presumption. But this rule does not shift the burden of persuasion, which remains on the party who had it originally.

RULE 302. APPLYING STATE LAW TO PRESUMPTIONS IN CIVIL CASES

In a civil case, state law governs the effect of a presumption regarding a claim or defense for which state law supplies the rule of decision.

ARTICLE IV. RELEVANCE AND ITS LIMITS

RULE 401. TEST FOR RELEVANT EVIDENCE

Evidence is relevant if:

(a) it has any tendency to make a fact more or less probable than it would be without the evidence; and

(b) the fact is of consequence in determining the action.

NOTES OF ADVISORY COMMITTEE ON PROPOSED RULES (1973)

Problems of relevancy call for an answer to the question whether an item of evidence, when tested by the processes of legal reasoning, possesses sufficient probative value to justify receiving it in evidence. Thus, assessment of the probative value of evidence that a person purchased a revolver shortly prior to a fatal shooting with which he is charged is a matter of analysis and reasoning.

The variety of relevancy problems is coextensive with the ingenuity of counsel in using circumstantial evidence as a means of proof. An enormous number of cases fall in no set pattern, and this rule is designed as a guide for handling them. On the other hand, some situations recur with sufficient frequency to create patterns susceptible of treatment by specific rules. Rule 404 and those following it are of that variety; they also serve as illustrations of the application of the present rule as limited by the exclusionary principles of Rule 403.

Passing mention should be made of so-called "conditional" relevancy. Morgan, Basic Problems of Evidence 45–46 (1962). In this situation, probative value depends not only upon satisfying the basic requirement of relevancy as described above but also upon the existence of some matter of fact. For example, if evidence of a spoken statement is relied upon to prove notice, probative value is lacking unless the person sought to be charged heard the statement. The problem is one of fact, and the only rules needed are for the purpose of determining the respective functions of judge and jury. See Rules 104(b) and 901. The discussion which follows in the present note is concerned with relevancy generally, not with any particular problem of conditional relevancy.

Relevancy is not an inherent characteristic of any item of evidence but exists only as a relation between an item of evidence and a matter properly provable in the case. Does the item of evidence tend to prove the matter sought to be proved? Whether the relationship exists depends upon principles evolved by experience or science, applied logically to the situation at hand. James, Relevancy, Probability and the Law, 29 Calif.L.Rev. 689, 696,

n. 15 (1941), in Selected Writings on Evidence and Trial 610, 615, n. 15 (Fryer ed. 1957). The rule summarizes this relationship as a "tendency to make the existence" of the fact to be proved "more probable or less probable." Compare Uniform Rule 1(2) which states the crux of relevancy as "a tendency in reason," thus perhaps emphasizing unduly the logical process and ignoring the need to draw upon experience or science to validate the general principle upon which relevancy in a particular situation depends.

The standard of probability under the rule is "more * * * probable than it would be without the evidence." Any more stringent requirement is unworkable and unrealistic. As McCormick §152, p. 317, says, "A brick is not a wall," or, as Falknor, Extrinsic Policies Affecting Admissibility, 10 Rutgers L.Rev. 574, 576 (1956), quotes Professor McBaine, "* * * [I]t is not to be supposed that every witness can make a home run." Dealing with probability in the language of the rule has the added virtue of avoiding confusion between questions of admissibility and questions of the sufficiency of the evidence.

The rule uses the phrase "fact that is of consequence to the determination of the action" to describe the kind of fact to which proof may properly be directed. The language is that of California Evidence Code §210; it has the advantage of avoiding the loosely used and ambiguous word "material." Tentative Recommendation and a Study Relating to the Uniform Rules of Evidence (Art. I. General Provisions), Cal. Law Revision Comm'n, Rep., Rec. & Studies, 10–11 (1964). The fact to be proved may be ultimate, intermediate, or evidentiary; it matters not, so long as it is of consequence in the determination of the action. Cf. Uniform Rule 1(2) which requires that the evidence relate to a "material" fact.

The fact to which the evidence is directed need not be in dispute. While situations will arise which call for the exclusion of evidence offered to prove a point conceded by the opponent, the ruling should be made on the basis of such considerations as waste of time and undue prejudice (see Rule 403), rather than under any general requirement that evidence is admissible only if directed to matters in dispute. Evidence which is essentially background in nature can scarcely be said to involve disputed matter, yet it is universally offered and admitted as an aid to understanding. Charts, photographs, views of real estate, murder weapons, and many other items of evidence fall in this category. A rule limiting admissibility to evidence directed to a controversial point would invite the exclusion of this helpful evidence, or at least the raising of endless questions over its admission. Cf. California Evidence Code §210, defining relevant evidence in terms of tendency to prove a disputed fact.

RULE 402. GENERAL ADMISSIBILITY OF RELEVANT EVIDENCE

Relevant evidence is admissible unless any of the following provides otherwise:

- the United States Constitution;
- a federal statute;
- these rules; or
- other rules prescribed by the Supreme Court.

Irrelevant evidence is not admissible.

RULE 403. EXCLUDING RELEVANT EVIDENCE FOR PREJUDICE, CONFUSION, WASTE OF TIME, OR OTHER REASONS.

The court may exclude relevant evidence if its probative value is substantially outweighed by a danger of one or more of the following: unfair prejudice, confusing the issues, misleading the jury, undue delay, wasting time, or needlessly presenting cumulative evidence.

NOTES OF ADVISORY COMMITTEE ON PROPOSED RULES (1973)

The case law recognizes that certain circumstances call for the exclusion of evidence which is of unquestioned relevance. These circumstances entail risks which range all the way from inducing decision on a purely emotional basis, at one extreme, to nothing more harmful than merely wasting time, at the other extreme. Situations in this area call for balancing the probative value of and need for the evidence against the harm likely to result from its admission. Slough, Relevancy Unraveled, 5 Kan. L. Rev. 1, 12–15 (1956); Trautman, Logical or Legal Relevancy—A Conflict in Theory, 5 Van. L. Rev. 385, 392 (1952); McCormick §152, pp. 319–321. The rules which follow in this Article are concrete applications evolved for particular situations. However, they reflect the policies underlying the present rule, which is designed as a guide for the handling of situations for which no specific rules have been formulated.

Exclusion for risk of unfair prejudice, confusion of issues, misleading the jury, or waste of time, all find ample support in the authorities. "Unfair prejudice" within its context means an undue tendency to suggest decision on an improper basis, commonly, though not necessarily, an emotional one.

The rule does not enumerate surprise as a ground for exclusion, in this respect following Wigmore's view of the common law. 6 Wigmore §1849. Cf. McCormick §152, p. 320, n. 29, listing unfair surprise as a ground for exclusion but stating that it is usually "coupled with the danger of prejudice and confusion of issues." While Uniform Rule 45 incorporates surprise as a ground and is followed in Kansas Code of Civil Procedure §60–445, surprise is not included in California Evidence Code §352 or New Jersey Rule 4, though both the latter otherwise substantially embody Uniform Rule 45. While it can scarcely be doubted that claims of unfair surprise may still be justified despite procedural requirements of notice and instrumentalities of discovery, the granting of a continuance is a more appropriate remedy than exclusion of the evidence. Tentative Recommendation and a Study Relating to the Uniform Rules of Evidence (Art. VI. Extrinsic Policies Affecting Admissibility), Cal. Law Revision Comm'n, Rep., Rec. & Studies, 612 (1964). Moreover, the impact of a rule excluding evidence on the ground of surprise would be difficult to estimate.

In reaching a decision whether to exclude on grounds of unfair prejudice, consideration should be given to the probable effectiveness or lack of effectiveness of a limiting instruction. See Rule 106 [now 105] and Advisory Committee's Note thereunder. The availability of other means of proof may also be an appropriate factor.

RULE 404. CHARACTER EVIDENCE; OTHER CRIMES, WRONGS, OR ACTS

(a) Character Evidence.

(1) Prohibited Uses. Evidence of a person's character or character trait is not admissible to prove that on a particular occasion the person acted in accordance with the character or trait.

(2) Exceptions for a Defendant or Victim in a Criminal Case. The following exceptions apply in a criminal case:

(A) a defendant may offer evidence of the defendant's pertinent trait, and if the evidence is admitted, the prosecutor may offer evidence to rebut it;

(B) subject to the limitations in Rule 412, a defendant may offer evidence of an alleged victim's pertinent trait, and if the evidence is admitted, the prosecutor may:

(i) offer evidence to rebut it; and

(ii) offer evidence of the defendant's same trait; and

(C) in a homicide case, the prosecutor may offer evidence of the alleged victim's trait of peacefulness to rebut evidence that the victim was the first aggressor.

(3) Exceptions for a Witness. Evidence of a witness's character may be admitted under Rules 607, 608, and 609.

(b) Other Crimes, Wrongs, or Acts.

(1) Prohibited Uses. Evidence of any other crime, wrong, or act is not admissible to prove a person's character in order to show that on a particular occasion the person acted in accordance with the character.

(2) Permitted Uses. This evidence may be admissible for another purpose, such as proving motive, opportunity, intent, preparation, plan, knowledge, identity, absence of mistake, or lack of accident.

(3) Notice in a Criminal Case. In a criminal case, the prosecutor must:

(A) provide reasonable notice of any such evidence that the prosecutor intends to offer at trial, so that the defendant has a fair opportunity to meet it;

(B) articulate in the notice the permitted purpose for which the prosecutor intends to offer the evidence and the reasoning that supports the purpose; and

(C) do so in writing before trial—or in any form during trial if the court, for good cause, excuses lack of pretrial notice.

NOTES OF ADVISORY COMMITTEE ON PROPOSED RULES (1973)

Subdivision (a). This subdivision deals with the basic question whether character evidence should be admitted. Once the admissibility of character evidence in some form is established under this rule, reference must then be made to Rule 405, which follows, in order to determine the appropriate method of proof. If the character is that of a witness, see Rules 608 and 610 for methods of proof.

Character questions arise in two fundamentally different ways. (1) Character may itself be an element of a crime, claim, or defense. A situation of this kind is commonly referred to as "character in issue." Illustrations are: the chastity of the victim under a statute specifying her chastity as an element of the crime of seduction, or the competency of the driver in an action for negligently entrusting a motor vehicle to an incompetent driver. No problem of the general relevancy of character evidence is involved, and the present rule therefore has no provision on the subject. The only question relates to allowable methods of proof, as to which see Rule 405, immediately following. (2) Character evidence is susceptible of being used for the purpose of suggesting an inference that the person acted on the occasion in question consistently with his character. This use of character is often described as "circumstantial." Illustrations are: evidence of a violent disposition to prove that the person was the aggressor in an affray, or evidence of honesty in disproof of a charge of theft. This circumstantial use of character evidence raises questions of relevancy as well as questions of allowable methods of proof.

In most jurisdictions today, the circumstantial use of character is rejected but with important exceptions: (1) an accused may introduce pertinent evidence of good character (often misleadingly described as "putting his character in issue"), in which event the prosecution may rebut with evidence of bad character; (2) an accused may introduce pertinent evidence of the character of the victim, as in support of a claim of self-defense to a charge of homicide or consent in a case of rape, and the prosecution may introduce similar evidence in rebuttal of the character evidence, or, in a homicide case, to rebut a claim that deceased was the first aggressor, however proved; and (3) the character of a witness may be gone into as bearing on his credibility. McCormick §§155–161. This pattern is incorporated in the rule. While its basis lies more in history and experience than in logic as underlying justification can fairly be found in terms of the relative presence and absence of prejudice in the various situations. Falknor, Extrinsic Policies Affecting Admissibility, 10 Rutgers L.Rev. 574, 584 (1956); McCormick §157. In any event, the criminal rule is so deeply imbedded [sic] in our jurisprudence as to assume almost constitutional proportions and to override doubts of the basic relevancy of the evidence.

The limitation to pertinent traits of character, rather than character generally, in paragraphs (1) and (2) is in accordance with the prevailing view. McCormick §158, p. 334. A similar provision in Rule 608, to which reference is made in paragraph (3), limits character evidence respecting witnesses to the trait of truthfulness or untruthfulness.

The argument is made that circumstantial use of character ought to be allowed in civil cases to the same extent as in criminal cases, i.e., evidence of good (nonprejudicial) character would be admissible in the first instance, subject to rebuttal by evidence of bad character. Falknor, Extrinsic Policies Affecting Admissibility, 10 Rutgers L.Rev. 574, 581–583 (1956); Tentative Recommendation and a Study Relating to the Uniform Rules of Evidence (Art. VI. Extrinsic Policies Affecting Admissibility), Cal. Law Revision Comm'n, Rep., Rec. & Studies, 657–658 (1964). Uniform Rule 47 goes farther, in that it assumes that character evidence in general satisfies the conditions of relevancy, except as provided in Uniform Rule 48. The difficulty with expanding the use of character evidence in civil cases is set forth by the California Law Revision Commission in its ultimate rejection of Uniform Rule 47, *Id.*, 615:

"Character evidence is of slight probative value and may be very prejudicial. It tends to distract the trier of fact from the main question of what actually happened on the particular occasion. It subtly permits the trier of fact to reward the good man to punish the bad man because of their respective characters despite what the evidence in the case shows actually happened."

Much of the force of the position of those favoring greater use of character evidence in civil cases is dissipated by their support of Uniform Rule 48 which excludes the evidence in negligence cases, where it could be expected to achieve its maximum usefulness. Moreover, expanding concepts of "character," which seem of necessity to extend into such areas as psychiatric evaluation and psychological testing, coupled with expanded admissibility, would open up such vistas of mental examinations as caused the Court concern in *Schlagenhauf v. Holder,* 379 U.S. 104, 85 S.Ct. 234, 13 L.Ed. 2d 152 (1964). It is believed that those espousing change have not met the burden of persuasion.

Subdivision (b). deals with a specialized but important application of the general rule excluding circumstantial use of character evidence. Consistently with that rule, evidence of other crimes, wrongs, or acts is not admissible to prove character as a basis for suggesting the inference that conduct on a particular occasion was in conformity with it. However, the evidence may be offered for another purpose, such as proof of motive, opportunity, and so on, which does not fall within the prohibition. In this situation the rule does not require that the evidence be excluded. No mechanical solution is offered. The determination must be made whether the danger of undue prejudice outweighs the probative value of the evidence in view of the availability of other means of proof and other factors appropriate for making decisions of this kind under Rule 403. Slough and Knightly, Other Vices, Other Crimes, 41 Iowa L.Rev. 325 (1956).

NOTES OF ADVISORY COMMITTEE ON RULES – 1991 AMENDMENT

Rule 404(b) has emerged as one of the most cited Rules in the Rules of Evidence. And in many criminal cases evidence of an accused's extrinsic acts is viewed as an important asset in the prosecution's case against an accused. Although there are a few reported decisions on use of such evidence by the defense, *see, e.g., United States v. McClure,* 546 F.2nd 670 (5th Cir. 19[77]) (acts of informant offered in entrapment defense), the overwhelming number of cases involve introduction of that evidence by the prosecution.

The amendment to Rule 404(b) adds a pretrial notice requirement in criminal cases and is intended to reduce surprise and promote early resolution on the issue of admissibility. The notice requirement thus places Rule 404(b) in the mainstream with notice and disclosure provisions in other rules of evidence. *See, e.g.,* Rule 412 (written motion of intent to offer evidence under rule), Rule 609 (written notice of intent to offer conviction older than 10 years), Rule 803(24) and 804(b)(5) (notice of intent to use residual hearsay exceptions).

The Rule expects that counsel for both the defense and the prosecution will submit the necessary request and information in a reasonable and timely fashion. Other than requiring pretrial notice, no specific time limits are stated in recognition that what constitutes a reasonable request or disclosure will depend largely on the circumstances of each case. *Compare* Fla. Stat. Ann §90.404 (2)(b) (notice must be given at least 10 days before trial) *with* Tex. R. Evid. 404(b) (no time limit).

Likewise, no specific form of notice is required. The Committee considered and rejected a requirement that the notice satisfy the particularity requirements normally required of language used in a charging instrument. *Cf.* Fla. Stat. Ann §90.404 (2)(b) (written disclosure must describe uncharged misconduct with particularity required of an indictment or information). Instead, the Committee opted for a generalized notice provision which requires the prosecution to apprise the defense of the general nature of the evidence of extrinsic acts. The Committee does not intend that the amendment will supercede [sic] other rules of admissibility or disclosure, such as the Jencks Act, 18 U.S.C. §3500, et seq., nor require the prosecution to disclose directly or indirectly the names and addresses of its witnesses, something it is currently not required to do under Federal Rule of Criminal Procedure 16.

The amendment requires the prosecution to provide notice, regardless of how it intends to use the extrinsic act evidence at trial, i.e., during its case-in-chief, for impeachment, or for possible rebuttal. The court in its discretion may, under the facts, decide that the particular request or notice was not reasonable, either because of the lack of timeliness or completeness. Because the notice requirement serves as condition precedent to admissibility of 404(b) evidence, the offered evidence is inadmissible if the court decides that the notice requirement has not been met.

Nothing in the amendment precludes the court from requiring the government to provide it with an opportunity to rule *in limine* on 404(b) evidence before it is offered or even mentioned during trial. When ruling *in limine*, the court may require the government to disclose to it the specifics of such evidence which the court must consider in determining admissibility.

The amendment does not extend to evidence of acts which are "intrinsic" to the charged offense, see *United States v. Williams*, 900 F.2d 823 (5th Cir. 1990) (noting distinction between 404(b) evidence and intrinsic offense evidence). Nor is the amendment intended to redefine what evidence would otherwise be admissible under Rule 404(b). Finally, the Committee does not intend through the amendment to affect the role of the court and the jury in considering such evidence. See *United States v. Huddleston*, 485 U.S. 681, 108 S.Ct 1496 (1988).

COMMITTEE NOTES ON RULES – 2000 AMENDMENT

Rule 404(a)(1) has been amended to provide that when the accused attacks the character of an alleged victim under subdivision (a)(2) of this Rule, the door is opened to an attack on the same character trait of the accused. Current law does not allow the government to introduce negative character evidence as to the accused unless the accused introduces evidence of good character. *See, e.g., United States v. Fountain*, 768 F.2d 790

(7th Cir. 1985) (when the accused offers proof of self-defense, this permits proof of the alleged victim's character trait for peacefulness, but it does not permit proof of the accused's character trait for violence).

The amendment makes clear that the accused cannot attack the alleged victim's character and yet remain shielded from the disclosure of equally relevant evidence concerning the same character trait of the accused. For example, in a murder case with a claim of self-defense, the accused, to bolster this defense, might offer evidence of the alleged victim's violent disposition. If the government has evidence that the accused has a violent character, but is not allowed to offer this evidence as part of its rebuttal, the jury has only part of the information it needs for an informed assessment of the probabilities as to who was the initial aggressor. This may be the case even if evidence of the accused's prior violent acts is admitted under Rule 404(b), because such evidence can be admitted only for limited purposes and not to show action in conformity with the accused's character on a specific occasion. Thus, the amendment is designed to permit a more balanced presentation of character evidence when an accused chooses to attack the character of the alleged victim.

The amendment does not affect the admissibility of evidence of specific acts of uncharged misconduct offered for a purpose other than proving character under Rule 404(b). Nor does it affect the standards for proof of character by evidence of other sexual behavior or sexual offenses under Rules 412–415. By its placement in Rule 404(a)(1), the amendment covers only proof of character by way of reputation or opinion.

The amendment does not permit proof of the accused's character if the accused merely uses character evidence for a purpose other than to prove the alleged victim's propensity to act in a certain way. See *United States v. Burks*, 470 F.2d 432, 434–5 (D.C. Cir. 1972) (evidence of the alleged victim's violent character, when known by the accused, was admissible "on the issue of whether or not the defendant reasonably feared he was in danger of imminent great bodily harm"). Finally, the amendment does not permit proof of the accused's character when the accused attacks the alleged victim's character as a witness under Rule 608 or 609.

The term "alleged" is inserted before each reference to "victim" in the Rule, in order to provide consistency with Evidence Rule 412.

COMMITTEE NOTES ON RULES – 2006 AMENDMENT

The Rule has been amended to clarify that in a civil case evidence of a person's character is never admissible to prove that the person acted in conformity with the character trait. The amendment resolves the dispute in the case law over whether the exceptions in subdivisions (a)(1) and (2) permit the circumstantial use of character evidence in civil cases. *Compare Carson v. Polley*, 689 F.2d 562, 576 (5th Cir. 1982) ("when a central issue in a case is close to one of a criminal nature, the exceptions to the Rule 404(a) ban on character evidence may be invoked"), *with SEC v. Towers Financial Corp.*, 966 F.Supp. 203 (S.D.N.Y. 1997) (relying on the terms "accused" and "prosecution" in Rule 404(a) to conclude that the exceptions in subdivisions (a)(1) and (2) are inapplicable in civil cases). The amendment is consistent with the original intent of the Rule, which was to prohibit the circumstantial use of character evidence in civil cases, even where closely related to criminal charges. *See Ginter v. Northwestern Mut. Life Ins. Co.*, 576 F. Supp. 627, 629–30 (D. Ky. 1984) ("It seems beyond peradventure of doubt that the drafters of F.R.Evi. 404(a) explicitly intended that all character evidence, except where 'character is at issue' was to be excluded" in civil cases).

The circumstantial use of character evidence is generally discouraged because it carries serious risks of prejudice, confusion, and delay. *See Michelson v. United States*, 335 U.S. 469, 476 (1948) ("The overriding policy of excluding such evidence, despite its admitted probative value, is the practical experience that its disallowance tends to prevent confusion of issues, unfair surprise and undue prejudice."). In criminal cases, the so-called "mercy rule" permits a criminal defendant to introduce evidence of pertinent character traits of the defendant and the victim. But that is because the accused, whose liberty is at stake, may need "a counterweight against the strong investigative and prosecutorial resources of the government." C. Mueller & L. Kirkpatrick, *Evidence: Practice Under the Rules*, pp. 264–5 (2d ed. 1999). See also Richard Uviller, *Evidence of Character to Prove Conduct: Illusion, Illogic, and Injustice in the Courtroom*, 130 U. Pa. L. Rev. 845, 855 (1982) (the rule prohibiting circumstantial use of character evidence "was relaxed to allow the criminal defendant with so much at stake and so little available in the way of conventional proof to have special dispensation to tell the factfinder just what sort of person he really is"). Those concerns do not apply to parties in civil cases.

The amendment also clarifies that evidence otherwise admissible under Rule 404(a)(2) may nonetheless be excluded in a criminal case involving sexual misconduct. In such a case, the admissibility of evidence of the victim's sexual behavior and predisposition is governed by the more stringent provisions of Rule 412.

Nothing in the amendment is intended to affect the scope of Rule 404(b). While Rule 404(b) refers to the "accused," the "prosecution," and a "criminal case," it does so only in the context of a notice requirement. The admissibility standards of Rule 404(b) remain fully applicable to both civil and criminal cases.

RULE 405. METHODS OF PROVING CHARACTER

(a) By Reputation or Opinion. When evidence of a person's character or character trait is admissible, it may be proved by testimony about the person's reputation or by testimony in the form of an opinion. On cross-examination of the character witness, the court may allow an inquiry into relevant specific instances of the person's conduct.

(b) By Specific Instances of Conduct. When a person's character or character trait is an essential element of a charge, claim, or defense, the character or trait may also be proved by relevant specific instances of the person's conduct.

NOTES OF ADVISORY COMMITTEE OF PROPOSED RULES (1973)

The rule deals only with allowable methods of proving character, not with the admissibility of character evidence, which is covered in Rule 404.

Of the three methods of proving character provided by the rule, evidence of specific instances of conduct is the most convincing. At the same time it possesses the greatest capacity to arouse prejudice, to confuse, to surprise, and to consume time. Consequently, the rule confines the use of evidence of this kind to cases in which character is, in the strict sense, in issue and hence deserving of a searching inquiry. When character is used circumstantially and hence occupies a lesser status in the case, proof may be only by reputation and opinion. These latter methods are also available when character is in issue. This treatment is, with respect to specific instances of conduct and reputation, conventional contemporary common law doctrine. McCormick §153.

In recognizing opinion as a means of proving character, the rule departs from usual contemporary practice in favor of that of an earlier day. See 7 Wigmore §1986, pointing out that the earlier practice permitted opinion and arguing strongly for evidence based on personal knowledge and belief as contrasted with "the secondhand, irresponsible product of multiplied guesses and gossip which we term 'reputation'." It seems likely that the persistence of reputation evidence is due to its largely being opinion in disguise. Traditionally character has been regarded primarily in moral overtones of good and bad: chaste, peaceable, truthful, honest. Nevertheless, on occasion nonmoral considerations crop up, as in the case of the incompetent driver, and this seems bound to happen increasingly. If character is defined as the kind of person one is, then account must be taken of varying ways of arriving at the estimate. These may range from the opinion of the employer who has found the man honest to the opinion of the psychiatrist based upon examination and testing. No effective dividing line exists between character and mental capacity, and the latter traditionally has been provable by opinion.

According to the great majority of cases, on cross-examination inquiry is allowable as to whether the reputation witness has heard of particular instances of conduct pertinent to the trait in question. *Michelson v. United States*, 335 U.S. 469, 69 S.Ct. 213, 93 L.Ed. 168 (1948); Annot., 47 A.L.R.2d 1258. The theory is that, since the reputation witness relates what he has heard, the inquiry tends to shed light on the accuracy of his hearing and reporting. Accordingly, the opinion witness would be asked whether he knew, as well as whether he had heard. The fact is, of course, that these distinctions are of slight if any practical significance, and the second sentence of subdivision (a) eliminates them as a factor in formulating questions. This recognition of the propriety of inquiring into specific instances of conduct does not circumscribe inquiry otherwise into the bases of opinion and reputation testimony.

The express allowance of inquiry into specific instances of conduct on cross-examination in subdivision (a) and the express allowance of it as part of a case in chief when character is actually in issue in subdivision (b) contemplate that testimony of specific instances is not generally permissible on the direct examination of an ordinary opinion witness to character. Similarly as to witnesses to the character of witnesses under Rule 608(b). Opinion testimony on direct in these situations ought in general to correspond to reputation testimony as now given, i.e., be confined to the nature and extent of observation and acquaintance upon which the opinion is based. See Rule 701.

RULE 406. HABIT; ROUTINE PRACTICE

Evidence of a person's habit or an organization's routine practice may be admitted to prove that on a particular occasion the person or organization acted in accordance with the habit or routine practice. The court may admit this evidence regardless of whether it is corroborated or whether there was an eyewitness.

NOTES OF ADVISORY COMMITTEE ON PROPOSED RULES (1973)

An oft-quoted paragraph, McCormick, §162, p. 340, describes habit in terms effectively contrasting it with character:

"Character and habit are close akin. Character is a generalized description of one's disposition, or of one's disposition in respect to a general trait, such as honesty, temperance, or peacefulness. 'Habit,' in modern usage, both lay and psychological, is more specific. It describes one's regular response to a repeated specific situation. If we speak of character for care, we think of the person's tendency to act prudently in all the varying situations of life, in business, family life, in handling automobiles and in walking across the street. A habit, on the other hand, is the person's regular practice of meeting a particular kind of situation with a specific type of conduct, such as the habit of going down a particular stairway two stairs at a time, or of giving the hand-signal for a left turn, or of alighting from railway cars while they are moving. The doing of the habitual acts may become semi-automatic."

Equivalent behavior on the part of a group is designated "routine practice of an organization" in the rule. Agreement is general that habit evidence is highly persuasive as proof of conduct on a particular occasion. Again quoting McCormick §162, p. 341:

"Character may be thought of as the sum of one's habits though doubtless it is more than this. But unquestionably the uniformity of one's response to habit is far greater than the consistency with which one's conduct conforms to character or disposition. Even though character comes in only exceptionally as evidence of an act, surely any sensible man in investigating whether X did a particular act would be greatly helped in his inquiry by evidence as to whether he was in the habit of doing it."

When disagreement has appeared, its focus has been upon the question what constitutes habit, and the reason for this is readily apparent. The extent to which instances must be multiplied and consistency of behavior maintained in order to rise to the status of habit inevitably gives rise to differences of opinion. Lewan, Rationale of Habit Evidence, 16 Syracuse L.Rev. 39, 49 (1964). While adequacy of sampling and uniformity of response are key factors, precise standards for measuring their sufficiency for evidence purposes cannot be formulated.

The rule is consistent with prevailing views. Much evidence is excluded simply because of failure to achieve the status of habit. Thus, evidence of intemperate "habits" is generally excluded when offered as proof of drunkenness in accident cases, Annot., 46 A.L.R.2d 103, and evidence of other assaults is inadmissible to prove the instant one in a civil assault action, Annot., 66 A.L.R.2d 806. In *Levin v. United States,* 119 U.S. App. D.C. 156, 338 F.2d 265 (1964), testimony as to the religious "habits" of the accused, offered as tending to prove that he was at home observing the Sabbath rather than out obtaining money through larceny by trick, was held properly excluded;

"It seems apparent to us that an individual's religious practices would not be the type of activities which would lend themselves to the characterization of 'invariable regularity.' [1 Wigmore 520.] Certainly the very volitional basis of the activity raises serious questions as to its invariable nature, and hence its probative value." *Id.* at 272.

These rulings are not inconsistent with the trend towards admitting evidence of business transactions between one of the parties and a third person as tending to prove that he made the same bargain or proposal in the litigated situation. Slough, Relevancy Unraveled, 6 Kan.L.Rev. 38–41

(1957). Nor are they inconsistent with such cases as *Whittemore v. Lockheed Aircraft Corp.*, 65 Cal.App.2d 737, 151 P.2d 670 (1944), upholding the admission of evidence that plaintiff's intestate had on four other occasions flown planes from defendant's factory for delivery to his employer airline, offered to prove that he was piloting rather than a guest on a plane which crashed and killed all on board while en route for delivery.

A considerable body of authority has required that evidence of the routine practice of an organization be corroborated as a condition precedent to its admission in evidence. Slough, Relevancy Unraveled, 5 Kan.L.Rev. 404, 449 (1957). This requirement is specifically rejected by the rule on the ground that it relates to the sufficiency of the evidence rather than admissibility. A similar position is taken in New Jersey Rule 49. The rule also rejects the requirement of the absence of eyewitnesses, sometimes encountered with respect to admitting habit evidence to prove freedom from contributory negligence in wrongful death cases. For comment critical of the requirements see Frank, J., in *Cereste v. New York, N.H. & H.R. Co.*, 231 F.2d 50 (2d Cir. 1956), cert. denied 351 U.S. 951, 76 S.Ct. 848, 100 L. Ed. 1475, 10 Vand.L.Rev. 447 (1957); McCormick §162, p. 342. The omission of the requirement from the California Evidence Code is said to have effected its elimination. Comment, Cal. Ev. Code §1105.

RULE 407. SUBSEQUENT REMEDIAL MEASURES

When measures are taken that would have made an earlier injury or harm less likely to occur, evidence of the subsequent measures is not admissible to prove:

- negligence;
- culpable conduct;
- a defect in a product or its design; or
- a need for a warning or instruction.

But the court may admit this evidence for another purpose, such as impeachment or—if disputed—proving ownership, control, or the feasibility of precautionary measures.

NOTES OF ADVISORY COMMITTEE ON PROPOSED RULES (1973)

The rule incorporates conventional doctrine which excludes evidence of subsequent remedial measures as proof of an admission of fault. The rule rests on two grounds. (1) The conduct is not in fact an admission, since the conduct is equally consistent with injury by mere accident or through contributory negligence. Or, as Baron Bramwell put it, the rule rejects the notion that "because the world gets wiser as it gets older, therefore it was foolish before." *Hart v. Lancashire & Yorkshire Ry. Co.*, 21 L.T.R. N.S. 261, 263 (1869). Under a liberal theory of relevancy this ground alone would not support exclusion as the inference is still a possible one. (2) The other, and more impressive, ground for exclusion rests on a social policy of encouraging people to take, or at least not discouraging them from taking, steps in furtherance of added safety. The courts have applied this principle to exclude evidence of subsequent repairs, installation of safety devices, changes in company rules, and discharge of employees, and the language of the present rules is broad enough to encompass all of them. See Falknor, Extrinsic Policies Affecting Admissibility, 10 Rutgers L.Rev. 574, 590 (1956).

The second sentence of the rule directs attention to the limitations of the rule. Exclusion is called for only when the evidence of subsequent remedial measures is offered as proof of negligence or culpable conduct. In effect it rejects the suggested inference that fault is admitted. Other purposes are, however, allowable, including ownership or control, existence of duty, and feasibility of precautionary measures, if controverted, and impeachment. 2 Wigmore §283; Annot., 64 A.L.R.2d 1296. Two recent federal cases are illustrative. *Boeing Airplane Co. v. Brown*, 291 F.2d 310 (9th Cir. 1961), an action against an airplane manufacturer for using an allegedly defectively designed alternator shaft which caused a plane crash, upheld the admission of evidence of subsequent design modification for the purpose of showing that design changes and safeguards were feasible. And *Powers v. J. B. Michael & Co.*, 329 F.2d 674 (6th Cir. 1964), an action against a road contractor for negligent failure to put out warning signs, sustained the admission of evidence that defendant subsequently put out signs to show that the portion of the road in question was under defendant's control. The requirement that the other purpose be controverted calls for automatic exclusion unless a genuine issue be present and allows the opposing party to lay the groundwork for exclusion by making an admission. Otherwise the factors of undue prejudice, confusion of issues, misleading the jury, and waste of time remain for consideration under Rule 403.

For comparable rules, see Uniform Rule 51; California Evidence Code §1151; Kansas Code of Civil Procedure §60–451; New Jersey Evidence Rule 51.

NOTES OF ADVISORY COMMITTEE ON RULES – 1997 AMENDMENT

The amendment to Rule 407 makes two changes in the rule. First, the words "an injury or harm allegedly caused by" were added to clarify that the rule applies only to changes made after the occurrence that produced the damages giving rise to the action. Evidence of measures taken by the defendant prior to the "event" causing "injury or harm" do not fall within the exclusionary scope of Rule 407 even if they occurred after the manufacture or design of the product. See *Chase v. General Motors Corp.*, 856 F.2d 17, 21–22 (4th Cir. 1988).

Second, Rule 407 has been amended to provide that evidence of subsequent remedial measures may not be used to prove "a defect in a product or its design, or that a warning or instruction should have accompanied a product." This amendment adopts the view of a majority of the circuits that have interpreted Rule 407 to apply to products liability actions. See *Raymond v. Raymond Corp.*, 938 F.2d 1518, 1522 (1st Cir. 1991); *In re Joint Eastern District and Southern District Asbestos Litigation v. Armstrong World Industries, Inc.*, 995 F.2d 343 (2d Cir. 1993); *Cann v. Ford Motor Co.*, 658 F.2d 54, 60 (2d Cir. 1981), cert. denied, 456 U.S. 960 (1982); *Kelly v. Crown Equipment Co.*, 970 F.2d 1273, 1275 (3d Cir. 1992); *Werner v. Upjohn, Inc.*, 628 F.2d 848 (4th Cir. 1980), cert. denied, 449 U.S. 1080 (1981); *Grenada Steel Industries, Inc. v. Alabama Oxygen Co., Inc.*, 695 F.2d 883 (5th Cir. 1983); *Bauman v. Volkswagenwerk Aktiengesellschaft*, 621 F.2d 230, 232 (6th Cir. 1980); *Flaminio v. Honda Motor Company, Ltd.*, 733 F.2d 463, 469 (7th Cir. 1984); *Gauthier v. AMF, Inc.*, 788 F.2d 634, 636–37 (9th Cir. 1986).

Although this amendment adopts a uniform federal rule, it should be noted that evidence of subsequent remedial measures may be admissible pursuant to the second sentence of Rule 407. Evidence of subsequent measures that is not barred by Rule 407 may still be subject to exclusion on Rule 403 grounds when the dangers of prejudice or confusion substantially outweigh the probative value of the evidence.

GAP Report on Rule 407. The words "injury or harm" were substituted for the word "event" in line 3. The stylization changes in the second sentence of the rule were eliminated. The words "causing 'injury or harm'" were added to the Committee Note.

RULE 408. COMPROMISE OFFERS AND NEGOTIATIONS

(a) Prohibited Uses. Evidence of the following is not admissible—on behalf of any party—either to prove or disprove the validity or amount of a disputed claim or to impeach by a prior inconsistent statement or a contradiction:

(1) furnishing, promising, or offering—or accepting, promising to accept, or offering to accept—a valuable consideration in compromising or attempting to compromise the claim; and

(2) conduct or a statement made during compromise negotiations about the claim—except when offered in a criminal case and when the negotiations related to a claim by a public office in the exercise of its regulatory, investigative, or enforcement authority.

(b) Exceptions. The court may admit this evidence for another purpose, such as proving a witness's bias or prejudice, negating a contention of undue delay, or proving an effort to obstruct a criminal investigation or prosecution.

NOTES OF ADVISORY COMMITTEE ON PROPOSED RULES (1973)

As a matter of general agreement, evidence of an offer-to compromise a claim is not receivable in evidence as an admission of, as the case may be, the validity or invalidity of the claim. As with evidence of subsequent remedial measures, dealt with in Rule 407, exclusion may be based on two grounds. (1) The evidence is irrelevant, since the offer may be motivated by a desire for peace rather than from any concession of weakness of position. The validity of this position will vary as the amount of the offer varies in relation to the size of the claim and may also be influenced by other circumstances. (2) a more consistently impressive ground is promotion of the public policy favoring the compromise and settlement of disputes. McCormick §§76, 251. While the rule is ordinarily phrased in terms of offers of compromise, it is apparent that a similar attitude must be taken with respect to completed compromises when offered against a party thereto. This latter situation will not, of course, ordinarily occur except when a party to the present litigation has compromised with a third person.

The same policy underlies the provision of Rule 68 of the Federal Rules of Civil Procedure that evidence of an unaccepted offer of judgment is not admissible except in a proceeding to determine costs.

The practical value of the common law rule has been greatly diminished by its inapplicability to admissions of fact, even though made in the course of compromise negotiations, unless hypothetical, stated to be "without prejudice," or so connected with the offer as to be inseparable from it. McCormick §251, pp. 540–541. An inevitable effect is to inhibit freedom of communication with respect to compromise, even among lawyers. Another effect is the generation of controversy over whether a given statement falls within or without the protected area. These considerations account for the expansion of the rule herewith to include evidence of conduct or statements made in compromise negotiations, as well as the offer or completed compromise itself. For similar provisions, see California Evidence Code §§1152, 1154.

The policy considerations which underlie the rule do not come into play when the effort is to induce a creditor to settle an admittedly due amount for a lessor [sic] sum. McCormick §251, p. 540. Hence the rule requires that the claim be disputed as to either validity or amount.

The final sentence of the rule serves to point out some limitations upon its applicability. Since the rule excludes only when the purpose is proving the validity or invalidity of the claim or its amount, an offer for another purpose is not within the rule. The illustrative situations mentioned in the rule are supported by the authorities. As to proving bias or prejudice of a witness, see Annot., 161 A.L.R. 395, *contra, Fenberg v. Rosenthal,* 348 Ill. App. 510, 109 N.E.2d 402 (1952), and negativing a contention of lack of due diligence in presenting a claim, 4 Wigmore §1061. An effort to "buy off" the prosecution or a prosecuting witness in a criminal case is not within the policy of the rule of exclusion. McCormick §251, p. 542.

For other rules of similar import, see Uniform Rules 52 and 53; California Evidence Code §1152, 1154; Kansas Code of Civil Procedure §§60–452, 60–453; New Jersey Evidence Rules 52 and 53.

COMMITTEE NOTES ON RULES – 2006 AMENDMENT

Rule 408 has been amended to settle some questions in the courts about the scope of the Rule, and to make it easier to read. First, the amendment provides that Rule 408 does not prohibit the introduction in a criminal case of statements or conduct during compromise negotiations regarding a civil dispute by a government regulatory, investigative, or enforcement agency. See, e.g., *United States v. Prewitt,* 34 F.3d 436, 439 (7th Cir. 1994) (admissions of fault made in compromise of a civil securities enforcement action were admissible against the accused in a subsequent criminal action for mail fraud). Where an individual makes a statement in the presence of government agents, its subsequent admission in a criminal case should not be unexpected. The individual can seek to protect against subsequent disclosure through negotiation and agreement with the civil regulator or an attorney for the government.

Statements made in compromise negotiations of a claim by a government agency may be excluded in criminal cases where the circumstances so warrant under Rule 403. For example, if an individual was unrepresented at the time the statement was made in a civil enforcement proceeding, its probative value in a subsequent criminal case may be minimal. But there is no absolute exclusion imposed by Rule 408.

In contrast, statements made during compromise negotiations of other disputed claims are not admissible in subsequent criminal litigation, when offered to prove liability for, invalidity of, or amount of those claims. When private parties enter into compromise negotiations they cannot protect against the subsequent use of statements in criminal cases by way of private ordering. The inability to guarantee protection against subsequent use could lead to parties refusing to admit fault, even if by doing so they could favorably settle the private matter. Such a chill on settlement negotiations would be contrary to the policy of Rule 408.

The amendment distinguishes statements and conduct (such as a direct admission of fault) made in compromise negotiations of a civil claim by a government agency from an offer or acceptance of a compromise of such a claim. An offer or acceptance of a compromise of any civil claim is excluded under the Rule if offered against the defendant as an admission of fault. In that case, the predicate for the evidence would be that the defendant, by compromising with the government agency, has admitted the validity and amount of the civil claim, and that this admission has sufficient probative value to be considered as evidence of guilt. But unlike a direct statement of fault, an offer or acceptance of a compromise is not very probative of the defendant's guilt. Moreover, admitting such an offer or acceptance could deter a defendant from settling a civil regulatory action, for fear of evidentiary use in a subsequent criminal action. *See, e.g.*, Fishman, *Jones on Evidence, Civil and Criminal*, §22:16 at 199, n.83 (7th ed. 2000) ("A target of a potential criminal investigation may be unwilling to settle civil claims against him if by doing so he increases the risk of prosecution and conviction.").

The amendment retains the language of the original rule that bars compromise evidence only when offered as evidence of the "validity," "invalidity," or "amount" of the disputed claim. The intent is to retain the extensive case law finding Rule 408 inapplicable when compromise evidence is offered for a purpose other than to prove the validity, invalidity, or amount of a disputed claim. *See, e.g., Athey v. Farmers Ins. Exchange*, 234 F.3d 357 (8th Cir. 2000) (evidence of settlement offer by insurer was properly admitted to prove insurer's bad faith); *Coakley & Williams v. Structural Concrete Equip.*, 973 F.2d 349 (4th Cir. 1992) (evidence of settlement is not precluded by Rule 408 where offered to prove a party's intent with respect to the scope of a release); *Cates v. Morgan Portable Bldg. Corp.*, 708 F.2d 683 (7th Cir. 1985) (Rule 408 does not bar evidence of a settlement when offered to prove a breach of the settlement agreement, as the purpose of the evidence is to prove the fact of settlement as opposed to the validity or amount of the underlying claim); *Uforma/Shelby Bus. Forms, Inc. v. NLRB*, 111 F.3d 1284 (6th Cir. 1997) (threats made in settlement negotiations were admissible; Rule 408 is inapplicable when the claim is based upon a wrong that is committed during the course of settlement negotiations). So for example, Rule 408 is inapplicable if offered to show that a party made fraudulent statements in order to settle a litigation.

The amendment does not affect the case law providing that Rule 408 is inapplicable when evidence of the compromise is offered to prove notice. *See, e.g., United States v. Austin*, 54 F.3d 394 (7th Cir. 1995) (no error to admit evidence of the defendant's settlement with the FTC, because it was offered to prove that the defendant was on notice that subsequent similar conduct was wrongful); *Spell v. McDaniel*, 824 F.2d 1380 (4th Cir. 1987) (in a civil rights action alleging that an officer used excessive force, a prior settlement by the City of another brutality claim was properly admitted to prove that the City was on notice of aggressive behavior by police officers).

The amendment prohibits the use of statements made in settlement negotiations when offered to impeach by prior inconsistent statement or through contradiction. Such broad impeachment would tend to swallow the exclusionary rule and would impair the public policy of promoting settlements. *See McCormick on Evidence* at 186 (5th ed. 1999) ("Use of statements made in compromise negotiations to impeach the testimony of a party, which is not specifically treated in Rule 408, is fraught with danger of misuse of the statements to prove liability, threatens frank interchange of information during negotiations, and generally should not be permitted."). *See also EEOC v. Gear Petroleum, Inc.*, 948 F.2d 1542 (10th Cir. 1991) (letter sent as part of settlement negotiation cannot be used to impeach defense witnesses by way of contradiction or prior inconsistent statement; such broad impeachment would undermine the policy of encouraging uninhibited settlement negotiations).

The amendment makes clear that Rule 408 excludes compromise evidence even when a party seeks to admit its own settlement offer or statements made in settlement negotiations. If a party were to reveal its own statement or offer, this could itself reveal the fact that the adversary entered into settlement negotiations. The protections of Rule 408 cannot be waived unilaterally because the Rule, by definition, protects both parties from having the fact of negotiation disclosed to the jury. Moreover, proof of statements and offers made in settlement would often have to be made through the testimony of attorneys, leading to the risks and costs of disqualification. *See generally Pierce v. F.R. Tripler & Co.*, 955 F.2d 820, 828 (2d Cir. 1992) (settlement offers are excluded under Rule 408 even if it is the offeror who seeks to admit them; noting that the "widespread admissibility of the substance of settlement offers could bring with it a rash of motions for disqualification of a party's chosen counsel who would likely become a witness at trial").

The sentence of the Rule referring to evidence "otherwise discoverable" has been deleted as superfluous. *See, e.g.*, Advisory Committee Note to Maine Rule of Evidence 408 (refusing to include the sentence in the Maine version of Rule 408 and noting that the sentence "seems to state what the law would be if it were omitted"); Advisory Committee Note to Wyoming Rule of Evidence 408 (refusing to include the sentence in Wyoming Rule 408 on the ground that it was "superfluous"). The intent of the sentence was to prevent a party from trying to immunize admissible information, such as a pre-existing document, through the pretense of disclosing it during compromise negotiations. *See Ramada Development Co. v. Rauch*, 644 F.2d 1097 (5th Cir. 1981). But even without the sentence, the Rule cannot be read to protect pre-existing information simply because it was presented to the adversary in compromise negotiations.

Changes Made After Publication and Comments. In response to public comment, the proposed amendment was changed to provide that statements and conduct during settlement negotiations are to be admissible in subsequent criminal litigation only when made during settlement discussions of a claim brought by a government regulatory agency. Stylistic changes were made in accordance with suggestions from the Style Subcommittee of the Standing Committee. The Committee Note was altered to accord with the change in the text, and also to clarify that fraudulent statements made during settlement negotiations are not protected by the Rule.

RULE 409. OFFERS TO PAY MEDICAL AND SIMILAR EXPENSES

Evidence of furnishing, promising to pay, or offering to pay medical, hospital, or similar expenses resulting from an injury is not admissible to prove liability for the injury.

NOTES OF ADVISORY COMMITTEE ON PROPOSED RULES (1973)

The considerations underlying this rule parallel those underlying Rules 407 and 408, which deal respectively with subsequent remedial measures and offers of compromise. As stated in Annot., 20 A.L.R.2d 291, 293:

"[G]enerally, evidence of payment of medical, hospital, or similar expenses of an injured party by the opposing party, is not admissible, the reason often given being that such payment or offer is usually made from humane impulses and not from an admission of liability, and that to hold otherwise would tend to discourage assistance to the injured person."

Contrary to Rule 408, dealing with offers of compromise, the present rule does not extend to conduct or statements not a part of the act of furnishing or offering or promising to pay. This difference in treatment arises from fundamental differences in nature. Communication is essential if compromises are to be effected, and consequently broad protection of statements is needed. This is not so in cases of payments or offers or promises to pay medical expenses, where factual statements may be expected to be incidental in nature.

For rules on the same subject, but phrased in terms of "humanitarian motives," see Uniform Rule 52; California Evidence Code §1152; Kansas Code of Civil Procedure §60–452; New Jersey Evidence Rule 52.

RULE 410. PLEAS, PLEA DISCUSSIONS, RELATED STATEMENTS

(a) Prohibited Uses. In a civil or criminal case, evidence of the following is not admissible against the defendant who made the plea or participated in the plea discussions:

(1) a guilty plea that was later withdrawn;

(2) a nolo contendere plea;

(3) a statement made during a proceeding on either of those pleas under Federal Rule of Criminal Procedure 11 or a comparable state procedure; or

(4) a statement made during plea discussions with an attorney for the prosecuting authority if the discussions did not result in a guilty plea or they resulted in a later-withdrawn guilty plea.

(b) Exceptions. The court may admit a statement described in Rule 410(a)(3) or (4):

(1) in any proceeding in which another statement made during the same plea or plea discussions has been introduced, if in fairness the statements ought to be considered together; or

(2) in a criminal proceeding for perjury or false statement, if the defendant made the statement under oath, on the record, and with counsel present.

NOTES OF ADVISORY COMMITTEE ON PROPOSED RULES (1973)

Withdrawn pleas of guilty were held inadmissible in federal prosecutions in *Kercheval v. United States*, 274 U.S. 220, 47 S.Ct. 582, 71 L.Ed. 1009 (1927). The Court pointed out that to admit the withdrawn plea would effectively set at naught the allowance of withdrawal and place the accused in a dilemma utterly inconsistent with the decision to award him a trial. The New York Court of Appeals, in *People v. Spitaleri*, 9 N.Y.2d 168, 212 N.Y.S.2d 53, 173 N.E.2d 35 (1961), reexamined and overturned its earlier decisions which had allowed admission. In addition to the reasons set forth in Kercheval, which was quoted at length, the court pointed out that the effect of admitting the plea was to compel defendant to take the stand by way of explanation and to open the way for the prosecution to call the lawyer who had represented him at the time of entering the plea. State court decisions for and against admissibility are collected in Annot., 86 A.L.R.2d 326.

Pleas of *nolo contendere* are recognized by Rule 11 of the Rules of Criminal Procedure, although the law of numerous States is to the contrary. The present rule gives effect to the principal traditional characteristic of the *nolo* plea, i.e., avoiding the admission of guilt which is inherent in pleas of guilty. This position is consistent with the construction of Section 5 of the Clayton Act, 15 U.S.C. §16(a), recognizing the inconclusive and compromise nature of judgments based on *nolo* pleas. *General Electric Co. v. City of San Antonio*, 334 F.2d 480 (5th Cir. 1964); *Commonwealth Edison Co. v. Allis-Chalmers Mfg. Co.*, 323 F.2d 412 (7th Cir. 1963), cert. denied 376 U.S. 939, 84 S.Ct. 794, 11 L.Ed. 2d 659; *Armco Steel Corp. v. North Dakota*, 376 F.2d 206 (8th Cir. 1967); *City of Burbank v. General Electric Co.*, 329 F.2d 825 (9th Cir. 1964). See also state court decisions in Annot., 18 A.L.R.2d 1287, 1314.

Exclusion of offers to plead guilty or nolo has as its purpose the promotion of disposition of criminal cases by compromise. As pointed out in McCormick §251, p. 543:

"Effective criminal law administration in many localities would hardly be possible if a large proportion of the charges were not disposed of by such compromises."

See also *People v. Hamilton*, 60 Cal. 2d 105, 32 Cal.Rptr. 4, 383 P.2d 412 (1963), discussing legislation designed to achieve this result. As with compromise offers generally, Rule 408, free communication is needed, and security against having an offer of compromise or related statement admitted in evidence effectively encourages it.

Limiting the exclusionary rule to use against the accused is consistent with the purpose of the rule, since the possibility of use for or against other persons will not impair the effectiveness of withdrawing pleas or the freedom of discussion which the rule is designed to foster. See A.B.A. Standards Relating to Pleas of Guilty §2.2 (1968). See also the narrower provisions of New Jersey Evidence Rule 52(2) and the unlimited exclusion provided in California Evidence Code §1153.

RULE 411. LIABILITY INSURANCE

Evidence that a person was or was not insured against liability is not admissible to prove whether the person acted negligently or otherwise wrongfully. But the court may admit this evidence for another purpose, such as proving a witness's bias or prejudice or proving agency, ownership, or control.

NOTES OF ADVISORY COMMITTEE ON PROPOSED RULES (1973)

The courts have with substantial unanimity rejected evidence of liability insurance for the purpose of proving fault, and absence of liability insurance as proof of lack of fault. At best the inference of fault from the fact of insurance coverage is a tenuous one, as is its converse. More important, no doubt, has been the feeling that knowledge of the presence or absence of liability insurance would induce juries to decide cases on improper grounds. McCormick §168; Annot., 4 A.L.R.2d 761. The rule is drafted in broad terms so as to include contributory negligence or other fault of a plaintiff as well as fault of a defendant.

The second sentence points out the limits of the rule, using well established illustrations. *Id.*

For similar rules see Uniform Rule 54; California Evidence Code §1155; Kansas Code of Civil Procedure §60–454; New Jersey Evidence Rule 54.

RULE 412. SEX-OFFENSE CASES: THE VICTIM

(a) Prohibited Uses. The following evidence is not admissible in a civil or criminal proceeding involving alleged sexual misconduct:

(1) evidence offered to prove that a victim engaged in other sexual behavior; or

(2) evidence offered to prove a victim's sexual predisposition.

(b) Exceptions.

(1) *Criminal Cases.* The court may admit the following evidence in a criminal case:

(A) evidence of specific instances of a victim's sexual behavior, if offered to prove that someone other than the defendant was the source of semen, injury, or other physical evidence;

(B) evidence of specific instances of a victim's sexual behavior with respect to the person accused of the sexual misconduct, if offered by the defendant to prove consent or if offered by the prosecutor; and

(C) evidence whose exclusion would violate the defendant's constitutional rights.

(2) *Civil Cases.* In a civil case, the court may admit evidence offered to prove a victim's sexual behavior or sexual predisposition if its probative value substantially outweighs the danger of harm to any victim and of unfair prejudice to any party. The court may admit evidence of a victim's reputation only if the victim has placed it in controversy.

(c) Procedure to Determine Admissibility.

(1) *Motion.* If a party intends to offer evidence under Rule 412(b), the party must:

(A) file a motion that specifically describes the evidence and states the purpose for which it is to be offered;

(B) do so at least 14 days before trial unless the court, for good cause, sets a different time;

(C) serve the motion on all parties; and

(D) notify the victim or, when appropriate, the victim's guardian or representative.

(2) *Hearing.* Before admitting evidence under this rule, the court must conduct an in camera hearing and give the victim and parties a right to attend and be heard. Unless the court orders otherwise, the motion, related materials, and the record of the hearing must be and remain sealed.

(d) Definition of "Victim." In this rule, "victim" includes an alleged victim.

NOTES OF ADVISORY COMMITTEE ON RULES – 1994 AMENDMENT

Rule 412 has been revised to diminish some of the confusion engendered by the original rule and to expand the protection afforded alleged victims of sexual misconduct. Rule 412 applies to both civil and criminal proceedings. The rule aims to safeguard the alleged victim against the invasion of privacy, potential embarrassment and sexual stereotyping that is associated with public disclosure of intimate sexual details and the infusion of sexual innuendo into the factfinding process. By affording victims protection in most instances, the rule also encourages victims of sexual misconduct to institute and to participate in legal proceedings against alleged offenders.

Rule 412 seeks to achieve these objectives by barring evidence relating to the alleged victim's sexual behavior or alleged sexual predisposition, whether offered as substantive evidence or for impeachment, except in designated circumstances in which the probative value of the evidence significantly outweighs possible harm to the victim.

The revised rule applies in all cases involving sexual misconduct without regard to whether the alleged victim or person accused is a party to the litigation. Rule 412 extends to "pattern" witnesses in both criminal and civil cases whose testimony about other instances of sexual misconduct by the person accused is otherwise admissible. When the case does not involve alleged sexual misconduct, evidence relating to a third-party witness' alleged sexual activities is not within the ambit of Rule 412. The witness will, however, be protected by other rules such as Rules 404 and 608, as well as Rule 403.

The terminology "alleged victim" is used because there will frequently be a factual dispute as to whether sexual misconduct occurred. It does not connote any requirement that the misconduct be alleged in the pleadings. Rule 412 does not, however, apply unless the person against whom the evidence is offered can reasonably be characterized as a "victim of alleged sexual misconduct." When this is not the case, as for instance in a defamation action involving statements concerning sexual misconduct in which the evidence is offered to show that the alleged defamatory statements were true or did not damage the plaintiff's reputation, neither Rule 404 nor this rule will operate to bar the evidence; Rule 401 and 403 will continue to control. Rule 412 will, however, apply in a Title VII action in which the plaintiff has alleged sexual harassment.

The reference to a person "accused" is also used in a non-technical sense. There is no requirement that there be a criminal charge pending against the person or even that the misconduct would constitute a criminal offense. Evidence offered to prove allegedly false prior claims by the victim is not barred by Rule 412. However, this evidence is subject to the requirements of Rule 404.

Subdivision (a). As amended, Rule 412 bars evidence offered to prove the victim's sexual behavior and alleged sexual predisposition. Evidence, which might otherwise be admissible under Rules 402, 404(b), 405, 607, 608, 609, or some other evidence rule, must be excluded if Rule 412 so requires. The word "other" is used to suggest some flexibility in admitting evidence "intrinsic" to the alleged sexual misconduct. *Cf.* Committee Note to 1991 amendment to Rule 404(b).

Past sexual behavior connotes all activities that involve actual physical conduct, i.e. sexual intercourse and sexual contact, or that imply sexual intercourse or sexual contact. *See, e.g., United States v. Galloway,* 937 F.2d 542 (10th Cir. 1991), *cert. denied,* 113 S.Ct. 418 (1992) (use of contraceptives inadmissible since use implies sexual activity); *United States v. One Feather,* 702 F.2d 736 (8th Cir. 1983) (birth of an illegitimate child inadmissible); *State v. Carmichael,* 727 P.2d 918, 925 (Kan. 1986) (evidence of venereal disease inadmissible). In addition, the word "behavior" should be construed to include activities of the mind, such as fantasies or dreams. See 23 C. Wright & K. Graham, Jr., *Federal Practice and Procedure,* §5384 at p. 548 (1980) ("While there may be some doubt under statutes that require 'conduct,' it would seem that the language of Rule 412 is broad enough to encompass the behavior of the mind.").

The rule has been amended to also exclude all other evidence relating to an alleged victim of sexual misconduct that is offered to prove a sexual predisposition. This amendment is designed to exclude evidence that does not directly refer to sexual activities or thoughts but that the proponent believes may have a sexual connotation for the factfinder. Admission of such evidence would contravene Rule 412's objectives of shielding the alleged victim from potential embarrassment and safeguarding the victim against stereotypical thinking. Consequently, unless the (b)(2) exception is satisfied, evidence such as that relating to the alleged victim's mode of dress, speech, or lifestyle will not be admissible.

The introductory phrase in subdivision (a) was deleted because it lacked clarity and contained no explicit reference to the other provisions of law that were intended to be overridden. The conditional clause, "except as provided in subdivisions (b) and (c)" is intended to make clear that evidence of the types described in subdivision (a) is admissible only under the strictures of those sections.

The reason for extending the rule to all criminal cases is obvious. The strong social policy of protecting a victim's privacy and encouraging victims to come forward to report criminal acts is not confined to cases that involve a charge of sexual assault. The need to protect the victim is equally great when a defendant is charged with kidnapping, and evidence is offered, either to prove motive or as background, that the defendant sexually assaulted the victim.

The reason for extending Rule 412 to civil cases is equally obvious. The need to protect alleged victims against invasions of privacy, potential embarrassment, and unwarranted sexual stereotyping, and the wish to encourage victims to come forward when they have been sexually molested do not disappear because the context has shifted from a criminal prosecution to a claim for damages or injunctive relief. There is a strong social policy in not only punishing those who engage in sexual misconduct, but in also providing relief to the victim. Thus, Rule 412 applies in any civil case in which a person claims to be the victim of sexual misconduct, such as actions for sexual battery or sexual harassment.

Subdivision (b). Subdivision (b) spells out the specific circumstances in which some evidence may be admissible that would otherwise be barred by the general rule expressed in subdivision (a). As amended, Rule 412 will be virtually unchanged in criminal cases, but will provide protection to any person alleged to be a victim of sexual misconduct regardless of the charge actually brought against an accused. A new exception has been added for civil cases.

In a criminal case, evidence may be admitted under subdivision (b)(1) pursuant to three possible exceptions, provided the evidence also satisfies other requirements for admissibility specified in the Federal Rules of Evidence, including Rule 403. Subdivisions (b)(1)(A) and (b)(1)(B) require proof in the form of specific instances of sexual behavior in recognition of the limited probative value and dubious reliability of evidence of reputation or evidence in the form of an opinion.

Under subdivision (b)(1)(A), evidence of specific instances of sexual behavior with persons other than the person whose sexual misconduct is alleged may be admissible if it is offered to prove that another person was the source of semen, injury or other physical evidence. Where the prosecution has directly or indirectly asserted that the physical evidence originated with the accused, the defendant must be afforded an opportunity to prove that another person was responsible. See *United States v. Begay*, 937 F.2d 515, 523 n. 10 (10th Cir. 1991). Evidence offered for the specific purpose identified in this subdivision may still be excluded if it does not satisfy Rules 401 or 403. *See, e.g., United States v. Azure*, 845 F.2d 1503, 1505–06 (8th Cir. 1988) (10 year old victim's injuries indicated recent use of force; court excluded evidence of consensual sexual activities with witness who testified at in camera hearing that he had never hurt victim and failed to establish recent activities).

Under the exception in subdivision (b)(1)(B), evidence of specific instances of sexual behavior with respect to the person whose sexual misconduct is alleged is admissible if offered to prove consent, or offered by the prosecution. Admissible pursuant to this exception might be evidence of prior instances of sexual activities between the alleged victim and the accused, as well as statements in which the alleged victim expressed an intent to engage in sexual intercourse with the accused, or voiced sexual fantasies involving the specific accused. In a prosecution for child sexual abuse, for example, evidence of uncharged sexual activity between the accused and the alleged victim offered by the prosecution may be admissible pursuant to Rule 404(b) to show a pattern of behavior. Evidence relating to the victim's alleged sexual predisposition is not admissible pursuant to this exception.

Under subdivision (b)(1)(C), evidence of specific instances of conduct may not be excluded if the result would be to deny a criminal defendant the protections afforded by the Constitution. For example, statements in which the victim has expressed an intent to have sex with the first person encountered on a particular occasion might not be excluded without violating the due process right of a rape defendant seeking to prove consent. Recognition of this basic principle was expressed in subdivision (b)(1) of the original rule. The United States Supreme Court has recognized that in various circumstances a defendant may have a right to introduce evidence otherwise precluded by an evidence rule under the Confrontation Clause. *See, e.g., Olden v. Kentucky*, 488 U.S. 227 (1988) (defendant in rape cases had right to inquire into alleged victim's cohabitation with another man to show bias).

Subdivision (b)(2) governs the admissibility of otherwise proscribed evidence in civil cases. It employs a balancing test rather than the specific exceptions stated in subdivision (b)(1) in recognition of the difficulty of foreseeing future developments in the law. Greater flexibility is needed to accommodate evolving causes of action such as claims for sexual harassment.

The balancing test requires the proponent of the evidence, whether plaintiff or defendant, to convince the court that the probative value of the proffered evidence "substantially outweighs the danger of harm to any victim and of unfair prejudice of any party." This test for admitting evidence offered to prove sexual behavior or sexual propensity in civil cases differs in three respects from the general rule governing admissibility set forth in Rule 403. First, it reverses the usual procedure spelled out in Rule 403 by shifting the burden to the proponent to demonstrate admissibility rather than making the opponent justify exclusion of the evidence. Second, the standard expressed in subdivision (b)(2) is more stringent than in the original rule; it raises the threshold for admission by requiring that the probative value of the evidence *substantially* outweigh the specified dangers. Finally, the Rule 412 test puts "harm to the victim" on the scale in addition to prejudice to the parties.

Evidence of reputation may be received in a civil case only if the alleged victim has put his or her reputation into controversy. The victim may do so without making a specific allegation in a pleading. Cf. Fed.R.Civ.P. 35 (a).

Subdivision (c). Amended subdivision (c) is more concise and understandable than the subdivision it replaces. The requirement of a motion before trial is continued in the amended rule, as is the provision that a late motion may be permitted for good cause shown. In deciding whether to permit late filing, the court may take into account the conditions previously included in the rule: namely whether the evidence is newly discovered and could not have been obtained earlier through the existence of due diligence, and whether the issue to which such evidence relates has newly arisen in the case. The rule recognizes that in some instances the circumstances that justify an application to introduce evidence otherwise barred by Rule 412 will not become apparent until trial.

The amended rule provides that before admitting evidence that falls within the prohibition of Rule 412(a), the court must hold a hearing in camera at which the alleged victim and any party must be afforded the right to be present and an opportunity to be heard. All papers connected with the motion and any record of a hearing on the motion must be kept and remain under seal during the course of trial and appellate proceedings unless otherwise ordered. This is to assure that the privacy of the alleged victim is preserved in all cases in which the court rules that proffered evidence is not admissible, and in which the hearing refers to matters that are not received, or are received in another form.

The procedures set forth in subdivision (c) do not apply to discovery of a victim's past sexual conduct or predisposition in civil cases, which will be continued to be governed by Fed. R. Civ. P. 26. In order not to undermine the rationale of Rule 412, however, courts should enter appropriate orders pursuant to Fed. R. Civ. P. 26 (c) to protect the victim against unwarranted inquiries and to ensure confidentiality. Courts should presumptively issue protective orders barring discovery unless the party seeking discovery makes a showing that the evidence sought to be discovered would be relevant under the facts and theories of the particular case, and cannot be obtained except through discovery. In an action for sexual harassment, for instance, while some evidence of the alleged victim's sexual behavior and/or predisposition in the workplace may perhaps be relevant, non-workplace conduct will usually be irrelevant. *Cf. Burns v. McGregor Electronic Industries, Inc.*, 989 F.2d 959, 962–63 (8th Cir. 1993) (posing for a nude magazine outside work hours is irrelevant to issue of unwelcomeness of sexual advances at work). Confidentiality orders should be presumptively granted as well.

One substantive change made in subdivision (c) is the elimination of the following sentence: "Notwithstanding subdivision (b) of Rule 104, if the relevancy of the evidence which the accused seeks to offer in the trial depends upon the fulfillment of a condition of fact, the court, at the hearing in chambers or at a subsequent hearing in chambers scheduled for such purpose, shall accept evidence on the issue of whether such condition of fact is fulfilled and shall determine such issue." On its face, this language would appear to authorize a trial judge to exclude evidence of past sexual conduct between an alleged victim and an accused or a defendant in a civil case based upon the judge's belief that such past acts did not occur. Such an authorization raises questions of invasion of the right to a jury trial under the Sixth and Seventh Amendments. *See* 1 S. Saltzburg & M. Martin, *Federal Rules Of Evidence Manual*, 396–97 (5th ed. 1990).

The Advisory Committee concluded that the amended rule provided adequate protection for all persons claiming to be the victims of sexual misconduct, and that it was inadvisable to continue to include a provision in the rule that has been confusing and that raises substantial constitutional issues.

[The Supreme Court withheld that portion of the proposed amendment to Rule 412 transmitted to the Court by the Judicial Conference of the United States which would apply that Rule to civil cases. This Note was not revised to account for the Court's action, because the Note is the commentary of the advisory committee. The proposed amendment to Rule 412 was subsequently amended by section 40141(b) of Pub. L. 103–322. See below.]

RULE 413. SIMILAR CRIMES IN SEXUAL-ASSAULT CASES

(a) Permitted Uses. In a criminal case in which a defendant is accused of a sexual assault, the court may admit evidence that the defendant committed any other sexual assault. The evidence may be considered on any matter to which it is relevant.

(b) Disclosure to the Defendant. If the prosecutor intends to offer this evidence, the prosecutor must disclose it to the defendant, including witnesses' statements or a summary of the expected testimony. The prosecutor must do so at least 15 days before trial or at a later time that the court allows for good cause.

(c) Effect on Other Rules. This rule does not limit the admission or consideration of evidence under any other rule.

(d) Definition of "Sexual Assault." In this rule and Rule 415, "sexual assault" means a crime under federal law or under state law (as "state" is defined in 18 U.S.C. § 513) involving:

(1) any conduct prohibited by 18 U.S.C. chapter 109A;

(2) contact, without consent, between any part of the defendant's body—or an object—and another person's genitals or anus;

(3) contact, without consent, between the defendant's genitals or anus and any part of another person's body;

(4) deriving sexual pleasure or gratification from inflicting death, bodily injury, or physical pain on another person; or

(5) an attempt or conspiracy to engage in conduct described in subparagraphs (1)– (4).

RULE 414. SIMILAR CRIMES IN CHILD MOLESTATION CASES

(a) Permitted Uses. In a criminal case in which a defendant is accused of child molestation, the court may admit evidence that the defendant committed any other child molestation. The evidence may be considered on any matter to which it is relevant.

(b) Disclosure to the Defendant. If the prosecutor intends to offer this evidence, the prosecutor must disclose it to the defendant, including witnesses' statements or a summary of the expected testimony. The prosecutor must do so at least 15 days before trial or at a later time that the court allows for good cause.

(c) Effect on Other Rules. This rule does not limit the admission or consideration of evidence under any other rule.

(d) Definition of "Child" and "Child Molestation." In this rule and Rule 415:

(1) "child" means a person below the age of 14; and

(2) "child molestation" means a crime under federal law or under state law (as "state" is defined in 18 U.S.C. § 513) involving:

(A) any conduct prohibited by 18 U.S.C. chapter 109A and committed with a child;

(B) any conduct prohibited by 18 U.S.C. chapter 110;

(C) contact between any part of the defendant's body—or an object—and a child's genitals or anus;

(D) contact between the defendant's genitals or anus and any part of a child's body;

(E) deriving sexual pleasure or gratification from inflicting death, bodily injury, or physical pain on a child; or

(F) an attempt or conspiracy to engage in conduct described in subparagraphs (A)–(E).

RULE 415. SIMILAR ACTS IN CIVIL CASES INVOLVING SEXUAL ASSAULT OR CHILD MOLESTATION

(a) Permitted Uses. In a civil case involving a claim for relief based on a party's alleged sexual assault or child molestation, the court may admit evidence that the party committed any other sexual assault or child molestation. The evidence may be considered as provided in Rules 413 and 414 .

(b) Disclosure to the Opponent. If a party intends to offer this evidence, the party must disclose it to the party against whom it will be offered, including witnesses' statements or a summary of the expected testimony. The party must do so at least 15 days before trial or at a later time that the court allows for good cause.

(c) Effect on Other Rules. This rule does not limit the admission or consideration of evidence under any other rule.

ARTICLE V. PRIVILEGES

RULE 501. PRIVILEGE IN GENERAL

The common law—as interpreted by United States courts in the light of reason and experience—governs a claim of privilege unless any of the following provides otherwise:

- the United States Constitution;
- a federal statute; or
- rules prescribed by the Supreme Court.

But in a civil case, state law governs privilege regarding a claim or defense for which state law supplies the rule of decision.

RULE 502. ATTORNEY-CLIENT PRIVILEGE AND WORK PRODUCT; LIMITATIONS ON WAIVER

The following provisions apply, in the circumstances set out, to disclosure of a communication or information covered by the attorney-client privilege or work-product protection.

(a) Disclosure Made in a Federal Proceeding or to a Federal Office or Agency; Scope of a Waiver. When the disclosure is made in a federal proceeding or to a federal office or agency and waives the attorney-client privilege or work-product protection, the waiver extends to an undisclosed communication or information in a federal or state proceeding only if:

(1) the waiver is intentional;

(2) the disclosed and undisclosed communications or information concern the same subject matter; and

(3) they ought in fairness to be considered together.

(b) Inadvertent Disclosure. When made in a federal proceeding or to a federal office or agency, the disclosure does not operate as a waiver in a federal or state proceeding if:

(1) the disclosure is inadvertent;

(2) the holder of the privilege or protection took reasonable steps to prevent disclosure; and

(3) the holder promptly took reasonable steps to rectify the error, including (if applicable) following Federal Rule of Civil Procedure 26 (b)(5)(B).

(c) Disclosure Made in a State Proceeding. When the disclosure is made in a state proceeding and is not the subject of a state-court order concerning waiver, the disclosure does not operate as a waiver in a federal proceeding if the disclosure:

(1) would not be a waiver under this rule if it had been made in a federal proceeding; or

(2) is not a waiver under the law of the state where the disclosure occurred.

(d) Controlling Effect of a Court Order. A federal court may order that the privilege or protection is not waived by disclosure connected with the litigation pending before the court—in which event the disclosure is also not a waiver in any other federal or state proceeding.

(e) Controlling Effect of a Party Agreement. An agreement on the effect of disclosure in a federal proceeding is binding only on the parties to the agreement, unless it is incorporated into a court order.

(f) Controlling Effect of this Rule. Notwithstanding Rules 101 and 1101, this rule applies to state proceedings and to federal court-annexed and federal court-mandated arbitration proceedings, in the circumstances set out in the rule. And notwithstanding Rule 501, this rule applies even if state law provides the rule of decision.

(g) Definitions. In this rule:

(1) "attorney-client privilege" means the protection that applicable law provides for confidential attorney-client communications; and

(2) "work-product protection" means the protection that applicable law provides for tangible material (or its intangible equivalent) prepared in anticipation of litigation or for trial.

ARTICLE VI. WITNESSES

RULE 601. COMPETENCY TO TESTIFY IN GENERAL

Every person is competent to be a witness unless these rules provide otherwise. But in a civil case, state law governs the witness's competency regarding a claim or defense for which state law supplies the rule of decision.

RULE 602. NEED FOR PERSONAL KNOWLEDGE

A witness may testify to a matter only if evidence is introduced sufficient to support a finding that the witness has personal knowledge of the matter. Evidence to prove personal knowledge may consist of the witness's own testimony. This rule does not apply to a witness's expert testimony under Rule 703.

RULE 603. OATH OR AFFIRMATION TO TESTIFY TRUTHFULLY

Before testifying, a witness must give an oath or affirmation to testify truthfully. It must be in a form designed to impress that duty on the witness's conscience.

RULE 604. INTERPRETER

An interpreter must be qualified and must give an oath or affirmation to make a true translation.

RULE 605. JUDGE'S COMPETENCY AS A WITNESS

The presiding judge may not testify as a witness at the trial. A party need not object to preserve the issue.

NOTES OF ADVISORY COMMITTEE ON PROPOSED RULES (1973)

In view of the mandate of 28 U.S.C. §455 that a judge disqualify himself in "any case in which he * * * is or has been a material witness," the likelihood that the presiding judge in a federal court might be called to testify in the trial over which he is presiding is slight. Nevertheless the possibility is not totally eliminated.

The solution here presented is a broad rule of incompetency, rather than such alternatives as incompetency only as to material matters, leaving the matter to the discretion of the judge, or recognizing no incompetency. The choice is the result of inability to evolve satisfactory answers to questions which arise when the judge abandons the bench for the witness stand. Who rules on objections? Who compels him to answer? Can he rule impartially on the weight and admissibility of his own testimony? Can he be impeached or cross-examined effectively? Can he, in a jury trial, avoid conferring his seal of approval on one side in the eyes of the jury? Can he, in a bench trial, avoid an involvement destructive of impartiality? The rule of general incompetency has substantial support. See Report of the Special Committee on the Propriety of Judges Appearing as Witnesses, 36 A.B.A.J. 630 (1950); cases collected in Annot. 157 A.L.R. 311; McCormick §68, p. 147; Uniform Rule 42; California Evidence Code §703; Kansas Code of Civil Procedure §60–442; New Jersey Evidence Rule 42. Cf. 6 Wigmore §1909, which advocates leaving the matter to the discretion of the judge, and statutes to that effect collected in Annot. 157 A.L.R. 311.

The rule provides an "automatic" objection. To require an actual objection would confront the opponent with a choice between not objecting, with the result of allowing the testimony, and objecting, with the probable result of excluding the testimony but at the price of continuing the trial before a judge likely to feel that his integrity had been attacked by the objector.

RULE 606. JUROR'S COMPETENCY AS A WITNESS

(a) At the Trial. A juror may not testify as a witness before the other jurors at the trial. If a juror is called to testify, the court must give a party an opportunity to object outside the jury's presence.

(b) During an Inquiry into the Validity of a Verdict or Indictment.

(1) *Prohibited Testimony or Other Evidence.* During an inquiry into the validity of a verdict or indictment, a juror may not testify about any statement made or incident that occurred during the jury's deliberations; the effect of anything on that juror's or another juror's vote; or any juror's mental processes concerning the verdict or indictment. The court may not receive a juror's affidavit or evidence of a juror's statement on these matters.

(2) *Exceptions.* A juror may testify about whether:

(A) extraneous prejudicial information was improperly brought to the jury's attention;

(B) an outside influence was improperly brought to bear on any juror; or

(C) a mistake was made in entering the verdict on the verdict form.

RULE 607. WHO MAY IMPEACH A WITNESS

Any party, including the party that called the witness, may attack the witness's credibility.

RULE 608. A WITNESS'S CHARACTER FOR TRUTHFULNESS OR UNTRUTHFULNESS

(a) Reputation or Opinion Evidence. A witness's credibility may be attacked or supported by testimony about the witness's reputation for having a character for truthfulness or untruthfulness, or by testimony in the form of an opinion about that character. But evidence of truthful character is admissible only after the witness's character for truthfulness has been attacked.

(b) Specific Instances of Conduct. Except for a criminal conviction under Rule 609, extrinsic evidence is not admissible to prove specific instances of a witness's conduct in order to attack or support the witness's character for truthfulness. But the court may, on cross-examination, allow them to be inquired into if they are probative of the character for truthfulness or untruthfulness of:

(1) the witness; or

(2) another witness whose character the witness being cross-examined has testified about.

By testifying on another matter, a witness does not waive any privilege against self-incrimination for testimony that relates only to the witness's character for truthfulness.

NOTES OF ADVISORY COMMITTEE ON PROPOSED RULES (1973)

Subdivision (a). In Rule 404(a) the general position is taken that character evidence is not admissible for the purpose of proving that the person acted in conformity therewith, subject, however, to several exceptions, one of which is character evidence of a witness as bearing upon his credibility. The present rule develops that exception.

In accordance with the bulk of judicial authority, the inquiry is strictly limited to character for veracity, rather than allowing evidence as to character generally. The result is to sharpen relevancy, to reduce surprise, waste of time, and confusion, and to make the lot of the witness somewhat less unattractive. McCormick §44.

The use of opinion and reputation evidence as means of proving the character of witnesses is consistent with Rule 405(a). While the modern practice has purported to exclude opinion witnesses who testify to reputation seem in fact often to be giving their opinions, disguised somewhat misleadingly as reputation. See McCormick §44. And even under the modern practice, a common relaxation has allowed inquiry as to whether the witnesses would believe the principal witness under oath. *United States v. Walker*, 313 F.2d 236 (6th Cir. 1963), and cases cited therein; McCormick §44, pp. 94–95, n. 3.

Character evidence in support of credibility is admissible under the rule only after the witness' character has first been attacked, as has been the case at common law. Maguire, Weinstein, et al., Cases on Evidence 295 (5th ed. 1965); McCormick §49, p. 105; 4 Wigmore §1104. The enormous needless consumption of time which a contrary practice would entail justifies the limitation. Opinion or reputation that the witness is untruthful specifically qualifies as an attack under the rule, and evidence or misconduct, including conviction of crime, and of corruption also fall within this category. Evidence of bias or interest does not. McCormick §49; 4 Wigmore §§1106, 1107. Whether evidence in the form of contradiction is an attack upon the character of the witness must depend[.] §§1108, 1109.

As to the use of specific instances on direct by an opinion witness, see the Advisory Committee's Note to Rule 405, supra.

Subdivision (b). In conformity with Rule 405, which forecloses use of evidence of specific incidents as proof in chief of character unless character is an issue in the case, the present rule generally bars evidence of specific instances of conduct of a witness for the purpose of attacking or supporting his credibility. There are, however, two exceptions: (1) specific instances are provable when they have been the subject of criminal conviction, and (2) specific instances may be inquired into on cross-examination of the principal witness or of a witness giving an opinion of his character for truthfulness.

(1) Conviction of crime as a technique of impeachment is treated in detail in Rule 609, and here is merely recognized as an exception to the general rule excluding evidence of specific incidents for impeachment purposes.

(2) Particular instances of conduct, though not the subject of criminal conviction, may be inquired into on cross-examination of the principal witness himself or of a witness who testifies concerning his character for truthfulness. Effective cross-examination demands that some allowance be made for going into matters of this kind, but the possibilities of abuse are substantial. Consequently safeguards are erected in the form of specific requirements that the instances inquired into be probative of truthfulness or its opposite and not remote in time. Also, the overriding protection of Rule 403 requires that probative value not be outweighed by danger of unfair prejudice, confusion of issues, or misleading the jury, and that of Rule 611 bars harassment and undue embarrassment.

The final sentence constitutes a rejection of the doctrine of such cases as *People v. Sorge*, 301 N.Y. 198, 93 N.E.2d 637 (1950), that any past criminal act relevant to credibility may be inquired into on cross-examination, in apparent disregard of the privilege against self-incrimination. While it is clear that an ordinary witness cannot make a partial disclosure of incriminating matter and then invoke the privilege on cross-examination, no tenable contention can be made that merely by testifying he waives his right to foreclose inquiry on cross-examination into criminal activities for the purpose of attacking his credibility. So to hold would reduce the privilege to a nullity. While it is true that an accused, unlike an ordinary witness, has an option whether to testify, if the option can be exercised only at the price of opening up inquiry as to any and all criminal acts committed during his lifetime, the right to testify could scarcely be said to possess much vitality. In *Griffin v. California*, 380 U.S. 609, 85 S.Ct. 1229, 14 L.Ed. 2d 106 (1965), the Court held that allowing comment on the election of an accused not to testify exacted a constitutionally impermissible price, and so here. While no specific provision in terms confers constitutional status on the right of an accused to take the stand in his own defense, the existence of the right is so completely recognized that a denial of it or substantial infringement upon it would surely be of due process dimensions. See *Ferguson v. Georgia*, 365 U.S. 570, 81 S.Ct. 756, 5 L.Ed. 2d 783 (1961); McCormick §131; 8 Wigmore §2276 (McNaughton Rev. 1961). In any event, wholly aside from constitutional considerations, the provision represents a sound policy.

COMMITTEE NOTES ON RULES – 2003 AMENDMENT

The Rule has been amended to clarify that the absolute prohibition on extrinsic evidence applies only when the sole reason for proffering that evidence is to attack or support the witness' character for truthfulness. *See United States v. Abel*, 469 U.S. 45 (1984); *United States v. Fusco*, 748 F.2d 996 (5th Cir. 1984) (Rule 608(b) limits the use of evidence "designed to show that the witness has done things, unrelated to the suit being tried, that make him more or less believable per se"); Ohio R. Evid. 608(b). On occasion the Rule's use of the overbroad term "credibility" has been read "to bar extrinsic evidence for bias, competency and contradiction impeachment since they too deal with credibility." American Bar Association Section of Litigation, *Emerging Problems Under the Federal Rules of Evidence* at 161 (3d ed. 1998). The amendment conforms the language of the Rule to its original intent, which was to impose an absolute bar on extrinsic evidence only if the sole purpose for offering the evidence was to prove the witness' character for veracity. *See* Advisory Committee Note to Rule 608(b) (stating that the Rule is "[i]n conformity with Rule 405, which forecloses use of evidence of specific incidents as proof in chief of character unless character is in issue in the case . . .").

By limiting the application of the Rule to proof of a witness' character for truthfulness, the amendment leaves the admissibility of extrinsic evidence offered for other grounds of impeachment (such as contradiction, prior inconsistent statement, bias and mental capacity) to Rules 402 and 403 . *See, e.g., United States v. Winchenbach*, 197 F.3d 548 (1st Cir. 1999) (admissibility of a prior inconsistent statement offered for impeachment is governed by Rules 402 and 403, not Rule 608(b)); *United States v. Tarantino*, 846 F.2d 1384 (D.C. Cir. 1988) (admissibility of extrinsic evidence offered to contradict a witness is governed by Rules 402 and 403); *United States v. Lindemann*, 85 F.3d 1232 (7th Cir. 1996) (admissibility of extrinsic evidence of bias is governed by Rules 402 and 403).

It should be noted that the extrinsic evidence prohibition of Rule 608(b) bars any reference to the consequences that a witness might have suffered as a result of an alleged bad act. For example, Rule 608(b) prohibits counsel from mentioning that a witness was suspended or disciplined for the conduct that is the subject of impeachment, when that conduct is offered only to prove the character of the witness. See *United States v. Davis*, 183 F.3d 231, 257 n.12 (3d Cir. 1999) (emphasizing that in attacking the defendant's character for truthfulness "the government cannot make reference to Davis's forty-four day suspension or that Internal Affairs found that he lied about" an incident because "[s]uch evidence would not only be hearsay to the extent it contains assertion of fact, it would be inadmissible extrinsic evidence under Rule 608(b)"). *See also* Stephen A. Saltzburg, *Impeaching the Witness: Prior Bad Acts and Extrinsic Evidence*, 7 Crim. Just. 28, 31 (Winter 1993) ("counsel should not be permitted to circumvent the no-extrinsic-evidence provision by tucking a third person's opinion about prior acts into a question asked of the witness who has denied the act.").

For purposes of consistency the term "credibility" has been replaced by the term "character for truthfulness" in the last sentence of subdivision (b). The term "credibility" is also used in subdivision (a). But the Committee found it unnecessary to substitute "character for truthfulness" for "credibility" in Rule 608(a), because subdivision (a)(1) already serves to limit impeachment to proof of such character.

Rules 609(a) and 610 also use the term "credibility" when the intent of those Rules is to regulate impeachment of a witness' character for truthfulness. No inference should be derived from the fact that the Committee proposed an amendment to Rule 608(b) but not to Rules 609 and 610.

Changes Made After Publication and Comments. The last sentence of Rule 608(b) was changed to substitute the term "character for truthfulness" for the existing term "credibility." This change was made in accordance with public comment suggesting that it would be helpful to provide uniform terminology throughout Rule 608(b). A stylistic change was also made to the last sentence of Rule 608(b).

RULE 609. IMPEACHMENT BY EVIDENCE OF A CRIMINAL CONVICTION

(a) In General. The following rules apply to attacking a witness's character for truthfulness by evidence of a criminal conviction:

(1) for a crime that, in the convicting jurisdiction, was punishable by death or by imprisonment for more than one year, the evidence:

(A) must be admitted, subject to Rule 403, in a civil case or in a criminal case in which the witness is not a defendant; and

(B) must be admitted in a criminal case in which the witness is a defendant, if the probative value of the evidence outweighs its prejudicial effect to that defendant; and

(2) for any crime regardless of the punishment, the evidence must be admitted if the court can readily determine that establishing the elements of the crime required proving—or the witness's admitting—a dishonest act or false statement.

(b) Limit on Using the Evidence After 10 Years. This subdivision (b) applies if more than 10 years have passed since the witness's conviction or release from confinement for it, whichever is later. Evidence of the conviction is admissible only if:

(1) its probative value, supported by specific facts and circumstances, substantially outweighs its prejudicial effect; and

(2) the proponent gives an adverse party reasonable written notice of the intent to use it so that the party has a fair opportunity to contest its use.

(c) Effect of a Pardon, Annulment, or Certificate of Rehabilitation. Evidence of a conviction is not admissible if:

(1) the conviction has been the subject of a pardon, annulment, certificate of rehabilitation, or other equivalent procedure based on a finding that the person has been rehabilitated, and the person has not been convicted of a later crime punishable by death or by imprisonment for more than one year; or

(2) the conviction has been the subject of a pardon, annulment, or other equivalent procedure based on a finding of innocence.

(d) Juvenile Adjudications. Evidence of a juvenile adjudication is admissible under this rule only if:

(1) it is offered in a criminal case;

(2) the adjudication was of a witness other than the defendant;

(3) an adult's conviction for that offense would be admissible to attack the adult's credibility; and

(4) admitting the evidence is necessary to fairly determine guilt or innocence.

(e) Pendency of an Appeal. A conviction that satisfies this rule is admissible even if an appeal is pending. Evidence of the pendency is also admissible.

RULE 610. RELIGIOUS BELIEFS OR OPINIONS

Evidence of a witness's religious beliefs or opinions is not admissible to attack or support the witness's credibility.

RULE 611. MODE AND ORDER OF EXAMINING WITNESSES AND PRESENTING EVIDENCE

(a) Control by the Court; Purposes. The court should exercise reasonable control over the mode and order of examining witnesses and presenting evidence so as to:

(1) make those procedures effective for determining the truth;

(2) avoid wasting time; and

(3) protect witnesses from harassment or undue embarrassment.

(b) Scope of Cross-Examination. Cross-examination should not go beyond the subject matter of the direct examination and matters affecting the witness's credibility. The court may allow inquiry into additional matters as if on direct examination.

(c) Leading Questions. Leading questions should not be used on direct examination except as necessary to develop the witness's testimony. Ordinarily, the court should allow leading questions:

(1) on cross-examination; and

(2) when a party calls a hostile witness, an adverse party, or a witness identified with an adverse party.

RULE 612. WRITING USED TO REFRESH A WITNESS'S MEMORY

(a) Scope. This rule gives an adverse party certain options when a witness uses a writing to refresh memory:

(1) while testifying; or

(2) before testifying, if the court decides that justice requires the party to have those options.

(b) Adverse Party's Options; Deleting Unrelated Matter. Unless 18 U.S.C. § 3500 provides otherwise in a criminal case, an adverse party is entitled to have the writing produced at the hearing, to inspect it, to cross-examine the witness about it, and to introduce in evidence any portion that relates to the witness's testimony. If the producing party claims that the writing includes unrelated matter, the court must examine the writing in camera, delete any unrelated portion, and order that the rest be delivered to the adverse party. Any portion deleted over objection must be preserved for the record.

(c) Failure to Produce or Deliver the Writing. If a writing is not produced or is not delivered as ordered, the court may issue any appropriate order. But if the prosecution does not comply in a criminal case, the court must strike the witness's testimony or—if justice so requires—declare a mistrial.

RULE 613. WITNESS'S PRIOR STATEMENT

(a) Showing or Disclosing the Statement During Examination. When examining a witness about the witness's prior statement, a party need not show it or disclose its contents to the witness. But the party must, on request, show it or disclose its contents to an adverse party's attorney.

(b) Extrinsic Evidence of a Prior Inconsistent Statement. Unless the court orders otherwise, extrinsic evidence of a witness's prior inconsistent statement may not be admitted until after the witness is given an opportunity to explain or deny the statement and an adverse party is given an opportunity to examine the witness about it. This subdivision (b) does not apply to an opposing party's statement under Rule 801(d)(2).

RULE 614. COURT'S CALLING OR EXAMINING A WITNESS

(a) Calling. The court may call a witness on its own or at a party's request. Each party is entitled to cross-examine the witness.

(b) Examining. The court may examine a witness regardless of who calls the witness.

(c) Objections. A party may object to the court's calling or examining a witness either at that time or at the next opportunity when the jury is not present.

RULE 615. EXCLUDING WITNESSES

(a) Excluding Witnesses. At a party's request, the court must order witnesses excluded from the courtroom so that they cannot hear other witnesses' testimony. Or the court may do so on its own. But this rule does not authorize excluding:

(1) a party who is a natural person;

(2) one officer or employee of a party that is not a natural person, if that officer or employee has been designated as the party's representative by its attorney;

(3) any person whose presence a party shows to be essential to presenting the party's claim or defense; or

(4) a person authorized by statute to be present.

(b) Additional Orders to Prevent Disclosing and Accessing Testimony. An order under (a) operates only to exclude witnesses from the courtroom. But the court may also, by order:

(1) prohibit disclosure of trial testimony to witnesses who are excluded from the courtroom; and

(2) prohibit excluded witnesses from accessing trial testimony.

ARTICLE VII. OPINIONS AND EXPERT TESTIMONY

RULE 701. OPINION TESTIMONY BY LAY WITNESSES

If a witness is not testifying as an expert, testimony in the form of an opinion is limited to one that is:

(a) rationally based on the witness's perception;

(b) helpful to clearly understanding the witness's testimony or to determining a fact in issue; and

(c) not based on scientific, technical, or other specialized knowledge within the scope of Rule 702.

NOTES OF ADVISORY COMMITTEE ON PROPOSED RULES (1973)

The rule retains the traditional objective of putting the trier of fact in possession of an accurate reproduction of the event.

Limitation (a) is the familiar requirement of first-hand knowledge or observation.

Limitation (b) is phrased in terms of requiring testimony to be helpful in resolving issues. Witnesses often find difficulty in expressing themselves in language which is not that of an opinion or conclusion. While the courts have made concessions in certain recurring situations, necessity as a standard for permitting opinions and conclusions has proved too elusive and too unadaptable to particular situations for purposes of satisfactory judicial administration. McCormick §11. Moreover, the practical impossibility of determining by rule what is a "fact," demonstrated by a century of litigation of the question of what is a fact for purposes of pleading under the Field Code, extends into evidence also. 7 Wigmore §1919. The rule assumes that the natural characteristics of the adversary system will generally lead to an acceptable result, since the detailed account carries more conviction than the broad assertion, and a lawyer can be expected to display his witness to the best advantage. If he fails to do so, cross-examination and argument will point up the weakness. See Ladd, Expert Testimony, 5 Vand.L.Rev. 414, 415–417 (1952). If, despite these considerations, attempts are made to introduce meaningless assertions which amount to little more than choosing up sides, exclusion for lack of helpfulness is called for by the rule.

The language of the rule is substantially that of Uniform. Rule 56(1). Similar provisions are California Evidence Code §800; Kansas Code of Civil Procedure §60–456(a); New Jersey Evidence Rule 56(1).

COMMITTEE NOTES ON RULES – 2000 AMENDMENT

Rule 701 has been amended to eliminate the risk that the reliability requirements set forth in Rule 702 will be evaded through the simple expedient of proffering an expert in lay witness clothing. Under the amendment, a witness' testimony must be scrutinized under the rules regulating expert opinion to the extent that the witness is providing testimony based on scientific, technical, or other specialized knowledge within the scope of Rule 702. *See generally Asplundh Mfg. Div. v. Benton Harbor Eng'g*, 57 F.3d 1190 (3d Cir. 1995). By channeling testimony that is actually expert testimony to Rule 702, the amendment also ensures that a party will not evade the expert witness disclosure requirements set forth in Fed. R. Civ. P. 26 and Fed. R. Crim. P. 16 by simply calling an expert witness in the guise of a layperson. *See* Joseph, *Emerging Expert Issues Under the 1993 Disclosure Amendments to the Federal Rules of Civil Procedure*, 164 F.R.D. 97, 108 (1996) (noting that "there is no good reason to allow what is essentially surprise expert testimony," and that "the Court should be vigilant to preclude manipulative conduct designed to thwart the expert disclosure and discovery process"). See also *United States v. Figueroa-Lopez*, 125 F.3d 1241, 1246 (9th Cir. 1997) (law enforcement agents testifying that the defendant's conduct was consistent with that of a drug trafficker could not testify as lay witnesses; to permit such testimony under Rule 701 "subverts the requirements of Federal Rule of Criminal Procedure 16 (a)(1)(E)").

The amendment does not distinguish between expert and lay *witnesses*, but rather between expert and lay *testimony*. Certainly it is possible for the same witness to provide both lay and expert testimony in a single case. *See, e.g., United States v. Figueroa-Lopez*, 125 F.3d 1241, 1246 (9th Cir. 1997) (law enforcement agents could testify that the defendant was acting suspiciously, without being qualified as experts; however, the rules on experts were applicable where the agents testified on the basis of extensive experience that the defendant was using code words to refer to drug quantities and prices). The amendment makes clear that any part of a witness' testimony that is based upon scientific, technical, or other specialized knowledge within the scope of Rule 702 is governed by the standards of Rule 702 and the corresponding disclosure requirements of the Civil and Criminal Rules.

The amendment is not intended to affect the "prototypical example[s] of the type of evidence contemplated by the adoption of Rule 701 relat[ing] to the appearance of persons or things, identity, the manner of conduct, competency of a person, degrees of light or darkness, sound, size, weight, distance, and an endless number of items that cannot be described factually in words apart from inferences." *Asplundh Mfg. Div. v. Benton Harbor Eng'g*, 57 F.3d 1190, 1196 (3d Cir. 1995).

For example, most courts have permitted the owner or officer of a business to testify to the value or projected profits of the business, without the necessity of qualifying the witness as an accountant, appraiser, or similar expert. *See, e.g., Lightning Lube, Inc. v. Witco Corp.*, 4 F.3d 1153 (3d Cir. 1993) (no abuse of discretion in permitting the plaintiff's owner to give lay opinion testimony as to damages, as it was based on his knowledge and participation in the day-to-day affairs of the business). Such opinion testimony is admitted not because of experience, training or specialized knowledge within the realm of an expert, but because of the particularized knowledge that the witness has by virtue of his or her position in the business. The amendment does not purport to change this analysis. Similarly, courts have permitted lay witnesses to testify that a substance appeared to be a narcotic, so long as a foundation of familiarity with the substance is established. *See, e.g., United States v. Westbrook*, 896 F.2d 330 (8th Cir. 1990) (two lay witnesses who were heavy amphetamine users were properly permitted to testify that a substance was amphetamine; but it was error to permit another witness to make such an identification where she had no experience with amphetamines). Such testimony is not based on specialized knowledge within the scope of Rule 702, but rather is based upon a layperson's personal knowledge. If, however, that witness were to describe how a narcotic was manufactured, or to describe the intricate workings of a narcotic distribution network, then the witness would have to qualify as an expert under Rule 702. *United States v. Figueroa-Lopez, supra.*

The amendment incorporates the distinctions set forth in *State v. Brown*, 836 S.W.2d 530, 549 (1992), a case involving former Tennessee Rule of Evidence 701, a rule that precluded lay witness testimony based on "special knowledge." In *Brown*, the court declared that the distinction between lay and expert witness testimony is that lay testimony "results from a process of reasoning familiar in everyday life," while expert testimony "results from a process of reasoning which can be mastered only by specialists in the field." The court in *Brown* noted that a lay witness with experience could testify that a substance appeared to be blood, but that a witness would have to qualify as an expert before he could testify that bruising around the eyes is indicative of skull trauma. That is the kind of distinction made by the amendment to this Rule.

GAP Report—Proposed Amendment to Rule 701. The Committee made the following changes to the published draft of the proposed amendment to Evidence Rule 701:

1. The words "within the scope of Rule 702" were added at the end of the proposed amendment, to emphasize that the Rule does not require witnesses to qualify as experts unless their testimony is of the type

traditionally considered within the purview of Rule 702. The Committee Note was amended to accord with this textual change.

2. The Committee Note was revised to provide further examples of the kind of testimony that could and could not be proffered under the limitation imposed by the proposed amendment.

RULE 702. TESTIMONY BY EXPERT WITNESSES

A witness who is qualified as an expert by knowledge, skill, experience, training, or education may testify in the form of an opinion or otherwise if the proponent demonstrates to the court that it is more likely than not that:

(a) the expert's scientific, technical, or other specialized knowledge will help the trier of fact to understand the evidence or to determine a fact in issue;

(b) the testimony is based on sufficient facts or data;

(c) the testimony is the product of reliable principles and methods; and

(d) the expert's opinion reflects a reliable application of the principles and methods to the facts of the case.

NOTES OF ADVISORY COMMITTEE ON PROPOSED RULES (1973)

An intelligent evaluation of facts is often difficult or impossible without the application of some scientific, technical, or other specialized knowledge. The most common source of this knowledge is the expert witness, although there are other techniques for supplying it.

Most of the literature assumes that experts testify only in the form of opinions. The assumption is logically unfounded. The rule accordingly recognizes that an expert on the stand may give a dissertation or exposition of scientific or other principles relevant to the case, leaving the trier of fact to apply them to the facts. Since much of the criticism of expert testimony has centered upon the hypothetical question, it seems wise to recognize that opinions are not indispensable and to encourage the use of expert testimony in non-opinion form when counsel believes the trier can itself draw the requisite inference. The use of opinions is not abolished by the rule, however. It will continue to be permissible for the experts to take the further step of suggesting the inference which should be drawn from applying the specialized knowledge to the facts. See Rules 703 to 705.

Whether the situation is a proper one for the use of expert testimony is to be determined on the basis of assisting the trier. "There is no more certain test for determining when experts may be used than the common sense inquiry whether the untrained layman would be qualified to determine intelligently and to the best possible degree the particular issue without enlightenment from those having a specialized understanding of the subject involved in the dispute." Ladd, Expert Testimony, 5 Vand.L.Rev. 414, 418 (1952). When opinions are excluded, it is because they are unhelpful and therefore superfluous and a waste of time. 7 Wigmore §1918.

The rule is broadly phrased. The fields of knowledge which may be drawn upon are not limited merely to the "scientific" and "technical" but extend to all "specialized" knowledge. Similarly, the expert is viewed, not in a narrow sense, but as a person qualified by "knowledge, skill, experience, training or education." Thus within the scope of the rule are not only experts in the strictest sense of the word, e.g., physicians, physicists, and architects, but also the large group sometimes called "skilled" witnesses, such as bankers or landowners testifying to land values.

COMMITTEE NOTES ON RULES – 2000 AMENDMENT

Rule 702 has been amended in response to *Daubert v. Merrell Dow Pharmaceuticals, Inc.*, 509 U.S. 579 (1993), and to the many cases applying Daubert, including *Kumho Tire Co. v. Carmichael*, 119 S.Ct. 1167 (1999). In *Daubert* the Court charged trial judges with the responsibility of acting as gatekeepers to exclude unreliable expert testimony, and the Court in *Kumho* clarified that this gatekeeper function applies to all expert testimony, not just testimony based in science. *See also Kumho*, 119 S.Ct. at 1178 (citing the Committee Note to the proposed amendment to Rule 702, which had been released for public comment before the date of the *Kumho* decision). The amendment affirms the trial court's role as gatekeeper and provides some general standards that the trial court must use to assess the reliability and helpfulness of proffered expert testimony. Consistently with *Kumho*, the Rule as amended provides that all types of expert testimony present questions of admissibility for the trial court in deciding whether the evidence is reliable and helpful. Consequently, the admissibility of all expert testimony is governed by the principles of Rule 104(a). Under that Rule, the proponent has the burden of establishing that the pertinent admissibility requirements are met by a preponderance of the evidence. See *Bourjaily v. United States*, 483 U.S. 171 (1987).

Daubert set forth a non-exclusive checklist for trial courts to use in assessing the reliability of scientific expert testimony. The specific factors explicated by the *Daubert* Court are (1) whether the expert's technique or theory can be or has been tested—that is, whether the expert's theory can be challenged in some objective sense, or whether it is instead simply a subjective, conclusory approach that cannot reasonably be assessed for reliability; (2) whether the technique or theory has been subject to peer review and publication; (3) the known or potential rate of error of the technique or theory when applied; (4) the existence and maintenance of standards and controls; and (5) whether the technique or theory has been generally accepted in the scientific community. The Court in *Kumho* held that these factors might also be applicable in assessing the reliability of nonscientific expert testimony, depending upon "the particular circumstances of the particular case at issue." 119 S.Ct. at 1175.

No attempt has been made to "codify" these specific factors. *Daubert* itself emphasized that the factors were neither exclusive nor dispositive. Other cases have recognized that not all of the specific *Daubert* factors can apply to every type of expert testimony. In addition to *Kumho,* 119 S.Ct. at 1175, see *Tyus v. Urban Search Management,* 102 F.3d 256 (7th Cir. 1996) (noting that the factors mentioned by the Court in Daubert do not neatly apply to expert testimony from a sociologist). *See also Kannankeril v. Terminix Int'l, Inc.,* 128 F.3d 802, 809 (3d Cir. 1997) (holding that lack of peer review or publication was not dispositive where the expert's opinion was supported by "widely accepted scientific knowledge"). The standards set forth in the amendment are broad enough to require consideration of any or all of the specific *Daubert* factors where appropriate.

Courts both before and after *Daubert* have found other factors relevant in determining whether expert testimony is sufficiently reliable to be considered by the trier of fact. These factors include:

(1) Whether experts are "proposing to testify about matters growing naturally and directly out of research they have conducted independent of the litigation, or whether they have developed their opinions expressly for purposes of testifying." *Daubert v. Merrell Dow Pharmaceuticals,* Inc ., 43 F.3d 1311, 1317 (9th Cir. 1995).

(2) Whether the expert has unjustifiably extrapolated from an accepted premise to an unfounded conclusion. *See General Elec. Co. v. Joiner,* 522 U.S. 136, 146 (1997) (noting that in some cases a trial court "may conclude that there is simply too great an analytical gap between the data and the opinion proffered").

(3) Whether the expert has adequately accounted for obvious alternative explanations. *See Claar v. Burlington N.R.R.,* 29 F.3d 499 (9th Cir. 1994) (testimony excluded where the expert failed to consider other obvious causes for the plaintiff's condition). Compare *Ambrosini v. Labarraque,* 101 F.3d 129 (D.C.Cir. 1996) (the possibility of some uneliminated causes presents a question of weight, so long as the most obvious causes have been considered and reasonably ruled out by the expert).

(4) Whether the expert "is being as careful as he would be in his regular professional work outside his paid litigation consulting." *Sheehan v. Daily Racing Form, Inc.,* 104 F.3d 940, 942 (7th Cir. 1997). See *Kumho Tire*

Co. v. Carmichael, 119 S.Ct. 1167, 1176 (1999) (*Daubert* requires the trial court to assure itself that the expert "employs in the courtroom the same level of intellectual rigor that characterizes the practice of an expert in the relevant field").

(5) Whether the field of expertise claimed by the expert is known to reach reliable results for the type of opinion the expert would give. See *Kumho Tire Co. v. Carmichael,* 119 S.Ct. 1167, 1175 (1999) (*Daubert's* general acceptance factor does not "help show that an expert's testimony is reliable where the discipline itself lacks reliability, as, for example, do theories grounded in any so-called generally accepted principles of astrology or necromancy."); *Moore v. Ashland Chemical, Inc.,* 151 F.3d 269 (5th Cir. 1998) (en banc) (clinical doctor was properly precluded from testifying to the toxicological cause of the plaintiff's respiratory problem, where the opinion was not sufficiently grounded in scientific methodology); *Sterling v. Velsicol Chem. Corp.,* 855 F.2d 1188 (6th Cir. 1988) (rejecting testimony based on "clinical ecology" as unfounded and unreliable).

All of these factors remain relevant to the determination of the reliability of expert testimony under the Rule as amended. Other factors may also be relevant. *See Kumho,* 119 S.Ct. 1167, 1176 ("[W]e conclude that the trial judge must have considerable leeway in deciding in a particular case how to go about determining whether particular expert testimony is reliable."). Yet no single factor is necessarily dispositive of the reliability of a particular expert's testimony. *See, e.g., Heller v. Shaw Industries, Inc.,* 167 F.3d 146, 155 (3d Cir. 1999) ("not only must each stage of the expert's testimony be reliable, but each stage must be evaluated practically and flexibly without bright-line exclusionary (or inclusionary) rules."); *Daubert v. Merrell Dow Pharmaceuticals, Inc.,* 43 F.3d 1311, 1317, n.5 (9th Cir. 1995) (noting that some expert disciplines "have the courtroom as a principal theatre of operations" and as to these disciplines "the fact that the expert has developed an expertise principally for purposes of litigation will obviously not be a substantial consideration.").

A review of the caselaw after *Daubert* shows that the rejection of expert testimony is the exception rather than the rule. Daubert did not work a "seachange over federal evidence law," and "the trial court's role as gatekeeper is not intended to serve as a replacement for the adversary system." *United States v. 14.38 Acres of Land Situated in Leflore County, Mississippi,* 80 F.3d 1074, 1078 (5th Cir. 1996). As the Court in *Daubert* stated: "Vigorous cross-examination, presentation of contrary evidence, and careful instruction on the burden of proof are the traditional and appropriate means of attacking shaky but admissible evidence." 509 U.S. at 595. Likewise, this amendment is not intended to provide an excuse for an automatic challenge to the testimony of every expert. See *Kumho Tire Co. v. Carmichael,* 119 S.Ct. 1167, 1176 (1999) (noting that the trial judge has the discretion "both to avoid unnecessary 'reliability' proceedings in ordinary cases where the reliability of an expert's methods is properly taken for granted, and to require appropriate proceedings in the less usual or more complex cases where cause for questioning the expert's reliability arises.").

When a trial court, applying this amendment, rules that an expert's testimony is reliable, this does not necessarily mean that contradictory expert testimony is unreliable. The amendment is broad enough to permit testimony that is the product of competing principles or methods in the same field of expertise. *See, e.g., Heller v. Shaw Industries, Inc.*, 167 F.3d 146, 160 (3d Cir. 1999) (expert testimony cannot be excluded simply because the expert uses one test rather than another, when both tests are accepted in the field and both reach reliable results). As the court stated in *In re Paoli R.R. Yard PCB Litigation,* 35 F.3d 717, 744 (3d Cir. 1994), proponents "do not have to demonstrate to the judge by a preponderance of the evidence that the assessments of their experts are correct, they only have to demonstrate by a preponderance of evidence that their opinions are reliable. . . . The evidentiary requirement of reliability is lower than the merits standard of correctness." *See also Daubert v. Merrell Dow Pharmaceuticals, Inc.*, 43 F.3d 1311, 1318 (9th Cir. 1995) (scientific experts might be permitted to testify if they could show that the methods they used were also employed by "a recognized minority of scientists in their field."); *Ruiz-Troche v. Pepsi Cola,* 161 F.3d 77, 85 (1st Cir. 1998) ("*Daubert* neither requires nor empowers trial courts to determine which of several competing scientific theories has the best provenance.").

The Court in *Daubert* declared that the "focus, of course, must be solely on principles and methodology, not on the conclusions they generate." 509 U.S. at 595. Yet as the Court later recognized, "conclusions and methodology are not entirely distinct from one another." *General Elec. Co. v. Joiner,* 522 U.S. 136, 146 (1997). Under the amendment, as under *Daubert,* when an expert purports to apply principles and methods in accordance with professional standards, and yet reaches a conclusion that other experts in the field would not reach, the trial court may fairly suspect that the principles and methods have not been faithfully applied. *See Lust v. Merrell Dow Pharmaceuticals, Inc.*, 89 F.3d 594, 598 (9th Cir. 1996). The amendment specifically provides that the trial court must scrutinize not only the principles and methods used by the expert, but also whether those principles and methods have been properly applied to the facts of the case. As the court noted in *In re Paoli R.R. Yard PCB Litig.*, 35 F.3d 717, 745 (3d Cir. 1994), "*any* step that renders the analysis unreliable . . . renders the expert's testimony inadmissible. *This is true whether the step completely changes a reliable methodology or merely misapplies that methodology.*"

If the expert purports to apply principles and methods to the facts of the case, it is important that this application be conducted reliably. Yet it might also be important in some cases for an expert to educate the factfinder about general principles, without ever attempting to apply these principles to the specific facts of the case. For example, experts might instruct the factfinder on the principles of thermodynamics, or bloodclotting, or on how financial markets respond to corporate reports, without ever knowing about or trying to tie their testimony into the facts of the case. The amendment does not alter the venerable practice of using expert testimony to educate the factfinder on general principles. For this kind of generalized testimony, Rule 702 simply requires that: (1) the expert be qualified; (2) the testimony address a subject matter on which the factfinder can be assisted by an expert; (3) the testimony be reliable; and (4) the testimony "fit" the facts of the case.

As stated earlier, the amendment does not distinguish between scientific and other forms of expert testimony. The trial court's gatekeeping function applies to testimony by any expert. *See Kumho Tire Co. v. Carmichael,* 119 S.Ct. 1167, 1171 (1999) ("We conclude that *Daubert's* general holding—setting forth the trial judge's general 'gatekeeping' obligation—applies not only to testimony based on 'scientific' knowledge, but also to testimony based on 'technical' and 'other specialized' knowledge."). While the relevant factors for determining reliability will vary from expertise to expertise, the amendment rejects the premise that an expert's testimony should be treated more permissively simply because it is outside the realm of science. An opinion from an expert who is not a scientist should receive the same degree of scrutiny for reliability as an opinion from an expert who purports to be a scientist. See *Watkins v. Telsmith, Inc.*, 121 F.3d 984, 991 (5th Cir. 1997) ("[I]t seems exactly backwards that experts who purport to rely on general engineering principles and practical experience might escape screening by the district court simply by stating that their conclusions were not reached by any particular method or technique."). Some types of expert testimony will be more objectively verifiable, and subject to the expectations of falsifiability, peer review, and publication, than others. Some types of expert testimony will not rely on anything like a scientific method, and so will have to be evaluated by reference to other standard principles attendant to the particular area of expertise. The trial judge in all cases of proffered expert testimony must find that it is properly grounded, well-reasoned, and not speculative before it can be admitted. The expert's testimony must be grounded in an accepted body of learning or experience in the expert's field, and the expert must explain how the conclusion is so grounded. *See, e.g.*, American College of Trial Lawyers, *Standards and Procedures for Determining the Admissibility of Expert Testimony after Daubert,* 157 F.R.D. 571, 579 (1994) ("[W]hether the testimony concerns economic principles, accounting standards, property valuation or other non-scientific subjects, it should be evaluated by reference to the 'knowledge and experience' of that particular field.").

The amendment requires that the testimony must be the product of reliable principles and methods that are reliably applied to the facts of the case. While the terms "principles" and "methods" may convey a certain impression when applied to scientific knowledge, they remain relevant when applied to testimony based on technical or other specialized knowledge. For example, when a law enforcement agent testifies regarding the use of code words in a drug transaction, the principle used by the agent is that participants in such transactions regularly use code words to conceal the nature of their activities. The method used by the agent is the application of extensive experience to analyze the meaning of the conversations. So long as the principles and methods are reliable and applied reliably to the facts of the case, this type of testimony should be admitted.

Nothing in this amendment is intended to suggest that experience alone—or experience in conjunction with other knowledge, skill, training or education—may not provide a sufficient foundation for expert testimony. To the contrary, the text of Rule 702 expressly contemplates that an expert may be qualified on the basis of experience. In certain fields, experience is the predominant, if not sole, basis for a great deal of reliable expert testimony. *See, e.g., United States v. Jones,* 107 F.3d 1147 (6th Cir. 1997) (no abuse of discretion in admitting the testimony of a handwriting examiner who had years of practical experience and extensive training, and who explained his methodology in detail); *Tassin v. Sears Roebuck,* 946 F.Supp. 1241, 1248 (M.D. La. 1996) (design engineer's testimony can be admissible when the expert's opinions "are based on facts, a reasonable investigation, and traditional technical/mechanical expertise, and he provides a reasonable link between the information and procedures he uses and the conclusions he reaches"). *See also Kumho Tire Co. v. Carmichael,* 119 S.Ct. 1167, 1178 (1999) (stating that "no one denies that an expert might draw a conclusion from a set of observations based on extensive and specialized experience.").

If the witness is relying solely or primarily on experience, then the witness must explain how that experience leads to the conclusion reached, why that experience is a sufficient basis for the opinion, and how that experience is reliably applied to the facts. The trial court's gatekeeping function requires more than simply "taking the expert's word for it." *See Daubert v. Merrell Dow Pharmaceuticals, Inc.,* 43 F.3d 1311, 1319 (9th Cir. 1995) ("We've been presented with only the experts' qualifications, their conclusions and their assurances of reliability. Under *Daubert,* that's not enough."). The more subjective and controversial the expert's inquiry, the more likely the testimony should be excluded as unreliable. *See O'Conner v. Commonwealth Edison Co.,* 13 F.3d 1090 (7th Cir. 1994) (expert testimony based on a completely subjective methodology held properly excluded). *See also Kumho Tire Co. v. Carmichael,* 119 S.Ct. 1167, 1176 (1999) ("[I]t will at times be useful to ask even of a witness whose expertise is based purely on experience, say, a perfume tester able to distinguish among 140 odors at a sniff, whether his preparation is of a kind that others in the field would recognize as acceptable.").

Subpart (1) of Rule 702 calls for a quantitative rather than qualitative analysis. The amendment requires that expert testimony be based on sufficient underlying "facts or data." The term "data" is intended to encompass the reliable opinions of other experts. See the original Advisory Committee Note to Rule 703. The language "facts or data" is broad enough to allow an expert to rely on hypothetical facts that are supported by the evidence. *Id.*

When facts are in dispute, experts sometimes reach different conclusions based on competing versions of the facts. The emphasis in the amendment on "sufficient facts or data" is not intended to authorize a trial court to exclude an expert's testimony on the ground that the court believes one version of the facts and not the other.

There has been some confusion over the relationship between Rules 702 and 703 . The amendment makes clear that the sufficiency of the basis of an expert's testimony is to be decided under Rule 702. Rule 702 sets forth the overarching requirement of reliability, and an analysis of the sufficiency of the expert's basis cannot be divorced from the ultimate reliability of the expert's opinion. In contrast, the "reasonable reliance" requirement of Rule 703 is a relatively narrow inquiry. When an expert relies on inadmissible information, Rule 703 requires the trial court to determine whether that information is of a type reasonably relied on by other experts in the field. If so, the expert can rely on the information in reaching an opinion. However, the question whether the expert is relying on a sufficient basis of information—whether admissible information or not—is governed by the requirements of Rule 702.

The amendment makes no attempt to set forth procedural requirements for exercising the trial court's gatekeeping function over expert testimony. *See* Daniel J. Capra, *The Daubert Puzzle*, 38 Ga.L.Rev. 699, 766 (1998) ("Trial courts should be allowed substantial discretion in dealing with *Daubert* questions; any attempt to codify procedures will likely give rise to unnecessary changes in practice and create difficult questions for appellate review."). Courts have shown considerable ingenuity and flexibility in considering challenges to expert testimony under *Daubert*, and it is contemplated that this will continue under the amended Rule. *See, e.g., Cortes-Irizarry v. Corporacion Insular*, 111 F.3d 184 (1st Cir. 1997) (discussing the application of *Daubert* in ruling on a motion for summary judgment); *In re Paoli R.R. Yard PCB Litig.*, 35 F.3d 717, 736, 739 (3d Cir. 1994) (discussing the use of *in limine* hearings); *Claar v. Burlington N.R.R.*, 29 F.3d 499, 502–05 (9th Cir. 1994) (discussing the trial court's technique of ordering experts to submit serial affidavits explaining the reasoning and methods underlying their conclusions).

The amendment continues the practice of the original Rule in referring to a qualified witness as an "expert." This was done to provide continuity and to minimize change. The use of the term "expert" in the Rule does not, however, mean that a jury should actually be informed that a qualified witness is testifying as an "expert." Indeed, there is much to be said for a practice that prohibits the use of the term "expert" by both the parties and the court at trial. Such a practice "ensures that trial courts do not inadvertently put their stamp of authority" on a witness's opinion, and protects against the jury's being "overwhelmed by the so-called 'experts'." Hon. Charles Richey, *Proposals to Eliminate the Prejudicial Effect of the Use of the Word "Expert" Under the Federal Rules of Evidence in Criminal and Civil Jury Trials*, 154 F.R.D. 537, 559 (1994) (setting forth limiting instructions and a standing order employed to prohibit the use of the term "expert" in jury trials).

GAP Report—Proposed Amendment to Rule 702. The Committee made the following changes to the published draft of the proposed amendment to Evidence Rule 702:

1. The word "reliable" was deleted from Subpart (1) of the proposed amendment, in order to avoid an overlap with Evidence Rule 703, and to clarify that an expert opinion need not be excluded simply because it is based on hypothetical facts. The Committee Note was amended to accord with this textual change.
2. The Committee Note was amended throughout to include pertinent references to the Supreme Court's decision in *Kumho Tire Co. v. Carmichael*, which was rendered after the proposed amendment was released for public comment. Other citations were updated as well.
3. The Committee Note was revised to emphasize that the amendment is not intended to limit the right to jury trial, nor to permit a challenge to the testimony of every expert, nor to preclude the testimony of experience-based experts, nor to prohibit testimony based on competing methodologies within a field of expertise.
4. Language was added to the Committee Note to clarify that no single factor is necessarily dispositive of the reliability inquiry mandated by Evidence Rule 702.

COMMITTEE NOTES ON RULES – 2011 AMENDMENT

The language of Rule 702 has been amended as part of the restyling of the Evidence Rules to make them more easily understood and to make style and terminology consistent throughout the rules. These changes are intended to be stylistic only. There is no intent to change any result in any ruling on evidence admissibility.

COMMITTEE NOTES ON RULES – 2023 AMENDMENT

Rule 702 has been amended in two respects:

(1) First, the rule has been amended to clarify and emphasize that expert testimony may not be admitted unless the proponent demonstrates to the court that it is more likely than not that the proffered testimony meets the admissibility requirements set forth in the rule. See Rule 104(a). This is the preponderance of the evidence standard that applies to most of the admissibility requirements set forth in the evidence rules. See *Bourjaily v. United States,* 483 U.S. 171, 175 (1987) ("The preponderance standard ensures that before admitting evidence, the court will have found it more likely than not that the technical issues and policy concerns addressed by the Federal Rules of Evidence have been afforded due consideration."); Huddleston v. United States, 485 U.S. 681, 687 n.5 (1988) ("preliminary factual findings under Rule 104(a) are subject to the preponderance-of-the-evidence standard"). But many courts have held that the critical questions of the sufficiency of an expert's basis, and the application of the expert's methodology, are questions of weight and not admissibility. These rulings are an incorrect application of Rules 702 and 104(a).

There is no intent to raise any negative inference regarding the applicability of the Rule 104(a) standard of proof for other rules. The Committee concluded that emphasizing the preponderance standard in Rule 702 specifically was made necessary by the courts that have failed to apply correctly the reliability requirements of that rule. Nor does the amendment require that the court make a finding of reliability in the absence of objection.

The amendment clarifies that the preponderance standard applies to the three reliability-based requirements added in 2000—requirements that many courts have incorrectly determined to be governed by the more permissive Rule 104(b) standard. But it remains the case that other admissibility requirements in the rule (such as that the expert must be qualified and the expert's testimony must help the trier of fact) are governed by the Rule 104(a) standard as well.

Some challenges to expert testimony will raise matters of weight rather than admissibility even under the Rule 104(a) standard. For example, if the court finds it more likely than not that an expert has a sufficient basis to support an opinion, the fact that the expert has not read every single study that exists will raise a question of weight and not admissibility. But this does not mean, as certain courts have held, that arguments about the sufficiency of an expert's basis always go to weight and not admissibility. Rather it means that once the court has found it more likely than not that the admissibility requirement has been met, any attack by the opponent will go only to the weight of the evidence.

It will often occur that experts come to different conclusions based on contested sets of facts. Where that is so, the Rule 104(a) standard does not necessarily require exclusion of either side's experts. Rather, by deciding the disputed facts, the jury can decide which side's experts to credit. "[P]roponents 'do not have to demonstrate to the judge by a preponderance of the evidence that the assessments of their experts are correct, they only have to demonstrate by a preponderance of evidence that their opinions are reliable. . . . The evidentiary requirement of reliability is lower than the merits standard of correctness.'" Advisory Committee Note to the 2000 amendment to Rule 702, quoting *In re Paoli R.R. Yard PCB Litigation*, 35 F.3d 717, 744 (3d Cir. 1994).

Rule 702 requires that the expert's knowledge "help" the trier of fact to understand the evidence or to determine a fact in issue. Unfortunately, some courts have required the expert's testimony to "appreciably help" the trier of fact. Applying a higher standard than helpfulness to otherwise reliable expert testimony is unnecessarily strict.

(2) Rule 702(d) has also been amended to emphasize that each expert opinion must stay within the bounds of what can be concluded from a reliable application of the expert's basis and methodology. Judicial gatekeeping is essential because just as jurors may be unable, due to lack of specialized knowledge, to evaluate meaningfully the reliability of scientific and other methods underlying expert opinion, jurors may also lack the specialized knowledge to determine whether the conclusions of an expert go beyond what the expert's basis and methodology may reliably support.

The amendment is especially pertinent to the testimony of forensic experts in both criminal and civil cases. Forensic experts should avoid assertions of absolute or one hundred percent certainty—or to a reasonable degree of scientific certainty—if the methodology is subjective and thus potentially subject to error. In deciding whether to admit forensic expert testimony, the judge should (where possible) receive an estimate of the known or potential rate of error of the methodology employed, based (where appropriate) on studies that reflect how often the method produces accurate results. Expert opinion testimony regarding the weight of feature comparison evidence (i.e., evidence that a set of features corresponds between two examined items) must be limited to those inferences that can reasonably be drawn from a reliable application of the principles and methods. This amendment does not, however, bar testimony that comports with substantive law requiring opinions to a particular degree of certainty.

Nothing in the amendment imposes any new, specific procedures. Rather, the amendment is simply intended to clarify that Rule 104(a)'s requirement applies to expert opinions under Rule 702. Similarly, nothing in the amendment requires the court to nitpick an expert's opinion in order to reach a perfect expression of what the basis and methodology can support. The Rule 104(a) standard does not require perfection. On the other hand, it does not permit the expert to make claims that are unsupported by the expert's basis and methodology.

RULE 703. BASES OF AN EXPERT'S OPINION TESTIMONY

An expert may base an opinion on facts or data in the case that the expert has been made aware of or personally observed. If experts in the particular field would reasonably rely on those kinds of facts or data in forming an opinion on the subject, they need not be admissible for the opinion to be admitted. But if the facts or data would otherwise be inadmissible, the proponent of the opinion may disclose them to the jury only if their probative value in helping the jury evaluate the opinion substantially outweighs their prejudicial effect.

NOTES OF ADVISORY COMMITTEE ON PROPOSED RULES (1973)

Facts or data upon which expert opinions are based may, under the rule, be derived from three possible sources. The first is the firsthand observation of the witness, with opinions based thereon traditionally allowed. A treating physician affords an example. Rheingold, The Basis of Medical Testimony, 15 Vand. L. Rev. 473, 489 (1962). Whether he must first relate his observations is treated in Rule 705. The second source, presentation at the trial, also reflects existing practice. The technique may be the familiar hypothetical question or having the expert attend the trial and hear the testimony establishing the facts. Problems of determining what testimony the expert relied upon, when the latter technique is employed and the testimony is in conflict, may be resolved by resort to Rule 705. The third source contemplated by the rule consists of presentation of data to the expert outside of court and other than by his own perception. In this respect the rule is designed to broaden the basis for expert opinions beyond that current in many jurisdictions and to bring the judicial practice into line with the practice of the experts themselves when not in court. Thus a physician in his own practice bases his diagnosis on information from numerous sources and of considerable variety, including statements by patients and relatives, reports and opinions from nurses, technicians and other doctors, hospital records, and X rays. Most of them are admissible in evidence, but only with the expenditure of substantial time in producing and examining various authenticating witnesses. The physician makes life-and-death decisions in reliance upon them. His validation, expertly performed and subject to cross-examination, ought to suffice for judicial purposes. Rheingold, *supra,* at 531; McCormick §15. A similar provision is California Evidence Code §801(b).

The rule also offers a more satisfactory basis for ruling upon the admissibility of public opinion poll evidence. Attention is directed to the validity of the techniques employed rather than to relatively fruitless inquiries whether hearsay is involved. See Judge Feinberg's careful analysis in *Zippo Mfg. Co. v. Rogers Imports, Inc.*, 216 F.Supp. 670 (S.D.N.Y. 1963) See also Blum et al, The Art of Opinion Research: A Lawyer's Appraisal of an Emerging Service, 24 U. Chi.L.Rev. 1 (1956); Bonynge, Trademark Surveys and Techniques and Their Use in Litigation, 48 A.B.A.J. 329 (1962); Zeisel, The Uniqueness of Survey Evidence, 45 Cornell L.Q. 322 (1960); Annot., 76 A.L.R.2d 919.

If it be feared that enlargement of permissible data may tend to break down the rules of exclusion unduly, notice should be taken that the rule requires that the facts or data "be of a type reasonably relied upon by experts in the particular field." The language would not warrant admitting in evidence the opinion of an "accidentologist" as to the point of impact in an automobile collision based on statements of bystanders, since this requirement is not satisfied. See Comment, Cal. Law Rev. Comm'n, Recommendation Proposing an Evidence Code 148–150 (1965).

COMMITTEE NOTES ON RULES – 2000 AMENDMENT

Rule 703 has been amended to emphasize that when an expert reasonably relies on inadmissible information to form an opinion or inference, the underlying information is not admissible simply because the opinion or inference is admitted. Courts have reached different results on how to treat inadmissible information when it is reasonably relied upon by an expert in forming an opinion or drawing an inference. *Compare United States v. Rollins,* 862 F.2d 1282 (7th Cir. 1988) (admitting, as part of the basis of an FBI agent's expert opinion on the meaning of code language, the hearsay statements of an informant), *with United States v. 0.59 Acres of Land,* 109 F.3d 1493 (9th Cir. 1997) (error to admit hearsay offered as the basis of an expert opinion, without a limiting instruction). Commentators have also taken differing views. *See, e.g.,* Ronald Carlson, Policing the Bases of Modern Expert Testimony, 39 Vand.L.Rev. 577 (1986) (advocating limits on the jury's consideration of otherwise inadmissible evidence used as the basis for an expert opinion); Paul Rice, Inadmissible Evidence as a Basis for Expert Testimony: A Response to Professor Carlson, 40 Vand.L.Rev. 583 (1987) (advocating unrestricted use of information reasonably relied upon by an expert).

When information is reasonably relied upon by an expert and yet is admissible only for the purpose of assisting the jury in evaluating an expert's opinion, a trial court applying this Rule must consider the information's probative value in assisting the jury to weigh the expert's opinion on the one hand, and the risk of prejudice resulting from the jury's potential misuse of the information for substantive purposes on the other. The information may be disclosed to the jury, upon objection, only if the trial court finds that the probative value of the information in assisting the jury to evaluate the expert's opinion substantially outweighs its prejudicial effect. If the otherwise inadmissible information is admitted under this balancing test, the trial judge must give a limiting instruction upon request, informing the jury that the underlying information must not be used for substantive purposes. *See* Rule 105. In determining the appropriate course, the trial court should consider the probable effectiveness or lack of effectiveness of a limiting instruction under the particular circumstances.

The amendment governs only the disclosure to the jury of information that is reasonably relied on by an expert, when that information is not admissible for substantive purposes. It is not intended to affect the admissibility of an expert's testimony. Nor does the amendment prevent an expert from relying on information that is inadmissible for substantive purposes.

Nothing in this Rule restricts the presentation of underlying expert facts or data when offered by an adverse party. *See* Rule 705. Of course, an adversary's attack on an expert's basis will often open the door to a proponent's rebuttal with information that was reasonably relied upon by the expert, even if that information would not have been disclosable initially under the balancing test provided by this amendment. Moreover, in some circumstances the proponent might wish to disclose information that is relied upon by the expert in order to "remove the sting" from the opponent's anticipated attack, and thereby prevent the jury from drawing an unfair negative inference. The trial court should take this consideration into account in applying the balancing test provided by this amendment.

This amendment covers facts or data that cannot be admitted for any purpose other than to assist the jury to evaluate the expert's opinion. The balancing test provided in this amendment is not applicable to facts or data that are admissible for any other purpose but have not yet been offered for such a purpose at the time the expert testifies.

The amendment provides a presumption against disclosure to the jury of information used as the basis of an expert's opinion and not admissible for any substantive purpose, when that information is offered by the proponent of the expert. In a multi-party case, where one party proffers an expert whose testimony is also beneficial to other parties, each such party should be deemed a "proponent" within the meaning of the amendment.

GAP Report—Proposed Amendment to Rule 703. The Committee made the following changes to the published draft of the proposed amendment to Evidence Rule 703:

1. A minor stylistic change was made in the text, in accordance with the suggestion of the Style Subcommittee of the Standing Committee on Rules of Practice and Procedure.

2. The words "in assisting the jury to evaluate the expert's opinion" were added to the text, to specify the proper purpose for offering the otherwise inadmissible information relied on by an expert. The Committee Note was revised to accord with this change in the text.
3. Stylistic changes were made to the Committee Note.
4. The Committee Note was revised to emphasize that the balancing test set forth in the proposal should be used to determine whether an expert's basis may be disclosed to the jury either (1) in rebuttal or (2) on direct examination to "remove the sting" of an opponent's anticipated attack on an expert's basis.

RULE 704. OPINION ON AN ULTIMATE ISSUE

(a) In General—Not Automatically Objectionable. An opinion is not objectionable just because it embraces an ultimate issue.

(b) Exception. In a criminal case, an expert witness must not state an opinion about whether the defendant did or did not have a mental state or condition that constitutes an element of the crime charged or of a defense. Those matters are for the trier of fact alone.

NOTES OF ADVISORY COMMITTEE ON PROPOSED RULES (1973)

The basic approach to opinions, lay and expert, in these rules is to admit them when helpful to the trier of fact. In order to render this approach fully effective and to allay any doubt on the subject, the so-called "ultimate issue" rule is specifically abolished by the instant rule.

The older cases often contained strictures against allowing witnesses to express opinions upon ultimate issues, as a particular aspect of the rule against opinions. The rule was unduly restrictive, difficult of application, and generally served only to deprive the trier of fact of useful information. 7 Wigmore §§1920, 1921; McCormick §12. The basis usually assigned for the rule, to prevent the witness from "usurping the province of the jury," is aptly characterized as "empty rhetoric." 7 Wigmore §1920, p. 17. Efforts to meet the felt needs of particular situations led to odd verbal circumlocutions which were said not to violate the rule. Thus a witness could express his estimate of the criminal responsibility of an accused in terms of sanity or insanity, but not in terms of ability to tell right from wrong or other more modern standard. And in cases of medical causation, witnesses were sometimes required to couch their opinions in cautious phrases of "might or could," rather than "did," though the result was to deprive many opinions of the positiveness to which they were entitled, accompanied by the hazard of a ruling of insufficiency to support a verdict. In other instances the rule was simply disregarded, and, as concessions to need, opinions were allowed upon such matters as intoxication, speed, handwriting, and value, although more precise coincidence with an ultimate issue would scarcely be possible.

Many modern decisions illustrate the trend to abandon the rule completely. *People v. Wilson*, 25 Cal.2d 341, 153 P.2d 720 (1944), whether abortion necessary to save life of patient; *Clifford-Jacobs Forging Co. v. Industrial Comm.*, 19 Ill.2d 236, 166 N.E.2d 582 (1960), medical causation; *Dowling v. L. H. Shattuck, Inc.*, 91 N.H. 234, 17 A.2d 529 (1941), proper method of shoring ditch; *Schweiger v. Solbeck*, 191 Or. 454, 230 P.2d 195 (1951), cause of landslide. In each instance the opinion was allowed.

The abolition of the ultimate issue rule does not lower the bars so as to admit all opinions. Under Rules 701 and 702, opinions must be helpful to the trier of fact, and Rule 403 provides for exclusion of evidence which wastes time. These provisions afford ample assurances against the admission of opinions which would merely tell the jury what result to reach, somewhat in the manner of the oath-helpers of an earlier day. They also stand ready to exclude opinions phrased in terms of inadequately explored legal criteria. Thus the question, "Did T have capacity to make a will?" would be excluded, while the question, "Did T have sufficient mental capacity to know the nature and extent of his property and the natural objects of his bounty and to formulate a rational scheme of distribution?" would be allowed. McCormick §12.

For similar provisions, *see* Uniform Rule 56(4); California Evidence Code §805; Kansas Code of Civil Procedures §60–456(d); New Jersey Evidence Rule 56(3).

RULE 705. DISCLOSING THE FACTS OR DATA UNDERLYING AN EXPERT'S OPINION

Unless the court orders otherwise, an expert may state an opinion—and give the reasons for it—without first testifying to the underlying facts or data. But the expert may be required to disclose those facts or data on cross-examination.

RULE 706. COURT-APPOINTED EXPERT WITNESSES

(a) Appointment Process. On a party's motion or on its own, the court may order the parties to show cause why expert witnesses should not be appointed and may ask the parties to submit nominations. The court may appoint any expert that the parties agree on and any of its own choosing. But the court may only appoint someone who consents to act.

(b) Expert's Role. The court must inform the expert of the expert's duties. The court may do so in writing and have a copy filed with the clerk or may do so orally at a conference in which the parties have an opportunity to participate. The expert:

(1) must advise the parties of any findings the expert makes;

(2) may be deposed by any party;

(3) may be called to testify by the court or any party; and

(4) may be cross-examined by any party, including the party that called the expert.

(c) Compensation. The expert is entitled to a reasonable compensation, as set by the court. The compensation is payable as follows:

(1) in a criminal case or in a civil case involving just compensation under the Fifth Amendment, from any funds that are provided by law; and

(2) in any other civil case, by the parties in the proportion and at the time that the court directs—and the compensation is then charged like other costs.

(d) Disclosing the Appointment to the Jury. The court may authorize disclosure to the jury that the court appointed the expert.

(e) Parties' Choice of Their Own Experts. This rule does not limit a party in calling its own experts.

ARTICLE VIII. HEARSAY

RULE 801. DEFINITIONS THAT APPLY TO THIS ARTICLE; EXCLUSIONS FROM HEARSAY

(a) Statement. "Statement" means a person's oral assertion, written assertion, or nonverbal conduct, if the person intended it as an assertion.

(b) Declarant. "Declarant" means the person who made the statement.

(c) Hearsay. "Hearsay" means a statement that:

(1) the declarant does not make while testifying at the current trial or hearing; and

(2) a party offers in evidence to prove the truth of the matter asserted in the statement.

(d) Statements That Are Not Hearsay. A statement that meets the following conditions is not hearsay:

(1) *A Declarant-Witness's Prior Statement.* The declarant testifies and is subject to cross-examination about a prior statement, and the statement:

(A) is inconsistent with the declarant's testimony ~~and was given under penalty of perjury at a trial, hearing, or other proceeding or in a deposition~~;

> ***Author's Note:*** *Before December 1, 2026, FRE 801(d)(1)(A) allowed prior inconsistent statements as substantive evidence only if given under oath at a trial, hearing, or deposition (as set forth in the text). However, amendments effective December 1, 2026 (and reflected in the set if the strike-through text is omitted) eliminate the latter requirements, thereby broadening this exception to allow for the admission of extrinsic evidence of any inconsistent statement as substantive evidence (regardless of whether it was made under oath or at a specified proceeding), provided the witness gets a chance to explain or deny it.*

(B) is consistent with the declarant's testimony and is offered:

(i) to rebut an express or implied charge that the declarant recently fabricated it or acted from a recent improper influence or motive in so testifying; or

(ii) to rehabilitate the declarant's credibility as a witness when attacked on another ground; or

(C) identifies a person as someone the declarant perceived earlier.

(2) *An Opposing Party's Statement.* The statement is offered against an opposing party and:

(A) was made by the party in an individual or representative capacity;

(B) is one the party manifested that it adopted or believed to be true;

(C) was made by a person whom the party authorized to make a statement on the subject;

(D) was made by the party's agent or employee on a matter within the scope of that relationship and while it existed; or

(E) was made by the party's coconspirator during and in furtherance of the conspiracy.

The statement must be considered but does not by itself establish the declarant's authority under (C); the existence or scope of the relationship under (D); or the existence of the conspiracy or participation in it under (E).

If a party's claim, defense, or potential liability is directly derived from a declarant or the declarant's principal, a statement that would be admissible against the declarant or the principal under this rule is also admissible against the party.

NOTES OF ADVISORY COMMITTEE ON PROPOSED RULES (1973)

Subdivision (a). The definition of "statement" assumes importance because the term is used in the definition of hearsay in subdivision (c). The effect of the definition of "statement" is to exclude from the operation of the hearsay rule all evidence of conduct, verbal or nonverbal, not intended as an assertion. The key to the definition is that nothing is an assertion unless intended to be one.

It can scarcely be doubted that an assertion made in words is intended by the declarant to be an assertion. Hence verbal assertions readily fall into the category of "statement." Whether nonverbal conduct should be regarded as a statement for purposes of defining hearsay requires further consideration. Some nonverbal conduct, such as the act of pointing to identify a suspect in a lineup, is clearly the equivalent of words, assertive in nature, and to be regarded as a statement. Other nonverbal conduct, however, may be offered as evidence that the person acted as he did because of his belief in the existence of the condition sought to be proved, from which belief the existence of the condition may be inferred. This sequence is, arguably, in effect an assertion of the existence of the condition and hence properly includable within the hearsay concept. See Morgan, Hearsay Dangers and the Application of the Hearsay Concept, 62 Harv. L. Rev. 177, 214, 217 (1948), and the elaboration in Finman, Implied Assertions as Hearsay: Some Criticisms of the Uniform Rules of Evidence, 14 Stan.L.Rev. 682 (1962). Admittedly evidence of this character is untested with respect to the perception, memory, and narration (or their equivalents) of the actor, but the Advisory Committee is of the view that these dangers are minimal in the absence of an intent to assert and do not justify the loss of the evidence on hearsay grounds. No class of evidence is free of the possibility of fabrication, but the likelihood is less with nonverbal than with assertive verbal conduct. The situations giving rise to the nonverbal conduct are such as virtually to eliminate questions of sincerity. Motivation, the nature of the conduct, and the presence or absence of reliance will bear heavily upon the weight to be given the evidence. Falknor, The "Hear-Say" Rule as a "See-Do" Rule: Evidence of Conduct, 33 Rocky Mt.L.Rev. 133 (1961). Similar considerations govern nonassertive verbal conduct and verbal conduct which is assertive but offered as a basis for inferring something other than the matter asserted, also excluded from the definition of hearsay by the language of subdivision (c).

When evidence of conduct is offered on the theory that it is not a statement, and hence not hearsay, a preliminary determination will be required to determine whether an assertion is intended. The rule is so worded as to place the burden upon the party claiming that the intention existed; ambiguous and doubtful cases will be resolved against him and in favor of admissibility. The determination involves no greater difficulty than many other preliminary questions of fact. Maguire, The Hearsay System: Around and Through the Thicket, 14 Vand.L.Rev. 741, 765–767 (1961).

For similar approaches, see Uniform Rule 62(1); California Evidence Code §§225, 1200; Kansas Code of Civil Procedure §60–459(a); New Jersey Evidence Rule 62(1).

Subdivision (c). The definition follows along familiar lines in including only statements offered to prove the truth of the matter asserted. McCormick §225; 5 Wigmore §1361, 6 *id.* §1766. If the significance of an offered statement lies solely in the fact that it was made, no issue is raised as to the truth of anything asserted, and the statement is not hearsay. *Emich Motors Corp. v. General Motors Corp.*, 181 F.2d 70 (7th Cir. 1950), rev'd on other grounds 340 U.S. 558, 71 S.Ct. 408, 95 L.Ed 534, letters of complaint from customers offered as a reason for cancellation of dealer's franchise, to rebut contention that franchise was revoked for refusal to finance sales through affiliated finance company. The effect is to exclude from hearsay the entire category of "verbal acts" and "verbal parts of an act," in which the statement itself affects the legal rights of the parties or is a circumstance bearing on conduct affecting their rights.

The definition of hearsay must, of course, be read with reference to the definition of statement set forth in subdivision (a).

Testimony given by a witness in the course of court proceedings is excluded since there is compliance with all the ideal conditions for testifying.

Subdivision (d). Several types of statements which would otherwise literally fall within the definition are expressly excluded from it:

(1) *Prior statement by witness.* Considerable controversy has attended the question whether a prior out-of-court statement by a person now available for cross-examination concerning it, under oath and in the presence of the trier of fact, should be classed as hearsay. If the witness admits on the stand that he made the statement and that it was true, he adopts the statement and there is no hearsay problem. The hearsay problem arises when the witness on the stand denies having made the statement or admits having made it but denies its truth. The argument in favor of treating these latter statements as hearsay is based upon the ground that the conditions of oath, cross-examination, and demeanor observation did not prevail at the time the statement was made and cannot adequately be supplied by the later examination. The logic of the situation is troublesome. So far as concerns the oath, its mere presence has never been regarded as sufficient to remove a statement from the hearsay category, and it receives much less emphasis than cross-examination as a truth-compelling device. While strong expressions are found to the effect that no conviction can be had or important right taken away on the basis of statements not made under fear of prosecution for perjury, *Bridges v. Wixon*, 326 U.S. 135, 65 S.Ct. 1443, 89

L.Ed. 2103 (1945), the fact is that, of the many common law exceptions to the hearsay rule, only that for reported testimony has required the statement to have been made under oath. Nor is it satisfactorily explained why cross-examination cannot be conducted subsequently with success. The decisions contending most vigorously for its inadequacy in fact demonstrate quite thorough exploration of the weaknesses and doubts attending the earlier statement. *State v. Saporen*, 205 Minn. 358, 285 N.W. 898 (1939); *Ruhala v. Roby*, 379 Mich. 102, 150 N.W.2d 146 (1967); *People v. Johnson*, 68 Cal.2d 646, 68 Cal.Rptr. 599, 441 P.2d 111 (1968). In respect to demeanor, as Judge Learned Hand observed in *Di Carlo v. United States*, 6 F.2d 364 (2d Cir. 1925), when the jury decides that the truth is not what the witness says now, but what he said before, they are still deciding from what they see and hear in court. The bulk of the case law nevertheless has been against allowing prior statements of witnesses to be used generally as substantive evidence. Most of the writers and Uniform Rule 63(1) have taken the opposite position.

The position taken by the Advisory Committee in formulating this part of the rule is founded upon an unwillingness to countenance the general use of prior prepared statements as substantive evidence, but with a recognition that particular circumstances call for a contrary result. The judgment is one more of experience than of logic. The rule requires in each instance, as a general safeguard, that the declarant actually testify as a witness, and it then enumerates three situations in which the statement is excepted from the category of hearsay. Compare Uniform Rule 63(1) which allows any out-of-court statement of a declarant who is present at the trial and available for cross-examination.

(A) Prior inconsistent statements traditionally have been admissible to impeach but not as substantive evidence. Under the rule they are substantive evidence. As has been said by the California Law Revision Commission with respect to a similar provision:

"Section 1235 admits inconsistent statements of witnesses because the dangers against which the hearsay rule is designed to protect are largely nonexistent. The declarant is in court and may be examined and cross-examined in regard to his statements and their subject matter. In many cases, the inconsistent statement is more likely to be true than the testimony of the witness at the trial because it was made nearer in time to the matter to which it relates and is less likely to be influenced by the controversy that gave rise to the litigation. The trier of fact has the declarant before it and can observe his demeanor and the nature of his testimony as he denies or tries to explain away the inconsistency. Hence, it is in as good a position to determine the truth or falsity of the prior statement as it is to determine the truth or falsity of the inconsistent testimony given in court. Moreover, Section 1235 will provide a party with desirable protection against the 'turncoat' witness who changes his story on the stand and deprives the party calling him of evidence essential to his case." Comment, California Evidence Code §1235. See also McCormick §39. The Advisory Committee finds these views more convincing than those expressed in *People v. Johnson*, 68 Cal. 2d 646, 68 Cal. Rptr. 599, 441 P.2d 111 (1968). The constitutionality of the Advisory Committee's view was upheld in *California v. Green*, 399 U.S. 149, 90 S.Ct. 1930, 26 L.Ed. 2d 489 (1970). Moreover, the requirement that the statement be inconsistent with the testimony given assures a thorough exploration of both versions while the witness is on the stand and bars any general and indiscriminate use of previously prepared statements.

(B) Prior consistent statements traditionally have been admissible to rebut charges of recent fabrication or improper influence or motive but not as substantive evidence. Under the rule they are substantive evidence. The prior statement is consistent with the testimony given on the stand, and, if the opposite party wishes to open the door for its admission in evidence, no sound reason is apparent why it should not be received generally.

(C) The admission of evidence of identification finds substantial support, although it falls beyond a doubt in the category of prior out-of-court statements. Illustrative are *People v. Gould*, 54 Cal. 2d 621, 7 Cal. Rptr. 273, 354 P.2d 865 (1960); *Judy v. State*, 218 Md. 168, 146 A.2d 29 (1958); *State v. Simmons*, 63 Wash.2d 17, 385 P.2d 389 (1963); California Evidence Code §1238; New Jersey Evidence Rule 63(1)(c); N.Y. Code of Criminal Procedure §393–b. Further cases are found in 4 Wigmore §1130. The basis is the generally unsatisfactory and inconclusive nature of courtroom identifications as compared with those made at an earlier time under less suggestive conditions. The Supreme Court considered the admissibility of evidence of prior identification in *Gilbert v. California*, 388 U.S. 263, 87 S.Ct. 1951, 18 L.Ed. 2d 1178 (1967). Exclusion of lineup identification was held to be required because the accused did not then have the assistance of counsel. Significantly, the Court carefully refrained from placing its decision on the ground that testimony as to the making of a prior out-of-court identification ("That's the man") violated either the hearsay rule or the right of confrontation because not made under oath, subject to immediate cross-examination, in the presence of the trier. Instead the Court observed:

"There is a split among the States concerning the admissibility of prior extra-judicial identifications, as independent evidence of identity, both by the witness and third parties present at the prior identification. See 71 ALR2d 449. It has been held that the prior identification is hearsay, and, when admitted through the testimony of the identifier, is merely a prior consistent statement. The recent trend, however, is to admit the prior identification under the exception that admits as substantive evidence a prior communication by a witness who is available for cross-examination at the trial. See 5 ALR2d Later Case Service 1225–1228. . . ." 388 U.S. at 272, n. 3, 87 S.Ct. at 1956.

(2) *Admissions.* Admissions by a party-opponent are excluded from the category of hearsay on the theory that their admissibility in evidence is the result of the adversary system rather than satisfaction of the conditions of the hearsay rule. Strahorn, A Reconsideration of the Hearsay Rule and Admissions, 85 U.Pa.L.Rev. 484, 564 (1937); Morgan, Basic Problems of Evidence 265 (1962); 4 Wigmore §1048. No guarantee of trustworthiness is required in the case of an admission. The freedom which admissions have enjoyed from technical demands of searching for an assurance of trustworthiness in some against-interest circumstance, and from the restrictive influences of the opinion rule and the rule requiring firsthand knowledge, when taken with the apparently prevalent satisfaction with the results, calls for generous treatment of this avenue to admissibility.

The rule specifies five categories of statements for which the responsibility of a party is considered sufficient to justify reception in evidence against him:

(A) A party's own statement is the classic example of an admission. If he has a representative capacity and the statement is offered against him in that capacity, no inquiry whether he was acting in the representative capacity in making the statement is required; the statement need only be relevant to represent affairs. To the same effect in California Evidence Code §1220. Compare Uniform Rule 63(7), requiring a statement to be made in a representative capacity to be admissible against a party in a representative capacity.

(B) Under established principles an admission may be made by adopting or acquiescing in the statement of another. While knowledge of contents would ordinarily be essential, this is not inevitably so: "X is a reliable person and knows what he is talking about." See McCormick §246, p. 527, n. 15. Adoption or acquiescence may be manifested in any appropriate manner. When silence is relied upon, the theory is that the person would, under the circumstances, protest the statement made in his presence, if untrue. The decision in each case calls for an evaluation in terms of probable human behavior. In civil cases, the results have generally been satisfactory. In criminal cases, however, troublesome questions have been raised by decisions holding that failure to deny is an admission: the inference is a fairly weak one, to begin with; silence may be motivated by advice of counsel or realization that "anything you say may be used against you"; unusual opportunity is afforded to manufacture evidence; and encroachment upon the privilege against self-incrimination seems inescapably to be involved. However, recent decisions of the Supreme Court relating to custodial interrogation and the right to counsel appear to resolve these difficulties. Hence the rule contains no special provisions concerning failure to deny in criminal cases.

(C) No authority is required for the general proposition that a statement authorized by a party to be made should have the status of an admission by the party. However, the question arises whether only statements to third persons should be so regarded, to the exclusion of statements by the agent to the principal. The rule is phrased broadly so as to encompass both. While it may be argued that the agent authorized to make statements to his principal does not speak for him, Morgan, Basic Problems of Evidence 273 (1962), communication to an outsider has not generally been thought to be an essential characteristic of an admission. Thus a party's books or records are usable against him, without regard to any intent to disclose to third persons. 5 Wigmore §1557. *See also* McCormick §78, pp. 159–161. In accord is New Jersey Evidence Rule 63(8)(a). Cf. Uniform Rule 63(8)(a) and California Evidence Code §1222 which limit status as an admission in this regard to statements authorized by the party to be made "for" him, which is perhaps an ambiguous limitation to statements to third persons. Falknor, Vicarious Admissions and the Uniform Rules, 14 Vand. L. Rev. 855, 860–861 (1961).

(D) The tradition has been to test the admissibility of statements by agents, as admissions, by applying the usual test of agency. Was the admission made by the agent acting in the scope of his employment? Since few principals employ agents for the purpose of making damaging statements, the usual result was exclusion of the statement. Dissatisfaction with this loss of valuable and helpful evidence has been increasing. A substantial trend favors admitting statements related to a matter within the scope of the agency or employment. *Grayson v. Williams*, 256 F.2d 61 (10th Cir. 1958); *Koninklijke Luchtvaart Maatschappij N.V. KLM Royal Dutch Airlines v. Tuller*, 110 U.S. App. D.C. 282, 292 F.2d 775, 784 (1961); *Martin v. Savage Truck Lines, Inc.*, 121 F.Supp. 417 (D.D.C. 1054), and numerous state court decisions collected in 4 Wigmore, 1964 Supp., pp. 66–73, with comments by the editor that the statements should have been excluded as not within scope of agency. For the traditional view see *Northern Oil Co. v. Socony Mobile Oil Co.*, 347 F.2d 81, 85 (2d Cir. 1965) and cases cited therein. Similar provisions are found in Uniform Rule 63(9)(a), Kansas Code of Civil Procedure §60–460(i)(1), and New Jersey Evidence Rule 63(9)(a).

(E) The limitation upon the admissibility of statements of co-conspirators to those made "during the course and in furtherance of the conspiracy" is in the accepted pattern. While the broadened view of agency taken in item (iv) might suggest wider admissibility of statements of co-conspirators, the agency theory of conspiracy is at best a fiction and ought not to serve as a basis for admissibility beyond that already established. See Levie, Hearsay and Conspiracy, 52 Mich.L.Rev. 1159 (1954); Comment, 25 U.Chi.L.Rev. 530 (1958). The rule is consistent with the position of the Supreme Court in denying admissibility to statements made after the objectives of the conspiracy have either failed or been achieved. *Krulewitch v. United States,* 336 U.S. 440, 69 S.Ct. 716, 93 L.Ed. 790 (1949); *Wong Sun v. United States,* 371 U.S. 471, 490, 83 S.Ct. 407, 9 L.Ed. 2d 441 (1963). For similarly limited provisions, see California Evidence Code §1223 and New Jersey Rule 63(9)(b). Cf. Uniform Rule 63(9)(b).

NOTES OF ADVISORY ON COMMITTEE RULES – 1997 AMENDMENT

Rule 801(d)(2) has been amended in order to respond to three issues raised by *Bourjaily v. United States,* 483 U.S. 171 (1987). First, the amendment codifies the holding in *Bourjaily* by stating expressly that a court shall consider the contents of a coconspirator's statement in determining "the existence of the conspiracy and the participation therein of the declarant and the party against whom the statement is offered." According to *Bourjaily,* Rule 104(a) requires these preliminary questions to be established by a preponderance of the evidence.

Second, the amendment resolves an issue on which the Court had reserved decision. It provides that the contents of the declarant's statement do not alone suffice to establish a conspiracy in which the declarant and the defendant participated. The court must consider in addition the circumstances surrounding the statement, such as the identity of the speaker, the context in which the statement was made, or evidence corroborating the contents of the statement in making its determination as to each preliminary question. This amendment is in accordance with existing practice. Every court of appeals that has resolved this issue requires some evidence in addition to the contents of the statement. *See, e.g., United States v. Beckham,* 968 F.2d 47, 51 (D.C. Cir. 1992); *United States v. Sepulveda,* 15 F.3d 1161, 1181–82 (1st Cir. 1993), *cert. denied,* 114 S.Ct. 2714 (1994); *United States v. Daly,* 842 F.2d 1380, 1386 (2d Cir.), *cert. denied,* 488 U.S. 821 (1988); *United States v. Clark,* 18 F.3d 1337, 1341–42 (6th Cir.), *cert. denied,* 115 S. Ct. 152 (1994); *United States v. Zambrana,* 841 F.2d 1320, 1344–45 (7th Cir. 1988); *United States v. Silverman,* 861 F.2d 571, 577 (9th Cir. 1988); *United States v. Gordon,* 844 F.2d 1397, 1402 (9th Cir. 1988); *United States v. Hernandez,* 829 F.2d 988, 993 (10th Cir. 1987), *cert. denied,* 485 U.S. 1013 (1988); *United States v. Byrom,* 910 F.2d 725, 736 (11th Cir. 1990).

Third, the amendment extends the reasoning of *Bourjaily* to statements offered under subdivisions (C) and (D) of Rule 801(d)(2). In *Bourjaily,* the Court rejected treating foundational facts pursuant to the law of agency in favor of an evidentiary approach governed by Rule 104(a). The Advisory Committee believes it appropriate to treat analogously preliminary questions relating to the declarant's authority under subdivision (C), and the agency or employment relationship and scope thereof under subdivision (D).

GAP Report on Rule 801. The word "shall" was substituted for the word "may" in line 19. The second sentence of the committee note was changed accordingly.

COMMITTEE NOTES ON RULES – 2014 AMENDMENT

Rule 801(d)(1)(B), as originally adopted, provided for substantive use of certain prior consistent statements of a witness subject to cross-examination. As the Advisory Committee noted, "[t]he prior statement is consistent with the testimony given on the stand, and, if the opposite party wishes to open the door for its admission in evidence, no sound reason is apparent why it should not be received generally."

Though the original Rule 801(d)(1)(B) provided for substantive use of certain prior consistent statements, the scope of that Rule was limited. The Rule covered only those consistent statements that were offered to rebut charges of recent fabrication or improper motive or influence. The Rule did not, for example, provide for substantive admissibility of consistent statements that are probative to explain what otherwise appears to be an inconsistency in the witness's testimony. Nor did it cover consistent statements that would be probative to rebut a charge of faulty memory. Thus, the Rule left many prior consistent statements potentially admissible only for the limited purpose of rehabilitating a witness's credibility. The original Rule also led to some conflict in the cases; some courts distinguished between substantive and rehabilitative use for prior consistent statements, while others appeared to hold that prior consistent statements must be admissible under Rule 801(d)(1)(B) or not at all.

The amendment retains the requirement set forth in *Tome v. United States,* 513 U.S. 150 (1995): that under Rule 801(d)(1)(B), a consistent statement offered to rebut a charge of recent fabrication of improper influence or motive must have been made before the alleged fabrication or improper inference or motive arose. The intent of the amendment is to extend substantive effect to consistent statements that rebut other attacks on a witness – such as the charges of inconsistency or faulty memory.

The amendment does not change the traditional and well-accepted limits on bringing prior consistent statements before the factfinder for credibility purposes. It does not allow impermissible bolstering of a witness.

As before, prior consistent statements under the amendment may be brought before the factfinder only if they properly rehabilitate a witness whose credibility has been attacked. As before, to be admissible for rehabilitation, a prior consistent statement must satisfy the strictures of Rule 403. As before, the trial court has ample discretion to exclude prior consistent statements that are cumulative accounts of an event. The amendment does not make any consistent statement admissible that was not admissible previously – the only difference is that prior consistent statements otherwise admissible for rehabilitation are now admissible substantively as well.

RULE 802. THE RULE AGAINST HEARSAY

Hearsay is not admissible unless any of the following provides otherwise:

- a federal statute;
- these rules; or
- other rules prescribed by the Supreme Court.

RULE 803. EXCEPTIONS TO THE RULE AGAINST HEARSAY – REGARDLESS OF WHETHER THE DECLARANT IS AVAILABLE AS A WITNESS

The following are not excluded by the rule against hearsay, regardless of whether the declarant is available as a witness:

(1) Present Sense Impression. A statement describing or explaining an event or condition, made while or immediately after the declarant perceived it.

(2) Excited Utterance. A statement relating to a startling event or condition, made while the declarant was under the stress of excitement that it caused.

(3)Then-Existing Mental, Emotional, or Physical Condition. A statement of the declarant's then-existing state of mind (such as motive, intent, or plan) or emotional, sensory, or physical condition (such as mental feeling, pain, or bodily health), but not including a statement of memory or belief to prove the fact remembered or believed unless it relates to the validity or terms of the declarant's will.

(4) Statement Made for Medical Diagnosis or Treatment. A statement that:

(A) is made for—and is reasonably pertinent to—medical diagnosis or treatment; and

(B) describes medical history; past or present symptoms or sensations; their inception; or their general cause.

(5) Recorded Recollection. A record that:

(A) is on a matter the witness once knew about but now cannot recall well enough to testify fully and accurately;

(B) was made or adopted by the witness when the matter was fresh in the witness's memory; and

(C) accurately reflects the witness's knowledge.

If admitted, the record may be read into evidence but may be received as an exhibit only if offered by an adverse party.

(6) Records of a Regularly Conducted Activity. A record of an act, event, condition, opinion, or diagnosis if:

(A) the record was made at or near the time by—or from information transmitted by—someone with knowledge;

(B) the record was kept in the course of a regularly conducted activity of a business, organization, occupation, or calling, whether or not for profit;

(C) making the record was a regular practice of that activity;

(D) all these conditions are shown by the testimony of the custodian or another qualified witness, or by a certification that complies with Rule 902(11) or (12) or with a statute permitting certification; and

(E) the opponent does not show that the source of information or the method or circumstances of preparation indicate a lack of trustworthiness.

(7) Absence of a Record of a Regularly Conducted Activity. Evidence that a matter is not included in a record described in paragraph (6) if:

(A) the evidence is admitted to prove that the matter did not occur or exist;

(B) a record was regularly kept for a matter of that kind; and

(C) the opponent does not show that the possible source of the information or other circumstances indicate a lack of trustworthiness.

(8) Public Records. A record or statement of a public office if:

(A) it sets out:

(i) the office's activities;

(ii) a matter observed while under a legal duty to report, but not including, in a criminal case, a matter observed by law-enforcement personnel; or

(iii) in a civil case or against the government in a criminal case, factual findings from a legally authorized investigation; and

(B) the opponent does not show that the source of information or other circumstances indicate a lack of trustworthiness.

(9) Public Records of Vital Statistics. A record of a birth, death, or marriage, if reported to a public office in accordance with a legal duty.

(10) Absence of a Public Record. Testimony—or a certification under Rule 902—that a diligent search failed to disclose a public record or statement if:

(A) the testimony or certification is admitted to prove that

(i) the record or statement does not exist; or

(ii) a matter did not occur or exist, if a public office regularly kept a record or statement for a matter of that kind; and

(B) in a criminal case, a prosecutor who intends to offer a certification provides written notice of that intent at least 14 days before trial, and the defendant does not object in writing within 7 days of receiving the notice—unless the court sets a different time for the notice or the objection.

(11) Records of Religious Organizations Concerning Personal or Family History. A statement of birth, legitimacy, ancestry, marriage, divorce, death, relationship by blood or marriage, or similar facts of personal or family history, contained in a regularly kept record of a religious organization.

(12) Certificates of Marriage, Baptism, and Similar Ceremonies. A statement of fact contained in a certificate:

(A) made by a person who is authorized by a religious organization or by law to perform the act certified;

(B) attesting that the person performed a marriage or similar ceremony or administered a sacrament; and

(C) purporting to have been issued at the time of the act or within a reasonable time after it.

(13) Family Records. A statement of fact about personal or family history contained in a family record, such as a Bible, genealogy, chart, engraving on a ring, inscription on a portrait, or engraving on an urn or burial marker.

(14) Records of Documents That Affect an Interest in Property. The record of a document that purports to establish or affect an interest in property if:

(A) the record is admitted to prove the content of the original recorded document, along with its signing and its delivery by each person who purports to have signed it;

(B) the record is kept in a public office; and

(C) a statute authorizes recording documents of that kind in that office.

(15) Statements in Documents That Affect an Interest in Property. A statement contained in a document that purports to establish or affect an interest in property if the matter stated was relevant to the document's purpose—unless later dealings with the property are inconsistent with the truth of the statement or the purport of the document.

(16) Statements in Ancient Documents. A statement in a document that was prepared before January 1, 1998, and whose authenticity is established.

(17) Market Reports and Similar Commercial Publications. Market quotations, lists, directories, or other compilations that are generally relied on by the public or by persons in particular occupations.

(18) Statements in Learned Treatises, Periodicals, or Pamphlets. A statement contained in a treatise, periodical, or pamphlet if:

(A) the statement is called to the attention of an expert witness on cross- examination or relied on by the expert on direct examination; and

(B) the publication is established as a reliable authority by the expert's admission or testimony, by another expert's testimony, or by judicial notice.

If admitted, the statement may be read into evidence but not received as an exhibit.

(19) Reputation Concerning Personal or Family History. A reputation among a person's family by blood, adoption, or marriage—or among a person's associates or in the community—concerning the person's birth, adoption, legitimacy, ancestry, marriage, divorce, death, relationship by blood, adoption, or marriage, or similar facts of personal or family history.

(20) Reputation Concerning Boundaries or General History. A reputation in a community—arising before the controversy—concerning boundaries of land in the community or customs that affect the land, or concerning general historical events important to that community, state, or nation.

(21) Reputation Concerning Character. A reputation among a person's associates or in the community concerning the person's character.

(22) Judgment of a Previous Conviction. Evidence of a final judgment of conviction if:

(A) the judgment was entered after a trial or guilty plea, but not a nolo contendere plea;

(B) the conviction was for a crime punishable by death or by imprisonment for more than a year;

(C) the evidence is admitted to prove any fact essential to the judgment; and

(D) when offered by the prosecutor in a criminal case for a purpose other than impeachment, the judgment was against the defendant.

The pendency of an appeal may be shown but does not affect admissibility.

(23) Judgments Involving Personal, Family, or General History, or a Boundary. A judgment that is admitted to prove a matter of personal, family, or general history, or boundaries, if the matter:

(A) was essential to the judgment; and

(B) could be proved by evidence of reputation.

(24) [*Other exceptions.*] [Transferred to Rule 807.]

NOTES OF ADVISORY COMMITTEE ON PROPOSED RULES (1973)

The exceptions are phrased in terms of nonapplication of the hearsay rule, rather than in positive terms of admissibility, in order to repel any implication that other possible grounds for exclusion are eliminated from consideration.

The present rule proceeds upon the theory that under appropriate circumstances a hearsay statement may possess circumstantial guarantees of trustworthiness sufficient to justify nonproduction of the declarant in person at the trial even though he may be available. The theory finds vast support in the many exceptions to the hearsay rule developed by the common law in which unavailability of the declarant is not a relevant factor. The present rule is a synthesis of them, with revision where modern developments and conditions are believed to make that course appropriate.

In a hearsay situation, the declarant is, of course, a witness, and neither this rule nor Rule 804 dispenses with the requirement of firsthand knowledge. It may appear from his statement or be inferable from circumstances.

See Rule 602.

Exceptions (1) and (2). In considerable measure these two examples overlap, though based on somewhat different theories. The most significant practical difference will lie in the time lapse allowable between event and statement.

The underlying theory of Exception (paragraph) (1) is that substantial contemporaneity of [the] event and [the] statement negat[e] the likelihood of deliberate of conscious misrepresentation. Moreover, if the witness is the declarant, he may be examined on the statement. If the witness is not the declarant, he may be examined as to the circumstances as an aid in evaluating the statement. Morgan, Basic Problems of Evidence 340–341 (1962).

The theory of Exception [paragraph] (2) is simply that circumstances may produce a condition of excitement which temporarily stills the capacity of reflection and produces utterances free of conscious fabrication. 6 Wigmore §1747, p. 135. Spontaneity is the key factor in each instance, though arrived at by somewhat different routes. Both are needed in order to avoid needless niggling.

While the theory of Exception [paragraph] (2) has been criticized on the ground that excitement impairs accuracy of observation as well as eliminating conscious fabrication, Hutchins and Slesinger, Some Observations on the Law of Evidence: Spontaneous Exclamations, 28 Colum.L.Rev. 432 (1928), it finds support in cases without number. See cases in 6 Wigmore §1750; Annot., 53 A.L.R.2d 1245 (statements as to cause of or responsibility for motor vehicle accident); Annot., 4 A.L.R.3d 149 (accusatory statements by homicide victims). Since unexciting events are less likely to evoke comment, decisions involving Exception (paragraph) (1) are far less numerous. Illustrative are *Tampa Elec. Co. v. Getrost,* 151 Fla. 558, 10

So. 2d 83 (1942); *Houston Oxygen Co. v. Davis,* 139 Tex. 1, 161 S.W.2d 474 (1942); and cases cited in McCormick §273, p. 585, n. 4.

With respect to the *time element,* Exception [paragraph] (1) recognizes that in many, if not most, instances precise contemporaneity is not possible, and hence a slight lapse is allowable. Under Exception (paragraph) (2) the standard of measurement is the duration of the state of excitement. "How long can excitement prevail? Obviously there are no pat answers and the character of the transaction or event will largely determine the significance of the time factor." Slough, Spontaneous Statements and State of Mind, 46 Iowa L.Rev. 224, 243 (1961); McCormick §272, p. 580.

Participation by the declarant is not required: a nonparticipant may be moved to describe what he perceives, and one may be startled by an event in which he is not an actor. Slough, supra; McCormick, supra; 6 Wigmore §1755; Annot., 78 A.L.R.2d 300.

Whether *proof of the startling event* may be made by the statement itself is largely an academic question, since in most cases there is present at least circumstantial evidence that something of a startling nature must have occurred. For cases in which the evidence consists of the condition of the declarant (injuries, state of shock), see *Insurance Co. v. Mosely,* 75 U.S. (8 Wall.), 397, 19 L.Ed. 437 (1869); *Wheeler v. United States,* 93 U.S.A. App. D.C. 159, 211 F.2d 19 (1953); cert. denied 347 U.S. 1019, 74 S.Ct. 876, 98 L.Ed. 1140; *Wetherbee v. Safety Casualty Co.,* 219 F.2d 274 (5th Cir. 1955); *Lampe v. United States,* 97 U.S. App. D.C. 160, 229 F.2d 43 (1956). Nevertheless, on occasion the only evidence may be the content of the statement itself, and rulings that it may be sufficient are described as "increasing," Slough, supra at 246, and as the "prevailing practice," McCormick §272, p. 579. *Illustrative are Armour & Co. v. Industrial Commission,* 78 Colo. 569, 243 P. 546 (1926); *Young v. Stewart,* 191 N.C. 297, 131 S.E. 735 (1926). Moreover, under Rule 104(a) the judge is not limited by the hearsay rule in passing upon preliminary questions of fact.

Proof of declarant's perception by his statement presents similar considerations when declarant is identified. *People v. Poland,* 22 Ill. 2d 175, 174 N.E.2d 804 (1961). However, when declarant is an unidentified bystander, the cases indicate hesitancy in upholding the statement alone as sufficient, *Garrett v. Howden,* 73 N.M. 307, 387 P.2d 874 (1963); *Beck v. Dye,* 200 Wash. 1, 92 P.2d 1113 (1939), a result which would under appropriate circumstances be consistent with the rule.

Permissible *subject matter* of the statement is limited under Exception (paragraph) (1) to description or explanation of the event or condition, the assumption being that spontaneity, in the absence of a startling event, may extend no farther. In Exception (paragraph) (2), however, the statement need only "relate" to the startling event or condition, thus affording a broader scope of subject matter coverage. 6 Wigmore §§1750, 1754. See *Sanitary Grocery Co. v. Snead,* 67 App.D.C. 129, 90 F.2d 374 (1937), slip-and-fall case sustaining admissibility of clerk's statement, "That has been on the floor for a couple of hours," *and Murphy Auto Parts Co., Inc. v. Ball,* 101 U.S. App. D.C. 416, 249 F.2d 508 (1957), upholding admission, on issue of driver's agency, of his statement that he had to call on a customer and was in a hurry to get home. Quick, Hearsay, Excitement, Necessity and the Uniform Rules: A Reappraisal of Rule 63(4), 6 Wayne L.Rev. 204, 206–209 (1960).

Similar provisions are found in Uniform Rule 63(4)(a) and (b); California Evidence Code §1240 (as to Exception (2) only); Kansas Code of Civil Procedure §60–460(d)(1) and (2); New Jersey Evidence Rule 63(4).

Exception (3) is essentially a specialized application of Exception (paragraph) (1), presented separately to enhance its usefulness and accessibility. See McCormick §§265, 268.

The exclusion of "statements of memory or belief to prove the fact remembered or believed" is necessary to avoid the virtual destruction of the hearsay rule which would otherwise result from allowing state of mind, provable by a hearsay statement, to serve as the basis for an inference of the happening of the event which produced the state of mind). *Shepard v. United States,* 290 U.S. 96, 54 S.Ct. 22, 78 L.Ed. 196 (1933); Maguire, The Hillmon Case—Thirty-three Years After, 38 Harv.L.Rev. 709, 719–731 (1925); Hinton, States of Mind and the Hearsay Rule, 1 U.Chi.L.Rev. 394, 421–423 (1934). The rule of *Mutual Life Ins. Co. v. Hillman,* 145 U.S. 285, 12 S.Ct. 909, 36 L.Ed. 706 (1892), allowing evidence of intention as tending to prove the doing of the act intended, is of course, left undisturbed.

The carving out, from the exclusion mentioned in the preceding paragraph, of declarations relating to the execution, revocation, identification, or terms of declarant's will represents an *ad hoc* judgment which finds ample reinforcement in the decisions, resting on practical grounds of necessity and expediency rather than logic. McCormick §271, pp. 577–578; Annot., 34 A.L.R.2d 588, 62 A.L.R.2d 855. A similar recognition of the need for and practical value of this kind of evidence is found in California Evidence Code §1260.

Exception (4). Even those few jurisdictions which have shied away from generally admitting statements of present condition have allowed them if made to a physician for purposes of diagnosis and treatment in view of the patient's strong motivation to be truthful. McCormick §266, p. 563. The same guarantee of trustworthiness extends to statements of past conditions and medical history, made for purposes of diagnosis or treatment. It also extends to statements as to causation, reasonably pertinent to the same purposes, in accord with the current trend, *Shell Oil Co. v. Industrial Commission,* 2 Ill. 2d 590, 119 N.E.2d 224 (1954); McCormick §266, p. 564; New Jersey Evidence Rule 63(12)(c). Statements as to fault would not ordinarily qualify under this latter language. Thus a patient's statement that he was struck by an automobile would qualify but not his statement that the car was driven through a red light. Under the exception the statement need not have been made to a physician. Statements to hospital attendants, ambulance drivers, or even members of the family might be included.

Conventional doctrine has excluded from the hearsay exception, as not within its guarantee of truthfulness, statements to a physician consulted only for the purpose of enabling him to testify. While these statements were not admissible as substantive evidence, the expert was allowed to state the basis of his opinion, including statements of this kind. The distinction thus called for was one most unlikely to be made by juries. The rule accordingly rejects the limitation. This position is consistent with the provision of Rule 703 that the facts on which expert testimony is based need not be admissible in evidence if of a kind ordinarily relied upon by experts in the field.

Exception (5). A hearsay exception for recorded recollection is generally recognized and has been described as having "long been favored by the federal and practically all the state courts that have had occasion to decide the question." *United States v. Kelly,* 349 F.2d 720, 770 (2d Cir. 1965), citing numerous cases and sustaining the exception against a claimed denial of the right of confrontation. Many additional cases are cited in Annot., 82 A.L.R.2d 473, 520. The guarantee of trustworthiness is found in the reliability inherent in a record made while events were still fresh in mind and accurately reflecting them. Owens v. State, 67 Md. 307, 316, 10 A. 210, 212 (1887).

The principal controversy attending the exception has centered, not upon the propriety of the exception itself, but upon the question whether a preliminary requirement of impaired memory on the part of the witness should be imposed. The authorities are divided. If regard be had only to the accuracy of the evidence, admittedly impairment of the memory of the witness adds nothing to it and should not be required. McCormick §277, p. 593; 3 Wigmore §738, p. 76; *Jordan v. People,* 151 Colo. 133, 376 P.2d 699 (1962), cert. denied 373 U.S. 944, 83 S.Ct. 1553, 10 L.Ed. 2d 699; *Hall v. State,* 223 Md. 158, 162 A.2d 751 (1960); *State v. Bindhammer,* 44 N.J. 372, 209 A.2d 124 (1965). Nevertheless, the absence of the requirement, it is believed, would encourage the use of statements carefully prepared for purposes of litigation under the supervision of attorneys, investigators, or claim adjusters. Hence the example includes a requirement that the witness not have "sufficient recollection to enable him to testify fully and accurately." To the same effect are California Evidence Code §1237 and New Jersey Rule 63(1)(b), and this has been the position of the federal courts. *Vicksburg & Meridian R.R. v. O'Brien,* 119 U.S. 99, 7 S.Ct. 118, 30 L.Ed. 299 (1886); *Ahern v. Webb,* 268 F.2d 45 (10th Cir. 1959); and see *N.L.R.B. v. Hudson Pulp and Paper Corp.,* 273 F.2d 660, 665 (5th Cir. 1960); *N.L.R.B. v. Federal Dairy Co.,* 297 F.2d 487 (1st Cir. 1962). But cf. *United States v. Adams,* 385 F.2d 548 (2d Cir. 1967).

No attempt is made in the exception to spell out the method of establishing the initial knowledge or the contemporaneity and accuracy of the record, leaving them to be dealt with as the circumstances of the particular case might indicate. Multiple person involvement in the process of observing and recording, as in *Rathbun v. Brancatella*, 93 N.J.L. 222, 107 A. 279 (1919), is entirely consistent with the exception.

Locating the exception at this place in the scheme of the rules is a matter of choice. There were two other possibilities. The first was to regard the statement as one of the group of prior statements of a testifying witness which are excluded entirely from the category of hearsay by Rule 801(d)(1). That category, however, requires that declarant be "subject to cross-examination," as to which the impaired memory aspect of the exception raises doubts. The other possibility was to include the exception among those covered by Rule 804. Since unavailability is required by that rule and lack of memory is listed as a species of unavailability by the definition of the term in Rule 804(a)(3), that treatment at first impression would seem appropriate. The fact is, however, that the unavailability requirement of the exception is of a limited and peculiar nature. Accordingly, the exception is located at this point rather than in the context of a rule where unavailability is conceived of more broadly.

Exception (6) represents an area which has received much attention from those seeking to improve the law of evidence. The Commonwealth Fund Act was the result of a study completed in 1927 by a distinguished committee under the chairmanship of Professor Morgan. Morgan et al., The Law of Evidence: Some Proposals for its Reform 63 (1927). With changes too minor to mention, it was adopted by Congress in 1936 as the rule for federal courts. 28 U.S.C. §1732. A number of states took similar action. The Commissioners on Uniform State Laws in 1936 promulgated the Uniform Business Records as Evidence Act, 9A U.L.A. 506, which has acquired a substantial following in the states. Model Code Rule 514 and Uniform Rule 63(13) also deal with the subject. Difference of varying degrees of importance exist among these various treatments.

These reform efforts were largely within the context of business and commercial records, as the kind usually encountered, and concentrated considerable attention upon relaxing the requirement of producing as witnesses, or accounting for the nonproduction of, all participants in the process of gathering, transmitting, and recording information which the common law had evolved as a burdensome and crippling aspect of using records of this type. In their areas of primary emphasis on witnesses to be called and the general admissibility of ordinary business and commercial records, the Commonwealth Fund Act and the Uniform Act appear to have worked well. The exception seeks to preserve their advantages.

On the subject of what witnesses must be called, the Commonwealth Fund Act eliminated the common law requirement of calling or accounting for all participants by failing to mention it. *United States v. Mortimer*, 118 F.2d 266 (2d Cir. 1941); *La Porte v. United States*, 300 F.2d 878 (9th Cir. 1962); McCormick §290, p. 608. Model Code Rule 514 and Uniform Rule

63(13) did likewise. The Uniform Act, however, abolished the common law requirement in express terms, providing that the requisite foundation testimony might be furnished by "the custodian or other qualified witness." Uniform Business Records as Evidence Act, §2; 9A U.L.A. 506. The exception follows the Uniform Act in this respect.

The element of unusual reliability of business records is said variously to be supplied by systematic checking, by regularity and continuity which produce habits of precision, by actual experience of business in relying upon them, or by a duty to make an accurate record as part of a continuing job or occupation. McCormick §§281, 286, 287; Laughlin, Business Entries and the Like, 46 Iowa L.Rev. 276 (1961). The model statutes and rules have sought to capture these factors and to extend their impact by employing the phrase "regular course of business," in conjunction with a definition of "business" far broader than its ordinarily accepted meaning. The result is a tendency unduly to emphasize a requirement of routineness and repetitiveness and an insistence that other types of records be squeezed into the fact patterns which give rise to traditional business records. The rule therefore adopts the phrase "the course of a regularly conducted activity" as capturing the essential basis of the hearsay exception as it has evolved and the essential element which can be abstracted from the various specifications of what is a "business."

Amplification of the kinds of activities producing admissible records has given rise to problems which conventional business records by their nature avoid. They are problems of the source of the recorded information, of entries in opinion form, of motivation, and of involvement as participant in the matters recorded.

Sources of information presented no substantial problem with ordinary business records. All participants, including the observer or participant furnishing the information to be recorded, were acting routinely, under a duty of accuracy, with employer reliance on the result, or in short "in the regular course of business." If, however, the supplier of the information does not act in the regular course, an essential link is broken; the assurance of accuracy does not extend to the information itself, and the fact that it may be recorded with scrupulous accuracy is of no avail. An illustration is the police report incorporating information obtained from a bystander: the officer qualifies as acting in the regular course but the informant does not. The leading case, *Johnson v. Lutz*, 253 N.Y. 124, 170 N.E. 517 (1930), held that a report thus prepared was inadmissible. Most of the authorities have agreed with the decision. *Gencarella v. Fyfe*, 171 F.2d 419 (1st Cir. 1948); *Gordon v. Robinson*, 210 F.2d 192 (3d Cir. 1954); *Standard Oil Co. of California v. Moore*, 251 F.2d 188, 214 (9th Cir. 1957), cert. denied 356 U.S. 975, 78 S.Ct. 1139, 2 L.Ed. 2d 1148; *Yates v. Bair Transport, Inc.*, 249 F.Supp. 681 (S.D.N.Y. 1965); Annot., 69 A.L.R.2d 1148. Cf. *Hawkins v. Gorea Motor Express, Inc.*, 360 F.2d 933 (2d Cir 1966). *Contra*, 5 Wigmore

§1530a, n. 1, pp. 391–392. The point is not dealt with specifically in the Commonwealth Fund Act, the Uniform Act, or Uniform Rule 63(13). However, Model Code Rule 514 contains the requirement "that it was the regular course of that business for one with personal knowledge * * * to make such a memorandum or record or to transmit information thereof to be included in such a memorandum or record * * *." The rule follows this lead in requiring an informant with knowledge acting in the course of the regularly conducted activity.

Entries in the form of opinions were not encountered in traditional business records in view of the purely factual nature of the items recorded, but they are now commonly encountered with respect to medical diagnoses, prognoses, and test results, as well as occasionally in other areas. The Commonwealth Fund Act provided only for records of an "act, transaction, occurrence, or event," while the Uniform Act, Model Code Rule 514, and Uniform Rule 63(13) merely added the ambiguous term "condition." The limited phrasing of the Commonwealth Fund Act, 28 U.S.C. §1732, may account for the reluctance of some federal decisions to admit diagnostic entries. *New York Life Ins. Co. v. Taylor,* 79 U.S. App. D.C. 66, 147 F.2d 297 (1945); *Lyles v. United States,* 103 U.S. App. D.C. 22, 254 F.2d 725 (1957), cert. denied 356 U.S. 961, 78 S.Ct. 997, 2 L.Ed. 2d 1067; *England v. United States,* 174 F.2d 466 (5th Cir. 1949); *Skogen v. Dow Chemical Co.,* 375 F.2d 692 (8th Cir. 1967). Other federal decisions, however, experienced no difficulty in freely admitting diagnostic entries. *Reed v. Order of United Commercial Travelers,* 123 F.2d 252 (2d Cir. 1941); *Buckminster's Estate v. Commissioner of Internal Revenue,* 147 F.2d 331 (2d Cir. 1944); *Medina v. Erickson,* 226 F.2d 475 (9th Cir. 1955); *Thomas v. Hogan,* 308 F.2d 355 (4th Cir. 1962); *Glawe v. Rulon,* 284 F.2d 495 (8th Cir. 1960). In the state courts, the trend favors admissibility. *Borucki v. MacKenzie Bros. Co.,* 125 Conn. 92, 3 A.2d 224 (1938); *Allen v. St. Louis Public Service Co.,* 365 Mo. 677, 285 S.W.2d 663, 55 A.L.R.2d 1022 (1956); *People v. Kohlmeyer,* 284 N.Y. 366, 31 N.E.2d 490 (1940); *Weis v. Weis,* 147 Ohio St. 416, 72 N.E.2d 245 (1947). In order to make clear its adherence to the latter position, the rule specifically includes both diagnoses and opinions, in addition to acts, events, and conditions, as proper subjects of admissible entries.

Problems of the motivation of the informant have been a source of difficulty and disagreement. In *Palmer v. Hoffman,* 318 U.S. 109, 63 S.Ct. 477, 87 L.Ed. 645 (1943), exclusion of an accident report made by the since deceased engineer, offered by defendant railroad trustees in a grade crossing collision case, was upheld. The report was not "in the regular course of business," not a record of the systematic conduct of the business as a business, said the Court. The report was prepared for use in litigating, not railroading. While the opinion mentions the motivation of the engineer only obliquely, the emphasis on records of routine operations is significant only by virtue of impact on motivation to be accurate. Absence of routineness raises lack of motivation to be accurate. The opinion of the Court of Appeals had gone beyond mere lack of motive to be accurate: the engineer's statement was "dripping with motivations to misrepresent." *Hoffman v. Palmer,* 129 F.2d 976, 991 (2d Cir. 1942). The direct introduction of motivation is a disturbing factor, since absence of motivation to misrepresent has not traditionally been a requirement of the rule; that records might be self-serving has not been a ground for exclusion. Laughlin, Business Records and the Like, 46 Iowa L.Rev. 276, 285 (1961). As Judge Clark said in his dissent, "I submit that there is hardly a grocer's account book which could not be excluded on that basis." 129 F.2d at 1002. A physician's evaluation report of a personal injury litigant would appear to be in the routine of his business. If the report is offered by the party at whose instance it was made, however, it has been held inadmissible, *Yates v. Bair Transport,* Inc., 249 F.Supp. 681 (S.D.N.Y. 1965), otherwise if offered by the opposite party, *Korte v. New York,* N.H. & H.R. Co., 191 F.2d 86 (2d Cir. 1951), cert. denied 342 U.S. 868, 72 S.Ct. 108, 96 L.Ed. 652.

The decisions hinge on motivation and which party is entitled to be concerned about it. Professor McCormick believed that the doctor's report or the accident report were sufficiently routine to justify admissibility. McCormick §287, p. 604. Yet hesitation must be experienced in admitting everything which is observed and recorded in the course of a regularly conducted activity. Efforts to set a limit are illustrated by *Hartzog v. United States,* 217 F.2d 706 (4th Cir. 1954), error to admit worksheets made by since deceased deputy collector in preparation for the instant income tax evasion prosecution, and *United States v. Ware,* 247 F.2d 698 (7th Cir. 1957), error to admit narcotics agents' records of purchases. See also Exception [paragraph] (8), *infra,* as to the public record aspects of records of this nature. Some decisions have been satisfied as to motivation of an accident report if made pursuant to statutory duty, *United States v. New York Foreign Trade Zone Operators,* 304 F.2d 792 (2d Cir. 1962); *Taylor v. Baltimore & O. R. Co.,* 344 F.2d 281 (2d Cir. 1965), since the report was oriented in a direction other than the litigation which ensued. Cf. *Matthews v. United States,* 217 F.2d 409 (5th Cir. 1954). The formulation of specific terms which would assure satisfactory results in all cases is not possible. Consequently the rule proceeds from the base that records made in the course of a regularly conducted activity will be taken as admissible but subject to authority to exclude if "the sources of information or other circumstances indicate lack of trustworthiness."

Occasional decisions have reached for enhanced accuracy by requiring involvement as a participant in matters reported. *Clainos v. United States,* 82 U.S. App. D.C. 278, 163 F.2d 593 (1947), error to admit police records of convictions; *Standard Oil Co. of California v. Moore,* 251 F.2d 188 (9th Cir. 1957), cert. denied 356 U.S. 975, 78 S.Ct. 1139, 2 L.Ed.2d 1148, error to admit employees' records of observed business practices of others. The rule includes no requirement of this nature. Wholly acceptable records may involve matters merely observed, e.g. the weather.

The form which the "record" may assume under the rule is described broadly as a "memorandum, report, record, or data compilation, in any form." The expression "data compilation" is used as broadly descriptive of any means of storing information other than the conventional words and figures in written or documentary form. It includes, but is by no means limited to, electronic computer storage. The term is borrowed from revised Rule 34(a) of the Rules of Civil Procedure.

Exception (7). Failure of a record to mention a matter which would ordinarily be mentioned is satisfactory evidence of its nonexistence. Uniform Rule 63(14), Comment. While probably not hearsay as defined in Rule 801, *supra,* decisions may be found which class the evidence not only as hearsay but also as not within any exception. In order to set the question at rest in favor of admissibility, it is specifically treated here. McCormick §289, p. 609; Morgan, Basic Problems of Evidence 314 (1962); 5 Wigmore §1531; Uniform Rule 63(14); California Evidence Code §1272; Kansas Code of Civil Procedure §60–460(n); New Jersey Evidence Rule 63(14).

Exception (8). Public records are a recognized hearsay exception at common law and have been the subject of statutes without number. McCormick §291. See, for example, 28 U.S.C. §1733, the relative narrowness of which is illustrated by its nonapplicability to nonfederal public agencies, thus necessitating report to the less appropriate business record exception to the hearsay rule. *Kay v. United States,* 255 F.2d 476 (4th Cir. 1958). The rule makes no distinction between federal and nonfederal offices and agencies.

Justification for the exception is the assumption that a public official will perform his duty properly and the unlikelihood that he will remember details independently of the record. *Wong Wing Foo v. McGrath,* 196 F.2d 120 (9th Cir. 1952), and see *Chesapeake & Delaware Canal Co. v. United States,* 250 U.S. 123, 39 S.Ct. 407, 63 L.Ed. 889 (1919). As to items (a) and (b), further support is found in the reliability factors underlying records of regularly conducted activities generally. See Exception (paragraph) (6), supra.

(a) Cases illustrating the admissibility of records of the office's or agency's own activities are numerous. *Chesapeake & Delaware Canal Co. v. United States,* 250 U.S. 123, 39 S.Ct. 407, 63 L.Ed. 889 (1919), Treasury records of miscellaneous receipts and disbursements; *Howard v. Perrin,* 200 U.S. 71, 26 S.Ct. 195, 50 L.Ed. 374 (1906), General Land Office records; *Ballew v. United States,* 160 U.S. 187, 16 S.Ct. 263, 40 L.Ed. 388 (1895), Pension Office records.

(b) Cases sustaining admissibility of records of matters observed are also numerous. *United States v. Van Hook,* 284 F.2d 489 (7th Cir. 1960), remanded for resentencing 365 U.S. 609, 81 S.Ct. 823, 5 L.Ed.2d 821, letter from induction officer to District Attorney, pursuant to army regulations, stating fact and circumstances of refusal to be inducted; *T'Kach v. United States,* 242 F.2d 937 (5th Cir. 1957), affidavit of White House personnel officer that search of records showed no employment of accused, charged with fraudulently representing himself as an envoy of the President; *Minnehaha County v. Kelley,* 150 F.2d 356 (8th Cir. 1945); Weather Bureau records of rainfall; *United States v. Meyer,* 113 F.2d 387 (7th Cir. 1940), cert. denied 311 U.S. 706, 61 S.Ct. 174, 85 L.Ed. 459, map prepared by government engineer from information furnished by men working under his supervision.

(c) The more controversial area of public records is that of the so-called "evaluative" report. The disagreement among the decisions has been due in part, no doubt, to the variety of situations encountered, as well as to differences in principle. Sustaining admissibility are such cases as *United States v. Dumas,* 149 U.S. 278, 13 S.Ct. 872, 37 L.Ed. 734 (1893), statement of account certified by Postmaster General in action against postmaster; *McCarty v. United States,* 185 F.2d 520 (5th Cir. 1950), reh. denied 187 F.2d 234, Certificate of Settlement of General Accounting Office showing indebtedness and letter from Army official stating Government had performed, in action on contract to purchase and remove waste food from Army camp; *Moran v. Pittsburgh-Des Moines Steel Co.,* 183 F.2d 467 (3d Cir. 1950), report of Bureau of Mines as to cause of gas tank explosion; Petition of W—, 164 F.Supp. 659 (E.D.Pa.1958), report by Immigration and Naturalization Service investigator that petitioner was known in community as wife of man to whom she was not married. To the opposite effect and denying admissibility are *Franklin v. Skelly Oil Co.,* 141 F.2d 568 (10th Cir. 1944), State Fire Marshal's report of cause of gas explosion; *Lomax Transp. Co. v. United States,* 183 F.2d 331 (9th Cir. 1950), Certificate of Settlement from General Accounting Office in action for naval supplies lost in warehouse fire; *Yung Jin Teung v. Dulles,* 229 F.2d 244 (2d Cir. 1956), "Status Reports" offered to justify delay in processing passport applications. Police reports have generally been excluded except to the extent to which they incorporate first-hand observations of the officer. Annot., 69 A.L.R.2d 1148. Various kinds of evaluative reports are admissible under federal statutes: 7 U.S.C. §78, findings of Secretary of Agriculture prima facie evidence of true grade of grain; 7 U.S.C. §210(f), findings of Secretary of Agriculture prima facie evidence in action for damages against stockyard owner; 7 U.S.C. §292, order by Secretary of Agriculture prima facie evidence in judicial enforcement proceedings against producers association monopoly; 7 U.S.C. §1622(h), Department of Agriculture inspection certificates of products shipped in interstate commerce prima facie evidence; 8 U.S.C. §1440(c), separation of alien from military service on conditions other than honorable provable by certificate from department in proceedings to revoke citizenship; 18 U.S.C. §4245, certificate of Director of Prisons that convicted person has been examined and found probably incompetent at time of trial prima facie evidence in court hearing on competency; 42 U.S.C. §269(b), bill of health by appropriate official prima facie evidence of vessel's sanitary history and condition and compliance with regulations; 46 U.S.C. §679, certificate of consul presumptive evidence of refusal of master to transport destitute seamen to United States. While these statutory exceptions to the hearsay rule are left undisturbed, Rule 802, the willingness of Congress to recognize a substantial measure of admissibility for evaluative reports is a helpful guide.

Factors which may be of assistance in passing upon the admissibility of evaluative reports include; (1) the timeliness of the investigation, McCormack, Can the Courts Make Wider Use of Reports of Official Investigations? 42 Iowa L.Rev. 363 (1957); (2) the special skill or experience of the official, id., (3) whether a hearing was held and the level at which conducted, *Franklin v. Skelly Oil Co.,* 141 F.2d 568 (10th Cir. 1944); (4) possible motivation problems suggested by *Palmer v. Hoffman,* 318 U.S. 109, 63 S.Ct. 477, 87 L.Ed. 645 (1943). Others no doubt could be added.

The formulation of an approach which would give appropriate weight to all possible factors in every situation is an obvious impossibility. Hence the rule, as in Exception (paragraph) (6), assumes admissibility in the first instance but with ample provision for escape if sufficient negative factors are present. In one respect, however, the rule with respect to evaluate reports under item (c) is very specific; they are admissible only in civil cases and against the government in criminal cases in view of the almost certain collision with confrontation rights which would result from their use against the accused in a criminal case.

Exception (9). Records of vital statistics are commonly the subject of particular statutes making them admissible in evidence. Uniform Vital Statistics Act, 9C U.L.A. 350 (1957). The rule is in principle narrower than Uniform Rule 63(16) which includes reports required of persons performing functions authorized by statute, yet in practical effect the two are substantially the same. Comment Uniform Rule 63(16). The exception as drafted is in the pattern of California Evidence Code §1281.

Exception (10). The principle of proving nonoccurrence of an event by evidence of the absence of a record which would regularly be made of its occurrence, developed in Exception (paragraph) (7) with respect to regularly conducted activities, is here extended to public records of the kind mentioned in Exceptions (paragraphs) (8) and (9). 5 Wigmore §1633(6), p. 519. Some harmless duplication no doubt exists with Exception (paragraph) (7). For instances of federal statutes recognizing this method of proof, see 8 U.S.C. §1284(b), proof of absence of alien crewman's name from outgoing manifest prima facie evidence of failure to detain or deport, and 42 U.S.C. §405(c)(3), (4)(B), (4)(C), absence of HEW (Department of Health, Education, and Welfare) record prima facie evidence of no wages or self-employment income.

The rule includes situations in which absence of a record may itself be the ultimate focal point of inquiry, e.g. *People v. Love,* 310 Ill. 558, 142 N.E. 204 (1923), certificate of Secretary of State admitted to show failure to file documents required by Securities Law, as well as cases where the absence of a record is offered as proof of the nonoccurrence of an event ordinarily recorded.

The refusal of the common law to allow proof by certificate of the lack of a record or entry has no apparent justification, 5 Wigmore §1678(7), p. 752. The rule takes the opposite position, as do Uniform Rule 63(17); California Evidence Code §1284; Kansas Code of Civil Procedure §60–460(c); New Jersey Evidence Rule 63(17). Congress has recognized certification as evidence of the lack of a record. 8 U.S.C. §1360(d), certificate of Attorney General or other designated officer that no record of Immigration and Naturalization Service of specified nature or entry therein is found, admissible in alien cases.

Exception (11). Records of activities of religious organizations are currently recognized as admissible at least to the extent of the business records exception to the hearsay rule, 5 Wigmore §1523, p. 371, and Exception (paragraph) (6) would be applicable. However, both the business record doctrine and Exception (paragraph) (6) require that the person furnishing the information be one in the business or activity. The result is such decisions as *Daily v. Grand Lodge,* 311 Ill. 184, 142 N.E. 478 (1924), holding a church record admissible to prove fact, date, and place of baptism, but not age of child except that he had at least been born at the time. In view of the unlikelihood that false information would be furnished on occasions of this kind, the rule contains no requirement that the informant be in the course of the activity. See California Evidence Code §1315 and Comment.

Exception (12). The principle of proof by certification is recognized as to public officials in Exceptions (paragraphs) (8) and (10), and with respect to authentication in Rule 902. The present exception is a duplication to the extent that it deals with a certificate by a public official, as in the case of a judge who performs a marriage ceremony. The area covered by the rule is, however, substantially larger and extends the certification procedure to clergymen and the like who perform marriages and other ceremonies or administer sacraments. Thus certificates of such matters as baptism or confirmation, as well as marriage, are included. In principle they are as acceptable evidence as certificates of public officers. See 5 Wigmore §1645, as to marriage certificates. When the person executing the certificate is not a public official, the self-authenticating character of documents purporting to emanate from public officials, see Rule 902, is lacking and proof is required that the person was authorized and did make the certificate. The time element, however, may safely be taken as supplied by the certificate, once authority and authenticity are established, particularly in view of the presumption that a document was executed on the date it bears.

For similar rules, some limited to certificates of marriage, with variations in foundation requirements, see Uniform Rule 63(18); California Evidence Code §1316; Kansas Code of Civil Procedure §60–460(p); New Jersey Evidence Rule 63(18).

Exception (13). Records of family history kept in family Bibles have by long tradition been received in evidence. 5 Wigmore §§1495, 1496, citing numerous statutes and decisions. See also Regulations, Social Security Administration, 20 C.F.R. §404.703(c), recognizing family Bible entries as proof of age in the absence of public or church records. Opinions in the area also include inscriptions on tombstones, publicly displayed pedigrees, and engravings on rings. Wigmore, supra. The rule is substantially identical in coverage with California Evidence Code §1312.

Exception (14). The recording of title documents is a purely statutory development. Under any theory of the admissibility of public records, the records would be receivable as evidence of the contents of the recorded document, else the recording process would be reduced to a nullity. When, however, the record is offered for the further purpose of proving execution and delivery, a problem of lack of first-hand knowledge by the recorder, not present as to contents, is presented. This problem is solved, seemingly in all jurisdictions, by qualifying for recording only those documents shown by a specified procedure, either acknowledgement or a form of probate, to have been executed and delivered. 5 Wigmore §§1647–1651. Thus what may appear in the rule, at first glance, as endowing the record with an effect independently of local law and inviting difficulties of an *Erie* nature under *Cities Service Oil Co. v. Dunlap*, 308 U.S. 208, 60 S.Ct. 201, 84 L.Ed. 196 (1939), is not present, since the local law in fact governs under the example.

Exception (15). Dispositive documents often contain recitals of fact. Thus a deed purporting to have been executed by an attorney in fact may recite the existence of the power of attorney, or a deed may recite that the grantors are all the heirs of the last record owner. Under the rule, these recitals are exempted from the hearsay rule. The circumstances under which dispositive documents are executed and the requirement that the recital be germane to the purpose of the document are believed to be adequate guarantees of trustworthiness, particularly in view of the nonapplicability of the rule if dealings with the property have been inconsistent with the document. The age of the document is of no significance, though in practical application the document will most often be an ancient one. See Uniform Rule 63(29), Comment.

Similar provisions are contained in Uniform Rule 63(29); California Evidence Code §1330; Kansas Code of Civil Procedure §60–460(aa); New Jersey Evidence Rule 63(29).

Exception (16). Authenticating a document as ancient, essentially in the pattern of the common law, as provided in Rule 901(b)(8), leaves open as a separate question the admissibility of assertive statements contained therein as against a hearsay objection. 7 Wigmore §2145a. Wigmore further states that the ancient document technique of authentication is universally conceded to apply to all sorts of documents, including letters, records, contracts, maps, and certificates, in addition to title documents, citing numerous decisions. Id. §2145. Since most of these items are significant evidentially only insofar as they are assertive, their admission in evidence must be as a hearsay exception. But see 5 id. §1573, p. 429, referring to recitals in ancient deeds as a "limited" hearsay exception. The former position is believed to be the correct one in reason and authority. As pointed out in McCormick §298, danger of mistake is minimized by authentication requirements, and age affords assurance that the writing antedates the present controversy. See *Dallas County v. Commercial Union Assurance Co.*, 286 F.2d 388 (5th Cir. 1961), upholding admissibility of 58-year-old newspaper story. Cf. Morgan, Basic Problems of Evidence 364 (1962), but see *id.* 254.

For a similar provision, but with the added requirement that "the statement has since generally been acted upon as true by persons having an interest in the matter," see California Evidence Code §1331.

Exception (17). Ample authority at common law supported the admission in evidence of items falling in this category. While Wigmore's text is narrowly oriented to lists, etc., prepared for the use of a trade or profession, 6 Wigmore §1702, authorities are cited which include other kinds of publications, for example, newspaper market reports, telephone directories, and city directories. *Id.* §§1702–1706. The basis of trustworthiness is general reliance by the public or by a particular segment of it, and the motivation of the compiler to foster reliance by being accurate.

For similar provisions, see Uniform Rule 63(30); California Evidence Code §1340; Kansas Code of Civil Procedure §60–460(bb); New Jersey Evidence Rule 63(30). Uniform Commercial Code §2–724 provides for admissibility in evidence of "reports in official publications or trade journals or in newspapers or periodicals of general circulation published as the reports of such (established commodity) market."

Exception (18). The writers have generally favored the admissibility of learned treatises, McCormick §296, p. 621; Morgan, Basic Problems of Evidence 366 (1962); 6 Wigmore §1692, with the support of occasional decisions and rules, *City of Dothan v. Hardy*, 237 Ala. 603, 188 So. 264 (1939); *Lewandowski v. Preferred Risk Mut. Ins. Co.*, 33 Wis.2d 69, 146 N.W.2d 505 (1966), 66 Mich.L.Rev. 183 (1967); Uniform Rule 63(31); Kansas Code of Civil Procedure §60–460(ce), but the great weight of authority has been that learned treatises are not admissible as substantive evidence though usable in the cross-examination of experts. The foundation of the minority view is that the hearsay objection must be regarded as unimpressive when directed against treatises since a high standard of accuracy is engendered by various factors: the treatise is written primarily and impartially for professionals, subject to scrutiny and exposure for inaccuracy, with the reputation of the writer at stake. 6 Wigmore §1692. Sound as this position may be with respect to trustworthiness, there is, nevertheless, an additional difficulty in the likelihood that the treatise will be misunderstood and misapplied without expert assistance and supervision. This difficulty is recognized in the cases demonstrating unwillingness to sustain findings relative to disability on the basis of judicially noticed medical texts. *Ross v. Gardner*, 365 F.2d 554 (6th Cir. 1966); *Sayers v. Gardner*, 380 F.2d 940 (6th Cir. 1967); *Colwell v. Gardner*, 386 F.2d 56 (6th Cir. 1967); *Glendenning v. Ribicoff*, 213 F.Supp. 301 (W.D.Mo. 1962); *Cook v. Celebrezze*, 217 F.Supp. 366 (W.D.Mo. 1963); *Sosna v. Celebrezze*, 234 F.Supp. 289 (E.D.Pa. 1964); and see *McDaniel v. Celebrezze*, 331 F.2d 426 (4th Cir. 1964). The rule avoids the danger of misunderstanding and misapplication by limiting the use of treatises as substantive evidence to situations in which an expert is on the stand and available to explain and assist in the application of the treatise if declared. The limitation upon receiving the publication itself physically in evidence, contained in the last sentence, is designed to further this policy.

The relevance of the use of treatises on cross-examination is evident. This use of treatises has been the subject of varied views. The most restrictive position is that the witness must have stated expressly on direct his reliance upon the treatise. A slightly more liberal approach still insists upon reliance but allows it to be developed on cross-examination. Further relaxation dispenses with reliance but requires recognition as an authority by the witness, developable on cross-examination. The greatest liberality is found in decisions allowing use of the treatise on cross-examination when its status as an authority is established by any means. Annot., 60 A.L.R.2d 77. The exception is hinged upon this last position, which is that of the Supreme Court, *Reilly v. Pinkus*, 338 U.S. 269, 70 S.Ct. 110, 94 L.Ed. 63 (1949), and of recent well considered state court decisions, *City of St. Petersburg v. Ferguson*, 193 So. 2d 648 (Fla. App. 1967), cert. denied Fla., 201 So.2d 556; *Darling v. Charleston Memorial Community Hospital*, 33 Ill.2d 326, 211 N.E.2d 253 (1965); *Dabroe v. Rhodes Co.*, 64 Wash.2d 431, 392 P.2d 317 (1964).

In *Reilly v. Pinkus, supra*, the Court pointed out that testing of professional knowledge was incomplete without exploration of the witness' knowledge of and attitude toward established treatises in the field. The process works equally well in reverse and furnishes the basis of the rule.

The rule does not require that the witness rely upon or recognize the treatise as authoritative, thus avoiding the possibility that the expert may at the outset block cross-examination by refusing to concede reliance or authoritativeness. *Dabroe v. Rhodes Co.*, supra. Moreover, the rule avoids the unreality of admitting evidence for the purpose of impeachment only, with an instruction to the jury not to consider it otherwise. The parallel to the treatment of prior inconsistent statements will be apparent. See Rules 6130(b) and 801(d)(1).

Exceptions (19), (20), and (21). Trustworthiness in reputation evidence is found "when the topic is such that the facts are likely to have been inquired about and that persons having personal knowledge have disclosed facts which have thus been discussed in the community; and thus the community's conclusion, if any has been formed, is likely to be a trustworthy one." 5 Wigmore §1580, p. 444, and see also §1583. On this common foundation, reputation as to land boundaries, customs, general history, character, and marriage have come to be regarded as admissible. The breadth of the underlying principle suggests the formulation of an equally broad exception, but tradition has in fact been much narrower and more particularized, and this is the pattern of these exceptions in the rule.

Exception [paragraph] (19) is concerned with matters of personal and family history. Marriage is universally conceded to be a proper subject of proof by evidence of reputation in the community. 5 Wigmore §1602. As to such items as legitimacy, relationship, adoption, birth, and death, the decisions are divided. *Id.* §1605. All seem to be susceptible to being the subject of well founded repute. The "world" in which the reputation may exist may be family, associates, or community. This world has proved capable of expanding with changing times from the single uncomplicated neighborhood, in which all activities take place, to the multiple and unrelated worlds of work, religious affiliation, and social activity, in each of which a reputation may be generated. *People v. Reeves*, 360 Ill. 55, 195 N.E. 443 (1935); *State v. Axilrod*, 248 Minn. 204, 79 N.W.2d 677 (1956); Mass. Stat. 1947, c. 410, M.G.L.A. c. 233 §21A; 5 Wigmore §1616. The family has often served as the point of beginning for allowing community reputation. 5 Wigmore §1488. For comparable provisions see Uniform Rule 63(26), (27)(c); California Evidence Code §§1313, 1314; Kansas Code of Civil Procedure §60–460(x), (y)(3); New Jersey Evidence Rule 63(26), (27)(c).

The first portion of Exception [paragraph] (20) is based upon the general admissibility of evidence of reputation as to land boundaries and land customs, expanded in this country to include private as well as public boundaries. McCormick §299, p. 625. The reputation is required to antedate the controversy, though not to be ancient. The second portion is likewise supported by authority, *id.*, and is designed to facilitate proof of events when judicial notice is not available The historical character of the subject matter dispenses with any need that the reputation antedate the controversy with respect to which it is offered. For similar provisions see Uniform Rule 63(27)(a), (b); California Evidence Code §§1320–1322;

Kansas Code of Civil Procedure §60–460(y), (1), (2); New Jersey Evidence Rule 63(27)(a), (b).

Exception [paragraph] (21) recognizes the traditional acceptance of reputation evidence as a means of proving human character. McCormick §§44, 158. The exception deals only with the hearsay aspect of this kind of evidence. Limitations upon admissibility based on other grounds will be found in Rules 404, relevancy of character evidence generally, and 608, character of witness. The exception is in effect a reiteration, in the context of hearsay, of Rule 405(a). Similar provisions are contained in Uniform Rule 63(28); California Evidence Code §1324; Kansas Code of Civil Procedure §60–460(z); New Jersey Evidence Rule 63(28).

Exception (22). When the status of a former judgment is under consideration in subsequent litigation, three possibilities must be noted: (1) the former judgment is conclusive under the doctrine of res judicata, either as a bar or a collateral estoppel; or (2) it is admissible in evidence for what it is worth; or (3) it may be of no effect at all. The first situation does not involve any problem of evidence except in the way that principles of substantive law generally bear upon the relevancy and materiality of evidence. The rule does not deal with the substantive effect of the judgment as a bar or collateral estoppel. When, however, the doctrine of res judicata does not apply to make the judgment either a bar or a collateral estoppel, a choice is presented between the second and third alternatives. The rule adopts the second for judgments of criminal conviction of felony grade. This is the direction of the decisions, Annot., 18 A.L.R.2d 1287, 1299, which manifest an increasing reluctance to reject in toto the validity of the law's factfinding processes outside the confines of res judicata and collateral estoppel. While this may leave a jury with the evidence of conviction but without means to evaluate it, as suggested by Judge Hinton, Note 27 Ill.L.Rev. 195 (1932), it seems safe to assume that the jury will give it substantial effect unless defendant offers a satisfactory explanation, a possibility not foreclosed by the provision. But see *North River Ins. Co. v. Militello,* 104 Colo. 28, 88 P.2d 567 (1939), in which the jury found for plaintiff on a fire policy despite the introduction of his conviction for arson. For supporting federal decisions see Clark, J., in *New York & Cuba Mail S.S. Co. v. Continental Cas. Co.,* 117 F.2d 404, 411 (2d Cir. 1941); *Connecticut Fire Ins. Co. v. Farrara,* 277 F.2d 388 (8th Cir. 1960).

Practical considerations require exclusion of convictions of minor offenses, not became the administration of justice in its lower echelons must be inferior, but because motivation to defend at this level is often minimal or nonexistent. *Cope v. Goble,* 39 Cal. App. 2d 448, 103 P.2d 598 (1940); *Jones v. Talbot,* 87 Idaho 498, 394 P.2d 316 (1964); *Warren v. Marsh,* 215 Minn. 615, 11 N.W.2d 528 (1943); Annot., 18 A.L.R.2d 1287, 1295–1297; 16 Brooklyn L.Rev. 286 (1950); 50 Colum.L.Rev. 529 (1950); 35

Cornell L.Q. 872 (1950). Hence the rule includes only convictions of felony grade, measured by federal standards.

Judgments of conviction based upon pleas of *nolo contendere* are not included. This position is consistent with the treatment of nolo pleas in Rule 410 and the authorities cited in the Advisory Committee's Note in support thereof.

While these rules do not in general purport to resolve constitutional issues, they have in general been drafted with a view to avoiding collision with constitutional principles. Consequently the exception does not include evidence of the conviction of a third person, offered against the accused in a criminal prosecution to prove any fact essential to sustain the judgment of conviction. A contrary position would seem clearly to violate the right of confrontation. *Kirby v. United States,* 174 U.S. 47, 19 S.Ct. 574, 43 L.Ed. 890 (1899), error to convict of possessing stolen postage stamps with the only evidence of theft being the record of conviction of the thieves The situation is to be distinguished from cases in which conviction of another person is an element of the crime, e.g. 15 U.S.C. §902(d), interstate shipment of firearms to a known convicted felon, and, as specifically provided, from impeachment.

For comparable provisions see Uniform Rule 63(20); California Evidence Code §1300; Kansas Code of Civil Procedure §60–460(r); New Jersey Evidence Rule 63(20).

Exception (23). A hearsay exception in this area was originally justified on the ground that verdicts were evidence of reputation. As trial by jury graduated from the category of neighborhood inquests, this theory lost its validity. It was never valid as to chancery decrees. Nevertheless the rule persisted, though the judges and writers shifted ground and began saying that the judgment or decree was as good evidence as reputation. See *City of London v. Clerke,* Carth. 181, 90 Eng. Rep. 710 (K.B. 1691); *Neill v. Duke of Devonshire,* 8 App. Cas. 135 (1882). The shift appears to be correct, since the process of inquiry, sifting, and scrutiny which is relied upon to render reputation reliable is present in perhaps greater measure in the process of litigation. While this might suggest a broader area of application, the affinity to reputation is strong, and paragraph (paragraph) (23) goes no further, not even including character.

The leading case in the *United States, Patterson v. Gaines,* 47 U.S. (6 How.) 550, 599, 12 L.Ed. 553 (1847), follows in the pattern of the English decisions, mentioning as illustrative matters thus provable: manorial rights, public rights of way, immemorial custom, disputed boundary, and pedigree. More recent recognition of the principle is found in *Grant Bros. Construction Co. v. United States,* 232 U.S. 647, 34 S.Ct. 452, 58 L.Ed. 776 (1914), in action for penalties under Alien Contract Labor Law, decision of board of inquiry of Immigration Service admissible to prove alienage of laborers, as a matter of pedigree; *United States v. Mid-Continent Petroleum Corp.*, 67 F.2d 37 (10th Cir. 1933), records of commission enrolling Indians admissible on pedigree; Jung Yen Loy v. Cahill, 81 F.2d 809 (9th Cir. 1936), board decisions as to citizenship of plaintiff's father admissible in proceeding for declaration of citizenship. *Contra,* In re Estate of Cunha, 49 Haw. 273, 414 P.2d 925 (1966).

COMMITTEE NOTES ON RULES – 2000 AMENDMENT

The amendment provides that the foundation requirements of Rule 803(6) can be satisfied under certain circumstances without the expense and inconvenience of producing time-consuming foundation witnesses. Under current law, courts have generally required foundation witnesses to testify. *See, e.g., Tongil Co., Ltd. v. Hyundai Merchant Marine Corp.*, 968 F.2d 999 (9th Cir. 1992) (reversing a judgment based on business records where a qualified person filed an affidavit but did not testify). Protections are provided by the authentication requirements of Rule 902(11) for domestic records, Rule 902(12) for foreign records in civil cases, and 18 U.S.C. §3505 for foreign records in criminal cases.

COMMITTEE NOTES ON RULES – 2013 AMENDMENT

Rule 803(10) has been amended in response to *Melendez-Diaz v. Massachusetts*, 557. U.S. 305 (2009). The *Melendez-Diaz* Court declared that a testimonial certificate could be admitted if the accused is given advance notice and does not timely demand the presence of the official who prepared the certificate. The amendment incorporates, with minor variations, a "notice-and-demand" procedure that was approved by the *Melendez-Diaz* Court. *See* Tex. Code Crim. P. Ann., art. 38.41.

COMMITTEE NOTES ON RULES – 2017 AMENDMENT

The ancient documents exception to the rule against hearsay has been limited to statements in documents prepared before January 1, 1998. The Committee has determined that the ancient documents exception should be limited due to the risk that it will be used as a vehicle to admit vast amounts of unreliable electronically stored information (ESI). Given the exponential development and growth of electronic information since 1998, the hearsay exception for ancient documents has now become a possible open door for large amounts of unreliable ESI, as no showing of reliability needs to be made to qualify under the exception.

The Committee is aware that in certain cases—such as cases involving latent diseases and environmental damage—parties must rely on hardcopy documents from the past. The ancient documents exception remains available for such cases for documents prepared before 1998. Going forward, it is anticipated that any need to admit old hardcopy documents produced after January 1, 1998 will decrease, because reliable ESI is likely to be available and can be offered under a reliability-based hearsay exception. Rule 803(6) may be used for many of these ESI documents, especially given its flexible standards on which witnesses might be qualified to provide an adequate foundation. And Rule 807 can be used to admit old documents upon a showing of reliability—which will often (though not always) be found by circumstances such as that document was prepared with no litigation motive in mind, close in time to the relevant events. The limitation of the ancient documents exception is not intended to raise an inference that 20-year-old documents are, as a class, unreliable, or that they should somehow not qualify for admissibility under Rule 807. Finally, many old documents can be admitted for the non-hearsay purpose of proving notice, or as party-opponent statements.

The limitation of the ancient documents hearsay exception is not intended to have any effect on authentication of ancient documents. The possibility of authenticating an old document under Rule 901(b)(8)—or under any ground available for any other document—remains unchanged.

The Committee carefully considered, but ultimately rejected, an amendment that would preserve the ancient documents exception for hardcopy evidence only. A party will often offer hardcopy that is derived from ESI. Moreover, a good deal of old information in hardcopy has been digitized or will be so in the future. Thus, the line between ESI and hardcopy was determined to be one that could not be drawn usefully.

The Committee understands that the choice of a cut-off date has a degree of arbitrariness. But January 1, 1998 is a rational date for treating concerns about old and unreliable ESI. And the date is no more arbitrary than the 20-year cutoff date in the original rule. See Committee Note to Rule 901(b)(8) ("Any time period selected is bound to be arbitrary.").

Under the amendment, a document is "prepared" when the statement proffered was recorded in that document. For example, if a hardcopy document is prepared in 1995, and a party seeks to admit a scanned copy of that document, the date of preparation is 1995 even though the scan was made long after that—the subsequent scan does not alter the document. The relevant point is the date on which the information is recorded, not when the information is prepared for trial. However, if the content of the document is itself altered after the cut-off date, then the hearsay exception will not apply to statements that were added in the alteration.

RULE 804. EXCEPTIONS TO THE RULE AGAINST HEARSAY – WHEN THE DECLARANT IS UNAVAILABLE AS A WITNESS

(a) Criteria for Being Unavailable. A declarant is considered to be unavailable as a witness if the declarant:

(1) is exempted from testifying about the subject matter of the declarant's statement because the court rules that a privilege applies;

(2) refuses to testify about the subject matter despite a court order to do so;

(3) testifies to not remembering the subject matter;

(4) cannot be present or testify at the trial or hearing because of death or a then-existing infirmity, physical illness, or mental illness; or

(5) is absent from the trial or hearing and the statement's proponent has not been able, by process or other reasonable means, to procure:

(A) the declarant's attendance, in the case of a hearsay exception under Rule 804(b)(1) or (6); or

(B) the declarant's attendance or testimony, in the case of a hearsay exception under Rule 804(b)(2), (3), or (4).

But this subdivision (a) does not apply if the statement's proponent procured or wrongfully caused the declarant's unavailability as a witness in order to prevent the declarant from attending or testifying.

(b) The Exceptions. The following are not excluded by the rule against hearsay if the declarant is unavailable as a witness:

(1) *Former Testimony.* Testimony that:

(A) was given as a witness at a trial, hearing, or lawful deposition, whether given during the current proceeding or a different one; and

(B) is now offered against a party who had—or, in a civil case, whose predecessor in interest had—an opportunity and similar motive to develop it by direct, cross-, or redirect examination.

(2) *Statement Under the Belief of Imminent Death.* In a prosecution for homicide or in a civil case, a statement that the declarant, while believing the declarant's death to be imminent, made about its cause or circumstances.

(3) *Statement Against Interest.* A statement that:

(A) a reasonable person in the declarant's position would have made only if the person believed it to be true because, when made, it was so contrary to the declarant's proprietary or pecuniary interest or had so great a tendency to invalidate the declarant's claim against someone else or to expose the declarant to civil or criminal liability; and

(B) if offered in a criminal case as one that tends to expose the declarant to criminal liability, is supported by corroborating circumstances that clearly indicate its trustworthiness after considering the totality of circumstances under which it was made and any evidence that supports or undermines it.

(4) *Statement of Personal or Family History.* A statement about:

(A) the declarant's own birth, adoption, legitimacy, ancestry, marriage, divorce, relationship by blood, adoption, or marriage, or similar facts of personal or family history, even though the declarant had no way of acquiring personal knowledge about that fact; or

(B) another person concerning any of these facts, as well as death, if the declarant was related to the person by blood, adoption, or marriage or was so intimately associated with the person's family that the declarant's information is likely to be accurate.

(5) [*Other Exceptions.*] [Transferred to Rule 807.]

(6) *Statement Offered Against a Party That Wrongfully Caused the Declarant's Unavailability.* A statement offered against a party that wrongfully caused—or acquiesced in wrongfully causing—the declarant's unavailability as a witness, and did so intending that result.

NOTES OF ADVISORY COMMITTEE ON PROPOSED RULES (1973)

As to firsthand knowledge on the part of hearsay declarants, see the introductory portion of the Advisory Committee's Note to Rule 803.

Subdivision (a). The definition of unavailability implements the division of hearsay exceptions into two categories by Rules 803 and 804(b).

At common law the unavailability requirement was evolved in connection with particular hearsay exceptions rather than along general lines. For example, see the separate explication of unavailability in relation to former testimony, declarations against interest, and statements of pedigree, separately developed in McCormick §§234, 257, and 297. However, no reason is apparent for making distinctions as to what satisfies unavailability for the different exceptions. The treatment in the rule is therefore uniform although differences in the range of process for witnesses between civil and criminal cases will lead to a less exacting requirement under item (5). See Rule 45(e) of the Federal Rules of Civil Procedure and Rule 17(e) of the Federal Rules of Criminal Procedure.

Five instances of unavailability are specified:

(1) Substantial authority supports the position that exercise of a claim of privilege by the declarant satisfies the requirement of unavailability (usually in connection with former testimony). *Wyatt v. State,* 35 Ala. App. 147, 46 So.2d 837 (1950); *State v. Stewart,* 85 Kan. 404, 116 P. 489 (1911); Annot., 45 A.L.R.2d 1354; Uniform Rule 62(7)

(a); California Evidence Code §240(a)(1); Kansas Code of Civil Procedure §60–459(g) (1). A ruling by the judge is required, which clearly implies that an actual claim of privilege must be made.

(2) A witness is rendered unavailable if he simply refuses to testify concerning the subject matter of his statement despite judicial pressures to do so, a position supported by similar considerations of practicality. *Johnson v. People,* 152 Colo. 586, 384 P.2d 454 (1963); *People v. Pickett,* 339 Mich. 294, 63 N.W.2d 681, 45 A.L.R.2d 1341 (1954). *Contra, Pleau v. State,* 255 Wis. 362, 38 N.W.2d 496 (1949).

(3) The position that a claimed lack of memory by the witness of the subject matter of his statement constitutes unavailability likewise finds support in the cases, though not without dissent. McCormick §234, p. 494. If the claim is successful, the practical effect is to put the testimony beyond reach, as in the other instances. In this instance, however, it will be noted that the lack of memory must be established by the testimony of the witness himself, which clearly contemplates his production and subjection to cross-examination.

(4) Death and infirmity find general recognition as ground. McCormick §§234, 257, 297; Uniform Rule 62(7)(c); California Evidence Code §240(a)(3); Kansas Code of Civil Procedure §60–459(g)(3); New Jersey Evidence Rule 62(6)(c). See also the provisions on use of depositions in Rule 32(a)(3) of the Federal Rules of Civil Procedure and Rule 15(e) of the Federal Rules of Criminal Procedure.

(5) Absence from the hearing coupled with inability to compel attendance by process or other reasonable means also satisfies the requirement. McCormick §234; Uniform Rule 62(7)(d) and (e); California Evidence Code §240(a)(4) and (5); Kansas Code of Civil Procedure §60–459(g)(4) and (5); New Jersey Rule 62(6)(b) and (d). See the discussion of procuring attendance of witnesses who are nonresidents or in custody in *Barber v. Page,* 390 U.S. 719, 88 S.Ct. 1318, 20 L.Ed.2d 255 (1968).

If the conditions otherwise constituting unavailability result from the procurement or wrongdoing of the proponent of the statement, the requirement is not satisfied. The rule contains no requirement that an attempt be made to take the deposition of a declarant.

Subdivision (b). Rule 803 *supra,* is based upon the assumption that a hearsay statement falling within one of its exceptions possesses qualities which justify the conclusion that whether the declarant is available or unavailable is not a relevant factor in determining admissibility. The instant rule proceeds upon a different theory: hearsay which admittedly is not equal in quality to testimony of the declarant on the stand may nevertheless be admitted if the declarant is unavailable and if his statement meets a specified standard. The rule expresses preferences: testimony given on the stand in person is preferred over hearsay, and hearsay, if of the specified quality, is preferred over complete loss of the evidence of the declarant. The exceptions evolved at common law with respect to declarations of unavailable declarants furnish the basis for the exceptions enumerated in the proposal. The term "unavailable" is defined in subdivision (a).

Exception (1). Former testimony does not rely upon some set of circumstances to substitute for oath and cross-examination, since both oath and opportunity to cross-examine were present in fact. The only missing one of the ideal conditions for the giving of testimony is the presence of trier and opponent ("demeanor evidence"). This is lacking with all hearsay exceptions. Hence it may be argued that former testimony is the strongest hearsay and should be included under Rule 803, supra. However, opportunity to observe demeanor is what in a large measure confers depth and meaning upon oath and cross-examination. Thus in cases under Rule 803 demeanor lacks the significance which it possesses with respect to testimony. In any event, the tradition, founded in experience, uniformly favors production of the witness if he is available. The exception indicates continuation of the policy. This preference for the presence of the witness is apparent also in rules and statutes on the use of depositions, which deal with substantially the same problem.

Under the exception, the testimony may be offered (1) against the party against whom it was previously offered or (2) against the party by whom it was previously offered. In each instance the question resolves itself into whether fairness allows imposing, upon the party against whom now offered, the handling of the witness on the earlier occasion. (1) If the party against whom now offered is the one against whom the testimony was offered previously, no unfairness is apparent in requiring him to accept his own prior conduct of cross-examination or decision not to cross-examine. Only demeanor has been lost, and that is inherent in the situation. (2) If the party against whom now offered is the one *by* whom the testimony was offered previously, a satisfactory answer becomes somewhat more difficult. One possibility is to proceed somewhat along the line of an adoptive admission, i.e. by offering the testimony proponent in effect adopts it. However, this theory savors of discarded concepts of witnesses' belonging to a party, of litigants' ability to pick and choose witnesses, and of vouching for one's own witnesses. Cf. McCormick §246, pp. 526–527; 4 Wigmore §1075. A more direct and acceptable approach is simply to recognize direct and redirect examination of one's own witness as the equivalent of cross-examining an opponent's witness. Falknor, Former Testimony and the Uniform Rules: A Comment, 38 N.Y.U.L.Rev. 651, n. 1 (1963); McCormick §231, p. 483. See also 5 Wigmore §1389. Allowable techniques for dealing with hostile, doublecrossing, forgetful, and mentally deficient witnesses leave no substance to a claim that one could not adequately develop his own witness at the former hearing. An even less appealing argument is presented when failure to develop fully was the result of a deliberate choice.

The common law did not limit the admissibility of former testimony to that given in an earlier trial of the same case, although it did require identity of issues as a means of insuring that the former handling of the witness was the equivalent of what would now be done if the opportunity were presented. Modern decisions reduce the requirement to "substantial" identity. McCormick §233. Since identity of issues is significant only in that it bears on motive and interest in developing fully the testimony of the witness, expressing the matter in the latter terms is preferable. Id. Testimony given at a preliminary hearing was held in *California v. Green,* 399 U.S. 149, 90 S.Ct. 1930, 26 L.Ed.2d 489 (1970), to satisfy confrontation requirements in this respect.

As a further assurance of fairness in thrusting upon a party the prior handling of the witness, the common law also insisted upon identity of parties, deviating only to the extent of allowing substitution of successors in a narrowly construed privity. Mutuality as an aspect of identity is now generally discredited, and the requirement of identity of the offering party disappears except as it might affect motive to develop the testimony. Falknor, supra, at 652; McCormick §232, pp. 487–488. The question remains whether strict identity, or privity, should continue as a requirement with respect to the party against whom offered. The rule departs to the extent of allowing substitution of one with the right and opportunity to develop the testimony with similar motive and interest. This position is supported by modern decisions. McCormick §232, pp. 489–490; 5 Wigmore §1388.

Provisions of the same tenor will be found in Uniform Rule 63(3)(b); California Evidence Code §§1290–1292; Kansas Code of Civil Procedure §60–460(c)(2); New Jersey Evidence Rule 63(3). Unlike the rule, the latter three provide either that former testimony is not admissible if the right of confrontation is denied or that it is not admissible if the accused was not a party to the prior hearing. The genesis of these limitations is a caveat in Uniform Rule 63(3) Comment that use of former testimony against an accused may violate his right of confrontation. *Mattox v. United States,* 156 U.S. 237, 15 S.Ct. 337, 39 L.Ed. 409 (1895), held that the right was not violated by the Government's use, on a retrial of the same case, of testimony given at the first trial by two witnesses since deceased. The decision leaves open the questions (1) whether direct and redirect are equivalent to cross-examination for purposes of confrontation, (2) whether testimony given in a different proceeding is acceptable, and (3) whether the accused must himself have been a party to the earlier proceeding or whether a similarly situated person will serve the purpose. Professor Falknor concluded that, if a dying declaration untested by cross-examination is constitutionally admissible, former testimony tested by the cross-examination of one similarly situated does not offend against confrontation. Falknor, *supra,* at

659–660. The constitutional acceptability of dying declarations has often been conceded. *Mattox v. United States,* 156 U.S. 237, 243, 15 S.Ct. 337, 39 L.Ed. 409 (1895); *Kirby v. United States,* 174 U.S. 47, 61, 19 S.Ct. 574, 43 L.Ed. 890 (1899); *Pointer v. Texas,* 380 U.S. 400, 407, 85 S.Ct. 1065, 13 L.Ed.2d 923 (1965).

Exception (2). The exception is the familiar dying declaration of the common law, expanded somewhat beyond its traditionally narrow limits. While the original religious justification for the exception may have lost its conviction for some persons over the years, it can scarcely be doubted that powerful psychological pressures are present. See 5 Wigmore §1443 and the classic statement of Chief Baron Eyre in *Rex v. Woodcock,* 1 Leach 500, 502, 168 Eng. Rep. 352, 353 (K.B. 1789).

The common law required that the statement be that of the victim, offered in a prosecution for criminal homicide. Thus declarations by victims in prosecutions for other crimes, e.g. a declaration by a rape victim who dies in childbirth, and all declarations in civil cases were outside the scope of the exception. An occasional statute has removed these restrictions, as in Colo. R.S. §52–1–20, or has expanded the area of offenses to include abortions, 5 Wigmore §1432, p. 224, n. 4. Kansas by decision extended the exception to civil cases. *Thurston v. Fritz,* 91 Kan. 468, 138 P. 625 (1914). While the common law exception no doubt originated as a result of the exceptional need for the evidence in homicide cases, the theory of admissibility applies equally in civil cases and in prosecutions for crimes other than homicide. The same considerations suggest abandonment of the limitation to circumstances attending the event in question, yet when the statement deals with matters other than the supposed death, its influence is believed to be sufficiently attenuated to justify the limitation. Unavailability is not limited to death. See subdivision (a) of this rule. Any problem as to declarations phrased in terms of opinion is laid at rest by Rule 701, and continuation of a requirement of first-hand knowledge is assured by Rule 602.

Comparable provisions are found in Uniform Rule 63 (5); California Evidence Code §1242; Kansas Code of Civil Procedure §60–460(e); New Jersey Evidence Rule 63(5).

Exception (3). The circumstantial guaranty of reliability for declarations against interest is the assumption that persons do not make statements which are damaging to themselves unless satisfied for good reason that they are true. *Hileman v. Northwest Engineering Co.,* 346 F.2d 668 (6th Cir. 1965). If the statement is that of a party, offered by his opponent, it comes in as an admission, Rule 803(d)(2), and there is no occasion to inquire whether it is against interest, this not being a condition precedent to admissibility of admissions by opponents.

The common law required that the interest declared against be pecuniary or proprietary but within this limitation demonstrated striking ingenuity in discovering an against-interest aspect. *Higham v. Ridgeway*, 10 East 109, 103 Eng.Rep. 717 (K.B. 1808); *Reg. v. Overseers of Birmingham*, 1 B. & S. 763, 121 Eng.Rep. 897 (Q.B. 1861); McCormick, §256, p. 551, nn. 2 and 3.

The exception discards the common law limitation and expands to the full logical limit. One result is to remove doubt as to the admissibility of declarations tending to establish a tort liability against the declarant or to extinguish one which might be asserted by him, in accordance with the trend of the decisions in this country. McCormick §254, pp. 548–549. Another is to allow statements tending to expose declarant to hatred, ridicule, or disgrace, the motivation here being considered to be as strong as when financial interests are at stake. McCormick §255, p. 551. And finally, exposure to criminal liability satisfies the against-interest requirement. The refusal of the common law to concede the adequacy of a penal interest was no doubt indefensible in logic, see the dissent of Mr. Justice Holmes in *Donnelly v. United States*, 228 U.S. 243, 33 S.Ct. 449, 57 L.Ed. 820 (1913), but one senses in the decisions a distrust of evidence of confessions by third persons offered to exculpate the accused arising from suspicions of fabrication either of the fact of the making of the confession or in its contents, enhanced in either instance by the required unavailability of the declarant. Nevertheless, an increasing amount of decisional law recognizes exposure to punishment for crime as a sufficient stake. *People v. Spriggs*, 60 Cal.2d 868, 36 Cal.Rptr. 841, 389 P.2d 377 (1964); *Sutter v. Easterly*, 354 Mo. 282, 189 S.W.2d 284 (1945); *Band's Refuse Removal, Inc. v. Fairlawn Borough*, 62 N.J. Super. 552, 163 A.2d 465 (1960); *Newberry v. Commonwealth*, 191 Va. 445, 61 S.E.2d 318 (1950); Annot., 162 A.L.R. 446. The requirement of corroboration is included in the rule in order to effect an accommodation between these competing considerations. When the statement is offered by the accused by way of exculpation, the resulting situation is not adapted to control by rulings as to the weight of the evidence and, hence the provision is cast in terms of a requirement preliminary to admissibility. Cf. Rule 406(a). The requirement of corroboration should be construed in such a manner as to effectuate its purpose of circumventing fabrication.

Ordinarily the third-party confession is thought of in terms of exculpating the accused, but this is by no means always or necessarily the case: it may include statements implicating him, and under the general theory of declarations against interest they would be admissible as related statements. *Douglas v. Alabama*, 380 U.S. 415, 85 S.Ct. 1074, 13 L.Ed.2d 934 (1965), and *Bruton v. United States*, 389 U.S. 818, 88 S.Ct. 126, 19 L.Ed.2d 70 (1968), both involved confessions by codefendants which implicated the accused. While the confession was not actually offered in evidence in *Douglas*, the procedure followed effectively put it before the jury, which the

Court ruled to be error. Whether the confession might have been admissible as a declaration against penal interest was not considered or discussed. Bruton assumed the inadmissibility, as against the accused, of the implicating confession of his codefendant, and centered upon the question of the effectiveness of a limiting instruction. These decisions, however, by no means require that all statements implicating another person be excluded from the category of declarations against interest. Whether a statement is in fact against interest must be determined from the circumstances of each case. Thus a statement admitting guilt and implicating another person, made while in custody, may well be motivated by a desire to curry favor with the authorities and hence fail to qualify as against interest. See the dissenting opinion of Mr. Justice White in *Bruton.* On the other hand, the same words spoken under different circumstances, *e.g.*, to an acquaintance, would have no difficulty in qualifying. The rule does not purport to deal with questions of the right of confrontation.

The balancing of self-serving against dissenting aspects of a declaration is discussed in McCormick §256.

For comparable provisions, see Uniform Rule 63(10): California Evidence Code §1230; Kansas Code of Civil Procedure §60–460(j); New Jersey Evidence Rule 63(10).

Exception (4). The general common law requirement that a declaration in this area must have been made *ante litem motam* has been dropped, as bearing more appropriately on weight than admissibility. See 5 Wigmore §1483. Item (i)[(A)] specifically disclaims any need of firsthand knowledge respecting declarant's own personal history. In some instances it is self-evident (marriage) and in others impossible and traditionally not required (date of birth). Item (ii)[(B)] deals with declarations concerning the history of another person. As at common law, declarant is qualified if related by blood or marriage. 5 Wigmore §1489. In addition, and contrary to the common law, declarant qualifies by virtue of intimate association with the family. *Id.*, §1487. The requirement sometimes encountered that when the subject of the statement is the relationship between two other persons the declarant must qualify as to both is omitted. Relationship is reciprocal. *Id.*, §1491.

For comparable provisions, see Uniform Rule 63 (23), (24), (25); California Evidence Code §§1310, 1311; Kansas Code of Civil Procedure §60–460(u), (v), (w); New Jersey Evidence Rules 63(23), 63(24), 63(25).

NOTES OF ADVISORY COMMITTEE ON RULES – 1997 AMENDMENT

Subdivision (b)(5). The contents of Rule 803(24) and Rule 804(b)(5) have been combined and transferred to a new Rule 807. This was done to facilitate additions to Rules 803 and 804. No change in meaning is intended.

Subdivision (b)(6). Rule 804(b)(6) has been added to provide that a party forfeits the right to object on hearsay grounds to the admission of a declarant's prior statement when the party's deliberate wrongdoing or acquiescence therein procured the unavailability of the declarant as a witness. This recognizes the need for a prophylactic rule to deal with abhorrent behavior "which strikes at the heart of the system of justice itself." *United States v. Mastrangelo,* 693 F.2d 269, 273 (2d Cir. 1982), *cert. denied,* 467 U.S. 1204 (1984). The wrongdoing need not consist of a criminal act. The rule applies to all parties, including the government.

Every circuit that has resolved the question has recognized the principle of forfeiture by misconduct, although the tests for determining whether there is a forfeiture have varied. *See, e.g., United States v. Aguiar,* 975 F.2d 45, 47 (2d Cir. 1992); *United States v. Potamitis,* 739 F.2d 784, 789 (2d Cir.), *cert. denied,* 469 U.S. 918 (1984); *Steele v. Taylor,* 684 F.2d 1193, 1199 (6th Cir. 1982), *cert. denied,* 460 U.S. 1053 (1983); *United States v. Balano,* 618 F.2d 624, 629 (10th Cir. 1979), *cert. denied,* 449 U.S. 840 (1980); *United States v. Carlson,* 547 F.2d 1346, 1358–59 (8th Cir.), *cert. denied,* 431 U.S. 914 (1977). The foregoing cases apply a preponderance of the evidence standard. *Contra United States v. Thevis,* 665 F.2d 616, 631 (5th Cir.) (clear and convincing standard), cert. denied, 459 U.S. 825 (1982). The usual Rule 104(a) preponderance of the evidence standard has been adopted in light of the behavior the new Rule 804(b)(6) seeks to discourage.

GAP Report on Rule 804(b)(5). The words "Transferred to Rule 807" were substituted for "Abrogated."

GAP Report on Rule 804(b)(6). The title of the rule was changed to "Forfeiture by wrongdoing." The word "who" in line 24 was changed to "that" to indicate that the rule is potentially applicable against the government. Two sentences were added to the first paragraph of the committee note to clarify that the wrongdoing need not be criminal in nature, and to indicate the rule's potential applicability to the government. The word "forfeiture" was substituted for "waiver" in the note.

NOTES OF ADVISORY COMMITTEE ON RULES – 2010 AMENDMENT

Subdivision (b)(3). Rule 804(b)(3) has been amended to provide that the corroborating circumstances requirement applies to all declarations against penal interest offered in criminal cases. A number of courts have applied the corroborating circumstances requirement to declarations against penal interest offered by the prosecution, even though the text of the Rule did not so provide. *See, e.g., United States v. Alvarez,* 584 F.2d 694, 701 (5th Cir. 1978) ("by transplanting the language governing exculpatory statements onto the analysis for admitting inculpatory hearsay, a unitary standard is derived which offers the most workable basis for applying Rule 804(b)(3)"); *United States v. Shukri,* 207 F.3d 412 (7th Cir. 2000) (requiring corroborating circumstances for against-penal-interest statements offered by the government). A unitary approach to declarations against penal interest assures both the prosecution and the accused that the Rule will not be abused and that only reliable hearsay statements will be admitted under the exception.

All other changes to the structure and wording of the Rule are intended to be stylistic only. There is no intent to change any other result in any ruling on evidence admissibility.

The amendment does not address the use of the corroborating circumstances for declarations against penal interest offered in civil cases.

In assessing whether corroborating circumstances exist, some courts have focused on the credibility of the witness who relates the hearsay statement in court. But the credibility of the witness who relates the statement is not a proper factor for the court to consider in assessing corroborating circumstances. To base admission or exclusion of a hearsay statement on the witness's credibility would usurp the jury's role of determining the credibility of testifying witnesses.

COMMITTEE NOTES ON RULES – 2011 AMENDMENT

The language of Rule 804 has been amended as part of the general restyling of the Evidence Rules to make them more easily understood and to make style and terminology consistent throughout the rules. These changes are intended to be stylistic only. There is no intent to change any result in any ruling on evidence admissibility.

The amendment to Rule 804(b)(3) provides that the corroborating circumstances requirement applies not only to declarations against penal interest offered by the defendant in a criminal case, but also to such statements offered by the government. The language in the original rule does not so provide, but a proposed amendment to Rule 804(b)(3)—released for public comment in 2008 and scheduled to be enacted before the restyled rules—explicitly extends the corroborating circumstances requirement to statements offered by the government.

Rule 804(b)(6) has been renumbered to fill a gap left when the original Rule 804(b)(5) was transferred to Rule 807.

RULE 805. HEARSAY WITHIN HEARSAY

Hearsay within hearsay is not excluded by the rule against hearsay if each part of the combined statements conforms with an exception to the rule.

RULE 806. ATTACKING AND SUPPORTING THE DECLARANT'S CREDIBILITY

When a hearsay statement—or a statement described in Rule 801(d)(2)(C), (D), or (E)—has been admitted in evidence, the declarant's credibility may be attacked, and then supported, by any evidence that would be admissible for those purposes if the declarant had testified as a witness. The court may admit evidence of the declarant's inconsistent statement or conduct, regardless of when it occurred or whether the declarant had an opportunity to explain or deny it. If the party against whom the statement was admitted calls the declarant as a witness, the party may examine the declarant on the statement as if on cross-examination.

RULE 807. RESIDUAL EXCEPTION

(a) In General. Under the following conditions, a hearsay statement is not excluded by the rule against hearsay even if the statement is not admissible under a hearsay exception in Rule 803 or 804:

(1) the statement is supported by sufficient guarantees of trustworthiness—after considering the totality of circumstances under which it was made and evidence, if any, corroborating the statement; and

(2) it is more probative on the point for which it is offered than any other evidence that the proponent can obtain through reasonable efforts.

(b) Notice. The statement is admissible only if the proponent gives an adverse party reasonable notice of the intent to offer the statement—including its substance and the declarant's name—so that the party has a fair opportunity to meet it. The notice must be provided in writing before the trial or hearing—or in any form during the trial or hearing if the court, for good cause, excuses a lack of earlier notice.

COMMITTEE NOTES ON RULES – 1997 AMENDMENT

The contents of Rule 803(24) and Rule 804(b)(5) have been combined and transferred to a new Rule 807. This was done to facilitate additions to Rules 803 and 804. No change in meaning is intended.

COMMITTEE NOTES ON RULES – 2019 AMENDMENT

Rule 807 has been amended to fix a number of problems that the courts have encountered in applying it.

Courts have had difficulty with the requirement that the proffered hearsay carry "equivalent" circumstantial guarantees of trustworthiness. The "equivalence" standard is difficult to apply, given the different types of guarantees of reliability, of varying strength, found among the categorical exceptions (as well as the fact that some hearsay exceptions, e.g., Rule 804(b)(6), are not based on reliability at all). The "equivalence" standard has not served to guide a court's discretion to admit hearsay, because the court is free to choose among a spectrum of exceptions for comparison. Moreover, experience has shown that some statements offered as residual hearsay cannot be compared usefully to any of the categorical exceptions and yet might well be trustworthy. Thus the requirement of an equivalence analysis has been eliminated. Under the amendment, the court should proceed directly to a determination of whether the hearsay is supported by guarantees of trustworthiness. See Rule 104(a). As with any hearsay statement offered under an exception, the court's threshold finding that admissibility requirements are met merely means that the jury may consider the statement and not that it must assume the statement to be true.

The amendment specifically requires the court to consider corroborating evidence in the trustworthiness enquiry. Most courts have required the consideration of corroborating evidence, though some courts have disagreed. The rule now provides for a uniform approach, and recognizes that the existence or absence of corroboration is relevant to, but not dispositive of, whether a statement should be admissible under this exception. Of course, the court must consider not only the existence of corroborating evidence but also the strength and quality of that evidence.

The amendment does not alter the case law prohibiting parties from proceeding directly to the residual exception, without considering the admissibility of the hearsay under Rules 803 and 804. A court is not required to make a finding that no other hearsay exception is applicable. But the opponent cannot seek admission under Rule 807 if it is apparent that the hearsay could be admitted under another exception.

The rule in its current form applies to hearsay "not specifically covered" by a Rule 803 or 804 exception. The amendment makes the rule applicable to hearsay "not admissible under" those exceptions. This clarifies that a court assessing guarantees of trustworthiness may consider whether the statement is a "near-miss" of one of the Rule 803 or 804 exceptions. If the court employs a "near-miss" analysis it should—in addition to evaluating all relevant guarantees of trustworthiness—take into account the reasons that the hearsay misses the admissibility requirements of the standard exception.

In deciding whether the statement is supported by sufficient guarantees of trustworthiness, the court should not consider the credibility of any witness who relates the declarant's hearsay statement in court. The credibility of an in-court witness does not present a hearsay question. To base admission or exclusion of a hearsay statement on the witness's credibility would usurp the jury's role of determining the credibility of testifying witnesses. The rule provides that the focus for trustworthiness is on circumstantial guarantees surrounding the making of the statement itself, as well as any independent evidence corroborating the statement. The credibility of the witness relating the statement is not a part of either enquiry.

Of course, even if the court finds sufficient guarantees of trustworthiness, the independent requirements of the Confrontation Clause must be satisfied if the hearsay statement is offered against a defendant in a criminal case.

The Committee decided to retain the requirement that the proponent must show that the hearsay statement is more probative than any other evidence that the proponent can reasonably obtain. This necessity requirement will continue to serve to prevent the residual exception from being used as a device to erode the categorical exceptions.

The requirements that residual hearsay must be evidence of a material fact and that its admission will best serve the purposes of these rules and the interests of justice have been deleted. These requirements have proved to be superfluous in that they are already found in other rules. See Rules 102, 401.

The notice provision has been amended to make four changes in the operation of the rule:

- First, the amendment requires the proponent to disclose the "substance" of the statement. This term is intended to require a description that is sufficiently specific under the circumstances to allow the opponent a fair opportunity to meet the evidence. See Rule 103(a)(2) (requiring the party making an offer of proof to inform the court of the "substance" of the evidence).
- Second, the prior requirement that the declarant's address must be disclosed has been deleted. That requirement was nonsensical when the declarant was unavailable, and unnecessary in the many cases in which the declarant's address was known or easily obtainable. If prior disclosure of the declarant's address is critical and cannot be obtained by the opponent through other means, then the opponent can seek relief from the court.
- Third, the amendment requires that the pretrial notice be in writing—which is satisfied by notice in electronic form. See Rule 101(b)(6). Requiring the notice to be in writing provides certainty and reduces arguments about whether notice was actually provided.
- Finally, the pretrial notice provision has been amended to provide for a good cause exception. Most courts have applied a good cause exception under Rule 807 even though the rule in its current form does not provide for it, while some courts have read the rule as it was written. Experience under the residual exception has shown

that a good cause exception is necessary in certain limited situations. For example, the proponent may not become aware of the existence of the hearsay statement until after the trial begins, or the proponent may plan to call a witness who without warning becomes unavailable during trial, and the proponent might then need to resort to residual hearsay.

The rule retains the requirement that the opponent receive notice in a way that provides a fair opportunity to meet the evidence. When notice is provided during trial after a finding of good cause, the court may need to consider protective measures, such as a continuance, to assure that the opponent is not prejudiced.

ARTICLE IX. AUTHENTICATION AND IDENTIFICATION

RULE 901. AUTHENTICATING OR IDENTIFYING EVIDENCE

(a) In General. To satisfy the requirement of authenticating or identifying an item of evidence, the proponent must produce evidence sufficient to support a finding that the item is what the proponent claims it is.

(b) Examples. The following are examples only—not a complete list—of evidence that satisfies the requirement:

(1) *Testimony of a Witness with Knowledge.* Testimony that an item is what it is claimed to be.

(2) *Nonexpert Opinion About Handwriting.* A nonexpert's opinion that handwriting is genuine, based on a familiarity with it that was not acquired for the current litigation.

(3) *Comparison by an Expert Witness or the Trier of Fact.* A comparison with an authenticated specimen by an expert witness or the trier of fact.

(4) *Distinctive Characteristics and the Like.* The appearance, contents, substance, internal patterns, or other distinctive characteristics of the item, taken together with all the circumstances.

(5) *Opinion About a Voice.* An opinion identifying a person's voice—whether heard firsthand or through mechanical or electronic transmission or recording—based on hearing the voice at any time under circumstances that connect it with the alleged speaker.

(6) *Evidence About a Telephone Conversation.* For a telephone conversation, evidence that a call was made to the number assigned at the time to:

(A) a particular person, if circumstances, including self-identification, show that the person answering was the one called; or

(B) a particular business, if the call was made to a business and the call related to business reasonably transacted over the telephone.

(7) *Evidence About Public Records.* Evidence that:

(A) a document was recorded or filed in a public office as authorized by law; or

(B) a purported public record or statement is from the office where items of this kind are kept.

(8) *Evidence About Ancient Documents or Data Compilations.* For a document or data compilation, evidence that it:

(A) is in a condition that creates no suspicion about its authenticity;

(B) was in a place where, if authentic, it would likely be; and

(C) is at least 20 years old when offered.

(9) *Evidence About a Process or System.* Evidence describing a process or system and showing that it produces an accurate result.

(10) *Methods Provided by a Statute or Rule.* Any method of authentication or identification allowed by a federal statute or a rule prescribed by the Supreme Court.

NOTES OF ADVISORY COMMITTEE ON PROPOSED RULES (1973)

Subdivision (a). Authentication and identification represent a special aspect of relevancy. Michael and Adler, Real Proof, 5 Vand.L.Rev. 344, 362 (1952); McCormick §§179, 185; Morgan, Basic Problems of Evidence 378. (1962). Thus a telephone conversation may be irrelevant because on an unrelated topic or because the speaker is not identified. The latter aspect is the one here involved. Wigmore describes the need for authentication as "an inherent logical necessity." 7 Wigmore §2129, p. 564.

This requirement of showing authenticity or identity fails in the category of relevancy dependent upon fulfillment of a condition of fact and is governed by the procedure set forth in Rule 104(b).

The common law approach to authentication of documents has been criticized as an "attitude of agnosticism," McCormick, Cases on Evidence 388, n. 4 (3rd ed. 1956), as one which "departs sharply from men's cus toms in ordinary affairs," and as presenting only a slight obstacle to the introduction of forgeries in comparison to the time and expense devoted to proving genuine writings which correctly show their origin on their face, McCormick §185, pp. 395, 396. Today, such available procedures as requests to admit and pretrial conference afford the means of eliminating much of the need for authentication or identification. Also, significant inroads upon the traditional insistence on authentication and identification have been made by accepting as at least prima facie genuine items of the kind treated in Rule 902, *infra.* However, the need for suitable methods of proof still remains, since criminal cases pose their own obstacles to the use of preliminary procedures, unforeseen contingencies may arise, and cases of genuine controversy will still occur.

Subdivision (b). The treatment of authentication and identification draws largely upon the experience embodied in the common law and in statutes to furnish illustrative applications of the general principle set forth in subdivision (a). The examples are not intended as an exclusive enumeration of allowable methods but are meant to guide and suggest, leaving room for growth and development in this area of the law.

The examples relate for the most part to documents, with some attention given to voice communications and computer print-outs. As Wigmore noted, no special rules have been developed for authenticating chattels. Wigmore, Code of Evidence §2086 (3rd ed. 1942).

It should be observed that compliance with requirements of authentication or identification by no means assures admission of an item into evidence, as other bars, hearsay for example, may remain.

Example (1). Example (1) contemplates a broad spectrum ranging from testimony of a witness who was present at the signing of a document to testimony establishing narcotics as taken from an accused and accounting for custody through the period until trial, including laboratory analysis. See California Evidence Code §1413, eyewitness to signing.

Example (2). Example (2) states conventional doctrine as to lay identification of handwriting, which recognizes that a sufficient familiarity with the handwriting of another person may be acquired by seeing him write, by exchanging correspondence, or by other means, to afford a basis for identifying it on subsequent occasions. McCormick §189. See also California Evidence Code §1416. Testimony based upon familiarity acquired for purposes of the litigation is reserved to the expert under the example which follows.

Example (3). The history of common law restrictions upon the technique of proving or disproving the genuineness of a disputed specimen of handwriting through comparison with a genuine specimen, by either the testimony of expert witnesses or direct viewing by the triers themselves, is detailed in 7 Wigmore §§1991–1994. In breaking away, the English Common Law Procedure Act of 1854, 17 and 18 Viet., c. 125, §27, cautiously allowed expert or trier to use exemplars "proved to the satisfaction of the judge to be genuine" for purposes of comparison. The language found its way into numerous statutes in this country, e.g., California Evidence Code §§1417, 1418. While explainable as a measure of prudence in the process of breaking with precedent in the handwriting situation, the reservation to the judge of the question of the genuineness of exemplars and the imposition of an unusually high standard of persuasion are at variance with the general treatment of relevancy which depends upon fulfillment of a condition of fact. Rule 104(b). No similar attitude is found in other comparison situations, e.g., ballistics comparison by jury, as in *Evans v. Commonwealth*, 230 Ky. 411, 19 S.W.2d 1091 (1929), or by experts, Annot. 26 A.L.R.2d 892, and no reason appears for its continued existence in handwriting cases. Consequently Example (3) sets no higher standard for handwriting specimens and treats all comparison situations alike, to be governed by Rule 104(b). This approach is consistent with 28 U.S.C. §1731: "The admitted or proved handwriting of any person shall be admissible, for purposes of comparison, to determine genuineness of other handwriting attributed to such person."

Precedent supports the acceptance of visual comparison as sufficiently satisfying preliminary authentication requirements for admission in evidence. *Brandon v. Collins*, 267 F.2d 731 (2d Cir. 1959); *Wausau Sulphate Fibre Co. v. Commissioner of Internal Revenue*, 61 F.2d 879 (7th Cir. 1932); *Desimone v. United States*, 227 F.2d 864 (9th Cir. 1955).

Example (4). The characteristics of the offered item itself, considered in the light of circumstances, afford authentication techniques in great variety. Thus a document or telephone conversation may be shown to have emanated from a particular person by virtue of its disclosing knowledge of facts known peculiarly to him; *Globe Automatic Sprinkler Co. v. Braniff*, 89 Okl. 105, 214 P. 127 (1923); California Evidence Code §1421; similarly, a letter may be authenticated by content and circumstances indicating it was in reply to a duly authenticated one. McCormick §192; California Evidence Code §1420. Language patterns may indicate authenticity or its opposite. *Magnuson v. State*, 187 Wis. 122, 203 N.W. 749 (1925); Arens and Meadow, Psycholinguistics and the Confession Dilemma, 56 Colum.L.Rev. 19 (1956).

Example (5). Since aural voice identification is not a subject of expert testimony, the requisite familiarity may be acquired either before or after the particular speaking which is the subject of the identification, in this respect resembling visual identification of a person rather than identification of handwriting. Cf. Example (2), *supra, People v. Nichols*, 378 Ill. 487, 38 N.E.2d 766 (1942); *McGuire v. State*, 200 Md. 601, 92 A.2d 582 (1952); *State v. McGee*, 336 Mo. 1082, 83 S.W.2d 98 (1935).

Example (6). The cases are in agreement that a mere assertion of his identity by a person talking on the telephone is not sufficient evidence of the authenticity of the conversation and that additional evidence of his identity is required. The additional evidence need not fall in any set pattern. Thus the content of his statements or the reply technique, under

Example (4), supra, or voice identification under Example (5), may furnish the necessary foundation. Outgoing calls made by the witness involve additional factors bearing upon authenticity. The calling of a number assigned by the telephone company reasonably supports the assumption that the listing is correct and that the number is the one reached. If the number is that of a place of business, the mass of authority allows an ensuing conversation if it relates to business reasonably transacted over the telephone, on the theory that the maintenance of the telephone connection is an invitation to do business without further identification. *Matton v. Hoover Co.*, 350 Mo. 506, 166 S.W.2d 557 (1942); *City of Pawhuska v. Crutchfield*, 147 Okl. 4. 293 P. 1095 (1930); *Zurich General Acc. & Liability Ins. Co. v. Baum*, 159 Va. 404, 165 S.E. 518 (1932). Otherwise, some additional circumstance of identification of the speaker is required. The authorities divide on the question whether the self-identifying statement of the person answering suffices. Example (6) answers in the affirmative on the assumption that usual conduct respecting telephone calls furnish adequate assurances of regularity, bearing in mind that the entire matter is open to exploration before the trier of fact. In general, see McCormick §193; 7 Wigmore §2155; Annot., 71 A.L.R. 5, 105 id. 326.

Example (7). Public records are regularly authenticated by proof of custody, without more. McCormick §191; 7 Wigmore §§2158, 2159. The example extends the principle to include data stored in computers and similar methods, of which increasing use in the public records area may be expected. See California Evidence Code §§1532, 1600.

Example (8). The familiar ancient document rule of the common law is extended to include data stored electronically or by other similar means. Since the importance of appearance diminishes in this situation, the importance of custody or place where found increases correspondingly. This expansion is necessary in view of the widespread use of methods of storing data in forms other than conventional written records.

Any time period selected is bound to be arbitrary. The common law period of 30 years is here reduced to 20 years, with some shift of emphasis from the probable unavailability of witnesses to the unlikeliness of a still viable fraud after the lapse of time. The shorter period is specified in the English Evidence Act of 1938, 1 & 2 Geo. 6, c. 28, and in Oregon R.S. 1963, §41.360(34). See also the numerous statutes prescribing periods of less than 30 years in the case of recorded documents. 7 Wigmore §2143.

The application of Example (8) is not subject to any limitation to title documents or to any requirement that possession, in the case of a title document, has been consistent with the document. See McCormick §190.

Example (9). Example (9) is designed for situations in which the accuracy of a result is dependent upon a process or system which produces it. X-rays afford a familiar instance. Among more recent developments is the computer, as to which see *Transport Indemnity Co. v. Seib,* 178 Neb. 253, 132 N.W.2d 871 (1965); *State v. Veres,* 7 Ariz. App. 117, 436 P.2d 629 (1968); *Merrick v. United States Rubber Co.,* 7 Ariz. App. 433, 440 P.2d 314 (1968); Freed, Computer Print-Outs as Evidence, 16 Am. Jur. Proof of Facts 273; Symposium, Law and Computers in the Mid-Sixties, ALI-ABA (1966); 37 Albany L.Rev. 61 (1967). Example (9) does not, of course, foreclose taking judicial notice of the accuracy of the process or system.

Example (10). The example makes clear that methods of authentication provided by Act of Congress and by the Rules of Civil and Criminal Procedure or by Bankruptcy Rules are not intended to be superseded. Illustrative are the provisions for authentication of official records in Civil Procedure Rule 44 and Criminal Procedure Rule 27, for authentication of records of proceedings by court reporters in 28 U.S.C. §753(b) and Civil Procedure Rule 80(c), and for authentication of depositions in Civil Procedure Rule 30(f).

RULE 902. EVIDENCE THAT IS SELF-AUTHENTICATING

The following items of evidence are self-authenticating; they require no extrinsic evidence of authenticity in order to be admitted:

(1) Domestic Public Documents That Are Sealed and Signed. A document that bears:

(A) a seal purporting to be that of the United States; any state, district, commonwealth, territory, or insular possession of the United States; the former Panama Canal Zone; the Trust Territory of the Pacific Islands; a political subdivision of any of these entities; or a department, agency, or officer of any entity named above; and

(B) a signature purporting to be an execution or attestation.

(2) Domestic Public Documents That Are Not Sealed but Are Signed and Certified. A document that bears no seal if:

(A) it bears the signature of an officer or employee of an entity named in Rule 902(1)(A); and

(B) another public officer who has a seal and official duties within that same entity certifies under seal—or its equivalent—that the signer has the official capacity and that the signature is genuine.

(3) Foreign Public Documents. A document that purports to be signed or attested by a person who is authorized by a foreign country's law to do so. The document must be accompanied by a final certification that certifies the genuineness of the signature and official position of the signer or attester—or of any foreign official whose certificate of genuineness relates to the signature or attestation or is in a chain of certificates of genuineness relating to the signature or attestation. The certification may be made by a secretary of a United States embassy or legation; by a consul general, vice consul, or consular agent of the United States; or by a diplomatic or consular official of the foreign country assigned or accredited to the United States. If all parties have been given a reasonable opportunity to investigate the document's authenticity and accuracy, the court may, for good cause, either:

(A) order that it be treated as presumptively authentic without final certification; or

(B) allow it to be evidenced by an attested summary with or without final certification.

(4) Certified Copies of Public Records. A copy of an official record—or a copy of a document that was recorded or filed in a public office as authorized by law—if the copy is certified as correct by:

(A) the custodian or another person authorized to make the certification; or

(B) a certificate that complies with Rule 902(1), (2), or (3), a federal statute, or a rule prescribed by the Supreme Court.

(5) Official Publications. A book, pamphlet, or other publication purporting to be issued by a public authority.

(6) Newspapers and Periodicals. Printed material purporting to be a newspaper or periodical.

(7) Trade Inscriptions and the Like. An inscription, sign, tag, or label purporting to have been affixed in the course of business and indicating origin, ownership, or control.

(8) Acknowledged Documents. A document accompanied by a certificate of acknowledgment that is lawfully executed by a notary public or another officer who is authorized to take acknowledgments.

(9) Commercial Paper and Related Documents. Commercial paper, a signature on it, and related documents, to the extent allowed by general commercial law.

(10) Presumptions Under a Federal Statute. A signature, document, or anything else that a federal statute declares to be presumptively or prima facie genuine or authentic.

(11) Certified Domestic Records of a Regularly Conducted Activity. The original or a copy of a domestic record that meets the requirements of Rule 803(6) (A)-(C), as shown by a certification of the custodian or another qualified person that complies with a federal statute or a rule prescribed by the Supreme Court. Before the trial or hearing, the proponent must give an adverse party reasonable written notice of the intent to offer the record—and must make the record and certification available for inspection—so that the party has a fair opportunity to challenge them.

(12) Certified Foreign Records of a Regularly Conducted Activity. In a civil case, the original or a copy of a foreign record that meets the requirements of Rule 902(11), modified as follows: the certification, rather than complying with a federal statute or Supreme Court rule, must be signed in a manner that, if falsely made, would subject the maker to a criminal penalty in the country where the certification is signed. The proponent must also meet the notice requirements of Rule 902(11) .

(13) Certified Records Generated by an Electronic Process or System. A record generated by an electronic process or system that produces an accurate result, as shown by a certification of a qualified person that complies with the certification requirements of Rule 902(11) or (12). The proponent must also meet the notice requirements of Rule 902(11).

(14) Certified Data Copied from an Electronic Device, Storage Medium, or File. Data copied from an electronic device, storage medium, or file, if authenticated by a process of digital identification, as shown by a certification of a qualified person that complies with the certification requirements of Rule 902(11) or (12). The proponent also must meet the notice requirements of Rule 902 (11).

NOTES OF ADVISORY COMMITTEE ON PROPOSED RULES (1973)

Case law and statutes have, over the years, developed a substantial body of instances in which authenticity is taken as sufficiently established for purposes of admissibility without extrinsic evidence to that effect, sometimes for reasons of policy but perhaps more often because practical considerations reduce the possibility of unauthenticity to a very small dimension. The present rule collects and incorporates these situations, in some instances expanding them to occupy a larger area which their underlying considerations justify. In no instance is the opposite party foreclosed from disputing authenticity.

Paragraph (1). The acceptance of documents bearing a public seal and signature, most often encountered in practice in the form of acknowledgments or certificates authenticating copies of public records, is actually of broad application. Whether theoretically based in whole or in part upon judicial notice, the practical underlying considerations are that forgery is a crime and detection is fairly easy and certain. 7 Wigmore §2161, p. 638; California Evidence Code §1452. More than 50 provisions for judicial notice of official seals are contained in the United States Code.

Paragraph (2). While statutes are found which raise a presumption of genuineness of purported official signatures in the absence of an official seal, 7 Wigmore §2167; California Evidence Code §1453, the greater ease of effecting a forgery under these circumstances is apparent. Hence this paragraph of the rule calls for authentication by an officer who has a seal. Notarial acts by members of the armed forces and other special situations are covered in paragraph (10).

Paragraph (3). provides a method for extending the presumption of authenticity to foreign official documents by a procedure of certification. It is derived from Rule 44(a)(2) of the Rules of Civil Procedure but is broader in applying to public documents rather than being limited to public records.

Paragraph (4). The common law and innumerable statutes have recognized the procedure of authenticating copies of public records by certificate. The certificate qualifies as a public document, receivable as authentic when in conformity with paragraph (1), (2), or (3). Rule 44(a) of the Rules of Civil Procedure and Rule 27 of the Rules of Criminal Procedure have provided authentication procedures of this nature for both domestic and foreign public records. It will be observed that the certification procedure here provided extends only to public records, reports, and recorded documents, all including data compilations, and does not apply to public documents generally. Hence documents provable when presented in original form under paragraphs (1), (2), or (3) may not be provable by certified copy under paragraph (4).

Paragraph (5). Dispensing with preliminary proof of the genuineness of purportedly official publications, most commonly encountered in connection with statutes, court reports, rules, and regulations, has been greatly enlarged by statutes and decisions. 5 Wigmore §1684. Paragraph (5), it will be noted, does not confer admissibility upon all official publications; it merely provides a means whereby their authenticity may be taken as established for purposes of admissibility. Rule 44(a) of the Rules of Civil Procedure has been to the same effect.

Paragraph (6). The likelihood of forgery of newspapers or periodicals is slight indeed. Hence no danger is apparent in receiving them. Establishing the authenticity of the publication may, of course, leave still open questions of authority and responsibility for items therein contained. See 7 Wigmore §2150. Cf. 39 U.S.C. §4005(b), public advertisement prima facie evidence of agency of person named, in postal fraud order proceeding; Canadian Uniform Evidence Act, Draft of 1936, printed copy of newspaper prima facie evidence that notices or advertisements were authorized.

Paragraph (7). Several factors justify dispensing with preliminary proof of genuineness of commercial and mercantile labels and the like.

The risk of forgery is minimal. Trademark infringement involves serious penalties. Great efforts are devoted to inducing the public to buy in reliance on brand names, and substantial protection is given them. Hence the fairness of this treatment finds recognition in the cases. *Curtiss Candy Co. v. Johnson,* 163 Miss. 426, 141 So. 762 (1932), Baby Ruth candy bar; *Doyle v. Continental Baking Co.,* 262 Mass. 516, 160 N.E. 325 (1928), loaf of bread; *Weiner v. Mager & Throne, Inc.,* 167 Misc. 338, 3 N.Y.S.2d 918 (1938), same. And see W.Va.Code 1966, §47–3–5, trade-mark on bottle prima facie evidence of ownership. *Contra, Keegan v. Green Giant Co.,* 150 Me. 283, 110 A.2d 599 (1954); *Murphy v. Campbell Soup Co.,* 62 F.2d 564 (1st Cir. 1933). Cattle brands have received similar acceptance in the western states. Rev. Code Mont.1947, §46–606; *State v. Wolfley,* 75 Kan. 406, 89 P. 1046 (1907); Annot., 11 L.R.A. (N.S.) 87. Inscriptions on trains and vehicles are held to be prima facie evidence of ownership or control. *Pittsburgh, Ft. W. & C. Ry. v. Callaghan,* 157 Ill. 406, 41 N.E. 909 (1895); 9 Wigmore §2510a. See also the provision of 19 U.S.C. §1615(2) that marks, labels, brands, or stamps indicating foreign origin are prima facie evidence of foreign origin of merchandise.

Paragraph (8). In virtually every state, acknowledged title documents are receivable in evidence without further proof. Statutes are collected in 5 Wigmore §1676. If this authentication suffices for documents of the importance of those affecting titles, logic scarcely permits denying this method when other kinds of documents are involved. Instances of broadly inclusive statutes are California Evidence Code §1451 and N.Y.C. PLR 4538, McKinney's Consol. Laws 1963.

Paragraph (9). Issues of the authenticity of commercial paper in federal courts will usually arise in diversity cases, will involve an element of a cause of action or defense, and with respect to presumptions and burden of proof will be controlled by *Erie Railroad Co. v. Tompkins,* 304 U.S. 64, 58 S.Ct. 817, 82 L.Ed. 1188 (1938). Rule 302, *supra.* There may, however, be questions of authenticity involving lesser segments of a case or the case may be one governed by federal common law. *Clearfield Trust Co. v. United States,* 318 U.S. 363, 63 S.Ct. 573, 87 L.Ed. 838 (1943). Cf. *United States v. Yazell,* 382 U.S. 341, 86 S.Ct. 500, 15 L.Ed.2d 404 (1966). In these situations, resort to the useful authentication provisions of the Uniform Commercial Code is provided for. While the phrasing is in terms of "general commercial law," in order to avoid the potential complication inherent in borrowing local statutes, today one would have difficulty in determining the general commercial law without referring to the Code. See *Williams v. Walker-Thomas-Furniture Co.,* 121 U.S. App. D.C. 315, 350 F.2d 445 (1965). Pertinent Code provisions are sections 1–202, 3–307, and 3–510, dealing with third-party documents, signatures on negotiable instruments, protests, and statements of dishonor.

Paragraph (10). The paragraph continues in effect dispensations with preliminary proof of genuineness provided in various Acts of Congress. See, for example, 10 U.S.C. §936, signature, without seal, together with title, prima facie evidence of authenticity of acts of certain military personnel who are given notarial power; 15 U.S.C. §77f(a), signature on SEC registration presumed genuine; 26 U.S.C. §6064, signature to tax return prima facie genuine.

COMMITTEE NOTES ON RULES – 2000 AMENDMENT

The amendment adds two new paragraphs to the rule on self-authentication. It sets forth a procedure by which parties can authenticate certain records of regularly conducted activity, other than through the testimony of a foundation witness. See the amendment to Rule 803(6). 18 U.S.C. §3505 currently provides a means for certifying foreign records of regularly conducted activity in criminal cases, and this amendment is intended to establish a similar procedure for domestic records, and for foreign records offered in civil cases.

A declaration that satisfies 28 U.S.C. §1746 would satisfy the declaration requirement of Rule 902(11), as would any comparable certification under oath.

The notice requirement in Rules 902(11) and (12) is intended to give the opponent of the evidence a full opportunity to test the adequacy of the foundation set forth in the declaration.

GAP Report—Proposed Amendment to Rule 902. The Committee made the following changes to the published draft of the proposed amendment to Evidence Rule 902:

1. Minor stylistic changes were made in the text, in accordance with suggestions of the Style Subcommittee of the Standing Committee on Rules of Practice and Procedure.
2. The phrase "in a manner complying with any Act of Congress or rule prescribed by the Supreme Court pursuant to statutory authority" was added to proposed Rule 902(11), to provide consistency with Evidence Rule 902(4). The Committee Note was amended to accord with this textual change.
3. Minor stylistic changes were made in the text to provide a uniform construction of the terms "declaration" and "certifying."
4. The notice provisions in the text were revised to clarify that the proponent must make both the declaration and the underlying record available for inspection.

COMMITTEE NOTES ON RULES – 2017 AMENDMENT

Paragraph (13). The amendment sets forth a procedure by which parties can authenticate certain electronic evidence other than through the testimony of a foundation witness. As with the provisions on business records in Rules 902(11) and (12), the Committee has found that the expense and inconvenience of producing a witness to authenticate an item of electronic evidence is often unnecessary. It is often the case that a party goes to the expense of producing an authentication witness, and then the adversary either stipulates authenticity before the witness is called or fails to challenge the authentication testimony once it is presented. The amendment provides a procedure under which the parties can determine in advance of trial whether a real challenge to authenticity will be made, and can then plan accordingly.

Nothing in the amendment is intended to limit a party from establishing authenticity of electronic evidence on any ground provided in these Rules, including through judicial notice where appropriate.

A proponent establishing authenticity under this Rule must present a certification containing information that would be sufficient to establish authenticity were that information provided by a witness at trial. If the certification provides information that would be insufficient to authenticate the record if the certifying person testified, then authenticity is not established under this Rule. The Rule specifically allows the authenticity foundation that satisfies Rule 901(b)(9) to be established by a certification rather than the testimony of a live witness.

The reference to the "certification requirements of Rule 902(11) or (12)" is only to the procedural requirements for a valid certification. There is no intent to require, or permit, a certification under this Rule to prove the requirements of Rule 803(6). Rule 902(13) is solely limited to authentication, and any attempt to satisfy a hearsay exception must be made independently.

A certification under this Rule can establish only that the proffered item has satisfied the admissibility requirements for authenticity. The opponent remains free to object to admissibility of the proffered item on other grounds—including hearsay, relevance, or in criminal cases the right to confrontation. For example, assume that a plaintiff in a defamation case offers what purports to be a printout of a webpage on which a defamatory statement was made. Plaintiff offers a certification under this Rule in which a qualified person describes the process by which the web page was retrieved. Even if that certification sufficiently establishes that the webpage is authentic, defendant remains free to object that the statement on the webpage was not placed there by defendant. Similarly, a certification authenticating a computer output, such as a spreadsheet, does not preclude an objection that the information produced is unreliable—the authentication establishes only that the output came from the computer.

A challenge to the authenticity of electronic evidence may require technical information about the system or process at issue, including possibly retaining a forensic technical expert; such factors will affect whether the opponent has a fair opportunity to challenge the evidence given the notice provided.

The reference to Rule 902(12) is intended to cover certifications that are made in a foreign country.

Paragraph (14). The amendment sets forth a procedure by which parties can authenticate data copied from an electronic device, storage medium, or an electronic file, other than through the testimony of a foundation witness. As with the provisions on business records in Rules 902(11) and (12), the Committee has found that the expense and inconvenience of producing an authenticating witness for this evidence is often unnecessary. It is often the case that a party goes to the expense of producing an authentication witness, and then the adversary either stipulates authenticity before the witness is called or fails to challenge the authentication testimony once it is presented. The amendment provides a procedure in which the parties can determine in advance of trial whether a real challenge to authenticity will be made, and can then plan accordingly.

Today, data copied from electronic devices, storage media, and electronic files are ordinarily authenticated by "hash value". A hash value is a number that is often represented as a sequence of characters and is produced by an algorithm based upon the digital contents of a drive, medium, or file. If the hash values for the original and copy are different, then the copy is not identical to the original. If the hash values for the original and copy are the same, it is highly improbable that the original and copy are not identical. Thus, identical hash values for the original and copy reliably attest to the fact that they are exact duplicates. This amendment allows self-authentication by a certification of a qualified person that she checked the hash value of the proffered item and that it was identical to the original. The rule is flexible enough to allow certifications through processes other than comparison of hash value, including by other reliable means of identification provided by future technology.

Nothing in the amendment is intended to limit a party from establishing authenticity of electronic evidence on any ground provided in these Rules, including through judicial notice where appropriate.

A proponent establishing authenticity under this Rule must present a certification containing information that would be sufficient to establish authenticity were that information provided by a witness at trial. If the certification provides information that would be insufficient to authenticate the record of the certifying person testified, then authenticity is not established under this Rule.

The reference to the "certification requirements of Rule 902(11) or (12)" is only to the procedural requirements for a valid certification. There is no intent to require, or permit, a certification under this Rule to prove the requirements of Rule 803(6). Rule 902(14) is solely limited to authentication, and any attempt to satisfy a hearsay exception must be made independently.

A certification under this Rule can only establish that the proffered item is authentic. The opponent remains free to object to admissibility of the proffered item on other grounds—including hearsay, relevance, or in criminal cases the right to confrontation. For example, in a criminal case in which data copied from a hard drive is proffered, the defendant can still challenge hearsay found in the hard drive, and can still challenge whether the information on the hard drive was placed there by the defendant.

A challenge to the authenticity of electronic evidence may require technical information about the system or process at issue, including possibly retaining a forensic technical expert; such factors will affect whether the opponent has a fair opportunity to challenge the evidence given the notice provided.

RULE 903. SUBSCRIBING WITNESS'S TESTIMONY

A subscribing witness's testimony is necessary to authenticate a writing only if required by the law of the jurisdiction that governs its validity.

ARTICLE X. CONTENTS OF WRITINGS, RECORDINGS, AND PHOTOGRAPHS

RULE 1001. DEFINITIONS THAT APPLY TO THIS ARTICLE

In this article:

(a) A "writing" consists of letters, words, numbers, or their equivalent set down in any form.

(b) A "recording" consists of letters, words, numbers, or their equivalent recorded in any manner.

(c) A "photograph" means a photographic image or its equivalent stored in any form.

(d) An "original" of a writing or recording means the writing or recording itself or any counterpart intended to have the same effect by the person who executed or issued it. For electronically stored information, "original" means any printout—or other output readable by sight—if it accurately reflects the information. An "original" of a photograph includes the negative or a print from it.

(e) A "duplicate" means a counterpart produced by a mechanical, photographic, chemical, electronic, or other equivalent process or technique that accurately reproduces the original.

NOTES OF ADVISORY COMMITTEE ON PROPOSED RULES (1973)

In an earlier day, when discovery and other related procedures were strictly limited, the misleading named "best evidence rule" afforded substantial guarantees against inaccuracies and fraud by its insistence upon production of original documents. The great enlargement of the scope of discovery and related procedures in recent times has measurably reduced the need for the rule. Nevertheless important areas of usefulness persist: discovery of documents outside the jurisdiction may require substantial outlay of time and money; the unanticipated document may not practically be discoverable; criminal cases have built-in limitations on discovery. Cleary and Strong, The Best Evidence Rule: An Evaluation in Context, 51 Iowa L.Rev. 825 (1966).

Paragraph [(a), formerly paragraph (1)]. Traditionally the rule requiring the original centered upon accumulations of data and expressions affecting legal relations set forth in words and figures. This meant that the rule was one essentially related to writings. Present day techniques have expanded methods of storing data, yet the essential form which the information ultimately assumes for usable purposes is words and figures. Hence the considerations underlying the rule dictate its expansion to include computers, photographic systems, and other modern developments.

Paragraph [(d), formerly paragraph (3)]. In most instances, what is an original will be self-evident and further refinement will be unnecessary. However, in some instances particularized definition is required. A carbon copy of a contract executed in duplicate becomes an original, as does a sales ticket carbon copy given to a customer. While strictly speaking the original of a photograph might be thought to be only the negative, practicality and common usage require that any print from the negative be regarded as an original. Similarly, practicality and usage confer the status of original upon any computer printout. *Transport Indemnity Co. v. Seib,* 178 Neb. 253, 132 N.W.2d 871 (1965).

Paragraph [(e), formerly paragraph (4)]. The definition describes "copies" produced by methods possessing an accuracy which virtually eliminates the possibility of error. Copies thus produced are given the status of originals in large measure by Rule 1003, *infra.* Copies subsequently produced manually, whether handwritten or typed, are not within the definition. It should be noted that what is an original for some purposes may be a duplicate for others. Thus a bank's microfilm record of checks cleared is the original as a record. However, a print offered as a copy of a check whose contents are in controversy is a duplicate. This result is substantially consistent with 28 U.S.C. §1732(b). Compare 26 U.S.C. §7513(c), giving full status as originals to photographic reproductions of tax returns and other documents, made by authority of the Secretary of the Treasury, and 44 U.S.C. §399(a), giving original status to photographic copies in the National Archives.

RULE 1002. REQUIREMENT OF THE ORIGINAL

An original writing, recording, or photograph is required in order to prove its content unless these rules or a federal statute provides otherwise.

NOTES OF ADVISORY COMMITTEE ON PROPOSED RULES (1973)

The rule is the familiar one requiring production of the original of a document to prove its contents, expanded to include writings, recordings, and photographs, as defined in Rule 1001(1) and (2), *supra.*

Application of the rule requires a resolution of the question whether contents are sought to be proved. Thus an event may be proved by non-documentary evidence, even though a written record of it was made. If, however, the event is sought to be proved by the written record, the rule applies. For example, payment may be proved without producing the written receipt which was given. Earnings may be proved without producing books of account in which they are entered. McCormick §198; 4 Wigmore §1245. Nor does the rule apply to testimony that books or records have been examined and found not to contain any reference to a designated matter.

The assumption should not be made that the rule will come into operation on every occasion when use is made of a photograph in evidence. On the contrary, the rule will seldom apply to ordinary photographs. In most instances a party *wishes* to introduce the item and the question raised is the propriety of receiving it in evidence. Cases in which an offer is made of the testimony of a witness as to what he saw in a photograph or motion picture, without producing the same, are most unusual. The usual course is for a witness on the stand to identify the photograph or motion picture as a correct representation of events which he saw or of a scene with which he is familiar. In fact he adopts the picture as his testimony, or, in common parlance, uses the picture to illustrate his testimony. Under these circumstances, no effort is made to prove the contents of the picture, and the rule is inapplicable. Paradis, The Celluloid Witness, 37 U. Colo. L. Rev. 235, 249–251 (1965).

On occasion, however, situations arise in which contents are sought to be proved. Copyright, defamation, and invasion of privacy by photograph or motion picture falls in this category. Similarly as to situations in which the picture is offered as having independent probative value, e.g. automatic photograph of bank robber. See *People v. Doggett,* 83 Cal. App. 2d 405, 188 P.2d 792 (1948) photograph of defendants engaged in indecent act; Mouser and Philbin, Photographic Evidence—Is There a Recognized Basis for Admissibility? 8 Hastings L.J. 310 (1957). The most commonly encountered of this latter group is of course, the X-ray, with substantial authority calling for production of the original. *Daniels v. Iowa City,* 191 Iowa 811, 183 N.W. 415 (1921); *Cellamare v. Third Acc. Transit Corp.*, 273 App. Div. 260, 77 N.Y.S.2d 91 (1948); *Patrick & Tilman v. Matkin,* 154 Okl. 232, 7 P.2d 414 (1932); *Mendoza v. Rivera,* 78 P.R.R. 569 (1955)

It should be noted, however, that Rule 703, supra, allows an expert to give an opinion based on matters not in evidence, and the present rule must be read as being limited accordingly in its application. Hospital records which may be admitted as business records under Rule 803(6) commonly contain reports interpreting X-rays by the staff radiologist, who qualifies as an expert, and these reports need not be excluded from the records by the instant rule.

The reference to Acts of Congress is made in view of such statutory provisions as 26 U.S.C. §7513, photographic reproductions of tax returns and documents, made by authority of the Secretary of the Treasury, treated as originals, and 44 U.S.C. §399(a), photographic copies in National Archives treated as originals.

RULE 1003. ADMISSIBILITY OF DUPLICATES

A duplicate is admissible to the same extent as the original unless a genuine question is raised about the original's authenticity or the circumstances make it unfair to admit the duplicate.

NOTES OF ADVISORY COMMITTEE ON PROPOSED RULES (1973)

When the only concern is with getting the words or other contents before the court with accuracy and precision, then a counterpart serves equally as well as the original, if the counterpart is the product of a method which insures accuracy and genuineness. By definition in Rule 1001(4), *supra,* a "duplicate" possesses this character.

Therefore, if no genuine issue exists as to authenticity and no other reason exists for requiring the original, a duplicate is admissible under the rule. This position finds support in the decisions, *Myrick v. United States,* 332 F.2d 279 (5th Cir. 1964), no error in admitting photostatic copies of checks instead of original microfilm in absence of suggestion to trial judge that photostats were incorrect; *Johns v. United States*, 323 F.2d 421 (5th Cir. 1963), not error to admit concededly accurate tape recording made from original wire recording; *Sauget v. Johnston*, 315 F.2d 816 (9th Cir. 1963), not error to admit copy of agreement when opponent had original and did not on appeal claim any discrepancy. Other reasons for requiring the original may be present when only a part of the original is reproduced and the remainder is needed for cross-examination or may disclose matters qualifying the part offered or otherwise useful to the opposing party. *United States v. Alexander*, 326 F.2d 736 (4th Cir. 1964). And see *Toho Bussan Kaisha, Ltd. v. American President Lines, Ltd.*, 265 F.2d 418, 76 A.L.R.2d 1344 (2d Cir. 1959).

RULE 1004. ADMISSIBILITY OF OTHER EVIDENCE OF CONTENT

An original is not required and other evidence of the content of a writing, recording, or photograph is admissible if:

(a) all the originals are lost or destroyed, and not by the proponent acting in bad faith;

(b) an original cannot be obtained by any available judicial process;

(c) the party against whom the original would be offered had control of the original; was at that time put on notice, by pleadings or otherwise, that the original would be a subject of proof at the trial or hearing; and fails to produce it at the trial or hearing; or

(d) the writing, recording, or photograph is not closely related to a controlling issue.

NOTES OF ADVISORY COMMITTEE ON PROPOSED RULES (1973)

Basically the rule requiring the production of the original as proof of contents has developed as a rule of preference: if failure to produce the original is satisfactory explained, secondary evidence is admissible. The instant rule specifies the circumstances under which production of the original is excused.

The rule recognizes no "degrees" of secondary evidence. While strict logic might call for extending the principle of preference beyond simply preferring the original, the formulation of a hierarchy of preferences and a procedure for making it effective is believed to involve unwarranted complexities. Most, if not all, that would be accomplished by an extended scheme of preferences will, in any event, be achieved through the normal motivation of a party to present the most convincing evidence possible and the arguments and procedures available to his opponent if he does not. Compare McCormick §207.

Paragraph (1). Loss or destruction of the original, unless due to bad faith of the proponent, is a satisfactory explanation of nonproduction. McCormick §201.

Paragraph (2). When the original is in the possession of a third person, inability to procure it from him by resort to process or other judicial procedure is sufficient explanation of nonproduction. Judicial procedure includes subpoena duces tecum as an incident to the taking of a deposition in another jurisdiction. No further showing is required. See McCormick §202.

Paragraph (3). A party who has an original in his control has no need for the protection of the rule if put on notice that proof of contents will be made. He can ward off secondary evidence by offering the original. The notice procedure here provided is not to be confused with orders to produce or other discovery procedures, as the purpose of the procedure under this rule is to afford the opposite party an opportunity to produce the original, not to compel him to do so. McCormick §203.

Paragraph (4). While difficult to define with precision, situations arise in which no good purpose is served by production of the original. Examples are the newspaper in an action for the price of publishing defendant's advertisement, *Foster-Holcomb Investment Co. v. Little Rock Publishing Co.*, 151 Ark. 449, 236 S.W. 597 (1922), and the streetcar transfer of plaintiff claiming status as a passenger, *Chicago City Ry. Co. v. Carroll*, 206 Ill. 318, 68 N.E. 1087 (1903). Numerous cases are collected in McCormick §200, p. 412, n. 1.

RULE 1005. COPIES OF PUBLIC RECORDS TO PROVE CONTENT

The proponent may use a copy to prove the content of an official record—or of a document that was recorded or filed in a public office as authorized by law—if these conditions are met: the record or document is otherwise admissible; and the copy is certified as correct in accordance with Rule 902(4) or is testified to be correct by a witness who has compared it with the original. If no such copy can be obtained by reasonable diligence, then the proponent may use other evidence to prove the content.

RULE 1006. SUMMARIES TO PROVE CONTENT

(a) Summaries of Voluminous Materials Admissible as Evidence. The court may admit as evidence a summary, chart, or calculation offered to prove the content of voluminous admissible writings, recordings, or photographs that cannot be conveniently examined in court, whether or not they have been introduced into evidence.

(b) Procedures. The proponent must make the underlying originals or duplicates available for examination or copying, or both, by other parties at a reasonable time and place. And the court may order the proponent to produce them in court.

(c) Illustrative Aids Not Covered. A summary, chart, or calculation that functions only as an illustrative aid is governed by Rule 107.

NOTES OF ADVISORY COMMITTEE ON PROPOSED RULES (1973)

The admission of summaries of voluminous books, records, or documents offers the only practicable means of making their contents available to judge and jury. The rule recognizes this practice, with appropriate safeguards. 4 Wigmore §1230.

COMMITTEE NOTES ON RULES – 2024 AMENDMENT

Rule 1006 has been amended to correct misperceptions about the operation of the rule by some courts. Some courts have mistakenly held that a Rule 1006 summary is "not evidence" and that it must be accompanied by limiting instructions cautioning against its substantive use. But the purpose of Rule 1006 is to permit alternative proof of the content of writings, recordings, or photographs too voluminous to be conveniently examined in court. To serve their intended purpose, therefore, Rule 1006 summaries must be admitted as substantive evidence and the rule has been amended to clarify that a party may offer a Rule 1006 summary "as evidence." The court may not instruct the jury that a summary admitted under this rule is not to be considered as evidence.

Rule 1006 has also been amended to clarify that a properly supported summary may be admitted into evidence whether or not the underlying voluminous materials reflected in the summary have been admitted. Some courts have mistakenly held that the underlying voluminous writings or recordings themselves must be admitted into evidence before a Rule 1006 summary may be used. Because Rule 1006 allows alternate proof of materials too voluminous to be conveniently examined during trial proceedings, admission of the underlying voluminous materials is not required and the amendment so states. Conversely, there are courts that deny resort to a properly supported Rule 1006 summary because the underlying writings or recordings—or a portion of them—have been admitted into evidence. Summaries that are otherwise admissible under Rule 1006 are not rendered inadmissible because the underlying documents have been admitted, in whole or in part, into evidence. In most cases, a Rule 1006 chart may be the only evidence the trier of fact will examine concerning a voluminous set of documents. In some instances, however, the summary may be admitted in addition to the underlying documents.

A summary admissible under Rule 1006 must also pass the balancing test of Rule 403. For example, if the summary does not accurately reflect the underlying voluminous evidence, or if it is argumentative, its probative value may be substantially outweighed by the risk of unfair prejudice or confusion.

Consistent with the original rule, the amendment requires that the proponent of a Rule 1006 summary make the underlying voluminous records available to other parties at a reasonable time and place. The trial judge has discretion in determining the reasonableness of the production in each case but must ensure that all parties have a fair opportunity to evaluate the summary. Cf. Fed. R. Evid. 404(b)(3) and 807(b).

Although Rule 1006 refers to materials too voluminous to be examined "in court" and permits the trial judge to order production of underlying materials "in court," the rule applies to virtual proceedings just as it does to proceedings conducted in person in a courtroom.

The amendment draws a distinction between summaries of voluminous admissible information offered to prove a fact, and illustrations offered solely to assist the trier of fact in understanding the evidence. The former are subject to the strictures of Rule 1006. The latter are illustrative aids, which are now regulated by Rule 107.

RULE 1007. TESTIMONY OR STATEMENT OF A PARTY TO PROVE CONTENT

The proponent may prove the content of a writing, recording, or photograph by the testimony, deposition, or written statement of the party against whom the evidence is offered. The proponent need not account for the original.

NOTES OF ADVISORY COMMITTEE ON PROPOSED RULES (1973)

While the parent case, *Slatterie v. Pooley*, 6 M. & W. 664, 151 Eng. Rep. 579 (Exch. 1840), allows proof of contents by evidence of an oral admission by the party against whom offered, without accounting for nonproduction of the original, the risk of inaccuracy is substantial and the decision is at odds with the purpose of the rule giving preference to the original. See 4 Wigmore §1255. The instant rule follows Professor McCormick's suggestion of limiting this use of admissions to those made in the course of giving testimony or in writing. McCormick §208, p. 424. The limitation, of course, does not call for excluding evidence of an oral admission when nonproduction of the original has been accounted for and secondary evidence generally has become admissible. Rule 1004, supra.

A similar provision is contained in New Jersey Evidence Rule 70(1)(h).

RULE 1008. FUNCTIONS OF THE COURT AND JURY

Ordinarily, the court determines whether the proponent has fulfilled the factual conditions for admitting other evidence of the content of a writing, recording, or photograph under Rule 1004 or 1005 . But in a jury trial, the jury determines—in accordance with Rule 104(b)—any issue about whether:

(a) an asserted writing, recording, or photograph ever existed;
(b) another one produced at the trial or hearing is the original; or
(c) other evidence of content accurately reflects the content.

ARTICLE XI. MISCELLANEOUS RULES

RULE 1101. APPLICABILITY OF THE RULES

(a) To Courts and Judges. These rules apply to proceedings before:

- United States district courts;
- United States bankruptcy and magistrate judges;
- United States courts of appeals;
- the United States Court of Federal Claims; and
- the district courts of Guam, the Virgin Islands, and the Northern Mariana Islands.

(b) To Cases and Proceedings. These rules apply in:

- civil cases and proceedings, including bankruptcy, admiralty, and maritime cases;
- criminal cases and proceedings; and
- contempt proceedings, except those in which the court may act summarily.

(c) Rules on Privilege. The rules on privilege apply to all stages of a case or proceeding.

(d) Exceptions. These rules—except for those on privilege—do not apply to the following:

(1) the court's determination, under Rule 104(a), on a preliminary question of fact governing admissibility;

(2) grand-jury proceedings; and

(3) miscellaneous proceedings such as:

- extradition or rendition;
- issuing an arrest warrant, criminal summons, or search warrant;
- a preliminary examination in a criminal case;
- sentencing;
- granting or revoking probation or supervised release; and
- considering whether to release on bail or otherwise.

(e) Other Statutes and Rules. A federal statute or a rule prescribed by the Supreme Court may provide for admitting or excluding evidence independently from these rules.

RULE 1102. AMENDMENTS

These rules may be amended as provided in 28 U.S.C. § 2072.

RULE 1103. TITLE

These rules may be cited as the Federal Rules of Evidence.

Part 2 EXCERPTS FROM THE CALIFORNIA EVIDENCE CODE (2026)

DIVISION 2: WORDS AND PHRASES DEFINED

§ 100. APPLICATION OF DEFINITIONS

Unless the provision or context otherwise requires, these definitions govern the construction of this code.

§ 105. "ACTION"

"Action" includes a civil action and a criminal action.

§ 110. "BURDEN OF PRODUCING EVIDENCE"

"Burden of producing evidence" means the obligation of a party to introduce evidence sufficient to avoid a ruling against him on the issue.

§ 115. "BURDEN OF PROOF"

"Burden of proof" means the obligation of a party to establish by evidence a requisite degree of belief concerning a fact in the mind of the trier of fact or the court. The burden of proof may require a party to raise a reasonable doubt concerning the existence or nonexistence of a fact or that he establish the existence or nonexistence of a fact by a preponderance of the evidence, by clear and convincing proof, or by proof beyond a reasonable doubt.

Except as otherwise provided by law, the burden of proof requires proof by a preponderance of the evidence.

§ 120. "CIVIL ACTION"

"Civil action" includes civil proceedings.

§ 125. "CONDUCT"

"Conduct" includes all active and passive behavior, both verbal and nonverbal.

§ 130. "CRIMINAL ACTION"

"Criminal action" includes criminal proceedings.

§ 135. "DECLARANT"

"Declarant" is a person who makes a statement.

§ 140. "EVIDENCE"

"Evidence" means testimony, writings, material objects, or other things presented to the senses that are offered to prove the existence or nonexistence of a fact.

§ 145. "THE HEARING"

"The hearing" means the hearing at which a question under this code arises, and not some earlier or later hearing.

§ 150. "HEARSAY EVIDENCE"

"Hearsay evidence" is defined in Section 1200.

§ 160. "LAW"

"Law" includes constitutional, statutory, and decisional law.

§ 165. "OATH"

"Oath" includes affirmation or declaration under penalty of perjury.

§ 170. "PERCEIVE"

"Perceive" means to acquire knowledge through one's senses.

§ 175. "PERSON"

"Person" includes a natural person, firm, association, organization, partnership, business trust, corporation, limited liability company, or public entity.

§ 177. "DEPENDENT PERSON"

"Dependent person" means a person, regardless of whether the person lives independently, who has a physical or mental impairment that substantially restricts his or her ability to carry out normal activities or to protect his or her rights, including, but not limited to, persons who have physical or developmental disabilities or whose physical or mental abilities have significantly diminished because of age. "Dependent person" includes any person who is admitted as an inpatient to a 24-hour health facility, as defined in Sections 1250, 1250.2, and 1250.3 of the Health and Safety Code.

§ 180. "PERSONAL PROPERTY"

"Personal property" includes money, goods, chattels, things in action, and evidences of debt.

§ 185. "PROPERTY"

"Property" includes both real and personal property.

§ 190. "PROOF"

"Proof" is the establishment by evidence of a requisite degree of belief concerning a fact in the mind of the trier of fact or the court.

§ 195. "PUBLIC EMPLOYEE"

"Public employee" means an officer, agent, or employee of a public entity.

§ 200. "PUBLIC ENTITY"

"Public entity" includes a nation, state, county, city and county, city, district, public authority, public agency, or any other political subdivision or public corporation, whether foreign or domestic.

§ 205. "REAL PROPERTY"

"Real property" includes lands, tenements, and hereditaments.

§ 210. "RELEVANT EVIDENCE"

"Relevant evidence" means evidence, including evidence relevant to the credibility of a witness or hearsay declarant, having any tendency in reason to prove or disprove any disputed fact that is of consequence to the determination of the action.

§ 215. "SPOUSE" TO INCLUDE REGISTERED DOMESTIC PARTNER

"Spouse" includes "registered domestic partner," as required by Section 297.5 of the Family Code.

§ 220. "STATE"

"State" means the State of California, unless applied to the different parts of the United States. In the latter case, it includes any state, district, commonwealth, territory, or insular possession of the United States.

§ 225. "STATEMENT"

"Statement" means (a) oral or written verbal expression or (b) nonverbal conduct of a person intended by him as a substitute for oral or written verbal expression.

§ 230. "STATUTE"

"Statute" includes a treaty and a constitutional provision.

§ 235. "TRIER OF FACT"

"Trier of fact" includes (a) the jury and (b) the court when the court is trying an issue of fact other than one relating to the admissibility of evidence.

§ 240. "UNAVAILABLE AS A WITNESS"

(a) Except as otherwise provided in subdivision (b), "unavailable as a witness" means that the declarant is any of the following:

(1) Exempted or precluded on the ground of privilege from testifying concerning the matter to which his or her statement is relevant.

(2) Disqualified from testifying to the matter.

(3) Dead or unable to attend or to testify at the hearing because of then-existing physical or mental illness or infirmity.

(4) Absent from the hearing and the court is unable to compel his or her attendance by its process.

(5) Absent from the hearing and the proponent of his or her statement has exercised reasonable diligence but has been unable to procure his or her attendance by the court's process.

(6) Persistent in refusing to testify concerning the subject matter of the declarant's statement despite having been found in contempt for refusal to testify.

(b) A declarant is not unavailable as a witness if the exemption, preclusion, disqualification, death, inability, or absence of the declarant was brought about by the procurement or wrongdoing of the proponent of his or her statement for the purpose of preventing the declarant from attending or testifying.

(c) Expert testimony that establishes that physical or mental trauma resulting from an alleged crime has caused harm to a witness of sufficient severity that the witness is physically unable to testify or is unable to testify without suffering substantial trauma may constitute a sufficient showing of unavailability pursuant to paragraph (3) of subdivision (a). As used in this section, the term "expert" means a physician and surgeon, including a psychiatrist, or any person described by subdivision (b), (c), or (e) of Section 1010.

The introduction of evidence to establish the unavailability of a witness under this subdivision shall not be deemed procurement of unavailability, in absence of proof to the contrary.

§ 250. "WRITING"

"Writing" means handwriting, typewriting, printing, photostating, photographing, photocopying, transmitting by electronic mail or facsimile, and every other means of recording upon any tangible thing, any form of communication or representation, including letters, words, pictures, sounds, or symbols, or combinations thereof, and any record thereby created, regardless of the manner in which the record has been stored.

§ 255. "ORIGINAL"

"Original" means the writing itself or any counterpart intended to have the same effect by a person executing or issuing it. An "original" of a photograph includes the negative or any print therefrom. If data are stored in a computer or similar device, any printout or other output readable by sight, shown to reflect the data accurately, is an "original."

§ 260. "DUPLICATE"

A "duplicate" is a counterpart produced by the same impression as the original, or from the same matrix, or by means of photography, including enlargements and miniatures, or by mechanical or electronic rerecording, or by chemical reproduction, or by other equivalent technique which accurately reproduces the original.

DIVISION 3: GENERAL PROVISIONS

Chapter 1: Applicability of Code

§ 300. APPLICABILITY OF CODE

Except as otherwise provided by statute, this code applies in every action before the Supreme Court or a court of appeal or superior court, including proceedings in such actions conducted by a referee, court commissioner, or similar officer, but does not apply in grand jury proceedings.

Chapter 2: Province of Court and Jury

§ 310. QUESTIONS OF LAW FOR COURT

(a) All questions of law (including but not limited to questions concerning the construction of statutes and other writings, the admissibility of evidence, and other rules of evidence) are to be decided by the court. Determination of issues of fact preliminary to the admission of evidence are to be decided by the court as provided in Article 2 (commencing with Section 400) of Chapter 4.

(b) Determination of the law of an organization of nations or of the law of a foreign nation or a public entity in a foreign nation is a question of law to be determined in the manner provided in Division 4 (commencing with Section 450).

§ 311. PROCEDURE WHEN FOREIGN OR SISTER-STATE LAW CANNOT BE DETERMINED

If the law of an organization of nations, a foreign nation or a state other than this state, or a public entity in a foreign nation or a state other than this state, is applicable and such law cannot be determined, the court may, as the ends of justice require, either:

(a) Apply the law of this state if the court can do so consistently with the Constitution of the United States and the Constitution of this state; or

(b) Dismiss the action without prejudice or, in the case of a reviewing court, remand the case to the trial court with directions to dismiss the action without prejudice.

§ 312. JURY AS TRIER OF FACT

Except as otherwise provided by law, where the trial is by jury:

(a) All questions of fact are to be decided by the jury.

(b) Subject to the control of the court, the jury is to determine the effect and value of the evidence addressed to it, including the credibility of witnesses and hearsay declarants.

Chapter 3: Order of Proof

§ 320. POWER OF COURT TO REGULATE ORDER OF PROOF

Except as otherwise provided by law, the court in its discretion shall regulate the order of proof.

Chapter 4: Admitting and Excluding Evidence

Article 1: General Provisions

§ 350. ONLY RELEVANT EVIDENCE ADMISSIBLE

No evidence is admissible except relevant evidence.

§ 351. ADMISSIBILITY OF RELEVANT EVIDENCE

Except as otherwise provided by statute, all relevant evidence is admissible.

§ 351.1. EXCLUSION OF RESULTS OF POLYGRAPH EXAMINATION

(a) Notwithstanding any other provision of law, the results of a polygraph examination, the opinion of a polygraph examiner, or any reference to an offer to take, failure to take, or taking of a polygraph examination, shall not be admitted into evidence in any criminal proceeding, including pretrial and post conviction motions and hearings, or in any trial or hearing of a juvenile for a criminal offense, whether heard in juvenile or adult court, unless all parties stipulate to the admission of such results.

(b) Nothing in this section is intended to exclude from evidence statements made during a polygraph examination which are otherwise admissible.

§ 351.2. IMMIGRATION STATUS INADMISSIBLE IN CIVIL ACTION FOR PERSONAL INJURY OR WRONGFUL DEATH

(a) In a civil action for personal injury or wrongful death, evidence of a person's immigration status shall not be admitted into evidence, nor shall discovery into a person's immigration status be permitted.

(b) This section does not affect the standards of relevance, admissibility, or discovery prescribed by Section 3339 of the Civil Code, Section 7285 of the Government Code, Section 24000 of the Health and Safety Code, and Section 1171.5 of the Labor Code.

§ 351.3. DISCLOSURE OF IMMIGRATION STATUS IN CIVIL ACTION

(a) In a civil action not governed by Section 351.2, evidence of a person's immigration status shall not be disclosed in open court by a party or their attorney unless the judge presiding over the matter first determines that the evidence is admissible in an in camera hearing requested by the party seeking disclosure of the person's immigration status.

(b) This section does not do any of the following:

(1) Apply to cases in which a person's immigration status is necessary to prove an element of a claim or an affirmative defense.

(2) Impact otherwise applicable laws governing the relevance of immigration status to liability or the standards applicable to inquiries regarding immigration status in discovery or proceedings in a civil action, including Section 3339 of the Civil Code, Section 7285 of the Government Code, Section 24000 of the Health and Safety Code, and Section 1171.5 of the Labor Code.

(3) Prohibit a person or their attorney from voluntarily revealing the person's immigration status to the court.

§ 351.4. DISCLOSURE OF IMMIGRATION STATUS IN CRIMINAL ACTION

(a) In a criminal action, evidence of a person's immigration status shall not be disclosed in open court by a party or their attorney unless the judge presiding over the matter first determines that the evidence is admissible in an in camera hearing requested by the party seeking disclosure of the person's immigration status.

(b) This section does not do any of the following:

(1) Apply to cases in which a person's immigration status is necessary to prove an element of an offense or an affirmative defense.

(2) Limit discovery in a criminal action.

(3) Prohibit a person or their attorney from voluntarily revealing the person's immigration status to the court.

§ 352. DISCRETION OF COURT TO EXCLUDE EVIDENCE

The court in its discretion may exclude evidence if its probative value is substantially outweighed by the probability that its admission will

(a) necessitate undue consumption of time or (b) create substantial danger of undue prejudice, of confusing the issues, or of misleading the jury.

§ 352.1 ADDRESS AND TELEPHONE NUMBER OF VICTIM OF CRIMINAL SEX ACT

In any criminal proceeding under Section 261, 262, or 264.1, subdivision (d) of Section 286, or subdivision (d) of Section 287 of, or former Section 288a of, the Penal Code, or in any criminal proceeding under subdivision (c) of Section 286 or subdivision (c) of Section 287 of, or former Section 288a of, the Penal Code in which the defendant is alleged to have compelled the participation of the victim by force, violence, duress, menace, or threat of great bodily harm, the district attorney may, upon written motion with notice to the defendant or the defendant's attorney, if he or she is represented by an attorney, within a reasonable time prior to any hearing, move to exclude from evidence the current address and telephone number of any victim at the hearing.

The court may order that evidence of the victim's current address and telephone number be excluded from any hearings conducted pursuant to the criminal proceeding if the court finds that the probative value of the evidence is outweighed by the creation of substantial danger to the victim.

Nothing in this section shall abridge or limit the defendant's right to discover or investigate the information.

§ 352.2. ADMISSION OF CREATIVE EXPRESSIONS

(a) In any criminal proceeding where a party seeks to admit as evidence a form of creative expression, the court, while balancing the probative value of that evidence against the substantial danger of undue prejudice under Section 352, shall consider, in addition to the factors listed in Section 352, that: (1) the probative value of such expression for its literal truth or as a truthful narrative is minimal unless that expression is created near in time to the charged crime or crimes, bears a sufficient level of similarity to the charged crime or crimes, or includes factual detail not otherwise publicly available; and (2) undue prejudice includes, but is not limited to, the possibility that the trier of fact will, in violation of Section 1101, treat the expression as evidence of the defendant's propensity for violence or general criminal disposition as well as the possibility that the evidence will explicitly or implicitly inject racial bias into the proceedings.

(b) If proffered and relevant to the issues in the case, the court shall consider the following as well as any additional relevant evidence offered by either party:

(1) Credible testimony on the genre of creative expression as to the social or cultural context, rules, conventions, and artistic techniques of the expression.

(2) Experimental or social science research demonstrating that the introduction of a particular type of expression explicitly or implicitly introduces racial bias into the proceedings.

(3) Evidence to rebut such research or testimony.

(c) For purposes of this section, "creative expression" means the expression or application of creativity or imagination in the production or arrangement of forms, sounds, words, movements, or symbols, including, but not limited to, music, dance, performance art, visual art, poetry, literature, film, and other such objects or media.

(d) The question of the admissibility of a form of creative expression shall be heard in limine and determined by the court, outside the presence and hearing of the jury, pursuant to Section 402. The court shall state on the record its ruling and its reasons therefor.

§ 353. EFFECT OF ERRONEOUS ADMISSION OF EVIDENCE

A verdict or finding shall not be set aside, nor shall the judgment or decision based thereon be reversed, by reason of the erroneous admission of evidence unless:

(a) There appears of record an objection to or a motion to exclude or to strike the evidence that was timely made and so stated as to make clear the specific ground of the objection or motion; and

(b) The court which passes upon the effect of the error or errors is of the opinion that the admitted evidence should have been excluded on the ground stated and that the error or errors complained of resulted in a miscarriage of justice.

§ 354. EFFECT OF ERRONEOUS EXCLUSION OF EVIDENCE

A verdict or finding shall not be set aside, nor shall the judgment or decision based thereon be reversed, by reason of the erroneous exclusion of evidence unless the court which passes upon the effect of the error or errors is of the opinion that the error or errors complained of resulted in a miscarriage of justice and it appears of record that:

(a) The substance, purpose, and relevance of the excluded evidence was made known to the court by the questions asked, an offer of proof, or by any other means;

(b) The rulings of the court made compliance with subdivision (a) futile; or

(c) The evidence was sought by questions asked during cross-examination or recross- examination.

§ 355. LIMITED ADMISSIBILITY

When evidence is admissible as to one party or for one purpose and is inadmissible as to another party or for another purpose, the court upon request shall restrict the evidence to its proper scope and instruct the jury accordingly.

§ 356. ENTIRE ACT, DECLARATION, CONVERSATION, OR WRITING MAY BE BROUGHT OUT TO ELUCIDATE PART OFFERED

Where part of an act, declaration, conversation, or writing is given in evidence by one party, the whole on the same subject may be inquired into by an adverse party; when a letter is read, the answer may be given; and when a detached act, declaration, conversation, or writing is given in evidence, any other act, declaration, conversation, or writing which is necessary to make it understood may also be given in evidence.

Article 2: Preliminary Determinations on Admissibility of Evidence

§ 400. "PRELIMINARY FACT"

As used in this article, "preliminary fact" means a fact upon the existence or nonexistence of which depends the admissibility or inadmissibility of evidence. The phrase "the admissibility or inadmissibility of evidence" includes the qualification or disqualification of a person to be a witness and the existence or nonexistence of a privilege.

§ 401. "PROFFERED EVIDENCE"

As used in this article, "proffered evidence" means evidence, the admissibility or inadmissibility of which is dependent upon the existence or nonexistence of a preliminary fact.

§ 402. PROCEDURE FOR DETERMINING FOUNDATIONAL AND OTHER PRELIMINARY FACTS

(a) When the existence of a preliminary fact is disputed, its existence or nonexistence shall be determined as provided in this article.

(b) The court may hear and determine the question of the admissibility of evidence out of the presence or hearing of the jury; but in a criminal action, the court shall hear and determine the question of the admissibility of a confession or admission of the defendant out of the presence and hearing of the jury if any party so requests.

(c) A ruling on the admissibility of evidence implies whatever finding of fact is prerequisite thereto; a separate or formal finding is unnecessary unless required by statute.

§ 403. DETERMINATION OF FOUNDATIONAL AND OTHER PRELIMINARY FACTS WHERE RELEVANCY, PERSONAL KNOWLEDGE, OR AUTHENTICITY IS DISPUTED

(a) The proponent of the proffered evidence has the burden of producing evidence as to the existence of the preliminary fact, and the proffered evidence is inadmissible unless the court finds that there is evidence sufficient to sustain a finding of the existence of the preliminary fact, when:

(1) The relevance of the proffered evidence depends on the existence of the preliminary fact;

(2) The preliminary fact is the personal knowledge of a witness concerning the subject matter of his testimony;

(3) The preliminary fact is the authenticity of a writing; or

(4) The proffered evidence is of a statement or other conduct of a particular person and the preliminary fact is whether that person made the statement or so conducted himself.

(b) Subject to Section 702, the court may admit conditionally the proffered evidence under this section, subject to evidence of the preliminary fact being supplied later in the course of the trial.

(c) If the court admits the proffered evidence under this section, the court:

(1) May, and on request shall, instruct the jury to determine whether the preliminary fact exists and to disregard the proffered evidence unless the jury finds that the preliminary fact does exist.

(2) Shall instruct the jury to disregard the proffered evidence if the court subsequently determines that a jury could not reasonably find that the preliminary fact exists.

§ 404. DETERMINATION OF WHETHER PROFFERED EVIDENCE IS INCRIMINATORY

Whenever the proffered evidence is claimed to be privileged under Section 940, the person claiming the privilege has the burden of showing that the proffered evidence might tend to incriminate him; and the proffered evidence is inadmissible unless it clearly appears to the court that the proffered evidence cannot possibly have a tendency to incriminate the person claiming the privilege.

§ 405. DETERMINATION OF FOUNDATIONAL AND OTHER PRELIMINARY FACTS IN OTHER CASES

With respect to preliminary fact determinations not governed by Section 403 or 404:

(a) When the existence of a preliminary fact is disputed, the court shall indicate which party has the burden of producing evidence and the burden of proof on the issue as implied by the rule of law under which the question arises. The court shall determine the existence or nonexistence of the preliminary fact and shall admit or exclude the proffered evidence as required by the rule of law under which the question arises.

(b) If a preliminary fact is also a fact in issue in the action:

(1) The jury shall not be informed of the court's determination as to the existence or nonexistence of the preliminary fact.

(2) If the proffered evidence is admitted, the jury shall not be instructed to disregard the evidence if its determination of the fact differs from the court's determination of the preliminary fact.

§ 406. EVIDENCE AFFECTING WEIGHT OR CREDIBILITY

This article does not limit the right of a party to introduce before the trier of fact evidence relevant to weight or credibility.

Chapter 5: Weight of Evidence Generally

§ 410. "DIRECT EVIDENCE"

As used in this chapter, "direct evidence" means evidence that directly proves a fact, without an inference or presumption, and which in itself, if true, conclusively establishes that fact.

§ 411. DIRECT EVIDENCE OF ONE WITNESS SUFFICIENT

Except where additional evidence is required by statute, the direct evidence of one witness who is entitled to full credit is sufficient for proof of any fact.

§ 412. PARTY HAVING POWER TO PRODUCE BETTER EVIDENCE

If weaker and less satisfactory evidence is offered when it was within the power of the party to produce stronger and more satisfactory evidence, the evidence offered should be viewed with distrust.

§ 413. PARTY'S FAILURE TO EXPLAIN OR DENY EVIDENCE

In determining what inferences to draw from the evidence or facts in the case against a party, the trier of fact may consider, among other things, the party's failure to explain or to deny by his testimony such evidence or facts in the case against him, or his willful suppression of evidence relating thereto, if such be the case.

DIVISION 4: JUDICIAL NOTICE

§ 450. JUDICIAL NOTICE MAY BE TAKEN ONLY AS AUTHORIZED BY LAW

Judicial notice may not be taken of any matter unless authorized or required by law.

§ 451. MATTERS WHICH MUST BE JUDICIALLY NOTICED

Judicial notice shall be taken of the following:

(a) The decisional, constitutional, and public statutory law of this state and of the United States and the provisions of any charter described in Section 3, 4, or 5 of Article XI of the California Constitution.

(b) Any matter made a subject of judicial notice by Section 11343.6, 11344.6, or 18576 of the Government Code or by Section 1507 of Title 44 of the United States Code.

(c) Rules of professional conduct for members of the bar adopted pursuant to Section 6076 of the Business and Professions Code and rules of practice and procedure for the courts of this state adopted by the Judicial Council.

(d) Rules of pleading, practice, and procedure prescribed by the United States Supreme Court, such as the Rules of the United States Supreme Court, the Federal Rules of Civil Procedure, the Federal Rules of Criminal Procedure, the Admiralty Rules, the Rules of the Court of Claims, the Rules of the Customs Court, and the General Orders and Forms in Bankruptcy.

(e) The true signification of all English words and phrases and of all legal expressions.

(f) Facts and propositions of generalized knowledge that are so universally known that they cannot reasonably be the subject of dispute.

§ 452. MATTERS WHICH MAY BE JUDICIALLY NOTICED

Judicial notice may be taken of the following matters to the extent that they are not embraced within Section 451:

(a) The decisional, constitutional, and statutory law of any state of the United States and the resolutions and private acts of the Congress of the United States and of the Legislature of this state.

(b) Regulations and legislative enactments issued by or under the authority of the United States or any public entity in the United States.

(c) Official acts of the legislative, executive, and judicial departments of the United States and of any state of the United States.

(d) Records of (1) any court of this state or (2) any court of record of the United States or of any state of the United States.

(e) Rules of court of (1) any court of this state or (2) any court of record of the United States or of any state of the United States.

(f) The law of an organization of nations and of foreign nations and public entities in foreign nations.

(g) Facts and propositions that are of such common knowledge within the territorial jurisdiction of the court that they cannot reasonably be the subject of dispute.

(h) Facts and propositions that are not reasonably subject to dispute and are capable of immediate and accurate determination by resort to sources of reasonably indisputable accuracy.

§ 452.5. COMPUTER-GENERATED RECORDS OR ELECTRONICALLY DIGITIZED COPIES; SEAL, SIGNATURE, OR OTHER INDICIA OF COURT AS ADEQUATE SHOWING

(a) The official acts and records specified in subdivisions (c) and (d) of Section 452 include any computer-generated official court records, as specified by the Judicial Council, that relate to criminal convictions, when the record is certified by a clerk of the superior court pursuant to Section 69844.5 of the Government Code at the time of computer entry.

(b)

(1) An official record of conviction certified in accordance with subdivision (a) of Section 1530, or an electronically digitized copy thereof, is admissible under Section 1280 to prove the commission, attempted commission, or solicitation of a criminal offense, prior conviction, service of a prison term, or other act, condition, or event recorded by the record.

(2) For purposes of this subdivision, "electronically digitized copy" means a copy that is made by scanning, photographing, or otherwise exactly reproducing a document, is stored or maintained in a digitized format, and meets either of the following requirements:

(A) The copy bears an electronic signature or watermark unique to the entity responsible for certifying the document.

(B) The copied document is an official record of conviction, certified in accordance with subdivision (a) of Section 1530, that is transmitted by the clerk of the superior court in a manner showing that the copy was prepared and transmitted by that clerk of the superior court. A seal, signature, or other indicia of the court shall constitute adequate showing.

§ 453. COMPULSORY JUDICIAL NOTICE UPON REQUEST

The trial court shall take judicial notice of any matter specified in Section 452 if a party requests it and:

(a) Gives each adverse party sufficient notice of the request, through the pleadings or otherwise, to enable such adverse party to prepare to meet the request; and

(b) Furnishes the court with sufficient information to enable it to take judicial notice of the matter.

§ 454. INFORMATION THAT MAY BE USED IN TAKING JUDICIAL NOTICES

(a) In determining the propriety of taking judicial notice of a matter, or the tenor thereof:

(1) Any source of pertinent information, including the advice of persons learned in the subject matter, may be consulted or used, whether or not furnished by a party.

(2) Exclusionary rules of evidence do not apply except for Section 352 and the rules of privilege.

(b) Where the subject of judicial notice is the law of an organization of nations, a foreign nation, or a public entity in a foreign nation and the court resorts to the advice of persons learned in the subject matter, such advice, if not received in open court, shall be in writing.

§ 455. OPPORTUNITY TO PRESENT INFORMATION TO COURT

With respect to any matter specified in Section 452 or in subdivision (f) of Section 451 that is of substantial consequence to the determination of the action:

(a) If the trial court has been requested to take or has taken or proposes to take judicial notice of such matter, the court shall afford each party reasonable opportunity, before the jury is instructed or before the cause is submitted for decision by the court, to present to the court information relevant to (1) the propriety of taking judicial notice of the matter and (2) the tenor of the matter to be noticed.

(b) If the trial court resorts to any source of information not received in open court, including the advice of persons learned in the subject matter, such information and its source shall be made a part of the record in the action and the court shall afford each party reasonable opportunity to meet such information before judicial notice of the matter may be taken.

§ 456. NOTING FOR RECORD DENIAL OF REQUEST TO TAKE JUDICIAL NOTICE

If the trial court denies a request to take judicial notice of any matter, the court shall at the earliest practicable time so advise the parties and indicate for the record that it has denied the request.

§ 457. INSTRUCTING JURY ON MATTER JUDICIALLY NOTICED

If a matter judicially noticed is a matter which would otherwise have been for determination by the jury, the trial court may, and upon request shall, instruct the jury to accept as a fact the matter so noticed.

§ 458. JUDICIAL NOTICE BY TRIAL COURT IN SUBSEQUENT PROCEEDINGS

The failure or refusal of the trial court to take judicial notice of a matter, or to instruct the jury with respect to the matter, does not preclude the trial court in subsequent proceedings in the action from taking judicial notice of the matter in accordance with the procedure specified in this division.

§ 459. JUDICIAL NOTICE BY REVIEWING COURT

(a) The reviewing court shall take judicial notice of (1) each matter properly noticed by the trial court and (2) each matter that the trial court was required to notice under Section 451 or 453. The reviewing court may take judicial notice of any matter specified in Section 452. The reviewing court may take judicial notice of a matter in a tenor different from that noticed by the trial court.

(b) In determining the propriety of taking judicial notice of a matter, or the tenor thereof, the reviewing court has the same power as the trial court under Section 454.

(c) When taking judicial notice under this section of a matter specified in Section 452 or in subdivision (f) of Section 451 that is of substantial consequence to the determination of the action, the reviewing court shall comply with the provisions of subdivision (a) of Section 455 if the matter was not theretofore judicially noticed in the action.

(d) In determining the propriety of taking judicial notice of a matter specified in Section 452 or in subdivision (f) of Section 451 that is of substantial consequence to the determination of the action, or the tenor thereof, if the reviewing court resorts to any source of information not received in open court or not included in the record of the action, including the advice of persons learned in the subject matter, the reviewing court shall afford each party reasonable opportunity to meet such information before judicial notice of the matter may be taken.

§ 460. APPOINTMENT OF EXPERT BY COURT

Where the advice of persons learned in the subject matter is required in order to enable the court to take judicial notice of a matter, the court on its own motion or on motion of any party may appoint one or more such persons to provide such advice. If the court determines to appoint such a person, he shall be appointed and compensated in the manner provided in Article 2 (commencing with Section 730) of Chapter 3 of Division 6.

DIVISION 5: BURDEN OF PROOF

Chapter 1: Burden of Proof

Article 1: General

§ 500. PARTY WHO HAS THE BURDEN OF PROOF

Except as otherwise provided by law, a party has the burden of proof as to each fact the existence or nonexistence of which is essential to the claim for relief or defense that he is asserting.

§ 501. BURDEN OF PROOF IN CRIMINAL ACTION GENERALLY

Insofar as any statute, except Section 522, assigns the burden of proof in a criminal action, such statute is subject to Penal Code Section 1096.

§ 502. INSTRUCTIONS ON BURDEN OF PROOF

The court on all proper occasions shall instruct the jury as to which party bears the burden of proof on each issue and as to whether that burden requires that a party raise a reasonable doubt concerning the existence or nonexistence of a fact or that he establish the existence or nonexistence of a fact by a preponderance of the evidence, by clear and convincing proof, or by proof beyond a reasonable doubt.

Article 2: Burden of Proof on Specific Issues

§ 520. CLAIM THAT PERSON GUILTY OF CRIME OR WRONGDOING

The party claiming that a person is guilty of crime or wrongdoing has the burden of proof on that issue.

§ 521. CLAIM THAT PERSON DID NOT EXERCISE CARE

The party claiming that a person did not exercise a requisite degree of care has the burden of proof on that issue.

§ 522. CLAIM THAT PERSON IS OR WAS INSANE

The party claiming that any person, including himself, is or was insane has the burden of proof on that issue.

Chapter 2: Burden of Producing Evidence

§ 550. PARTY WHO HAS THE BURDEN OF PRODUCING EVIDENCE

(a) The burden of producing evidence as to a particular fact is on the party against whom a finding on that fact would be required in the absence of further evidence.

(b) The burden of producing evidence as to a particular fact is initially on the party with the burden of proof as to that fact.

Chapter 3: Presumptions and Inferences

Article 1: General

§ 600. PRESUMPTION AND INFERENCE DEFINED

(a) A presumption is an assumption of fact that the law requires to be made from another fact or group of facts found or otherwise established in the action. A presumption is not evidence.

(b) An inference is a deduction of fact that may logically and reasonably be drawn from another fact or group of facts found or otherwise established in the action.

§ 601. CLASSIFICATION OF PRESUMPTIONS

A presumption is either conclusive or rebuttable. Every rebuttable presumption is either (a) a presumption affecting the burden of producing evidence or (b) a presumption affecting the burden of proof.

§ 602. STATUTE MAKING ONE FACT PRIMA FACIE EVIDENCE OF ANOTHER FACT

A statute providing that a fact or group of facts is prima facie evidence of another fact establishes a rebuttable presumption.

§ 603. PRESUMPTION AFFECTING THE BURDEN OF PRODUCING EVIDENCE DEFINED

A presumption affecting the burden of producing evidence is a presumption established to implement no public policy other than to facilitate the determination of the particular action in which the presumption is applied.

§ 604. EFFECT OF PRESUMPTION AFFECTING BURDEN OF PRODUCING EVIDENCE

The effect of a presumption affecting the burden of producing evidence is to require the trier of fact to assume the existence of the presumed fact unless and until evidence is introduced which would support a finding of its nonexistence, in which case the trier of fact shall determine the existence or nonexistence of the presumed fact from the evidence and without regard to the presumption. Nothing in this section shall be construed to prevent the drawing of any inference that may be appropriate.

§ 605. PRESUMPTION AFFECTING THE BURDEN OF PROOF DEFINED

A presumption affecting the burden of proof is a presumption established to implement some public policy other than to facilitate the determination of the particular action in which the presumption is applied, such as the policy in favor of establishment of a parent and child relationship, the validity of marriage, the stability of titles to property, or the security of those who entrust themselves or their property to the administration of others.

§ 606. EFFECT OF PRESUMPTION AFFECTING BURDEN OF PROOF

The effect of a presumption affecting the burden of proof is to impose upon the party against whom it operates the burden of proof as to the nonexistence of the presumed fact.

§ 607. EFFECT OF CERTAIN PRESUMPTION IN A CRIMINAL ACTION

When a presumption affecting the burden of proof operates in a criminal action to establish presumptively any fact that is essential to the defendant's guilt, the presumption operates only if the facts that give rise to the presumption have been found or otherwise established beyond a reasonable doubt and, in such case, the defendant need only raise a reasonable doubt as to the existence of the presumed fact.

Article 2: Conclusive Presumptions

§ 620. CONCLUSIVE PRESUMPTIONS

The presumptions established by this article, and all other presumptions declared by law to be conclusive, are conclusive presumptions.

§ 622. FACTS RECITED IN WRITTEN INSTRUMENT

The facts recited in a written instrument are conclusively presumed to be true as between the parties thereto, or their successors in interest; but this rule does not apply to the recital of a consideration.

§ 623. ESTOPPEL BY OWN STATEMENT OR CONDUCT

Whenever a party has, by his own statement or conduct, intentionally and deliberately led another to believe a particular thing true and to act upon such belief, he is not, in any litigation arising out of such statement or conduct, permitted to contradict it.

§ 624. ESTOPPEL OF TENANT TO DENY TITLE OF LANDLORD

A tenant is not permitted to deny the title of his landlord at the time of the commencement of the relation.

Article 3: Presumptions Affecting the Burden of Producing Evidence

§ 630. PRESUMPTION AFFECTING THE BURDEN OF PRODUCING EVIDENCE

The presumptions established by this article, and all other rebuttable presumptions established by law that fall within the criteria of Section 603, are presumptions affecting the burden of producing evidence.

§ 631. MONEY DELIVERED BY ONE TO ANOTHER

Money delivered by one to another is presumed to have been due to the latter.

§ 632. THING DELIVERED BY ONE TO ANOTHER

A thing delivered by one to another is presumed to have belonged to the latter.

§ 633. OBLIGATION DELIVERED UP TO THE DEBTOR

An obligation delivered up to the debtor is presumed to have been paid.

§ 634. PERSON IN POSSESSION OF ORDER ON HIMSELF

A person in possession of an order on himself for the payment of money, or delivery of a thing, is presumed to have paid the money or delivered the thing accordingly.

§ 635. OBLIGATION POSSESSED BY CREDITOR

An obligation possessed by the creditor is presumed not to have been paid.

§ 636. PAYMENT OF EARLIER RENT OR INSTALLMENTS

The payment of earlier rent or installments is presumed from a receipt for later rent or installments.

§ 637. OWNERSHIP OF THINGS POSSESSED

The things which a person possesses are presumed to be owned by him.

§ 638. OWNERSHIP OF PROPERTY BY PERSON WHO EXERCISES ACTS OF OWNERSHIP

A person who exercises acts of ownership over property is presumed to be the owner of it.

§ 639. JUDGMENT CORRECTLY DETERMINES RIGHTS OF PARTIES

A judgment, when not conclusive, is presumed to correctly determine or set forth the rights of the parties, but there is no presumption that the facts essential to the judgment have been correctly determined.

§ 640. WRITING TRULY DATED

A writing is presumed to have been truly dated.

§ 641. LETTER RECEIVED IN ORDINARY COURSE OF MAIL

A letter correctly addressed and properly mailed is presumed to have been received in the ordinary course of mail.

§ 642. CONVEYANCE BY PERSON HAVING DUTY TO CONVEY REAL PROPERTY

A trustee or other person, whose duty it was to convey real property to a particular person, is presumed to have actually conveyed to him when such presumption is necessary to perfect title of such person or his successor in interest.

§ 643. AUTHENTICITY OF ANCIENT DOCUMENT

A deed or will or other writing purporting to create, terminate, or affect an interest in real or personal property is presumed to be authentic if it:

(a) Is at least 30 years old;

(b) Is in such condition as to create no suspicion concerning its authenticity;

(c) Was kept, or if found was found, in a place where such writing, if authentic, would be likely to be kept or found; and

(d) Has been generally acted upon as authentic by persons having an interest in the matter.

§ 644. BOOK PURPORTING TO BE PUBLISHED BY PUBLIC AUTHORITY

A book, purporting to be printed or published by public authority, is presumed to have been so printed or published.

§ 645. BOOK PURPORTING TO CONTAIN REPORTS OF CASES

A book, purporting to contain reports of cases adjudged in the tribunals of the state or nation where the book is published, is presumed to contain correct reports of such cases.

§ 645.1 PRINTED MATERIALS PURPORTING TO BE PARTICULAR NEWSPAPER OR PERIODICAL

Printed materials, purporting to be a particular newspaper or periodical, are presumed to be that newspaper or periodical if regularly issued at average intervals not exceeding three months.

§ 646. RES IPSA LOQUITUR; INSTRUCTIONS TO JURY

(a) As used in this section, “defendant” includes any party against whom the res ipsa loquitur presumption operates.

(b) The judicial doctrine of res ipsa loquitur is a presumption affecting the burden of producing evidence.

(c) If the evidence, or facts otherwise established, would support a res ipsa loquitur presumption and the defendant has introduced evidence which would support a finding that he was not negligent or that any negligence on his part was not a proximate cause of the occurrence, the court may, and upon request shall, instruct the jury to the effect that:

> **(1)** If the facts which would give rise to res ipsa loquitur presumption are found or otherwise established, the jury may draw the inference from such facts that a proximate cause of the occurrence was some negligent conduct on the part of the defendant; and
>
> **(2)** The jury shall not find that a proximate cause of the occurrence was some negligent conduct on the part of the defendant unless the jury believes, after weighing all the evidence in the case and drawing such inferences therefrom as the jury believes are warranted, that it is more probable than not that the occurrence was caused by some negligent conduct on the part of the defendant.

§ 647. RETURN OF REGISTERED PROCESS SERVER

The return of a process server registered pursuant to Chapter 16 (commencing with Section 22350) of Division 8 of the Business and Professions Code upon process or notice establishes a presumption, affecting the burden of producing evidence, of the facts stated in the return.

Article 4: Presumptions Affecting the Burden of Proof

§ 660. PRESUMPTIONS AFFECTING THE BURDEN OF PROOF

The presumptions established by this article, and all other rebuttable presumptions established by law that fall within the criteria of Section 605, are presumptions affecting the burden of proof.

§ 662. OWNER OF LEGAL TITLE TO PROPERTY IS OWNER OF BENEFICIAL TITLE

The owner of the legal title to property is presumed to be the owner of the full beneficial title. This presumption may be rebutted only by clear and convincing proof.

§ 663. CEREMONIAL MARRIAGE

A ceremonial marriage is presumed to be valid.

§ 664. OFFICIAL DUTY REGULARLY PERFORMED

It is presumed that official duty has been regularly performed. This presumption does not apply on an issue as to the lawfulness of an arrest if it is found or otherwise established that the arrest was made without a warrant.

§ 665. ORDINARY CONSEQUENCES OF VOLUNTARY ACT

A person is presumed to intend the ordinary consequences of his voluntary act. This presumption is inapplicable in a criminal action to establish the specific intent of the defendant where specific intent is an element of the crime charged.

§ 666. JUDICIAL ACTION LAWFUL EXERCISE OF JURISDICTION

Any court of this state or the United States, or any court of general jurisdiction in any other state or nation, or any judge of such a court, acting as such, is presumed to have acted in the lawful exercise of its jurisdiction. This presumption applies only when the act of the court or judge is under collateral attack.

§ 667. DEATH OF PERSON NOT HEARD FROM IN FIVE YEARS

A person not heard from in five years is presumed to be dead.

§ 668. UNLAWFUL INTENT

An unlawful intent is presumed from the doing of an unlawful act. This presumption is inapplicable in a criminal action to establish the specific intent of the defendant where specific intent is an element of the crime charged.

§ 669. FAILURE TO EXERCISE DUE CARE

(a) The failure of a person to exercise due care is presumed if:

(1) He violated a statute, ordinance, or regulation of a public entity;

(2) The violation proximately caused death or injury to person or property;

(3) The death or injury resulted from an occurrence of the nature which the statute, ordinance, or regulation was designed to prevent; and

(4) The person suffering the death or the injury to his person or property was one of the class of persons for whose protection the statute, ordinance, or regulation was adopted.

(b) This presumption may be rebutted by proof that:

(1) The person violating the statute, ordinance, or regulation did what might reasonably be expected of a person of ordinary prudence, acting under similar circumstances, who desired to comply with the law; or

(2) The person violating the statute, ordinance, or regulation was a child and exercised the degree of care ordinarily exercised by persons of his maturity, intelligence, and capacity under similar circumstances, but the presumption may not be rebutted by such proof if the violation occurred in the course of an activity normally engaged in only by adults and requiring adult qualifications.

§ 669.1. GOVERNMENTAL RULE OR GUIDELINE FOR STANDARDS OF CONDUCT FOR PUBLIC EMPLOYEES

A rule, policy, manual, or guideline of state or local government setting forth standards of conduct or guidelines for its employees in the conduct of their public employment shall not be considered a statute, ordinance, or regulation of that public entity within the meaning of Section 669, unless the rule, manual, policy, or guideline has been formally adopted as a statute, as an ordinance of a local governmental entity in this state empowered to adopt ordinances, or as a regulation by an agency of the state pursuant to the Administrative Procedure Act (Chapter 3.5 (commencing with Section 11340) of Division 3 of Title 2 of the Government Code), or by an agency of the United States government pursuant to the federal Administrative Procedure Act (Chapter 5 (commencing with Section 5001) of Title 5 of the United States Code). This section affects only the presumption set forth in Section 669, and is not otherwise intended to affect the admissibility or inadmissibility of the rule, policy, manual, or guideline under other provisions of law.

§ 670. PRESUMPTION THAT CHECK HAS BEEN PAID

(a) In any dispute concerning payment by means of a check, a copy of the check produced in accordance with Section 1550 of the Evidence Code, together with the original bank statement that reflects payment of the check by the bank on which it was drawn or a copy thereof produced in the same manner, creates a presumption that the check has been paid.

(b) As used in this section:

(1) "Bank" means any person engaged in the business of banking and includes, in addition to a commercial bank, a savings and loan association, savings bank, or credit union.

(2) "Check" means a draft, other than a documentary draft, payable on demand and drawn on a bank, even though it is described by another term, such as "share draft" or "negotiable order of withdrawal."

DIVISION 6: WITNESSES

Chapter 1: Competency

§ 700. GENERAL RULE AS TO COMPETENCY

Except as otherwise provided by statute, every person, irrespective of age, is qualified to be a witness and no person is disqualified to testify to any matter.

§ 701. DISQUALIFICATION OF WITNESS

(a) A person is disqualified to be a witness if he or she is:

(1) Incapable of expressing himself or herself concerning the matter so as to be understood, either directly or through interpretation by one who can understand him; or

(2) Incapable of understanding the duty of a witness to tell the truth.

(b) In any proceeding held outside the presence of a jury, the court may reserve challenges to the competency of a witness until the conclusion of the direct examination of that witness.

§ 702. PERSONAL KNOWLEDGE OF WITNESS

(a) Subject to Section 801, the testimony of a witness concerning a particular matter is inadmissible unless he has personal knowledge of the matter. Against the objection of a party, such personal knowledge must be shown before the witness may testify concerning the matter.

(b) A witness' personal knowledge of a matter may be shown by any otherwise admissible evidence, including his own testimony.

§ 703. JUDGE AS WITNESS

(a) Before the judge presiding at the trial of an action may be called to testify in that trial as a witness, he shall, in proceedings held out of the presence and hearing of the jury, inform the parties of the information he has concerning any fact or matter about which he will be called to testify.

(b) Against the objection of a party, the judge presiding at the trial of an action may not testify in that trial as a witness. Upon such objection, the judge shall declare a mistrial and order the action assigned for trial before another judge.

(c) The calling of the judge presiding at a trial to testify in that trial as a witness shall be deemed a consent to the granting of a motion for mistrial, and an objection to such calling of a judge shall be deemed a motion for mistrial.

(d) In the absence of objection by a party, the judge presiding at the trial of an action may testify in that trial as a witness.

§ 703.5. JUDGE, ARBITRATOR OR MEDIATOR AS WITNESS IN SUBSEQUENT PROCEEDINGS

No person presiding at any judicial or quasi-judicial proceeding, and no arbitrator or mediator, shall be competent to testify, in any subsequent civil proceeding, as to any statement, conduct, decision, or ruling, occurring at or in conjunction with the prior proceeding, except as to a statement or conduct that could (a) give rise to civil or criminal contempt, (b) constitute a crime, (c) be the subject of investigation by the State Bar or Commission on Judicial Performance, or (d) give rise to disqualification proceedings under paragraph (1) or (6) of subdivision (a) of Section 170.1 of the Code of Civil Procedure. However, this section does not apply to a mediator with regard to any mediation under Chapter 11 (commencing with Section 3160) of Part 2 of Division 8 of the Family Code.

§ 704. JUROR AS WITNESS

(a) Before a juror sworn and impaneled in the trial of an action may be called to testify before the jury in that trial as a witness, he shall, in proceedings conducted by the court out of the presence and hearing of the remaining jurors, inform the parties of the information he has concerning any fact or matter about which he will be called to testify.

(b) Against the objection of a party, a juror sworn and impaneled in the trial of an action may not testify before the jury in that trial as a witness. Upon such objection, the court shall declare a mistrial and order the action assigned for trial before another jury.

(c) The calling of a juror to testify before the jury as a witness shall be deemed a consent to the granting of a motion for mistrial, and an objection to such calling of a juror shall be deemed a motion for mistrial.

(d) In the absence of objection by a party, a juror sworn and impaneled in the trial of an action may be compelled to testify in that trial as a witness.

Chapter 2: Oath and Confrontation

§ 710. OATH REQUIRED; EXCEPTION FOR CHILD OR DEPENDENT PERSON WITH COGNITIVE IMPAIRMENT

Every witness before testifying shall take an oath or make an affirmation or declaration in the form provided by law, except that a child under the age of 10 or a dependent person with a substantial cognitive impairment, in the court's discretion, may be required only to promise to tell the truth.

§ 711. CONFRONTATION

At the trial of an action, a witness can be heard only in the presence and subject to the examination of all the parties to the action, if they choose to attend and examine.

Chapter 3: Expert Witnesses

Article 1: Expert Witnesses Generally

§ 720. QUALIFICATION AS AN EXPERT WITNESS

(a) A person is qualified to testify as an expert if he has special knowledge, skill, experience, training, or education sufficient to qualify him as an expert on the subject to which his testimony relates. Against the objection of a party, such special knowledge, skill, experience, training, or education must be shown before the witness may testify as an expert.

(b) A witness' special knowledge, skill, experience, training, or education may be shown by any otherwise admissible evidence, including his own testimony.

§ 721. CROSS EXAMINATION OF EXPERT WITNESS

(a) Subject to subdivision (b), a witness testifying as an expert may be cross-examined to the same extent as any other witness and, in addition, may be fully cross-examined as to (1) his or her qualifications, (2) the subject to which his or her expert testimony relates, and (3) the matter upon which his or her opinion is based and the reasons for his or her opinion.

(b) If a witness testifying as an expert testifies in the form of an opinion, he or she may not be cross-examined in regard to the content or tenor of any scientific, technical, or professional text, treatise, journal, or similar publication unless any of the following occurs:

(1) The witness referred to, considered, or relied upon such publication in arriving at or forming his or her opinion.

(2) The publication has been admitted in evidence.

(3) The publication has been established as a reliable authority by the testimony or admission of the witness or by other expert testimony or by judicial notice.

If admitted, relevant portions of the publication may be read into evidence but may not be received as exhibits.

§ 722. CREDIBILITY OF EXPERT WITNESS

(a) The fact of the appointment of an expert witness by the court may be revealed to the trier of fact.

(b) The compensation and expenses paid or to be paid to an expert witness by the party calling him is a proper subject of inquiry by any adverse party as relevant to the credibility of the witness and the weight of his testimony.

§ 723. LIMIT ON NUMBER OF EXPERT WITNESSES

The court may, at any time before or during the trial of an action, limit the number of expert witnesses to be called by any party.

Article 2: Appointment of Expert Witnesses by Court

§ 730. APPOINTMENT BY COURT OF EXPERT; CONSTRUCTION REGARDING REQUIREMENT OF LICENSE

When it appears to the court, at any time before or during the trial of an action, that expert evidence is or may be required by the court or by any party to the action, the court on its own motion or on motion of any party may appoint one or more experts to investigate, to render a report as may be ordered by the court, and to testify as an expert at the trial of the action relative to the fact or matter as to which the expert evidence is or may be required. The court may fix the compensation for these services, if any, rendered by any person appointed under this section, in addition to any service as a witness, at the amount as seems reasonable to the court.

Nothing in this section shall be construed to permit a person to perform any act for which a license is required unless the person holds the appropriate license to lawfully perform that act.

§ 731. PAYMENT OF COURT-APPOINTED EXPERT

(a)

(1) In all criminal actions and juvenile court proceedings, the compensation fixed under Section 730 shall be a charge against the county in which the action or proceeding is pending and shall be paid out of the treasury of that county on order of the court.

(2) Notwithstanding paragraph (1), if the expert is appointed for the court's needs, the compensation shall be a charge against the court.

(b) In any county in which the superior court so provides, the compensation fixed under Section 730 for medical experts appointed for the court's needs in civil actions shall be a charge against the court. In any county in which the board of supervisors so provides, the compensation fixed under Section 730 for medical experts appointed in civil actions, for purposes other than the court's needs, shall be a charge against and paid out of the treasury of that county on order of the court.

(c) Except as otherwise provided in this section, in all civil actions, the compensation fixed under Section 730 shall, in the first instance, be apportioned and charged to the several parties in a proportion as the court may determine and may thereafter be taxed and allowed in like manner as other costs.

§ 732. CALLING AND EXAMINING COURT-APPOINTED EXPERT

Any expert appointed by the court under Section 730 may be called and examined by the court or by any party to the action. When such witness is called and examined by the court, the parties have the same right as is expressed in Section 775 to cross-examine the witness and to object to the questions asked and the evidence adduced.

§ 733. RIGHT TO PRODUCE OTHER EXPERT EVIDENCE

Nothing contained in this article shall be deemed or construed to prevent any party to any action from producing other expert evidence on the same fact or matter mentioned in Section 730; but, where other expert witnesses are called by a party to the action, their fees shall be paid by the party calling them and only ordinary witness fees shall be taxed as costs in the action.

Chapter 4: Interpreters and Translators

§ 750. RULES RELATING TO WITNESSES APPLY TO INTERPRETERS AND TRANSLATORS

A person who serves as an interpreter or translator in any action is subject to all the rules of law relating to witnesses.

§ 751. OATH REQUIRED OF INTERPRETERS AND TRANSLATORS

(a) An interpreter shall take an oath that he or she will make a true interpretation to the witness in a language that the witness understands and that he or she will make a true interpretation of the witness' answers to questions to counsel, court, or jury, in the English language, with his or her best skill and judgment.

(b) In any proceeding in which a deaf or hard-of-hearing person is testifying under oath, the interpreter certified pursuant to subdivision (f) of Section 754 shall advise the court whenever he or she is unable to comply with his or her oath taken pursuant to subdivision (a).

(c) A translator shall take an oath that he or she will make a true translation in the English language of any writing he or she is to decipher or translate.

(d) An interpreter regularly employed by the court and certified or registered in accordance with Article 4 (commencing with Section

68560) of Chapter 2 of Title 8 of the Government Code, or a translator regularly employed by the court, may file an oath as prescribed by this section with the clerk of the court. The filed oath shall serve for all subsequent court proceedings until the appointment is revoked by the court.

§ 752. INTERPRETERS FOR WITNESSES

(a) When a witness is incapable of understanding the English language or is incapable of expressing himself or herself in the English language so as to be understood directly by counsel, court, and jury, an interpreter whom the witness can understand and who can understand the witness shall be sworn to interpret for the witness.

(b) The record shall identify the interpreter, who may be appointed and compensated as provided in Article 2 (commencing with Section 730) of Chapter 3, with that compensation charged as follows:

(1) In all criminal actions and juvenile court proceedings, the compensation for an interpreter under this section shall be a charge against the court.

(2) In all civil actions, the compensation for an interpreter under this section shall, in the first instance, be apportioned and charged to the several parties in a proportion as the court may determine and may thereafter be taxed and allowed in a like manner as other costs.

§ 753. TRANSLATORS OF WRITINGS

(a) When the written characters in a writing offered in evidence are incapable of being deciphered or understood directly, a translator who can decipher the characters or understand the language shall be sworn to decipher or translate the writing.

(b) The record shall identify the translator, who may be appointed and compensated as provided in Article 2 (commencing with Section 730) of Chapter 3, with that compensation charged as follows:

(1) In all criminal actions and juvenile court proceedings, the compensation for a translator under this section shall be a charge against the court.

(2) In all civil actions, the compensation for a translator under this section shall, in the first instance, be apportioned and charged to the several parties in a proportion as the court may determine and may thereafter be taxed and allowed in like manner as other costs.

§ 754. INTERPRETERS FOR DEAF OR HARD OF HEARING IN CIVIL AND CRIMINAL CASES

(a) As used in this section, "individual who is deaf or hard of hearing" means an individual with a hearing loss so great as to prevent his or her understanding language spoken in a normal tone, but does not include an individual who is hard of hearing provided with, and able to fully participate in the proceedings through the use of, an assistive listening system or computer-aided transcription equipment provided pursuant to Section 54.8 of the Civil Code.

(b) In a civil or criminal action, including an action involving a traffic or other infraction, a small claims court proceeding, a juvenile court proceeding, a family court proceeding or service, or a proceeding to determine the mental competency of a person, in a court-ordered or court-provided alternative dispute resolution, including mediation and arbitration, or in an administrative hearing, where a party or witness is an individual who is deaf or hard of hearing and the individual who is deaf or hard of hearing is present and participating, the proceeding shall be interpreted in a language that the individual who is deaf or hard of hearing understands by a qualified interpreter appointed by the court or other appointing authority, or as agreed upon.

(c) For purposes of this section, "appointing authority" means a court, department, board, commission, agency, licensing or legislative body, or other body for proceedings requiring a qualified interpreter.

(d) For purposes of this section, "interpreter" includes an oral interpreter, a sign language interpreter, or a deaf-blind interpreter, depending upon the needs of the individual who is deaf or hard of hearing.

(e) For purposes of this section, "intermediary interpreter" means an individual who is deaf or hard of hearing, or a hearing individual who is able to assist in providing an accurate interpretation between spoken English and sign language or between variants of sign language or between American Sign Language and other foreign languages by acting as an intermediary between the individual who is deaf or hard of hearing and the qualified interpreter.

(f) For purposes of this section, "qualified interpreter" means an interpreter who has been certified as competent to interpret court proceedings by a testing organization, agency, or educational institution approved by the Judicial Council as qualified to administer tests to court interpreters for individuals who are deaf or hard of hearing.

(g) If the appointed interpreter is not familiar with the use of particular signs by the individual who is deaf or hard of hearing or his or her particular variant of sign language, the court or other appointing authority shall, in consultation with the individual who is deaf or hard of hearing or his or her representative, appoint an intermediary interpreter.

(h)

(1) Before July 1, 1992, the Judicial Council shall conduct a study to establish the guidelines pursuant to which it shall determine which testing organizations, agencies, or educational institutions will be approved to administer tests for certification of court interpreters for individuals who are deaf or hard of hearing. It is the intent of the Legislature that the study obtain the widest possible input from the public, including, but not limited to, educational institutions, the judiciary, linguists, members of the State Bar of California, court interpreters, members of professional interpreting organizations, and members of the deaf and hard of hearing communities. After obtaining public comment and completing its study, the Judicial Council shall publish these guidelines. By January 1, 1997, the Judicial Council shall approve one or more entities to administer testing for court interpreters for individuals who are deaf or hard of hearing. Testing entities may include educational institutions, testing organizations, joint powers agencies, or public agencies.

(2) Commencing July 1, 1997, court interpreters for individuals who are deaf or hard of hearing shall meet the qualifications specified in subdivision (f).

(i) Persons appointed to serve as interpreters under this section shall be paid, in addition to actual travel costs, the prevailing rate paid to persons employed by the court to provide other interpreter services unless such service is considered to be a part of the person's regular duties as an employee of the state, county, or other political subdivision of the state. Except as provided in subdivision (j), payment of the interpreter's fee shall be a charge against the court. Payment of the interpreter's fee in administrative proceedings shall be a charge against the appointing board or authority.

(j) Whenever a peace officer or any other person having a law enforcement or prosecutorial function in a criminal or quasi-criminal investigation or non-court proceeding questions or otherwise interviews an alleged victim or witness who demonstrates or alleges deafness or hearing loss, a good faith effort to secure the services of an interpreter shall be made without any unnecessary delay, unless either the individual who is deaf or hard of hearing affirmatively indicates that he or she does not need or cannot use an interpreter, or an interpreter is not otherwise required by Title II of the federal Americans with Disabilities Act of 1990 (Public Law 101-336) and federal regulations adopted thereunder. Payment of the interpreter's fee shall be a charge against the county, or other political subdivision of the state, in which the action is pending.

(k) A statement, written or oral, made by an individual who the court finds is deaf or hard of hearing in reply to a question of a peace officer, or any other person having a law enforcement or prosecutorial function in a criminal or quasi-criminal investigation or proceeding, shall not be used against that individual who is deaf or hard of hearing unless the question was accurately interpreted and the statement was made knowingly, voluntarily, and intelligently and was accurately interpreted, or the court finds that either the individual could not have used an interpreter or an interpreter was not otherwise required by Title II of the federal Americans with Disabilities Act of 1990 (Public Law 101-336) and federal regulations adopted thereunder and that the statement was made knowingly, voluntarily, and intelligently.

(l) In obtaining services of an interpreter for purposes of subdivision (j) or (k), priority shall be given to first obtaining a qualified interpreter.

(m) Subdivisions (j) and (k) shall not be deemed to supersede the requirement of subdivision (b) for use of a qualified interpreter for an individual who is deaf or hard of hearing participating as a party or witness in a trial or hearing.

(n) In an action or proceeding in which an individual who is deaf or hard of hearing is a participant, the appointing authority shall not commence the action or proceeding until the appointed interpreter is in full view of and spatially situated to assure proper communication with the participating individual who is deaf or hard of hearing.

(o) Each superior court shall maintain a current roster of qualified interpreters certified pursuant to subdivision (f).

§ 756. REIMBURSEMENT TO COURT INTERPRETER SERVICES IN CIVIL ACTIONS AND PROCEEDINGS

(a) To the extent required by other state or federal laws, the Judicial Council shall reimburse courts for court interpreter services provided in civil actions and proceedings to any party who is present in court and who does not proficiently speak or understand the English language for the purpose of interpreting the proceedings in a language the party understands, and assisting communications between the party, the party's attorney, and the court.

(b) If sufficient funds are not appropriated to provide an interpreter to every party that meets the standard of eligibility, court interpreter services in civil cases reimbursed by the Judicial Council, pursuant to subdivision (a), shall be prioritized by case type by each court in the following order:

(1) Actions and proceedings under Division 10 (commencing with Section 6200) of the Family Code, actions or proceedings under the Uniform Parentage Act (Part 3 (commencing with Section 7600) of Division 12 of the Family Code) in which a protective order has been granted or is being sought pursuant to Section 6221 of the Family Code, and actions and proceedings for dissolution or nullity of marriage or legal separation of the parties in which a protective order has been granted or is being sought pursuant to Section 6221 of the Family Code; actions and proceedings under subdivision (y) of Section 527.6 of the Code of Civil Procedure; and actions and proceedings for physical abuse or neglect under the Elder Abuse and Dependent Adult Civil Protection Act (Chapter 11 (commencing with Section 15600) of Part 3 of Division 9 of the Welfare and Institutions Code).

(2) Actions and proceedings relating to unlawful detainer.

(3) Actions and proceedings to terminate parental rights.

(4) Actions and proceedings relating to conservatorship or guardianship, including the appointment or termination of a probate guardian or conservator.

(5) Actions and proceedings by a parent to obtain sole legal or physical custody of a child or rights to visitation.

(6) All other actions and proceedings under Section 527.6 of the Code of Civil Procedure or the Elder Abuse and Dependent Adult Civil Protection Act (Chapter 11 (commencing with Section 15600) of Part 3 of Division 9 of the Welfare and Institutions Code).

(7) All other actions and proceedings related to family law.

(8) All other civil actions or proceedings.

(c)

(1) If funds are not available to provide an interpreter to every party that meets the standard of eligibility, preference shall be given for parties proceeding in forma pauperis pursuant to Section 68631 of the Government Code in any civil action or proceeding described in paragraph (3), (4), (5), (6), (7), or (8) of subdivision (b).

(2) Courts may provide an interpreter to a party outside the priority order listed in subdivision (b) when a qualified interpreter is present and available at the court location and no higher priority action that meets the standard of eligibility described in subdivision (a) is taking place at that location during the period of time for which the interpreter has already been compensated.

(d) A party shall not be charged a fee for the provision of a court interpreter.

(e) In seeking reimbursement for court interpreter services, the court shall identify to the Judicial Council the case types for which the interpretation to be reimbursed was provided. Courts shall regularly certify that in providing the interpreter services, they have complied with the priorities and preferences set forth in subdivisions (b) and (c), which shall be subject to review by the Judicial Council.

(f) This section shall not be construed to alter, limit, or negate any right to an interpreter in a civil action or proceeding otherwise provided by state or federal law, or the right to an interpreter in criminal, traffic, or other infraction, juvenile, or mental competency actions or proceedings.

(g) This section shall not result in a reduction in staffing or compromise the quality of interpreting services in criminal, juvenile, or other types of matters in which interpreters are provided.

Chapter 5: Method and Scope of Examination

Article 1: Definitions

§ 760. "DIRECT EXAMINATION"

"Direct examination" is the first examination of a witness upon a matter that is not within the scope of a previous examination of the witness.

§ 761. "CROSS-EXAMINATION"

"Cross-examination" is the examination of a witness by a party other than the direct examiner upon a matter that is within the scope of the direct examination of the witness.

§ 762. "REDIRECT EXAMINATION"

"Redirect examination" is an examination of a witness by the direct examiner subsequent to the cross-examination of the witness.

§ 763. "RECROSS-EXAMINATION"

"Recross-examination" is an examination of a witness by a cross-examiner subsequent to a redirect examination of the witness.

§ 764. "LEADING QUESTION"

A "leading question" is a question that suggests to the witness the answer that the examining party desires.

Article 2: Examination of Witnesses

§ 765. COURT TO CONTROL MODE OF INTERROGATION

(a) The court shall exercise reasonable control over the mode of interrogation of a witness so as to make interrogation as rapid, as distinct, and as effective for the ascertainment of the truth, as may be, and to protect the witness from undue harassment or embarrassment.

(b) With a witness under the age of 14 or a dependent person with a substantial cognitive impairment, the court shall take special care to protect him or her from undue harassment or embarrassment, and to restrict the unnecessary repetition of questions. The court shall also take special care to ensure that questions are stated in a form which is appropriate to the age or cognitive level of the witness. The court may, in the interests of justice, on objection by a party, forbid the asking of a question which is in a form that is not reasonably likely to be understood by a person of the age or cognitive level of the witness.

§ 766. RESPONSIVE ANSWERS

A witness must give responsive answers to questions, and answers that are not responsive shall be stricken on motion of any party.

§ 767. LEADING QUESTIONS

(a) Except under special circumstances where the interests of justice otherwise require:

(1) A leading question may not be asked of a witness on direct or redirect examination.

(2) A leading question may be asked of a witness on cross-examination or recross- examination.

(b) The court may, in the interests of justice permit a leading question to be asked of a child under 10 years of age or a dependent person with a substantial cognitive impairment in a case involving a prosecution under Section 273a, 273d, 288.5, 368, or any of the acts described in Section 11165.1 or 11165.2 of the Penal Code.

§ 768. WRITINGS

(a) In examining a witness concerning a writing, it is not necessary to show, read, or disclose to him any part of the writing.

(b) If a writing is shown to a witness, all parties to the action must be given an opportunity to inspect it before any question concerning it may be asked of the witness.

§ 769. INCONSISTENT STATEMENT OR CONDUCT

In examining a witness concerning a statement or other conduct by him that is inconsistent with any part of his testimony at the hearing, it is not necessary to disclose to him any information concerning the statement or other conduct.

§ 770. EVIDENCE OF INCONSISTENT STATEMENT OF WITNESS

Unless the interests of justice otherwise require, extrinsic evidence of a statement made by a witness that is inconsistent with any part of his testimony at the hearing shall be excluded unless:

(a) The witness was so examined while testifying as to give him an opportunity to explain or to deny the statement; or

(b) The witness has not been excused from giving further testimony in the action.

§ 771. PRODUCTION OF WRITING USED TO REFRESH MEMORY

(a) Subject to subdivision (c), if a witness, either while testifying or prior thereto, uses a writing to refresh his memory with respect to any matter about which he testifies, such writing must be produced at the hearing at the request of an adverse party and, unless the writing is so produced, the testimony of the witness concerning such matter shall be stricken.

(b) If the writing is produced at the hearing, the adverse party may, if he chooses, inspect the writing, cross-examine the witness concerning it, and introduce in evidence such portion of it as may be pertinent to the testimony of the witness.

(c) Production of the writing is excused, and the testimony of the witness shall not be stricken, if the writing:

(1) Is not in the possession or control of the witness or the party who produced his testimony concerning the matter; and

(2) Was not reasonably procurable by such party through the use of the court's process or other available means.

§ 772. ORDER OF EXAMINATION

(a) The examination of a witness shall proceed in the following phases: direct examination, cross-examination, redirect examination, recross-examination, and continuing thereafter by redirect and recross-examination.

(b) Unless for good cause the court otherwise directs, each phase of the examination of a witness must be concluded before the succeeding phase begins.

(c) Subject to subdivision (d), a party may, in the discretion of the court, interrupt his cross-examination, redirect examination, or recross-examination of a witness, in order to examine the witness upon a matter not within the scope of a previous examination of the witness.

(d) If the witness is the defendant in a criminal action, the witness may not, without his consent, be examined under direct examination by another party.

§ 773. CROSS-EXAMINATION

(a) A witness examined by one party may be cross-examined upon any matter within the scope of the direct examination by each other party to the action in such order as the court directs.

(b) The cross-examination of a witness by any party whose interest is not adverse to the party calling him is subject to the same rules that are applicable to the direct examination.

§ 774. REEXAMINATION

A witness once examined cannot be reexamined as to the same matter without leave of the court, but he may be reexamined as to any new matter upon which he has been examined by another party to the action. Leave may be granted or withheld in the court's discretion.

§ 775. COURT MAY CALL WITNESSES

The court, on its own motion or on the motion of any party, may call witnesses and interrogate them the same as if they had been produced by a party to the action, and the parties may object to the questions asked and the evidence adduced the same as if such witnesses were called and examined by an adverse party. Such witnesses may be cross-examined by all parties to the action in such order as the court directs.

§ 776. EXAMINATION OF ADVERSE PARTY OR WITNESS

(a) A party to the record of any civil action, or a person identified with such a party, may be called and examined as if under cross-examination by any adverse party at any time during the presentation of evidence by the party calling the witness.

(b) A witness examined by a party under this section may be cross-examined by all other parties to the action in such order as the court directs; but, subject to subdivision (e), the witness may be examined only as if under redirect examination by:

(1) In the case of a witness who is a party, his own counsel and counsel for a party who is not adverse to the witness.

(2) In the case of a witness who is not a party, counsel for the party with whom the witness is identified and counsel for a party who is not adverse to the party with whom the witness is identified.

(c) For the purpose of this section, parties represented by the same counsel are deemed to be a single party.

(d) For the purpose of this section, a person is identified with a party if he is:

(1) A person for whose immediate benefit the action is prosecuted or defended by the party.

(2) A director, officer, superintendent, member, agent, employee, or managing agent of the party or of a person specified in paragraph (1), or any public employee of a public entity when such public entity is the party.

(3) A person who was in any of the relationships specified in paragraph (2) at the time of the act or omission giving rise to the cause of action.

(4) A person who was in any of the relationships specified in paragraph (2) at the time he obtained knowledge of the matter concerning which he is sought to be examined under this section.

(e) Paragraph (2) of subdivision (b) does not require counsel for the party with whom the witness is identified and counsel for a party who is not adverse to the party with whom the witness is identified to examine the witness as if under redirect examination if the party who called the witness for examination under this section:

(1) Is also a person identified with the same party with whom the witness is identified.

(2) Is the personal representative, heir, successor, or assignee of a person identified with the same party with whom the witness is identified.

§ 777. EXCLUSION OF WITNESS

(a) Subject to subdivisions (b) and (c), the court may exclude from the courtroom any witness not at the time under examination so that such witness cannot hear the testimony of other witnesses.

(b) A party to the action cannot be excluded under this section.

(c) If a person other than a natural person is a party to the action, an officer or employee designated by its attorney is entitled to be present.

§ 778. RECALL OF WITNESS

After a witness has been excused from giving further testimony in the action, he cannot be recalled without leave of the court. Leave may be granted or withheld in the court's discretion.

Chapter 6: Credibility of Witnesses

Article 1: Credibility Generally

§ 780. GENERAL RULE AS TO CREDIBILITY

Except as otherwise provided by statute, the court or jury may consider in determining the credibility of a witness any matter that has any tendency in reason to prove or disprove the truthfulness of his testimony at the hearing, including but not limited to any of the following:

(a) His demeanor while testifying and the manner in which he testifies.

(b) The character of his testimony.

(c) The extent of his capacity to perceive, to recollect, or to communicate any matter about which he testifies.

(d) The extent of his opportunity to perceive any matter about which he testifies.

(e) His character for honesty or veracity or their opposites.

(f) The existence or nonexistence of a bias, interest, or other motive.

(g) A statement previously made by him that is consistent with his testimony at the hearing.

(h) A statement made by him that is inconsistent with any part of his testimony at the hearing.

(i) The existence or nonexistence of any fact testified to by him.

(j) His attitude toward the action in which he testifies or toward the giving of testimony.

(k) His admission of untruthfulness.

§ 782. EVIDENCE OF SEXUAL CONDUCT OF COMPLAINING WITNESS; WRITTEN MOTION; OFFER OF PROOF; AFFIDAVIT; PROCEDURE

(a) In any of the circumstances described in subdivision (c), if evidence of sexual conduct of the complaining witness is offered to attack the credibility of the complaining witness under Section 780, the following procedure shall be followed:

(1) A written motion shall be made by the defendant to the court and prosecutor stating that the defense has an offer of proof of the relevance of evidence of the sexual conduct of the complaining witness that is proposed to be presented and of its relevance in attacking the credibility of the complaining witness.

(2) The written motion shall be accompanied by an affidavit in which the offer of proof shall be stated. The affidavit shall be filed under seal and only unsealed by the court to determine if the offer of proof is sufficient to order a hearing pursuant to paragraph (3). After that determination, the affidavit shall be resealed by the court.

(3) If the court finds that the offer of proof is sufficient, the court shall order a hearing out of the presence of the jury, if any, and at the hearing allow the questioning of the complaining witness regarding the offer of proof made by the defendant.

(4) At the conclusion of the hearing, if the court finds that evidence proposed to be offered by the defendant regarding the sexual conduct of the complaining witness is relevant pursuant to Section 780, and is not inadmissible pursuant to Section 352, the court may make an order stating what evidence may be introduced by the defendant, and the nature of the questions to be permitted. The defendant may then offer evidence pursuant to the order of the court.

(5) An affidavit resealed by the court pursuant to paragraph (2) shall remain sealed, unless the defendant raises an issue on appeal or collateral review relating to the offer of proof contained in the sealed document. If the defendant raises that issue on appeal, the court shall allow the Attorney General and appellate counsel for the defendant access to the sealed affidavit. If the issue is raised on collateral review, the court shall allow the district attorney and defendant's counsel access to the sealed affidavit. The use of the information contained in the affidavit shall be limited solely to the pending proceeding.

(b)

(1) As used in this section, "complaining witness" means:

(A) The alleged victim of the crime charged, the prosecution of which is subject to this section, pursuant to paragraph (1) of subdivision (c).

(B) An alleged victim offering testimony pursuant to paragraph (2) or (3) of subdivision (c).

(2) As used in this section, "evidence of sexual conduct" includes those portions of a social media account about the complaining witness, including any text, image, video, or picture, which depict sexual content, sexual history, nudity or partial nudity, intimate sexual activity, communications about sex, sexual fantasies, and other information that appeals to a prurient interest, unless it is related to the alleged offense.

(c) The procedure provided by subdivision (a) shall apply in any of the following circumstances:

(1) In a prosecution under Section 261, 262, 264.1, 286, 287, 288, 288.5, or 289 of, or former Section 288a of, the Penal Code, or for assault with intent to commit, attempt to commit, or conspiracy to commit any crime defined in any of those sections, except if the crime is alleged to have occurred in a local detention facility, as defined in Section 6031.4 of the Penal Code, or in the state prison, as defined in Section 4504.

(2) When an alleged victim testifies pursuant to subdivision (b) of Section 1101 as a victim of a crime listed in Section 243.4, 261,

261.5, 269, 285, 286, 287, 288, 288.5, 289, 314, or 647.6 of, or former Section 288a of, the Penal Code, except if the crime is alleged to have occurred in a local detention facility, as defined in Section 6031.4 of the Penal Code, or in the state prison, as defined in Section 4504 of the Penal Code.

(3) When an alleged victim of a sexual offense testifies pursuant to Section 1108, except if the crime is alleged to have occurred in a local detention facility, as defined in Section 6031.4 of the Penal Code, or in the state prison, as defined in Section 4504 of the Penal Code.

§ 783. EVIDENCE OF SEXUAL CONDUCT TO ATTACK CREDIBILITY OF PLAINTIFF IN CIVIL ACTION ALLEGING SEXUAL HARASSMENT; PROCEDURE

In any civil action alleging conduct which constitutes sexual harassment, sexual assault, or sexual battery, if evidence of sexual conduct of the plaintiff is offered to attack credibility of the plaintiff under Section 780, the following procedures shall be followed:

(a) A written motion shall be made by the defendant to the court and the plaintiff's attorney stating that the defense has an offer of proof of the relevancy of evidence of the sexual conduct of the plaintiff proposed to be presented.

(b) The written motion shall be accompanied by an affidavit in which the offer of proof shall be stated.

(c) If the court finds that the offer of proof is sufficient, the court shall order a hearing out of the presence of the jury, if any, and at the hearing allow the questioning of the plaintiff regarding the offer of proof made by the defendant.

(d) At the conclusion of the hearing, if the court finds that evidence proposed to be offered by the defendant regarding the sexual conduct of the plaintiff is relevant pursuant to Section 780, and is not inadmissible pursuant to Section 352, the court may make an order stating what evidence may be introduced by the defendant, and the nature of the questions to be permitted. The defendant may then offer evidence pursuant to the order of the court.

Article 2: Attacking or Supporting Credibility

§ 785. PARTIES MAY ATTACK OR SUPPORT CREDIBILITY

The credibility of a witness may be attacked or supported by any party, including the party calling him.

§ 786. CHARACTER EVIDENCE GENERALLY

Evidence of traits of his character other than honesty or veracity, or their opposites, is inadmissible to attack or support the credibility of a witness.

§ 787. SPECIFIC INSTANCES OF CONDUCT

Subject to Section 788, evidence of specific instances of his conduct relevant only as tending to prove a trait of his character is inadmissible to attack or support the credibility of a witness.

§ 788. PRIOR FELONY CONVICTION

For the purpose of attacking the credibility of a witness, it may be shown by the examination of the witness or by the record of the judgment that he has been convicted of a felony unless:

(a) A pardon based on his innocence has been granted to the witness by the jurisdiction in which he was convicted.

(b) A certificate of rehabilitation and pardon has been granted to the witness under the provisions of Chapter 3.5 (commencing with Section 4852.01) of Title 6 of Part 3 of the Penal Code.

(c) The accusatory pleading against the witness has been dismissed under the provisions of Penal Code Section 1203.4, but this exception does not apply to any criminal trial where the witness is being prosecuted for a subsequent offense.

(d) The conviction was under the laws of another jurisdiction and the witness has been relieved of the penalties and disabilities arising from the conviction pursuant to a procedure substantially equivalent to that referred to in subdivision (b) or (c).

§ 789. RELIGIOUS BELIEF

Evidence of his religious belief or lack thereof is inadmissible to attack or support the credibility of a witness.

§ 790. GOOD CHARACTER OF WITNESS

Evidence of the good character of a witness is inadmissible to support his credibility unless evidence of his bad character has been admitted for the purpose of attacking his credibility.

§ 791. PRIOR CONSISTENT STATEMENT OF WITNESS

Evidence of a statement previously made by a witness that is consistent with his testimony at the hearing is inadmissible to support his credibility unless it is offered after:

(a) Evidence of a statement made by him that is inconsistent with any part of his testimony at the hearing has been admitted for the purpose of attacking his credibility, and the statement was made before the alleged inconsistent statement; or

(b) An express or implied charge has been made that his testimony at the hearing is recently fabricated or is influenced by bias or other improper motive, and the statement was made before the bias, motive for fabrication, or other improper motive is alleged to have arisen.

Chapter 7: Hypnosis of Witnesses

§ 795. ADMISSIBILITY OF TESTIMONY IN CRIMINAL PROCEEDING

(a) The testimony of a witness is not inadmissible in a criminal proceeding by reason of the fact that the witness has previously undergone hypnosis for the purpose of recalling events that are the subject of the witness's testimony, if all of the following conditions are met:

(1) The testimony is limited to those matters that the witness recalled and related prior to the hypnosis.

(2) The substance of the prehypnotic memory was preserved in a writing, audio recording or video recording prior to the hypnosis.

(3) The hypnosis was conducted in accordance with all of the following procedures:

(A) A written record was made prior to hypnosis documenting the subject's description of the event, and information that was provided to the hypnotist concerning the subject matter of the hypnosis.

(B) The subject gave informed consent to the hypnosis.

(C) The hypnosis session, including the pre- and post-hypnosis interviews, was video recorded for subsequent review.

(D) The hypnosis was performed by a licensed physician and surgeon, psychologist, licensed clinical social worker, licensed marriage and family therapist, or licensed professional clinical counselor experienced in the use of hypnosis and independent of and not in the presence of law enforcement, the prosecution, or the defense.

(4) Prior to admission of the testimony, the court holds a hearing pursuant to Section 402 at which the proponent of the evidence proves by clear and convincing evidence that the hypnosis did not so affect the witness as to render the witness's prehypnosis recollection unreliable or to substantially impair the ability to cross-examine the witness concerning the witness's prehypnosis recollection. At the hearing, each side shall have the right to present expert testimony and to cross-examine witnesses.

(b) Nothing in this section shall be construed to limit the ability of a party to attack the credibility of a witness who has undergone hypnosis, or to limit other legal grounds to admit or exclude the testimony of that witness.

DIVISION 7: OPINION TESTIMONY AND SCIENTIFIC EVIDENCE

Chapter 1: Expert and Other Opinion Testimony

Article 1: Expert and Other Opinion Testimony Generally

§ 800. OPINION TESTIMONY BY LAY WITNESS

If a witness is not testifying as an expert, his testimony in the form of an opinion is limited to such an opinion as is permitted by law, including but not limited to an opinion that is:

(a) Rationally based on the perception of the witness; and

(b) Helpful to a clear understanding of his testimony.

§ 801. OPINION TESTIMONY BY EXPERT WITNESSES

If a witness is testifying as an expert, his testimony in the form of an opinion is limited to such an opinion as is:

(a) Related to a subject that is sufficiently beyond common experience that the opinion of an expert would assist the trier of fact; and

(b) Based on matter (including his special knowledge, skill, experience, training, and education) perceived by or personally known to the witness or made known to him at or before the hearing, whether or not admissible, that is of a type that reasonably may be relied upon by an expert in forming an opinion upon the subject to which his testimony relates, unless an expert is precluded by law from using such matter as a basis for his opinion.

§ 801.1. EXPERT TESTIMONY REGARDING MEDICAL CAUSATION

(a) In a general civil case, as defined in Rule 1.6 of the California Rules of Court, where the party bearing the burden of proof proffers expert testimony regarding medical causation and where that party's expert is required as a condition of testifying to opine that causation exists to a reasonable medical probability, the party not bearing the burden of proof may offer a contrary expert only if its expert is able to opine that the proffered alternative cause or causes each exists to a reasonable medical probability, except as provided in subdivision (b).

(b) Subdivision (a) does not preclude a witness testifying as an expert from testifying that a matter cannot meet a reasonable degree of probability in the applicable field, and providing the basis for that opinion.

§ 802. STATEMENT OF BASIS OF OPINION

A witness testifying in the form of an opinion may state on direct examination the reasons for his opinion and the matter (including, in the case of an expert, his special knowledge, skill, experience, training, and education) upon which it is based, unless he is precluded by law from using such reasons or matter as a basis for his opinion. The court in its discretion may require that a witness before testifying in the form of an opinion be first examined concerning the matter upon which his opinion is based.

§ 803. OPINION BASED ON IMPROPER MATTER

The court may, and upon objection shall, exclude testimony in the form of an opinion that is based in whole or in significant part on matter that is not a proper basis for such an opinion. In such case, the witness may, if there remains a proper basis for his opinion, then state his opinion after excluding from consideration the matter determined to be improper.

§ 804. OPINION BASED ON OPINION OR STATEMENT OF ANOTHER

(a) If a witness testifying as an expert testifies that his opinion is based in whole or in part upon the opinion or statement of another person, such other person may be called and examined by any adverse party as if under cross-examination concerning the opinion or statement.

(b) This section is not applicable if the person upon whose opinion or statement the expert witness has relied is (1) a party, (2) a person identified with a party within the meaning of subdivision (d) of Section 776, or (3) a witness who has testified in the action concerning the subject matter of the opinion or statement upon which the expert witness has relied.

(c) Nothing in this section makes admissible an expert opinion that is inadmissible because it is based in whole or in part on the opinion or statement of another person.

(d) An expert opinion otherwise admissible is not made inadmissible by this section because it is based on the opinion or statement of a person who is unavailable for examination pursuant to this section.

§ 805. OPINION ON ULTIMATE ISSUE

Testimony in the form of an opinion that is otherwise admissible is not objectionable because it embraces the ultimate issue to be decided by the trier of fact.

Article 3: Opinion Testimony on Particular Subjects

§ 870. OPINION AS TO SANITY

A witness may state his opinion as to the sanity of a person when:

(a) The witness is an intimate acquaintance of the person whose sanity is in question;

(b) The witness was a subscribing witness to a writing, the validity of which is in dispute, signed by the person whose sanity is in question and the opinion relates to the sanity of such person at the time the writing was signed; or

(c) The witness is qualified under Section 800 or 801 to testify in the form of an opinion.

DIVISION 8: PRIVILEGES

Chapter 1: Definitions

§ 900. APPLICATION OF DEFINITIONS

Unless the provision or context otherwise requires, the definitions in this chapter govern the construction of this division. They do not govern the construction of any other division.

§ 901. "PROCEEDING"

"Proceeding" means any action, hearing, investigation, inquest, or inquiry (whether conducted by a court, administrative agency, hearing officer, arbitrator, legislative body, or any other person authorized by law) in which, pursuant to law, testimony can be compelled to be given.

§ 902. "CIVIL PROCEEDING"

"Civil proceeding" means any proceeding except a criminal proceeding.

§ 903. "CRIMINAL PROCEEDING"

"Criminal proceeding" means:

(a) A criminal action; and

(b) A proceeding pursuant to Article 3 (commencing with Section 3060) of Chapter 7 of Division 4 of Title 1 of the Government Code to determine whether a public officer should be removed from office for willful or corrupt misconduct in office.

§ 905. "PRESIDING OFFICER"

"Presiding officer" means the person authorized to rule on a claim of privilege in the proceeding in which the claim is made.

Chapter 2: Applicability of Division

§ 910. APPLICABILITY OF DIVISION

Except as otherwise provided by statute, the provisions of this division apply in all proceedings. The provisions of any statute making rules of evidence inapplicable in particular proceedings, or limiting the applicability of rules of evidence in particular proceedings, do not make this division inapplicable to such proceedings.

Chapter 3: General Provisions Relating to Privileges

§ 911. GENERAL RULE AS TO PRIVILEGES

Except as otherwise provided by statute:

(a) No person has a privilege to refuse to be a witness.

(b) No person has a privilege to refuse to disclose any matter or to refuse to produce any writing, object, or other thing.

(c) No person has a privilege that another shall not be a witness or shall not disclose any matter or shall not produce any writing, object, or other thing.

§ 912. WAIVER OF PRIVILEGE

(a) Except as otherwise provided in this section, the right of any person to claim a privilege provided by Section 954 (lawyer-client privilege), 966 (lawyer referral service-client privilege), 980 (privilege for confidential marital communications), 994 (physician-patient privilege), 1014 (psychotherapist-patient privilege), 1033 (privilege of penitent), 1034 (privilege of clergy member), 1035.8 (sexual assault counselor-victim privilege), 1037.5 (domestic violence counselor-victim privilege), or 1038 (human trafficking caseworker-victim privilege) is waived with respect to a communication protected by the privilege if any holder of the privilege, without coercion, has disclosed a significant part of the communication or has consented to disclosure made by anyone. Consent to disclosure is manifested by any statement or other conduct of the holder of the privilege indicating consent to the disclosure, including failure to claim the privilege in any proceeding in which the holder has legal standing and the opportunity to claim the privilege.

(b) Where two or more persons are joint holders of a privilege provided by Section 954 (lawyer-client privilege), 966 (lawyer referral service-client privilege), 994 (physician-patient privilege), 1014 (psychotherapist-patient privilege), 1035.8 (sexual assault counselor-victim privilege), 1037.5 (domestic violence counselor-victim privilege), or 1038 (human trafficking caseworker-victim privilege), a waiver of the right of a particular joint holder of the privilege to claim the privilege does not affect the right of another joint holder to claim the privilege. In the case of the privilege provided by Section 980 (privilege for confidential marital communications), a waiver of the right of one spouse to claim the privilege does not affect the right of the other spouse to claim the privilege.

(c) A disclosure that is itself privileged is not a waiver of any privilege.

(d) A disclosure in confidence of a communication that is protected by a privilege provided by Section 954 (lawyer-client privilege), 966 (lawyer referral service-client privilege), 994 (physician-patient privilege), 1014 (psychotherapist-patient privilege), 1035.8 (sexual assault counselor-victim privilege), 1037.5 (domestic violence counselor-victim privilege), or 1038 (human trafficking caseworker-victim privilege), when disclosure is reasonably necessary for the accomplishment of the purpose for which the lawyer, lawyer referral service, physician, psychotherapist, sexual assault counselor, domestic violence counselor, or human trafficking caseworker was consulted, is not a waiver of the privilege.

§ 913. COMMENT ON, AND INFERENCES FROM, EXERCISE OF PRIVILEGE

(a) If in the instant proceeding or on a prior occasion a privilege is or was exercised not to testify with respect to any matter, or to refuse to disclose or to prevent another from disclosing any matter, neither the presiding officer nor counsel may comment thereon, no presumption shall arise because of the exercise of the privilege, and the trier of fact may not draw any inference therefrom as to the credibility of the witness or as to any matter at issue in the proceeding.

(b) The court, at the request of a party who may be adversely affected because an unfavorable inference may be drawn by the jury because a privilege has been exercised, shall instruct the jury that no presumption arises because of the exercise of the privilege and that the jury may not draw any inference therefrom as to the credibility of the witness or as to any matter at issue in the proceeding.

§ 914. DETERMINATION OF CLAIM OF PRIVILEGE; LIMITATION ON PUNISHMENT FOR CONTEMPT

(a) The presiding officer shall determine a claim of privilege in any proceeding in the same manner as a court determines such a claim under Article 2 (commencing with Section 400) of Chapter 4 of Division 3.

(b) No person may be held in contempt for failure to disclose information claimed to be privileged unless he has failed to comply with an order of a court that he disclose such information. This subdivision does not apply to any governmental agency that has constitutional contempt power, nor does it apply to hearings and investigations of the Industrial Accident Commission, nor does it impliedly repeal Chapter 4 (commencing with Section 9400) of Part 1 of Division 2 of Title 2 of the Government Code. If no other statutory procedure is applicable, the procedure prescribed by Section 1991 of the Code of Civil Procedure shall be followed in seeking an order of a court that the person disclose the information claimed to be privileged.

§ 915. DISCLOSURE OF PRIVILEGED INFORMATION IN RULING ON CLAIM OF PRIVILEGE

(a) Subject to subdivision (b), the presiding officer may not require disclosure of information claimed to be privileged under this division or attorney work product under subdivision (a) of Section 2018.030 of the Code of Civil Procedure in order to rule on the claim of privilege; provided, however, that in any hearing conducted pursuant to subdivision (c) of Section 1524 of the Penal Code in which a claim of privilege is made and the court determines that there is no other feasible means to rule on the validity of the claim other than to require disclosure, the court shall proceed in accordance with subdivision (b).

(b) When a court is ruling on a claim of privilege under Article 9 (commencing with Section 1040) of Chapter 4 (official information and identity of informer) or under Section 1060 (trade secret) or under subdivision (b) of Section 2018.030 of the Code of Civil Procedure (attorney work product) and is unable to do so without requiring disclosure of the information claimed to be privileged, the court may require the person from whom disclosure is sought or the person authorized to claim the privilege, or both, to disclose the information in chambers out of the presence and hearing of all persons except the person authorized to claim the privilege and any other persons as the person authorized to claim the privilege is willing to have present. If the judge determines that the information is privileged, neither the judge nor any other person may ever disclose, without the consent of a person authorized to permit disclosure, what was disclosed in the course of the proceedings in chambers.

§ 916. EXCLUSION OF PRIVILEGED INFORMATION WHERE PERSONS AUTHORIZED TO CLAIM PRIVILEGE ARE NOT PRESENT

(a) The presiding officer, on his own motion or on the motion of any party, shall exclude information that is subject to a claim of privilege under this division if:

(1) The person from whom the information is sought is not a person authorized to claim the privilege; and

(2) There is no party to the proceeding who is a person authorized to claim the privilege.

(b) The presiding officer may not exclude information under this section if:

(1) He is otherwise instructed by a person authorized to permit disclosure; or

(2) The proponent of the evidence establishes that there is no person authorized to claim the privilege in existence.

§ 917. PRESUMPTION THAT CERTAIN COMMUNICATIONS ARE CONFIDENTIAL

(a) If a privilege is claimed on the ground that the matter sought to be disclosed is a communication made in confidence in the course of the lawyer-client, lawyer referral service-client, physician-patient, psychotherapist-patient, clergy-penitent, marital or domestic partnership, sexual assault counselor-victim, domestic violence counselor-victim, or human trafficking caseworker-victim relationship, the communication is presumed to have been made in confidence and the opponent of the claim of privilege has the burden of proof to establish that the communication was not confidential.

(b) A communication between persons in a relationship listed in subdivision (a) does not lose its privileged character for the sole reason that it is communicated by electronic means or because persons involved in the delivery, facilitation, or storage of electronic communication may have access to the content of the communication.

(c) For purposes of this section, "electronic" has the same meaning provided in Section 1633.2 of the Civil Code.

§ 918. EFFECT OF ERROR IN OVERRULING CLAIM OF PRIVILEGE

A party may predicate error on a ruling disallowing a claim of privilege only if he is the holder of the privilege, except that a party may predicate error on a ruling disallowing a claim of privilege by his spouse under Section 970 or 971.

§ 919. ADMISSIBILITY WHERE DISCLOSURE ERRONEOUSLY COMPELLED

(a) Evidence of a statement or other disclosure of privileged information is inadmissible against a holder of the privilege if:

(1) A person authorized to claim the privilege claimed it but nevertheless disclosure erroneously was required to be made; or

(2) The presiding officer did not exclude the privileged information as required by Section 916.

(b) If a person authorized to claim the privilege claimed it, whether in the same or a prior proceeding, but nevertheless disclosure erroneously was required by the presiding officer to be made, neither the failure to refuse to disclose nor the failure to seek review of the order of the presiding officer requiring disclosure indicates consent to the disclosure or constitutes a waiver and, under these circumstances, the disclosure is one made under coercion.

§ 920. NO IMPLIED REPEAL

Nothing in this division shall be construed to repeal by implication any other statute relating to privileges.

Chapter 4: Particular Privileges

Article 1: Privilege of Defendant in Criminal Case

§ 930. PRIVILEGE NOT TO BE CALLED AS A WITNESS AND NOT TO TESTIFY

To the extent that such privilege exists under the Constitution of the United States or the State of California, a defendant in a criminal case has a privilege not to be called as a witness and not to testify.

Article 2: Privilege Against Self-Incrimination

§ 940. PRIVILEGE AGAINST SELF-INCRIMINATION

To the extent that such privilege exists under the Constitution of the United States or the State of California, a person has a privilege to refuse to disclose any matter that may tend to incriminate him.

Article 3: Lawyer-Client Privilege

§ 950. "LAWYER"

As used in this article, "lawyer" means a person authorized, or reasonably believed by the client to be authorized, to practice law in any state or nation.

§ 951. "CLIENT"

As used in this article, "client" means a person who, directly or through an authorized representative, consults a lawyer for the purpose of retaining the lawyer or securing legal service or advice from him in his professional capacity, and includes an incompetent (a) who himself so consults the lawyer or (b) whose guardian or conservator so consults the lawyer in behalf of the incompetent.

§ 952. "CONFIDENTIAL COMMUNICATION BETWEEN CLIENT AND LAWYER"

As used in this article, "confidential communication between client and lawyer" means information transmitted between a client and his or her lawyer in the course of that relationship and in confidence by a means which, so far as the client is aware, discloses the information to no third persons other than those who are present to further the interest of the client in the consultation or those to whom disclosure is reasonably necessary for the transmission of the information or the accomplishment of the purpose for which the lawyer is consulted, and includes a legal opinion formed and the advice given by the lawyer in the course of that relationship.

§ 953. "HOLDER OF THE PRIVILEGE"

As used in this article, "holder of the privilege" means:

(a) The client, if the client has no guardian or conservator.

(b)

(1) A guardian or conservator of the client, if the client has a guardian or conservator, except as provided in paragraph (2).

(2) If the guardian or conservator has an actual or apparent conflict of interest with the client, then the guardian or conservator does not hold the privilege.

(c) The personal representative of the client if the client is dead, including a personal representative appointed pursuant to Section 12252 of the Probate Code.

(d) A successor, assign, trustee in dissolution, or any similar representative of a firm, association, organization, partnership, business trust, corporation, or public entity that is no longer in existence.

§ 954. LAWYER-CLIENT PRIVILEGE

Subject to Section 912 and except as otherwise provided in this article, the client, whether or not a party, has a privilege to refuse to disclose, and to prevent another from disclosing, a confidential communication between client and lawyer if the privilege is claimed by:

(a) The holder of the privilege;

(b) A person who is authorized to claim the privilege by the holder of the privilege; or

(c) The person who was the lawyer at the time of the confidential communication, but such person may not claim the privilege if there is no holder of the privilege in existence or if he is otherwise instructed by a person authorized to permit disclosure.

The relationship of attorney and client shall exist between a law corporation as defined in Article 10 (commencing with Section 6160) of Chapter 4 of Division 3 of the Business and Professions Code and the persons to whom it renders professional services, as well as between such persons and members of the State Bar employed by such corporation to render services to such persons. The word "persons" as used in this subdivision includes partnerships, corporations, limited liability companies, associations and other groups and entities.

§ 955. WHEN LAWYER REQUIRED TO CLAIM PRIVILEGE

The lawyer who received or made a communication subject to the privilege under this article shall claim the privilege whenever he is present when the communication is sought to be disclosed and is authorized to claim the privilege under subdivision (c) of Section 954.

§ 956. CRIME OR FRAUD

(a) There is no privilege under this article if the services of the lawyer were sought or obtained to enable or aid anyone to commit or plan to commit a crime or a fraud.

(b) This exception to the privilege granted by this article shall not apply to legal services rendered in compliance with state and local laws on medicinal cannabis or adult-use cannabis, and confidential communications provided for the purpose of rendering those services are confidential communications between client and lawyer, as defined in Section 952, provided the lawyer also advises the client on conflicts with respect to federal law.

§ 956.5. DISCLOSURE NECESSARY TO PREVENT CRIMINAL ACT LIKELY TO RESULT IN DEATH OR BODILY HARM

There is no privilege under this article if the lawyer reasonably believes that disclosure of any confidential communication relating to representation of a client is necessary to prevent a criminal act that the lawyer reasonably believes is likely to result in the death of, or substantial bodily harm to, an individual.

§ 957. PARTIES CLAIMING THROUGH DECEASED CLIENT

There is no privilege under this article as to a communication relevant to an issue between parties all of whom claim through a deceased client, regardless of whether the claims are by testate or intestate succession, nonprobate transfer, or inter vivos transaction.

§ 958. BREACH OF DUTY ARISING OUT OF LAWYER-CLIENT RELATIONSHIP

There is no privilege under this article as to a communication relevant to an issue of breach, by the lawyer or by the client, of a duty arising out of the lawyer-client relationship.

§ 959. LAWYER AS ATTESTING WITNESS

There is no privilege under this article as to a communication relevant to an issue concerning the intention or competence of a client executing an attested document of which the lawyer is an attesting witness, or concerning the execution or attestation of such a document.

§ 960. INTENTION OF DECEASED CLIENT CONCERNING WRITING AFFECTING PROPERTY INTEREST

There is no privilege under this article as to a communication relevant to an issue concerning the intention of a client, now deceased, with respect to a deed of conveyance, will, or other writing, executed by the client, purporting to affect an interest in property.

§ 961. VALIDITY OF WRITING AFFECTING PROPERTY INTEREST

There is no privilege under this article as to a communication relevant to an issue concerning the validity of a deed of conveyance, will, or other writing, executed by a client, now deceased, purporting to affect an interest in property.

§ 962. JOINT CLIENTS

Where two or more clients have retained or consulted a lawyer upon a matter of common interest, none of them, nor the successor in interest of any of them, may claim a privilege under this article as to a communication made in the course of that relationship when such communication is offered in a civil proceeding between one of such clients (or his successor in interest) and another of such clients (or his successor in interest).

Article 3.5: Lawyer Referral Service-Client Privilege

§ 965. DEFINITIONS

For purposes of this article, the following terms have the following meanings:

(a) "Client" means a person who, directly or through an authorized representative, consults a lawyer referral service for the purpose of retaining, or securing legal services or advice from, a lawyer in his or her professional capacity, and includes an incompetent who consults the lawyer referral service himself or herself or whose guardian or conservator consults the lawyer referral service on his or her behalf.

(b) "Confidential communication between client and lawyer referral service" means information transmitted between a client and a lawyer referral service in the course of that relationship and in confidence by a means that, so far as the client is aware, does not disclose the information to third persons other than those who are present to further the interests of the client in the consultation or those to whom disclosure is reasonably necessary for the transmission of the information or the accomplishment of the purpose for which the lawyer referral service is consulted.

(c) "Holder of the privilege" means any of the following:

(1) The client, if the client has no guardian or conservator.

(2) A guardian or conservator of the client, if the client has a guardian or conservator.

(3) The personal representative of the client if the client is dead, including a personal representative appointed pursuant to Section 12252 of the Probate Code.

(4) A successor, assign, trustee in dissolution, or any similar representative of a firm, association, organization, partnership, business trust, corporation, or public entity that is no longer in existence.

(d) "Lawyer referral service" means a lawyer referral service certified under, and operating in compliance with, Section 6155 of the Business and Professions Code or an enterprise reasonably believed by the client to be a lawyer referral service certified under, and operating in compliance with, Section 6155 of the Business and Professions Code.

§ 966. PRIVILEGE FOR CONFIDENTIAL COMMUNICATION BETWEEN CLIENT AND LAWYER REFERRAL SERVICE; WHO MAY CLAIM PRIVILEGE

(a) Subject to Section 912 and except as otherwise provided in this article, the client, whether or not a party, has a privilege to refuse to disclose, and to prevent another from disclosing, a confidential communication between client and lawyer referral service if the privilege is claimed by any of the following:

(1) The holder of the privilege.

(2) A person who is authorized to claim the privilege by the holder of the privilege.

(3) The lawyer referral service or a staff person thereof, but the lawyer referral service or a staff person thereof may not claim the privilege if there is no holder of the privilege in existence or if the lawyer referral service or a staff person thereof is otherwise instructed by a person authorized to permit disclosure.

(b) The relationship of lawyer referral service and client shall exist between a lawyer referral service, as defined in Section 965, and the persons to whom it renders services, as well as between such persons and anyone employed by the lawyer referral service to render services to such persons. The word "persons" as used in this subdivision includes partnerships, corporations, limited liability companies, associations, and other groups and entities.

§ 967. WHEN LAWYER REFERRAL SERVICE MUST CLAIM PRIVILEGE

A lawyer referral service that has received or made a communication subject to the privilege under this article shall claim the privilege if the communication is sought to be disclosed and the client has not consented to the disclosure.

§ 968. CRIME OR FRAUD; DISCLOSURE NECESSARY TO PREVENT CRIMINAL ACT LIKELY TO RESULT IN DEATH OR BODILY HARM

There is no privilege under this article if either of the following applies:

(a) The services of the lawyer referral service were sought or obtained to enable or aid anyone to commit or plan to commit a crime or a fraud.

(b) A staff person of the lawyer referral service who receives a confidential communication in processing a request for legal assistance reasonably believes that disclosure of the confidential communication is necessary to prevent a criminal act that the staff person of the lawyer referral service reasonably believes is likely to result in the death of, or substantial bodily harm to, an individual.

Article 4: Privilege Not to Testify Against Spouse

§ 970. PRIVILEGE NOT TO TESTIFY AGAINST SPOUSE

Except as otherwise provided by statute, a married person has a privilege not to testify against his spouse in any proceeding.

§ 971. PRIVILEGE NOT TO BE CALLED AS A WITNESS AGAINST SPOUSE

Except as otherwise provided by statute, a married person whose spouse is a party to a proceeding has a privilege not to be called as a witness by an adverse party to that proceeding without the prior express consent of the spouse having the privilege under this section unless the party calling the spouse does so in good faith without knowledge of the marital relationship.

§ 972. WHEN PRIVILEGE NOT APPLICABLE

A married person does not have a privilege under this article in:

(a) A proceeding brought by or on behalf of one spouse against the other spouse.

(b) A proceeding to commit or otherwise place his or her spouse or his or her spouse's property, or both, under the control of another because of the spouse's alleged mental or physical condition.

(c) A proceeding brought by or on behalf of a spouse to establish his or her competence.

(d) A proceeding under the Juvenile Court Law, Chapter 2 (commencing with Section 200) of Part 1 of Division 2 of the Welfare and Institutions Code.

(e) A criminal proceeding in which one spouse is charged with:

(1) A crime against the person or property of the other spouse or of a child, parent, relative, or cohabitant of either, whether committed before or during marriage.

(2) A crime against the person or property of a third person committed in the course of committing a crime against the person or property of the other spouse, whether committed before or during marriage.

(3) Bigamy.

(4) A crime defined by Section 270 or 270a of the Penal Code.

(f) A proceeding resulting from a criminal act which occurred prior to legal marriage of the spouses to each other regarding knowledge acquired prior to that marriage if prior to the legal marriage the witness spouse was aware that his or her spouse had been arrested for or had been formally charged with the crime or crimes about which the spouse is called to testify.

(g) A proceeding brought against the spouse by a former spouse so long as the property and debts of the marriage have not been adjudicated, or in order to establish, modify, or enforce a child, family or spousal support obligation arising from the marriage to the former spouse; in a proceeding brought against a spouse by the other parent in order to establish, modify, or enforce a child support obligation for a child of a nonmarital relationship of the spouse; or in a proceeding brought against a spouse by the guardian of a child of that spouse in order to establish, modify, or enforce a child support obligation of the spouse. The married person does not have a privilege under this subdivision to refuse to provide information relating to the issues of income, expenses, assets, debts, and employment of either spouse, but may assert the privilege s otherwise provided in this article if other information is requested by the former spouse, guardian, or other parent of the child.

Any person demanding the otherwise privileged information made available by this subdivision, who also has an obligation to support the child for whom an order to establish, modify, or enforce child support is sought, waives his or her marital privilege to the same extent as the spouse as provided in this subdivision.

§ 973. WAIVER OF PRIVILEGE

(a) Unless erroneously compelled to do so, a married person who testifies in a proceeding to which his spouse is a party, or who testifies against his spouse in any proceeding, does not have a privilege under this article in the proceeding in which such testimony is given.

(b) There is no privilege under this article in a civil proceeding brought or defended by a married person for the immediate benefit of his spouse or of himself and his spouse.

Article 5: Privilege for Confidential Marital Communications

§ 980. PRIVILEGE FOR CONFIDENTIAL MARITAL COMMUNICATIONS

Subject to Section 912 and except as otherwise provided in this article, a spouse (or his or her guardian or conservator when he or she has a guardian or conservator), whether or not a party, has a privilege during the marital or domestic partnership relationship and afterwards to refuse to disclose, and to prevent another from disclosing, a communication if he or she claims the privilege and the communication was made in confidence between him or her and the other spouse while they were spouses.

§ 981. CRIME OR FRAUD

There is no privilege under this article if the communication was made, in whole or in part, to enable or aid anyone to commit or plan to commit a crime or a fraud.

§ 982. COMMITMENT OR SIMILAR PROCEEDING

There is no privilege under this article in a proceeding to commit either spouse or otherwise place him or his property, or both, under the control of another because of his alleged mental or physical condition.

§ 983. PROCEEDING TO ESTABLISH COMPETENCE

There is no privilege under this article in a proceeding brought by or on behalf of either spouse to establish his competence.

§ 984. PROCEEDING BETWEEN SPOUSES

There is no privilege under this article in:

(a) A proceeding brought by or on behalf of one spouse against the other spouse.

(b) A proceeding between a surviving spouse and a person who claims through the deceased spouse, regardless of whether such claim is by testate or intestate succession or by inter vivos transaction.

§ 985. CERTAIN CRIMINAL PROCEEDINGS

There is no privilege under this article in a criminal proceeding in which one spouse is charged with:

(a) A crime committed at any time against the person or property of the other spouse or of a child of either.

(b) A crime committed at any time against the person or property of a third person committed in the course of committing a crime against the person or property of the other spouse.

(c) Bigamy.

(d) A crime defined by Section 270 or 270a of the Penal Code.

§ 986. JUVENILE COURT PROCEEDINGS

There is no privilege under this article in a proceeding under the Juvenile Court Law, Chapter 2 (commencing with Section 200) of Part 1 of Division 2 of the Welfare and Institutions Code.

§ 987. COMMUNICATION OFFERED BY SPOUSE WHO IS CRIMINAL DEFENDANT

There is no privilege under this article in a criminal proceeding in which the communication is offered in evidence by a defendant who is one of the spouses between whom the communication was made.

Article 6: Physician-Patient Privilege

§ 990. "PHYSICIAN"

As used in this article, "physician" means a person authorized, or reasonably believed by the patient to be authorized, to practice medicine in any state or nation.

§ 991. "PATIENT"

As used in this article, "patient" means a person who consults a physician or submits to an examination by a physician for the purpose of securing a diagnosis or preventive, palliative, or curative treatment of his physical or mental or emotional condition.

§ 992. "CONFIDENTIAL COMMUNICATION BETWEEN PATIENT AND PHYSICIAN"

As used in this article, "confidential communication between patient and physician" means information, including information obtained by an examination of the patient, transmitted between a patient and his physician in the course of that relationship and in confidence by a means which, so far as the patient is aware, discloses the information to no third persons other than those who are present to further the interest of the patient in the consultation or those to whom disclosure is reasonably necessary for the transmission of the information or the accomplishment of the purpose for which the physician is consulted, and includes a diagnosis made and the advice given by the physician in the course of that relationship.

§ 993. "HOLDER OF THE PRIVILEGE"

As used in this article, "holder of the privilege" means:

(a) The patient when he has no guardian or conservator.

(b) A guardian or conservator of the patient when the patient has a guardian or conservator.

(c) The personal representative of the patient if the patient is dead.

§ 994. PHYSICIAN-PATIENT PRIVILEGE

Subject to Section 912 and except as otherwise provided in this article, the patient, whether or not a party, has a privilege to refuse to disclose, and to prevent another from disclosing, a confidential communication between patient and physician if the privilege is claimed by:

(a) The holder of the privilege;

(b) A person who is authorized to claim the privilege by the holder of the privilege; or

(c) The person who was the physician at the time of the confidential communication, but such person may not claim the privilege if there is no holder of the privilege in existence or if he or she is otherwise instructed by a person authorized to permit disclosure.

The relationship of a physician and patient shall exist between a medical or podiatry corporation as defined in the Medical Practice Act and the patient to whom it renders professional services, as well as between such patients and licensed physicians and surgeons employed by such corporation to render services to such patients. The word "persons" as used in this subdivision includes partnerships, corporations, limited liability companies, associations, and other groups and entities.

§ 995. WHEN PHYSICIAN REQUIRED TO CLAIM PRIVILEGE

The physician who received or made a communication subject to the privilege under this article shall claim the privilege whenever he is present when the communication is sought to be disclosed and is authorized to claim the privilege under subdivision (c) of Section 994.

§ 996. PATIENT-LITIGANT EXCEPTION

There is no privilege under this article as to a communication relevant to an issue concerning the condition of the patient if such issue has been tendered by:

(a) The patient;

(b) Any party claiming through or under the patient;

(c) Any party claiming as a beneficiary of the patient through a contract to which the patient is or was a party; or

(d) The plaintiff in an action brought under Section 376 or 377 of the Code of Civil Procedure for damages for the injury or death of the patient.

§ 997. CRIME OR TORT

There is no privilege under this article if the services of the physician were sought or obtained to enable or aid anyone to commit or plan to commit a crime or a tort or to escape detection or apprehension after the commission of a crime or a tort.

§ 998. CRIMINAL PROCEEDING

There is no privilege under this article in a criminal proceeding.

§ 999. PROCEEDING TO RECOVER DAMAGES ON ACCOUNT OF CONDUCT OF PATIENT

There is no privilege under this article as to a communication relevant to an issue concerning the condition of the patient in a proceeding to recover damages on account of the conduct of the patient if good cause for disclosure of the communication is shown.

§ 1000. PARTIES CLAIMING THROUGH DECEASED PATIENT

There is no privilege under this article as to a communication relevant to an issue between parties all of whom claim through a deceased patient, regardless of whether the claims are by testate or intestate succession or by inter vivos transaction.

§ 1001. BREACH OF DUTY ARISING OUT OF PHYSICIAN-PATIENT RELATIONSHIP

There is no privilege under this article as to a communication relevant to an issue of breach, by the physician or by the patient, of a duty arising out of the physician-patient relationship.

§ 1002. INTENTION OF DECEASED PATIENT CONCERNING WRITING AFFECTING PROPERTY INTEREST

There is no privilege under this article as to a communication relevant to an issue concerning the intention of a patient, now deceased, with respect to a deed of conveyance, will, or other writing, executed by the patient, purporting to affect an interest in property.

§ 1003. VALIDITY OF WRITING AFFECTING PROPERTY INTEREST

There is no privilege under this article as to a communication relevant to an issue concerning the validity of a deed of conveyance, will, or other writing, executed by a patient, now deceased, purporting to affect an interest in property.

§ 1004. COMMITMENT OR SIMILAR PROCEEDING

There is no privilege under this article in a proceeding to commit the patient or otherwise place him or his property, or both, under the control of another because of his alleged mental or physical condition.

§ 1005. PROCEEDING TO ESTABLISH COMPETENCE

There is no privilege under this article in a proceeding brought by or on behalf of the patient to establish his competence.

§ 1006. REQUIRED REPORT

There is no privilege under this article as to information that the physician or the patient is required to report to a public employee, or as to information required to be recorded in a public office, if such report or record is open to public inspection.

§ 1007. PROCEEDING TO TERMINATE RIGHT, LICENSE, OR PRIVILEGE

There is no privilege under this article in a proceeding brought by a public entity to determine whether a right, authority, license, or privilege (including the right or privilege to be employed by the public entity or to hold a public office) should be revoked, suspended, terminated, limited, or conditioned.

Article 7: Psychotherapist-Patient Privilege

§ 1010. "PSYCHOTHERAPIST"

As used in this article, "psychotherapist" means a person who is, or is reasonably believed by the patient to be:

(a) A person authorized to practice medicine in any state or nation who devotes, or is reasonably believed by the patient to devote, a substantial portion of their time to the practice of psychiatry.

(b) A person licensed as a psychologist under Chapter 6.6 (commencing with Section 2900) of Division 2 of the Business and Professions Code.

(c) A person licensed as a clinical social worker under Chapter 14 (commencing with Section 4991) of Division 2 of the Business and Professions Code, when they are engaged in applied psychotherapy of a nonmedical nature.

(d) A person who is serving as a school psychologist and holds a credential authorizing that service issued by the state.

(e) A person licensed as a marriage and family therapist under Chapter 13 (commencing with Section 4980) of Division 2 of the Business and Professions Code.

(f) A person registered as a registered psychological associate who is under the supervision of a licensed psychologist as required by Section 2913 of the Business and Professions Code, or a person registered as an associate marriage and family therapist who is under the supervision of a licensed marriage and family therapist, a licensed clinical social worker, a licensed professional clinical counselor, a licensed psychologist, or a licensed physician and surgeon certified in psychiatry, as specified in Section 4980.44 of the Business and Professions Code.

(g) A person registered as an associate clinical social worker who is under supervision as specified in Section 4996.23 of the Business and Professions Code.

(h) A psychological intern as defined in Section 2911 of the Business and Professions Code who is under the primary supervision of a licensed psychologist.

(i) A trainee, as defined in subdivision (c) of Section 4980.03 of the Business and Professions Code, who is fulfilling their supervised practicum required by subparagraph (B) of paragraph (1) of subdivision (d) of Section 4980.36 of, or subdivision (c) of Section 4980.37 of, the Business and Professions Code and is supervised by a licensed psychologist, a board certified psychiatrist, a licensed clinical social worker, a licensed marriage and family therapist, or a licensed professional clinical counselor.

(j) A person licensed as a registered nurse pursuant to Chapter 6 (commencing with Section 2700) of Division 2 of the Business and Professions Code, who possesses a master's degree in psychiatric-mental health nursing and is listed as a psychiatric-mental health nurse by the Board of Registered Nursing.

(k) An advanced practice registered nurse who is certified as a clinical nurse specialist pursuant to Article 9 (commencing with Section 2838) of Chapter 6 of Division 2 of the Business and Professions Code and who participates in expert clinical practice in the specialty of psychiatric-mental health nursing.

(l) A person rendering mental health treatment or counseling services as authorized pursuant to Section 6924 of the Family Code.

(m) A person licensed as a professional clinical counselor under Chapter 16 (commencing with Section 4999.10) of Division 2 of the Business and Professions Code.

(n) A person registered as an associate professional clinical counselor who is under the supervision of a licensed professional clinical counselor, a licensed marriage and family therapist, a licensed clinical social worker, a licensed psychologist, or a licensed physician and surgeon certified in psychiatry, as specified in Sections 4999.42 to 4999.48, inclusive, of the Business and Professions Code.

(o) A clinical counselor trainee, as defined in subdivision (g) of Section 4999.12 of the Business and Professions Code, who is fulfilling their supervised practicum required by paragraph (3) of subdivision (c) of Section 4999.32 of, or paragraph (3) of subdivision (c) of Section 4999.33 of, the Business and Professions Code, and is supervised by a licensed psychologist, a board-certified psychiatrist, a licensed clinical social worker, a licensed marriage and family therapist, or a licensed professional clinical counselor.

§ 1010.5. COMMUNICATION BETWEEN PATIENT AND EDUCATIONAL PSYCHOLOGIST

A communication between a patient and an educational psychologist, licensed under Chapter 13.5 (commencing with Section 4989.10) of Division 2 of the Business and Professions Code, shall be privileged to the same extent, and subject to the same limitations, as a communication between a patient and a psychotherapist described in subdivisions (c), (d), and (e) of Section 1010.

§ 1011. "PATIENT"

As used in this article, "patient" means a person who consults a psychotherapist or submits to an examination by a psychotherapist for the purpose of securing a diagnosis or preventive, palliative, or curative treatment of his mental or emotional condition or who submits to an examination of his mental or emotional condition for the purpose of scientific research on mental or emotional problems.

§ 1012. "CONFIDENTIAL COMMUNICATION BETWEEN PATIENT AND PSYCHOTHERAPIST"

As used in this article, "confidential communication between patient and psychotherapist" means information, including information obtained by an examination of the patient, transmitted between a patient and his psychotherapist in the course of that relationship and in confidence by a means which, so far as the patient is aware, discloses the information to no third persons other than those who are present to further the interest of the patient in the consultation, or those to whom disclosure is reasonably necessary for the transmission of the information or the accomplishment of the purpose for which the psychotherapist is consulted, and includes a diagnosis made and the advice given by the psychotherapist in the course of that relationship.

§ 1013. "HOLDER OF THE PRIVILEGE"

As used in this article, "holder of the privilege" means:

(a) The patient when he has no guardian or conservator.

(b) A guardian or conservator of the patient when the patient has a guardian or conservator.

(c) The personal representative of the patient if the patient is dead.

§ 1014. PSYCHOTHERAPIST-PATIENT PRIVILEGE

Subject to Section 912 and except as otherwise provided in this article, the patient, whether or not a party, has a privilege to refuse to disclose, and to prevent another from disclosing, a confidential communication between patient and psychotherapist if the privilege is claimed by:

(a) The holder of the privilege.

(b) A person who is authorized to claim the privilege by the holder of the privilege.

(c) The person who was the psychotherapist at the time of the confidential communication, but the person may not claim the privilege if there is no holder of the privilege in existence or if he or she is otherwise instructed by a person authorized to permit disclosure.

The relationship of a psychotherapist and patient shall exist between a psychological corporation as defined in Article 9 (commencing with

Section 2995) of Chapter 6.6 of Division 2 of the Business and Professions Code, a marriage and family therapist corporation as defined in Article 6 (commencing with Section 4987.5) of Chapter 13 of Division 2 of the Business and Professions Code, a licensed clinical social workers corporation as defined in Article 5 (commencing with Section 4998) of Chapter 14 of Division 2 of the Business and Professions Code, or a professional clinical counselor corporation as defined in Article 7 (commencing with Section 4999.123) of Chapter 16 of Division 2 of the Business and Professions Code, and the patient to whom it renders professional services, as well as between those patients and psychotherapists employed by those corporations to render services to those patients. The word "persons" as used in this subdivision includes partnerships, corporations, limited liability companies, associations, and other groups and entities.

§ 1015. WHEN PSYCHOTHERAPIST REQUIRED TO CLAIM PRIVILEGE

The psychotherapist who received or made a communication subject to the privilege under this article shall claim the privilege whenever he is present when the communication is sought to be disclosed and is authorized to claim the privilege under subdivision (c) of Section 1014.

§ 1016. PATIENT-LITIGANT EXCEPTION

There is no privilege under this article as to a communication relevant to an issue concerning the mental or emotional condition of the patient if such issue has been tendered by:

(a) The patient;

(b) Any party claiming through or under the patient;

(c) Any party claiming as a beneficiary of the patient through a contract to which the patient is or was a party; or

(d) The plaintiff in an action brought under Section 376 or 377 of the Code of Civil Procedure for damages for the injury or death of the patient.

§ 1017. EXCEPTION WHERE PSYCHOTHERAPIST IS APPOINTED BY COURT OR BOARD OF PRISON TERMS

(a) There is no privilege under this article if the psychotherapist is appointed by order of a court to examine the patient, but this exception does not apply where the psychotherapist is appointed by order of the court upon the request of the lawyer for the defendant in a criminal proceeding in order to provide the lawyer with information needed so that he or she may advise the defendant whether to enter or withdraw a plea based on insanity or to present a defense based on his or her mental or emotional condition.

(b) There is no privilege under this article if the psychotherapist is appointed by the Board of Prison Terms to examine a patient pursuant to the provisions of Article 4 (commencing with Section 2960) of Chapter 7 of Title 1 of Part 3 of the Penal Code.

§ 1018. CRIME OR TORT

There is no privilege under this article if the services of the psychotherapist were sought or obtained to enable or aid anyone to commit or plan to commit a crime or a tort or to escape detention or apprehension after the commission of a crime or a tort.

§ 1019. PARTIES CLAIMING THROUGH DECEASED PATIENT

There is no privilege under this article as to a communication relevant to an issue between parties all of whom claim through a deceased patient, regardless of whether the claims are by testate or intestate succession or by inter vivos transaction.

§ 1020. BREACH OF DUTY ARISING OUT OF PSYCHOTHERAPIST-PATIENT RELATIONSHIP

There is no privilege under this article as to a communication relevant to an issue of breach, by the psychotherapist or by the patient, of a duty arising out of the psychotherapist-patient relationship.

§ 1021. INTENTION OF DECEASED PATIENT CONCERNING WRITING AFFECTING PROPERTY INTEREST

There is no privilege under this article as to a communication relevant to an issue concerning the intention of a patient, now deceased, with respect to a deed of conveyance, will, or other writing, executed by the patient, purporting to affect an interest in property.

§ 1022. VALIDITY OF WRITING AFFECTING PROPERTY INTEREST

There is no privilege under this article as to a communication relevant to an issue concerning the validity of a deed of conveyance, will, or other writing, executed by a patient, now deceased, purporting to affect an interest in property.

§ 1023. PROCEEDING TO DETERMINE SANITY OF CRIMINAL DEFENDANT

There is no privilege under this article in a proceeding under Chapter 6 (commencing with Section 1367) of Title 10 of Part 2 of the Penal Code initiated at the request of the defendant in a criminal action to determine his sanity.

§ 1024. PATIENT DANGEROUS TO SELF OR OTHERS

There is no privilege under this article if the psychotherapist has reasonable cause to believe that the patient is in such mental or emotional condition as to be dangerous to himself or to the person or property of another and that disclosure of the communication is necessary to prevent the threatened danger.

§ 1025. PROCEEDING TO ESTABLISH COMPETENCE

There is no privilege under this article in a proceeding brought by or on behalf of the patient to establish his competence.

§ 1026. REQUIRED REPORT

There is no privilege under this article as to information that the psychotherapist or the patient is required to report to a public employee or as to information required to be recorded in a public office, if such report or record is open to public inspection.

§ 1027. EXCEPTION; PATIENT UNDER 16 WHO IS VICTIM OF CRIME

There is no privilege under this article if all of the following circumstances exist:

(a) The patient is a child under the age of 16.

(b) The psychotherapist has reasonable cause to believe that the patient has been the victim of a crime and that disclosure of the communication is in the best interest of the child.

Article 8: Clergy Penitent Privileges

§ 1030. MEMBER OF THE CLERGY

As used in this article, a "member of the clergy" means a priest, minister, religious practitioner, or similar functionary of a church or of a religious denomination or religious organization.

§ 1031. "PENITENT"

As used in this article, "penitent" means a person who has made a penitential communication to a member of the clergy.

§ 1032. "PENITENTIAL COMMUNICATION"

As used in this article, "penitential communication" means a communication made in confidence, in the presence of no third person so far as the penitent is aware, to a member of the clergy who, in the course of the discipline or practice of the clergy member's church, denomination, or organization, is authorized or accustomed to hear those communications and, under the discipline or tenets of his or her church, denomination, or organization, has a duty to keep those communications secret.

§ 1033. PRIVILEGE OF PENITENT

Subject to Section 912, a penitent, whether or not a party, has a privilege to refuse to disclose, and to prevent another from disclosing, a penitential communication if he or she claims the privilege.

§ 1034. PRIVILEGE OF CLERGY MEMBER

Subject to Section 912, a member of the clergy, whether or not a party, has a privilege to refuse to disclose a penitential communication if he or she claims the privilege.

Article 8.5: Sexual Assault Counselor-Victim Privilege

§ 1035. "VICTIM"

As used in this article, "victim" means a person who consults a sexual assault counselor for the purpose of securing advice or assistance concerning a mental, physical, or emotional condition caused by a sexual assault.

§ 1035.2. "SEXUAL ASSAULT COUNSELOR"

As used in this article, "sexual assault counselor" means any of the following:

(a) A person who is engaged in any office, hospital, institution, or center commonly known as a rape crisis center, whose primary purpose is the rendering of advice or assistance to victims of sexual assault and who has received a certificate evidencing completion of a training program in the counseling of sexual assault victims issued by a counseling center that meets the criteria for the award of a grant established pursuant to Section 13837 of the Penal Code and who meets one of the following requirements:

(1) Is a psychotherapist as defined in Section 1010; has a master's degree in counseling or a related field; or has one year of counseling experience, at least six months of which is in rape crisis counseling.

(2) Has 40 hours of training as described below and is supervised by an individual who qualifies as a counselor under paragraph (1). The training, supervised by a person qualified under paragraph (1), shall include, but not be limited to, the following areas:

(A) Law.
(B) Medicine.
(C) Societal attitudes.
(D) Crisis intervention and counseling techniques.
(E) Role playing.
(F) Referral services.
(G) Sexuality.

(b) A person who is engaged in a program on the campus of a public or private institution of higher education, whose primary purpose is the rendering of advice or assistance to victims of sexual assault and who has received a certificate evidencing completion of a training program in the counseling of sexual assault victims issued by a counseling center that meets the criteria for the award of a grant established pursuant to Section 13837 of the Penal Code and who meets one of the following requirements:

(1) Is a psychotherapist as defined in Section 1010; has a master's degree in counseling or a related field; or has one year of counseling experience, at least six months of which is in rape crisis counseling.

(2) Has 40 hours of training as described below and is supervised by an individual who qualifies as a counselor under paragraph (1). The training, supervised by a person qualified under paragraph (1), shall include, but not be limited to, the following areas:

(A) Law.
(B) Medicine.
(C) Societal attitudes.
(D) Crisis intervention and counseling techniques.
(E) Role playing.
(F) Referral services.
(G) Sexuality.

(c) A person who is employed by any organization providing the programs specified in Section 13835.2 of the Penal Code, whether financially compensated or not, for the purpose of counseling and assisting sexual assault victims, and who meets one of the following requirements:

(1) Is a psychotherapist as defined in Section 1010; has a master's degree in counseling or a related field; or has one year of counseling experience, at least six months of which is in rape assault counseling.

(2) Has the minimum training for sexual assault counseling required by guidelines established by the employing agency pursuant to subdivision (c) of Section 13835.10 of the Penal Code, and is supervised by an individual who qualifies as a counselor under paragraph (1). The training, supervised by a person qualified under paragraph (1), shall include, but not be limited to, the following areas:

(A) Law.
(B) Victimology.
(C) Counseling.
(D) Client and system advocacy.
(E) Referral services.

§ 1035.4. "CONFIDENTIAL COMMUNICATION BETWEEN THE SEXUAL ASSAULT COUNSELOR AND THE VICTIM"

As used in this article, "confidential communication between the sexual assault counselor and the victim" means information transmitted between the victim and the sexual assault counselor in the course of their relationship and in confidence by a means which, so far as the victim is aware, discloses the information to no third persons other than those who are present to further the interests of the victim in the consultation or those to whom disclosures are reasonably necessary for the transmission of the information or an accomplishment of the purposes for which the sexual assault counselor is consulted. The term includes all information regarding the facts and circumstances involving the alleged sexual assault and also includes all information regarding the victim's prior or subsequent sexual conduct, and opinions regarding the victim's sexual conduct or reputation in sexual matters.

The court may compel disclosure of information received by the sexual assault counselor which constitutes relevant evidence of the facts and circumstances involving an alleged sexual assault about which the victim is complaining and which is the subject of a criminal proceeding if the court determines that the probative value outweighs the effect on the victim, the treatment relationship, and the treatment services if disclosure is compelled. The court may also compel disclosure in proceedings related to child abuse if the court determines the probative value outweighs the effect on the victim, the treatment relationship, and the treatment services if disclosure is compelled.

When a court is ruling on a claim of privilege under this article, the court may require the person from whom disclosure is sought or the person authorized to claim the privilege, or both, to disclose the information in chambers out of the presence and hearing of all persons except the person authorized to claim the privilege and such other persons as the person authorized to claim the privilege is willing to have present. If the judge determines that the information is privileged and must not be disclosed, neither he or she nor any other person may ever disclose, without the consent of a person authorized to permit disclosure, what was disclosed in the course of the proceedings in chambers.

If the court determines certain information shall be disclosed, the court shall so order and inform the defendant. If the court finds there is a reasonable likelihood that particular information is subject to disclosure pursuant to the balancing test provided in this section, the following procedure shall be followed:

(1) The court shall inform the defendant of the nature of the information which may be subject to disclosure.

(2) The court shall order a hearing out of the presence of the jury, if any, and at the hearing allow the questioning of the sexual assault counselor regarding the information which the court has determined may be subject to disclosure.

(3) At the conclusion of the hearing, the court shall rule which items of information, if any, shall be disclosed. The court may make an order stating what evidence may be introduced by the defendant and the nature of questions to be permitted. The defendant may then offer evidence pursuant to the order of the court. Admission of evidence concerning the sexual conduct of the complaining witness is subject to Sections 352, 782, and 1103.

§ 1035.6. "HOLDER OF THE PRIVILEGE"

As used in this article, "holder of the privilege" means:

(a) The victim when such person has no guardian or conservator.

(b) A guardian or conservator of the victim when the victim has a guardian or conservator.

(c) The personal representative of the victim if the victim is dead.

§ 1035.8. VICTIM'S PRIVILEGE

A victim of a sexual assault, whether or not a party, has a privilege to refuse to disclose, and to prevent another from disclosing, a confidential communication between the victim and a sexual assault counselor if the privilege is claimed by any of the following:

(a) The holder of the privilege;

(b) A person who is authorized to claim the privilege by the holder of the privilege; or

(c) The person who was the sexual assault counselor at the time of the confidential communication, but that person may not claim the privilege if there is no holder of the privilege in existence or if he or she is otherwise instructed by a person authorized to permit disclosure.

§ 1036. COUNSELOR'S PRIVILEGE

The sexual assault counselor who received or made a communication subject to the privilege under this article shall claim the privilege if he or she is present when the communication is sought to be disclosed and is authorized to claim the privilege under subdivision (c) of Section 1035.8.

§ 1036.2. "SEXUAL ASSAULT"

As used in this article, "sexual assault" includes all of the following:

(a) Rape, as defined in Section 261 of the Penal Code.

(b) Unlawful sexual intercourse, as defined in Section 261.5 of the Penal Code.

(c) Rape in concert with force and violence, as defined in Section 264.1 of the Penal Code.

(d) Sodomy, as defined in Section 286 of the Penal Code, except a violation of subdivision (e) of that section.

(e) A violation of Section 288 of the Penal Code.

(f) Oral copulation, as defined in Section 287 of, or former Section 288a of, the Penal Code, except a violation of subdivision (e) of those sections.

(g) Sexual penetration, as defined in Section 289 of the Penal Code.

(h) Annoying or molesting a child under 18 years of age, as defined in Section 647a of the Penal Code.

(i) Any attempt to commit any of the acts listed in this section.

Article 8.7: Domestic Violence Counselor-Victim Privilege

§ 1037. "VICTIM"

As used in this article, "victim" means any person who suffers domestic violence, as defined in Section 1037.7.

§ 1037.1. "DOMESTIC VIOLENCE COUNSELOR"; "DOMESTIC VIOLENCE VICTIM SERVICE ORGANIZATION"

(a)

(1) As used in this article, "domestic violence counselor" means a person who is employed by a domestic violence victim service organization, as defined in this article, whether financially compensated or not, for the purpose of rendering advice or assistance to victims of domestic violence and who has at least 40 hours of training as specified in paragraph (2).

(2) The 40 hours of training shall be supervised by an individual who qualifies as a counselor under paragraph (1), and who has at least one year of experience counseling domestic violence victims for the domestic violence victim service organization. The training shall include, but need not be limited to, the following areas: history of domestic violence, civil and criminal law as it relates to domestic violence, the domestic violence victim-counselor privilege and other laws that protect the confidentiality of victim records and information, societal attitudes towards domestic violence, peer counseling techniques, housing, public assistance and other financial resources available to meet the financial needs of domestic violence victims, and referral services available to domestic violence victims.

(3) A domestic violence counselor who has been employed by the domestic violence victim service organization for a period of less than six months shall be supervised by a domestic violence counselor who has at least one year of experience counseling domestic violence victims for the domestic violence victim service organization.

(b) As used in this article, "domestic violence victim service organization" means either of the following:

(1) A nongovernmental organization or entity that provides shelter, programs, or services to victims of domestic violence and their children, including, but not limited to, either of the following:

(A) Domestic violence shelter-based programs, as described in Section 18294 of the Welfare and Institutions Code.

(B) Other programs with the primary mission to provide services to victims of domestic violence whether or not that program exists in an agency that provides additional services.

(2) Programs on the campus of a public or private institution of higher education with the primary mission to provide support or advocacy services to victims of domestic violence.

§ 1037.2. "CONFIDENTIAL COMMUNICATION"; COMPELLING DISCLOSURE

(a) As used in this article, "confidential communication" means any information, including, but not limited to, written or oral communication, transmitted between the victim and the counselor in the course of their relationship and in confidence by a means which, so far as the victim is aware, discloses the information to no third persons other than those who are present to further the interests of the victim in the consultation or those to whom disclosures are reasonably necessary for the transmission of the information or an accomplishment of the purposes for which the domestic violence counselor is consulted. The term includes all information regarding the facts and circumstances involving all incidences of domestic violence, as well as all information about the children of the victim or abuser and the relationship of the victim with the abuser.

(b) The court may compel disclosure of information received by a domestic violence counselor which constitutes relevant evidence of the facts and circumstances involving a crime allegedly perpetrated against the victim or another household member and which is the subject of a criminal proceeding, if the court determines that the probative value of the information outweighs the effect of disclosure of the information on the victim, the counseling relationship, and the counseling services. The court may compel disclosure if the victim is either dead or not the complaining witness in a criminal action against the perpetrator. The court may also compel disclosure in proceedings related to child abuse if the court determines that the probative value of the evidence outweighs the effect of the disclosure on the victim, the counseling relationship, and the counseling services.

(c) When a court rules on a claim of privilege under this article, it may require the person from whom disclosure is sought or the person authorized to claim the privilege, or both, to disclose the information in chambers out of the presence and hearing of all persons except the person authorized to claim the privilege and such other persons as the person authorized to claim the privilege consents to have present. If the judge determines that the information is privileged and shall not be disclosed, neither he nor she nor any other person may disclose, without the consent of a person authorized to permit disclosure, any information disclosed in the course of the proceedings in chambers.

(d) If the court determines that information shall be disclosed, the court shall so order and inform the defendant in the criminal action. If the court finds there is a reasonable likelihood that any information is subject to disclosure pursuant to the balancing test provided in this section, the procedure specified in subdivisions (1), (2), and (3) of Section 1035.4 shall be followed.

§ 1037.3. EFFECT OF ARTICLE ON OBLIGATION TO REPORT CHILD ABUSE

Nothing in this article shall be construed to limit any obligation to report instances of child abuse as required by Section 11166 of the Penal Code.

§ 1037.4. "HOLDER OF THE PRIVILEGE"

As used in this article, "holder of the privilege" means:

(a) The victim when he or she has no guardian or conservator.

(b) A guardian or conservator of the victim when the victim has a guardian or conservator, unless the guardian or conservator is accused of perpetrating domestic violence against the victim.

§ 1037.5. WHO MAY CLAIM PRIVILEGE

A victim of domestic violence, whether or not a party to the action, has a privilege to refuse to disclose, and to prevent another from disclosing, a confidential communication between the victim and a domestic violence counselor in any proceeding specified in Section 901 if the privilege is claimed by any of the following persons:

(a) The holder of the privilege.

(b) A person who is authorized to claim the privilege by the holder of the privilege.

(c) The person who was the domestic violence counselor at the time of the confidential communication. However, that person may not claim the privilege if there is no holder of the privilege in existence or if he or she is otherwise instructed by a person authorized to permit disclosure.

§ 1037.6. WHEN DOMESTIC VIOLENCE COUNSELOR MUST CLAIM PRIVILEGE

The domestic violence counselor who received or made a communication subject to the privilege granted by this article shall claim the privilege whenever he or she is present when the communication is sought to be disclosed and he or she is authorized to claim the privilege under subdivision (c) of Section 1037.5.

§ 1037.7. "DOMESTIC VIOLENCE"

As used in this article, "domestic violence" means "domestic violence" as defined in Section 6211 of the Family Code.

§ 1037.8. INFORMING VICTIM OF LIMITATIONS ON CONFIDENTIALITY OF COMMUNICATIONS

A domestic violence counselor shall inform a domestic violence victim of any applicable limitations on confidentiality of communications between the victim and the domestic violence counselor. This information may be given orally.

Article 8.8: Human Trafficking Caseworker-Victim Privilege

§ 1038. RIGHT TO PREVENT DISCLOSURE OF CONFIDENTIAL COMMUNICATION BETWEEN VICTIM AND CASEWORKER; WHO MAY CLAIM PRIVILEGE; NOTICE TO VICTIM

(a) A trafficking victim, whether or not a party to the action, has a privilege to refuse to disclose, and to prevent another from disclosing, a confidential communication, whether made orally, in writing, or otherwise conveyed, between the victim and a human trafficking caseworker if the privilege is claimed by any of the following persons:

(1) The holder of the privilege.

(2) A person who is authorized to claim the privilege by the holder of the privilege.

(3) The person who was the human trafficking caseworker at the time of the confidential communication or is presently the human trafficking caseworker for the victim. However, that person may not claim the privilege if there is no holder of the privilege in existence or if the person is otherwise instructed by the court or by another person authorized to permit disclosure.

(b) The human trafficking caseworker shall claim the privilege whenever the caseworker is present when the communication is sought to be disclosed and the caseworker is authorized to claim the privilege under this section.

(c) A human trafficking caseworker shall inform a trafficking victim of any applicable limitations on confidentiality of communications between the victim and the caseworker. This information may be given orally.

§ 1038.1. WHEN COURT MAY COMPEL DISCLOSURE; RULING ON CLAIM OF PRIVILEGE

(a) The court may compel disclosure of information received by a human trafficking caseworker that constitutes relevant evidence of the facts and circumstances involving a crime allegedly perpetrated against the victim and that is the subject of a criminal proceeding, if the court determines that the probative value of the information outweighs the effect of disclosure of the information on the victim, the counseling relationship, and the counseling services.

(b) When a court rules on a claim of privilege under this article, it may require the person from whom disclosure is sought or the person authorized to claim the privilege, or both, to disclose the information in chambers out of the presence and hearing of all persons except the person authorized to claim the privilege and those other persons that the person authorized to claim the privilege consents to have present.

(c) If the judge determines that the information is privileged and shall not be disclosed, no person shall disclose, without the consent of a person authorized to permit disclosure, any information disclosed in the course of the proceedings in chambers. If the court determines that information shall be disclosed, the court shall so order and inform the defendant in the criminal action. If the court finds there is a reasonable likelihood that any information is subject to disclosure pursuant to the balancing test provided in this section, the procedure specified in paragraphs (1), (2), and (3) of Section 1035.4 shall be followed.

§ 1038.2. DEFINITIONS

As used in this article, the following terms have the following meanings:

(a) "Confidential communication" means all information, including, but not limited to, written and oral communication, transmitted between the victim and the human trafficking caseworker in the course of their relationship and in confidence by a means which, so far as the victim is aware, discloses the information to no third persons other than those who are present to further the interests of the victim in the consultation or those to whom disclosures are reasonably necessary for the transmission of the information or an accomplishment of the purposes for which the human trafficking caseworker is consulted and made with the victim's knowledge and consent. "Confidential communication" includes all information regarding the facts and circumstances relating to all incidences of human trafficking, as well as all information about the children of the victim and the relationship of the victim to the human trafficker.

(b) "Holder of the privilege" means:

(1) The victim if the victim has no guardian or conservator.

(2) A guardian or conservator of the victim if the victim has a guardian or conservator.

(3) The personal representative of the victim if the victim is deceased.

(c) "Human trafficking caseworker" means a person working for a human trafficking victim service organization, whether financially compensated or not, for the purpose of rendering advice or assistance to victims of human trafficking, who meets the requirements of paragraph (1) or (2) and who also meets the requirements of paragraph (3), if applicable:

(1) Has an advanced degree or license, such as a master's degree in counseling, social work, or a related field and at least one year of experience in a caseworker role working directly with victims of human trafficking.

(2) Has at least 40 hours of training as specified in this paragraph and is supervised by an individual who qualifies as a human trafficking caseworker under paragraph (1). The training, supervised by a person qualified under paragraph (1), shall include, but need not be limited to, the following areas:

(A) History of human trafficking.

(B) Civil and criminal law relating to human trafficking.

(C) Systems of oppression.

(D) Peer counseling techniques.

(E) Resources available to victims of human trafficking.

(F) Crisis intervention and counseling techniques.

(G) Role playing.

(H) Intersections of human trafficking and other crimes.

(I) Client and system advocacy.

(J) Referral services.

(K) Connecting to local, regional, and national human trafficking coalitions.

(L) Explaining privileged communications.

(3) If the caseworker has been employed by a human trafficking service organization for a period of less than six months, that caseworker is supervised by another human trafficking caseworker who has at least one year of experience working with human trafficking victims.

(d) "Human trafficking victim service organization" means a nongovernmental organization or entity that provides shelter, program, or other support services to victims of human trafficking and their children and that does all of the following:

(1) Employs staff that meet the requirements of a human trafficking caseworker as set forth in this section.

(2) Operates a telephone hotline, advertised to the public, for survivor crisis calls.

(3) Offers psychological support and peer counseling provided in accordance with this section.

(4) Makes staff available during normal business hours to assist victims of human trafficking who need shelter, programs, or other support services.

(e) "Victim" means a person who consults a human trafficking caseworker for the purpose of securing advice or assistance concerning a mental, physical, emotional, or other condition related to their experience as a victim of human trafficking.

§ 1038.3. NO LIMITATION ON OBLIGATION TO REPORT CHILD ABUSE

Nothing in this article shall be construed as limiting any obligation to report instances of child abuse as required by Section 11166 of the Penal Code.

Article 9: Official Information and Identity of Informer

§ 1040. PRIVILEGE FOR OFFICIAL INFORMATION

(a) As used in this section, "official information" means information acquired in confidence by a public employee in the course of his or her duty and not open, or officially disclosed, to the public prior to the time the claim of privilege is made.

(b) A public entity has a privilege to refuse to disclose official information, and to prevent another from disclosing official information, if the privilege is claimed by a person authorized by the public entity to do so and either of the following apply:

(1) Disclosure is forbidden by an act of the Congress of the United States or a statute of this state.

(2) Disclosure of the information is against the public interest because there is a necessity for preserving the confidentiality of the information that outweighs the necessity for disclosure in the interest of justice; but no privilege may be claimed under this paragraph if any person authorized to do so has consented that the information be disclosed in the proceeding. In determining whether disclosure of the information is against the public interest, the interest of the public entity as a party in the outcome of the proceeding may not be considered.

(c) Notwithstanding any other law, the Employment Development Department shall disclose to law enforcement agencies, in accordance with subdivision (i) of Section 1095 of the Unemployment Insurance Code, information in its possession relating to any person if an arrest warrant has been issued for the person for commission of a felony.

§ 1041. PRIVILEGE FOR IDENTITY OF INFORMER

(a) Except as provided in this section, a public entity has a privilege to refuse to disclose the identity of a person who has furnished information as provided in subdivision (b) purporting to disclose a violation of a law of the United States or of this state or of a public entity in this state, and to prevent another from disclosing the person's identity, if the privilege is claimed by a person authorized by the public entity to do so and either of the following apply:

(1) Disclosure is forbidden by an act of the Congress of the United States or a statute of this state.

(2) Disclosure of the identity of the informer is against the public interest because the necessity for preserving the confidentiality of his or her identity outweighs the necessity for disclosure in the interest of justice. The privilege shall not be claimed under this paragraph if a person authorized to do so has consented that the identity of the informer be disclosed in the proceeding. In determining whether disclosure of the identity of the informer is against the public interest, the interest of the public entity as a party in the outcome of the proceeding shall not be considered.

(b) The privilege described in this section applies only if the information is furnished in confidence by the informer to any of the following:

(1) A law enforcement officer.

(2) A representative of an administrative agency charged with the administration or enforcement of the law alleged to be violated.

(3) Any person for the purpose of transmittal to a person listed in paragraph (1) or (2). As used in this paragraph, "person" includes a volunteer or employee of a crime stopper organization.

(c) The privilege described in this section shall not be construed to prevent the informer from disclosing his or her identity.

(d) As used in this section, "crime stopper organization" means a private, nonprofit organization that accepts and expends donations used to reward persons who report to the organization information concerning alleged criminal activity, and forwards the information to the appropriate law enforcement agency.

§ 1042. ADVERSE ORDER OR FINDING IN CERTAIN CASES

(a) Except where disclosure is forbidden by an act of the Congress of the United States, if a claim of privilege under this article by the state or a public entity in this state is sustained in a criminal proceeding, the presiding officer shall make such order or finding of fact adverse to the public entity bringing the proceeding as is required by law upon any issue in the proceeding to which the privileged information is material.

(b) Notwithstanding subdivision (a), where a search is made pursuant to a warrant valid on its face, the public entity bringing a criminal proceeding is not required to reveal to the defendant official information or the identity of an informer in order to establish the legality of the search or the admissibility of any evidence obtained as a result of it.

(c) Notwithstanding subdivision (a), in any preliminary hearing, criminal trial, or other criminal proceeding, any otherwise admissible evidence of information communicated to a peace officer by a confidential informant, who is not a material witness to the guilt or innocence of the accused of the offense charged, is admissible on the issue of reasonable cause to make an arrest or search without requiring that the name or identity of the informant be disclosed if the judge or magistrate is satisfied, based upon evidence produced in open court, out of the presence of the jury, that such information was received from a reliable informant and in his discretion does not require such disclosure.

(d) When, in any such criminal proceeding, a party demands disclosure of the identity of the informant on the ground the informant is a material witness on the issue of guilt, the court shall conduct a hearing at which all parties may present evidence on the issue of disclosure. Such hearing shall be conducted outside the presence of the jury, if any. During the hearing, if the privilege provided for in Section 1041 is claimed by a person authorized to do so or if a person who is authorized to claim such privilege refuses to answer any question on the ground that the answer would tend to disclose the identity of the informant, the prosecuting attorney may request that the court hold an in camera hearing. If such a request is made, the court shall hold such a hearing outside the presence of the defendant and his counsel. At the in camera hearing, the prosecution may offer evidence which would tend to disclose or which discloses the identity of the informant to aid the court in its determination whether there is a reasonable possibility that nondisclosure might deprive the defendant of a fair trial. A reporter shall be present at the in camera hearing. Any transcription of the proceedings at the in camera hearing, as well as any physical evidence presented at the hearing, shall be ordered sealed by the court, and only a court may have access to its contents. The court shall not order disclosure, nor strike the testimony of the witness who invokes the privilege, nor dismiss the criminal proceeding, if the party offering the witness refuses to disclose the identity of the informant, unless, based upon the evidence presented at the hearing held in the presence of the defendant and his counsel and the evidence presented at the in camera hearing, the court concludes that there is a reasonable possibility that non-disclosure might deprive the defendant of a fair trial.

§ 1043. DISCOVERY OR DISCLOSURE OF PEACE OR CUSTODIAL OFFICER'S PERSONNEL RECORDS

(a) In any case in which discovery or disclosure is sought of peace or custodial officer personnel records or records maintained pursuant to Section 832.5 of the Penal Code or information from those records, the party seeking the discovery or disclosure shall file a written motion with the appropriate court or administrative body upon written notice to the governmental agency that has custody and control of the records, as follows:

(1) In a civil action, the written notice shall be given at the times prescribed by subdivision (b) of Section 1005 of the Code of Civil Procedure.

(2) In a criminal action, the written notice shall be served and filed at least 10 court days before the hearing. All papers opposing a motion so noticed shall be filed with the court at least five court days, and all reply papers at least two court days, before the hearing. Proof of service of the notice shall be filed no later than five court days before the hearing.

(b) The motion shall include all of the following:

(1) Identification of the proceeding in which discovery or disclosure is sought, the party seeking discovery or disclosure, the peace or custodial officer whose records are sought, the governmental agency that has custody and control of the records, and the time and place at which the motion for discovery or disclosure shall be heard.

(2) A description of the type of records or information sought.

(3) Affidavits showing good cause for the discovery or disclosure sought, setting forth the materiality thereof to the subject matter involved in the pending litigation and stating upon reasonable belief that the governmental agency identified has the records or information from the records.

(c) Upon receipt of a notice served pursuant to subdivision (a), the governmental agency shall immediately notify the individual whose records are sought.

(d) No hearing upon a motion for discovery or disclosure shall be held without full compliance with the notice provisions of this section except upon a showing by the moving party of good cause for noncompliance, or upon a waiver of the hearing by the governmental agency identified as having the records.

§ 1044. ACCESS TO MEDICAL OR PSYCHOLOGICAL HISTORY

Nothing in this article shall be construed to affect the right of access to records of medical or psychological history where such access would otherwise be available under Section 996 or 1016.

§ 1045. ACCESS TO RECORDS OF COMPLAINTS WHERE INVESTIGATIONS OR DISCIPLINE CONCERN PEACE OFFICER

(a) This article does not affect the right of access to records of complaints, or investigations of complaints, or discipline imposed as a result of those investigations, concerning an event or transaction in which the peace officer or custodial officer, as defined in Section 831.5 of the Penal Code, participated, or which the officer perceived, and pertaining to the manner in which the officer performed the officer's duties, provided that information is relevant to the subject matter involved in the pending litigation.

(b) In determining relevance, the court shall examine the information in chambers in conformity with Section 915, and shall exclude from disclosure both of the following:

(1) In any criminal proceeding the conclusions of any officer investigating a complaint filed pursuant to Section 832.5 of the Penal Code.

(2) Facts sought to be disclosed that are so remote as to make disclosure of little or no practical benefit.

(c) In determining relevance where the issue in litigation concerns the policies or pattern of conduct of the employing agency, the court shall consider whether the information sought may be obtained from other records maintained by the employing agency in the regular course of agency business which would not necessitate the disclosure of individual personnel records.

(d) Upon motion seasonably made by the governmental agency which has custody or control of the records to be examined or by the officer whose records are sought, and upon good cause showing the necessity thereof, the court may make any order which justice requires to protect the officer or agency from unnecessary annoyance, embarrassment or oppression.

(e) The court shall, in any case or proceeding permitting the disclosure or discovery of any peace or custodial officer records requested pursuant to Section 1043, order that the records disclosed or discovered may not be used for any purpose other than a court proceeding pursuant to applicable law.

§ 1046. MOTION TO INCLUDE COPY OF POLICE REPORT IN EXCESSIVE FORCE CASE

In any case, otherwise authorized by law, in which the party seeking disclosure is alleging excessive force by a peace officer or custodial officer, as defined in Section 831.5 of the Penal Code, in connection with the arrest of that party, or for conduct alleged to have occurred within a jail facility, the motion shall include a copy of the police report setting forth the circumstances under which the party was stopped and arrested, or a copy of the crime report setting forth the circumstances under which the conduct is alleged to have occurred within a jail facility.

§ 1047. POLICE RECORDS NOT SUBJECT TO DISCLOSURE; DISCLOSURE OF SUPERVISORIAL OFFICER'S RECORDS

(a) Records of peace officers or custodial officers, as defined in Section 831.5 of the Penal Code, including supervisorial officers, who either were not present during the arrest or had no contact with the party seeking disclosure from the time of the arrest until the time of booking, or who were not present at the time the conduct at issue is alleged to have occurred within a jail facility, shall not be subject to disclosure.

(b) Notwithstanding subdivision (a), if a supervisorial officer whose records are being sought had direct oversight of a peace officer or a custodial officer, as defined in Section 831.5 of the Penal Code and issued command directives or had command influence over the circumstances at issue, the supervisorial officer's records shall be subject to disclosure pursuant to Section 1045 if the peace officer or custodial officer under supervision was present during the arrest, had contact with the party seeking disclosure from the time of the arrest until the time of booking, or was present at the time the conduct at issue is alleged to have occurred within a jail facility.

Article 10: Political Vote

§ 1050. PRIVILEGE TO PROTECT SECRECY OF VOTE

If he claims the privilege, a person has a privilege to refuse to disclose the tenor of his vote at a public election where the voting is by secret ballot unless he voted illegally or he previously made an unprivileged disclosure of the tenor of his vote.

Article 11: Trade Secret

§ 1060. PRIVILEGE TO PROTECT TRADE SECRET

If he or his agent or employee claims the privilege, the owner of a trade secret has a privilege to refuse to disclose the secret, and to prevent another from disclosing it, if the allowance of the privilege will not tend to conceal fraud or otherwise work injustice.

§ 1061. "TRADE SECRET"; "ARTICLE"; PROCEDURE FOR ASSERTION OF TRADE SECRET PRIVILEGE; PROTECTIVE ORDER

(a) For purposes of this section, and Sections 1062 and 1063:

(1) "Trade secret" means "trade secret," as defined in subdivision (d) of Section 3426.1 of the Civil Code, or paragraph (9) of subdivision (a) of Section 499c of the Penal Code.

(2) "Article" means "article," as defined in paragraph (2) of subdivision (a) of Section 499c of the Penal Code.

(b) In addition to Section 1062, the following procedure shall apply whenever the owner of a trade secret wishes to assert his or her trade secret privilege, as provided in Section 1060, during a criminal proceeding:

(1) The owner of the trade secret shall file a motion for a protective order, or the people may file the motion on the owner's behalf and with the owner's permission. The motion shall include an affidavit based upon personal knowledge listing the affiant's qualifications to give an opinion concerning the trade secret at issue, identifying, without revealing, the alleged trade secret and articles which disclose the secret, and presenting evidence that the secret qualifies as a trade secret under either subdivision (d) of Section 3426.1 of the Civil Code or paragraph (9) of subdivision (a) of Section 499c of the Penal Code. The motion and affidavit shall be served on all parties in the proceeding.

(2) Any party in the proceeding may oppose the request for the protective order by submitting affidavits based upon the affiant's personal knowledge. The affidavits shall be filed under seal, but shall be provided to the owner of the trade secret and to all parties in the proceeding. Neither the owner of the trade secret nor any party in the proceeding may disclose the affidavit to persons other than to counsel of record without prior court approval.

(3) The movant shall, by a preponderance of the evidence, show that the issuance of a protective order is proper. The court may rule on the request without holding an evidentiary hearing. However, in its discretion, the court may choose to hold an in camera evidentiary hearing concerning disputed articles with only the owner of the trade secret, the people's representative, the defendant, and defendant's counsel present. If the court holds such a hearing, the parties' right to examine witnesses shall not be used to obtain discovery, but shall be directed solely toward the question of whether the alleged trade secret qualifies for protection.

(4) If the court finds that a trade secret may be disclosed during any criminal proceeding unless a protective order is issued and that the issuance of a protective order would not conceal a fraud or work an injustice, the court shall issue a protective order limiting the use and dissemination of the trade secret, including, but not limited to, articles disclosing that secret. The protective order may, in the court's discretion, include the following provisions:

(A) That the trade secret may be disseminated only to counsel for the parties, including their associate attorneys, paralegals, and investigators, and to law enforcement officials or clerical officials.

(B) That the defendant may view the secret only in the presence of his or her counsel, or if not in the presence of his or her counsel, at counsel's offices.

(C) That any party seeking to show the trade secret, or articles containing the trade secret, to any person not designated by the protective order shall first obtain court approval to do so:

(i) The court may require that the person receiving the trade secret do so only in the presence of counsel for the party requesting approval.

(ii) The court may require the person receiving the trade secret to sign a copy of the protective order and to agree to be bound by its terms. The order may include a provision recognizing the owner of the trade secret to be a third-party beneficiary of that agreement.

(iii) The court may require a party seeking disclosure to an expert to provide that expert's name, employment history, and any other relevant information to the court for examination. The court shall accept that information under seal, and the information shall not be disclosed by any court except upon termination of the action and upon a showing of good cause to believe the secret has been disseminated by a court-approved expert. The court shall evaluate the expert and determine whether the expert poses a discernible risk of disclosure. The court shall withhold approval if the expert's economic interests place the expert in a competitive position with the victim, unless no other experts are available. The court may interview the expert in camera in aid of its ruling. If the court rejects the expert, it shall state its reasons for doing so on the record and a transcript of those reasons shall be prepared and sealed.

(D) That no articles disclosing the trade secret shall be filed or otherwise made a part of the court record available to the public without approval of the court and prior notice to the owner of the secret. The owner of the secret may give either party permission to accept the notice on the owner's behalf.

(E) Other orders as the court deems necessary to protect the integrity of the trade secret.

(c) A ruling granting or denying a motion for a protective order filed pursuant to subdivision (b) shall not be construed as a determination that the alleged trade secret is or is not a trade secret as defined by subdivision (d) of Section 3426.1 of the Civil Code or paragraph (9) of subdivision (a) of Section 499c of the Penal Code. Such a ruling shall not have any effect on any civil litigation.

(d) This section shall have prospective effect only and shall not operate to invalidate previously entered protective orders.

§ 1062. EXCLUSION OF PUBLIC FROM PORTION OF CRIMINAL PROCEEDING IN WHICH TRADE SECRET MAY BE DISCLOSED

(a) Notwithstanding any other provision of law, in a criminal case, the court, upon motion of the owner of a trade secret, or upon motion by the People with the consent of the owner, may exclude the public from any portion of a criminal proceeding where the proponent of closure has demonstrated a substantial probability that the trade secret would otherwise be disclosed to the public during that proceeding and a substantial probability that the disclosure would cause serious harm to the owner of the secret, and where the court finds that there is no overriding public interest in an open proceeding. No evidence, however, shall be excluded during a criminal proceeding pursuant to this section if it would conceal a fraud, work an injustice, or deprive the People or the defendant of a fair trial.

(b) The motion made pursuant to subdivision (a) shall identify, without revealing, the trade secrets which would otherwise be disclosed to the public. A showing made pursuant to subdivision (a) shall be made during an in camera hearing with only the owner of the trade secret, the People's representative, the defendant, and defendant's counsel present. A court reporter shall be present during the hearing. Any transcription of the proceedings at the in camera hearing, as well as any articles presented at that hearing, shall be ordered sealed by the court and only a court may allow access to its contents upon a showing of good cause. The court, in ruling upon the motion made pursuant to subdivision (a), may consider testimony presented or affidavits filed in any proceeding held in that action.

(c) If, after the in camera hearing described in subdivision (b), the court determines that exclusion of trade secret information from the public is appropriate, the court shall close only that portion of the criminal proceeding necessary to prevent disclosure of the trade secret. Before granting the motion, however, the court shall find and state for the record that the moving party has met its burden pursuant to subdivision (b), and that the closure of that portion of the proceeding will not deprive the People or the defendant of a fair trial.

(d) The owner of the trade secret, the People, or the defendant may seek relief from a ruling denying or granting closure by petitioning a higher court for extraordinary relief.

(e) Whenever the court closes a portion of a criminal proceeding pursuant to this section, a transcript of that closed proceeding shall be made available to the public as soon as practicable. The court shall redact any information qualifying as a trade secret before making that transcript available.

(f) The court, subject to Section 867 of the Penal Code, may allow witnesses who are bound by a protective order entered in the criminal proceeding protecting trade secrets, pursuant to Section 1061, to remain within the courtroom during the closed portion of the proceeding.

§ 1063. PROVISIONS GOVERNING REQUESTS TO SEAL ARTICLES

The following provisions shall govern requests to seal articles which are protected by a protective order entered pursuant to Evidence Code Section 1060 or 1061:

(a) The People shall request sealing of articles reasonably expected to be filed or admitted into evidence as follows:

> **(1)** No less than 10 court days before trial, and no less than five court days before any other criminal proceeding, the People shall file with the court a list of all articles which the People reasonably expect to file with the court, or admit into evidence, under seal at that proceeding. That list shall be available to the public. The People may be relieved from providing timely notice upon showing that exigent circumstances prevent that notice.
>
> **(2)** The court shall not allow the listed articles to be filed, admitted into evidence, or in any way made a part of the court record otherwise open to the public before holding a hearing to consider any objections to the People's request to seal the articles. The court at that hearing shall allow those objecting to the sealing to state their objections.
>
> **(3)** After hearing any objections to sealing, the court shall conduct an in camera hearing with only the owner of the trade secret contained within those articles, the People's representative, defendant, and

defendant's counsel present. The court shall review the articles sought to be sealed, evaluate objections to sealing, and determine whether the People have satisfied the constitutional standards governing public access to articles which are part of the judicial record. The court may consider testimony presented or affidavits filed in any proceeding held in that action. The People, defendant, and the owner of the trade secret may file affidavits based on the affiant's personal knowledge to be considered at that hearing. Those affidavits are to be sealed and not released to the public, but shall be made available to the parties. The court may rule on the request to seal without taking testimony. If the court takes testimony, examination of witnesses shall not be used to obtain discovery, but shall be directed solely toward whether sealing is appropriate.

(4) If the court finds that the movant has satisfied appropriate constitutional standards with respect to sealing particular articles, the court shall seal those articles if and when they are filed, admitted into evidence, or in any way made a part of the court record otherwise open to the public. The articles shall not be unsealed absent an order of a court upon a showing of good cause. Failure to examine the court file for notice of a request to seal shall not constitute good cause to consider objections to sealing.

(b) The following procedure shall apply to other articles made a part of the court record:

(1) Where any articles protected by a protective order entered pursuant to Section 1060 or 1061 are filed, admitted into evidence, or in any way made a part of the court record in such a way as to be otherwise open to the public, the People, a defendant, or the owner of a trade secret contained within those articles may request the court to seal those articles.

(2) The request to seal shall be made by noticed motion filed with the court. It may also be made orally in court at the time the articles are made a part of the court record. Where the request is made orally, the movant must file within 24 hours a written description of that request, including a list of the articles which are the subject of that request. These motions and lists shall be available to the public.

(3) The court shall promptly conduct hearings as provided in paragraphs (2), (3), and (4) of subdivision (a). The court shall, pending the hearings, seal those articles which are the subject of the request. Where a request to seal is made orally, the court may conduct hearings at the time the articles are made a part of the court record, but shall reconsider its ruling in light of additional objections made by objectors within two court days after the written record of the request to seal is made available to the public.

(4) Any articles sealed pursuant to these hearings shall not be unsealed absent an order of a court upon a showing of good cause.

Failure to examine the court file for notice of a request to seal shall not constitute good cause to consider objections to sealing.

Chapter 5: Immunity of Newsman from Citation for Contempt

§ 1070. NEWSMAN'S REFUSAL TO DISCLOSE NEWS SOURCE

(a) A publisher, editor, reporter, or other person connected with or employed upon a newspaper, magazine, or other periodical publication, or by a press association or wire service, or any person who has been so connected or employed, cannot be adjudged in contempt by a judicial, legislative, administrative body, or any other body having the power to issue subpoenas, for refusing to disclose, in any proceeding as defined in Section 901, the source of any information procured while so connected or employed for publication in a newspaper, magazine or other periodical publication, or for refusing to disclose any unpublished information obtained or prepared in gathering, receiving or processing of information for communication to the public.

(b) Nor can a radio or television news reporter or other person connected with or employed by a radio or television station, or any person who has been so connected or employed, be so adjudged in contempt for refusing to disclose the source of any information procured while so connected or employed for news or news commentary purposes on radio or television, or for refusing to disclose any unpublished information obtained or prepared in gathering, receiving or processing of information for communication to the public.

(c) As used in this section, "unpublished information" includes information not disseminated to the public by the person from whom disclosure is sought, whether or not related information has been disseminated and includes, but is not limited to, all notes, outtakes, photographs, tapes or other data of whatever sort not itself disseminated to the public through a medium of communication, whether or not published information based upon or related to such material has been disseminated.

DIVISION 9: EVIDENCE AFFECTED OR EXCLUDED BY EXTRINSIC POLICIES

Chapter 1: Evidence of Character, Habit or Custom

§ 1100. MANNER OF PROOF OF CHARACTER

Except as otherwise provided by statute, any otherwise admissible evidence (including evidence in the form of an opinion, evidence of reputation, and evidence of specific instances of such person's conduct) is admissible to prove a person's character or a trait of his character.

§ 1101. EVIDENCE OF CHARACTER TO PROVE CONDUCT

(a) Except as provided in this section and in Sections 1102, 1103, 1108, and 1109, evidence of a person's character or a trait of his or her character (whether in the form of an opinion, evidence of reputation, or evidence of specific instances of his or her conduct) is inadmissible when offered to prove his or her conduct on a specified occasion.

(b) Nothing in this section prohibits the admission of evidence that a person committed a crime, civil wrong, or other act when relevant to prove some fact (such as motive, opportunity, intent, preparation, plan, knowledge, identity, absence of mistake or accident, or whether a defendant in a prosecution for an unlawful sexual act or attempted unlawful sexual act did not reasonably and in good faith believe that the victim consented) other than his or her disposition to commit such an act.

(c) Nothing in this section affects the admissibility of evidence offered to support or attack the credibility of a witness.

§ 1102. OPINION AND REPUTATION EVIDENCE OF CHARACTER OF CRIMINAL DEFENDANT TO PROVE CONDUCT

In a criminal action, evidence of the defendant's character or a trait of his character in the form of an opinion or evidence of his reputation is not made inadmissible by Section 1101 if such evidence is:

(a) Offered by the defendant to prove his conduct in conformity with such character or trait of character.

(b) Offered by the prosecution to rebut evidence adduced by the defendant under subdivision (a).

§ 1103. EVIDENCE OF CHARACTER OF VICTIM OF CRIME

(a) In a criminal action, evidence of the character or a trait of character (in the form of an opinion, evidence of reputation, or evidence of specific instances of conduct) of the victim of the crime for which the defendant is being prosecuted is not made inadmissible by Section 1101 if the evidence is:

(1) Offered by the defendant to prove conduct of the victim in conformity with the character or trait of character.

(2) Offered by the prosecution to rebut evidence adduced by the defendant under paragraph (1).

(b) In a criminal action, evidence of the defendant's character for violence or trait of character for violence (in the form of an opinion, evidence of reputation, or evidence of specific instances of conduct) is not made inadmissible by Section 1101 if the evidence is offered by the prosecution to prove conduct of the defendant in conformity with the character or trait of character and is offered after evidence that the victim had a character for violence or a trait of character tending to show violence has been adduced by the defendant under paragraph (1) of subdivision (a).

(c)

(1) Notwithstanding any other provision of this code to the contrary, and except as provided in this subdivision, in any prosecution under Section 261 or 264.1 of the Penal Code, or under Section 286, 287, or 289 of, or former Section 262 or 288a of, the Penal Code, or for assault with intent to commit, attempt to commit, or conspiracy to commit a crime defined in any of those sections, except where the crime is alleged to have occurred in a local detention facility, as defined in Section 6031.4, or in a state prison, as defined in Section 4504, opinion evidence, reputation evidence, and evidence of specific instances of the complaining witness' sexual conduct, or any of that evidence, is not admissible by the defendant in order to prove consent by the complaining witness.

(2) Notwithstanding paragraph (3), evidence of the manner in which the victim was dressed at the time of the commission of the offense is not admissible when offered by either party on the issue of consent in any prosecution for an offense specified in paragraph (1). For the purposes of this paragraph, "manner of dress" does not include the condition of the victim's clothing before, during, or after the commission of the offense.

(3) Paragraph (1) does not apply to evidence of the complaining witness' sexual conduct with the defendant.

(4) If the prosecutor introduces evidence, including testimony of a witness, or the complaining witness as a witness gives testimony, and that evidence or testimony relates to the complaining witness' sexual conduct, the defendant may cross-examine the witness who gives the testimony and offer relevant evidence limited specifically to the rebuttal of the evidence introduced by the prosecutor or given by the complaining witness.

(5) This subdivision does not make inadmissible any evidence offered to attack the credibility of the complaining witness as provided in Section 782.

(6) As used in this subdivision, "complaining witness" means the alleged victim of the crime charged, the prosecution of which is subject to this subdivision.

§ 1104. CHARACTER TRAIT FOR CARE OR SKILL

Except as provided in Sections 1102 and 1103, evidence of a trait of a person's character with respect to care or skill is inadmissible to prove the quality of his conduct on a specified occasion.

§ 1105. HABIT OR CUSTOM TO PROVE SPECIFIC BEHAVIOR

Any otherwise admissible evidence of habit or custom is admissible to prove conduct on a specified occasion in conformity with the habit or custom.

§ 1106. SPECIFIC INSTANCES OF PLAINTIFF'S SEXUAL CONDUCT IN CIVIL ACTION ALLEGING SEXUAL HARASSMENT

(a) In any civil action alleging conduct which constitutes sexual harassment, sexual assault, or sexual battery, opinion evidence, reputation evidence, and evidence of specific instances of the plaintiff's sexual conduct, or any of that evidence, is not admissible by the defendant in order to:

(1) Prove consent by the plaintiff.

(2) Prove absence of injury suffered by the plaintiff, unless the injury alleged by the plaintiff is in the nature of loss of consortium.

(3) Attack the credibility of the plaintiff's testimony on consent or the absence of injury suffered by the plaintiff.

(b) Subdivision (a) does not apply to evidence of the plaintiff's sexual conduct with the alleged perpetrator.

(c) Notwithstanding subdivision (b), in any civil action brought pursuant to Section 1708.5 of the Civil Code involving a minor and an adult as described in Section 1708.5.5 of the Civil Code, evidence of the plaintiff minor's sexual conduct with the defendant adult shall not be admissible to prove consent by the plaintiff or the absence of injury to the plaintiff.

(d) If the plaintiff introduces evidence, including testimony of a witness, or the plaintiff as a witness gives testimony, and the evidence or testimony relates to the plaintiff's sexual conduct, the defendant may cross-examine the witness who gives the testimony and offer relevant evidence limited specifically to the rebuttal of the evidence introduced by the plaintiff or given by the plaintiff.

(e) This section shall not be construed to make inadmissible any evidence offered to attack the credibility of the plaintiff's testimony as to something other than consent or absence of injury as provided in Section 783.

§ 1107. ADMISSIBILITY OF EXPERT EVIDENCE REGARDING INTIMATE PARTNER BATTERING

(a) In a criminal action, expert testimony is admissible by either the prosecution or the defense regarding intimate partner battering and its effects, including the nature and effect of physical, emotional, or mental abuse on the beliefs, perceptions, or behavior of victims of domestic violence, except when offered against a criminal defendant to prove the occurrence of the act or acts of abuse which form the basis of the criminal charge.

(b) The foundation shall be sufficient for admission of this expert testimony if the proponent of the evidence establishes its relevancy and the proper qualifications of the expert witness. Expert opinion testimony on intimate partner battering and its effects shall not be considered a new scientific technique whose reliability is unproven.

(c) For purposes of this section, "abuse" is defined in Section 6203 of the Family Code, and "domestic violence" is defined in Section 6211 of the Family Code and may include acts defined in Section 242, subdivision (e) of Section 243, Section 261, 273.5, 273.6, 422, or 653m of, or former Section 262 of, the Penal Code.

(d) This section is intended as a rule of evidence only and no substantive change affecting the Penal Code is intended.

(e) This section shall be known, and may be cited, as the Expert Witness Testimony on Intimate Partner Battering and Its Effects Section of the Evidence Code.

(f) The changes in this section that become effective on January 1, 2005, are not intended to impact any existing decisional law regarding this section, and that decisional law should apply equally to this section as it refers to "intimate partner battering and its effects" in place of "battered women's syndrome."

§ 1107.5. HUMAN TRAFFICKING; ADMISSIBILITY OF EXPERT TESTIMONY

(a) In a criminal action, expert testimony is admissible by either the prosecution or the defense regarding the effects of human trafficking on human trafficking victims, including the nature and effect of physical, emotional, or mental abuse on the beliefs, perceptions, or behavior of human trafficking victims.

(b) The foundation shall be sufficient for admission of this expert testimony if the proponent of the evidence establishes its relevancy and the proper qualifications of the expert witness.

(c) For purposes of this section, "human trafficking victim" is defined as a victim of an offense described in Section 236.1 of the Penal Code.

(d) This section is intended as a rule of evidence only and no substantive change affecting the Penal Code is intended.

§ 1108. EVIDENCE OF ANOTHER SEXUAL OFFENSE

(a) In a criminal action in which the defendant is accused of a sexual offense, evidence of the defendant's commission of another sexual offense or offenses is not made inadmissible by Section 1101, if the evidence is not inadmissible pursuant to Section 352.

(b) In an action in which evidence is to be offered under this section, the people shall disclose the evidence to the defendant, including statements of witnesses or a summary of the substance of any testimony that is expected to be offered in compliance with the requirements of Section 1054.7 of the Penal Code.

(c) This section does not limit the admission or consideration of evidence under any other section of this code.

(d) As used in this section, the following definitions shall apply:

(1) "Sexual offense" means a crime under the law of a state or of the United States that involved any of the following:

(A) Any conduct proscribed by subdivision (b) or (c) of Section 236.1, Section 243.4, 261, 261.5, 262, 264.1, 266c, 269, 286, 287, 288, 288.2, 288.5, or 289, or subdivision (b), (c), or (d) of Section 311.2 or Section 311.3, 311.4, 311.10, 311.11, 314, or 647.6 of, or former Section 288a of, the Penal Code.

(B) Any conduct proscribed by Section 220 of the Penal Code, except assault with intent to commit mayhem.

(C) Contact, without consent, between any part of the defendant's body or an object and the genitals or anus of another person.

(D) Contact, without consent, between the genitals or anus of the defendant and any part of another person's body.

(E) Deriving sexual pleasure or gratification from the infliction of death, bodily injury, or physical pain on another person.

(F) An attempt or conspiracy to engage in conduct described in this paragraph.

(2) "Consent" shall have the same meaning as provided in Section 261.6 of the Penal Code, except that it does not include consent which is legally ineffective because of the age, mental disorder, or developmental or physical disability of the victim.

§ 1109. DOMESTIC VIOLENCE, ABUSE OF ELDER OR DEPENDENT PERSON, AND CHILD ABUSE; WHEN EVIDENCE OF OTHER ACTS IS ADMISSIBLE; DISCLOSURE TO DEFENDANT

(a)

(1) Except as provided in subdivision (e) or (f), in a criminal action in which the defendant is accused of an offense involving domestic violence, evidence of the defendant's commission of other domestic violence is not made inadmissible by Section 1101 if the evidence is not inadmissible pursuant to Section 352.

(2) Except as provided in subdivision (e) or (f), in a criminal action in which the defendant is accused of an offense involving abuse of an elder or dependent person, evidence of the defendant's commission of other abuse of an elder or dependent person is not made inadmissible by Section 1101 if the evidence is not inadmissible pursuant to Section 352.

(3) Except as provided in subdivision (e) or (f) and subject to a hearing conducted pursuant to Section 352, which shall include consideration of any corroboration and remoteness in time, in a criminal action in which the defendant is accused of an offense involving child abuse, evidence of the defendant's commission of child abuse is not made inadmissible by Section 1101 if the evidence is not inadmissible pursuant to Section 352. Nothing in this paragraph prohibits or limits the admission of evidence pursuant to subdivision (b) of Section 1101.

(b) In an action in which evidence is to be offered under this section, the people shall disclose the evidence to the defendant, including statements of witnesses or a summary of the substance of any testimony that is expected to be offered, in compliance with the provisions of Section 1054.7 of the Penal Code.

(c) This section shall not be construed to limit or preclude the admission or consideration of evidence under any other statute or case law.

(d) As used in this section:

(1) "Abuse of an elder or dependent person" means physical or sexual abuse, neglect, financial abuse, abandonment, isolation, abduction, or other treatment that results in physical harm, pain, or mental suffering, the deprivation of care by a caregiver, or other deprivation by a custodian or provider of goods or services that are necessary to avoid physical harm or mental suffering.

(2) "Child abuse" means an act proscribed by Section 273d of the Penal Code.

(3) "Domestic violence" has the meaning set forth in Section 13700 of the Penal Code. Subject to a hearing conducted pursuant to Section

352, which shall include consideration of any corroboration and remoteness in time, "domestic violence" has the further meaning as set forth in Section 6211 of the Family Code, if the act occurred no more than five years before the charged offense.

(e) Evidence of acts occurring more than 10 years before the charged offense is inadmissible under this section, unless the court determines that the admission of this evidence is in the interest of justice.

(f) Evidence of the findings and determinations of administrative agencies regulating the conduct of health facilities licensed under Section 1250 of the Health and Safety Code is inadmissible under this section.

Chapter 2: Mediation

§ 1115. DEFINITIONS

For purposes of this chapter:

(a) "Mediation" means a process in which a neutral person or persons facilitate communication between the disputants to assist them in reaching a mutually acceptable agreement.

(b) "Mediator" means a neutral person who conducts a mediation. "Mediator" includes any person designated by a mediator either to assist in the mediation or to communicate with the participants in preparation for a mediation.

(c) "Mediation consultation" means a communication between a person and a mediator for the purpose of initiating, considering, or reconvening a mediation or retaining the mediator.

§ 1116. EFFECT OF CHAPTER

(a) Nothing in this chapter expands or limits a court's authority to order participation in a dispute resolution proceeding. Nothing in this chapter authorizes or affects the enforceability of a contract clause in which parties agree to the use of mediation.

(b) Nothing in this chapter makes admissible evidence that is inadmissible under Section 1152 or any other statute.

§ 1117. APPLICABILITY OF CHAPTER

(a) Except as provided in subdivision (b), this chapter applies to a mediation as defined in Section 1115.

(b) This chapter does not apply to either of the following:

(1) A proceeding under Part 1 (commencing with Section 1800) of Division 5 of the Family Code or Chapter 11 (commencing with Section 3160) of Part 2 of Division 8 of the Family Code.

(2) A settlement conference pursuant to Rule 3.1380 of the California Rules of Court.

§ 1118. ORAL AGREEMENT

An oral agreement "in accordance with Section 1118" means an oral agreement that satisfies all of the following conditions:

(a) The oral agreement is recorded by a court reporter or reliable means of audio recording.

(b) The terms of the oral agreement are recited on the record in the presence of the parties and the mediator, and the parties express on the record that they agree to the terms recited.

(c) The parties to the oral agreement expressly state on the record that the agreement is enforceable or binding, or words to that effect.

(d) The recording is reduced to writing and the writing is signed by the parties within 72 hours after it is recorded.

§ 1119. ADMISSIBILITY, DISCOVERY, OR DISCLOSURE OF EVIDENCE; CONFIDENTIALITY

Except as otherwise provided in this chapter:

(a) No evidence of anything said or any admission made for the purpose of, in the course of, or pursuant to, a mediation or a mediation consultation is admissible or subject to discovery, and disclosure of the evidence shall not be compelled, in any arbitration, administrative adjudication, civil action, or other noncriminal proceeding in which, pursuant to law, testimony can be compelled to be given.

(b) No writing, as defined in Section 250, that is prepared for the purpose of, in the course of, or pursuant to, a mediation or a mediation consultation, is admissible or subject to discovery, and disclosure of the writing shall not be compelled, in any arbitration, administrative adjudication, civil action, or other noncriminal proceeding in which, pursuant to law, testimony can be compelled to be given.

(c) All communications, negotiations, or settlement discussions by and between participants in the course of a mediation or a mediation consultation shall remain confidential.

§ 1120. EXCEPTIONS TO INADMISSIBILITY OR PROTECTION FROM DISCLOSURE

(a) Evidence otherwise admissible or subject to discovery outside of a mediation or a mediation consultation shall not be or become inadmissible or protected from disclosure solely by reason of its introduction or use in a mediation or a mediation consultation.

(b) This chapter does not limit any of the following:

(1) The admissibility of an agreement to mediate a dispute.

(2) The effect of an agreement not to take a default or an agreement to extend the time within which to act or refrain from acting in a pending civil action.

(3) Disclosure of the mere fact that a mediator has served, is serving, will serve, or was contacted about serving as a mediator in a dispute.

(4) The admissibility of declarations of disclosure required by Sections 2104 and 2105 of the Family Code, even if prepared for the purpose of, in the course of, or pursuant to, a mediation or a mediation consultation.

§ 1121. REPORTS

Neither a mediator nor anyone else may submit to a court or other adjudicative body, and a court or other adjudicative body may not consider, any report, assessment, evaluation, recommendation, or finding of any kind by the mediator concerning a mediation conducted by the mediator, other than a report that is mandated by court rule or other law and that states only whether an agreement was reached, unless all parties to the mediation expressly agree otherwise in writing, or orally in accordance with Section 1118.

§ 1122. CONDITIONS FOR ADMISSIBILITY OF COMMUNICATION OR WRITING

(a) A communication or a writing, as defined in Section 250, that is made or prepared for the purpose of, or in the course of, or pursuant to, a mediation or a mediation consultation, is not made inadmissible, or protected from disclosure, by provisions of this chapter if any of the following conditions are satisfied:

(1) All persons who conduct or otherwise participate in the mediation expressly agree in writing, or orally in accordance with Section 1118, to disclosure of the communication, document, or writing.

(2) The communication, document, or writing was prepared by or on behalf of fewer than all the mediation participants, those participants expressly agree in writing, or orally in accordance with Section 1118, to its disclosure, and the communication, document, or writing does not disclose anything said or done or any admission made in the course of the mediation.

(3) The communication, document, or writing is related to an attorney's compliance with the requirements described in Section 1129 and does not disclose anything said or done or any admission made in the course of the mediation, in which case the communication, document, or writing may be used in an attorney disciplinary proceeding to determine whether the attorney has complied with Section 1129.

(b) For purposes of subdivision (a), if the neutral person who conducts a mediation expressly agrees to disclosure, that agreement also binds any other person described in subdivision (b) of Section 1115.

§ 1123. ADMISSIBILITY OR DISCLOSURE OF WRITTEN SETTLEMENT AGREEMENT

A written settlement agreement prepared in the course of, or pursuant to, a mediation, is not made inadmissible, or protected from disclosure, by provisions of this chapter if the agreement is signed by the settling parties and any of the following conditions are satisfied:

(a) The agreement provides that it is admissible or subject to disclosure, or words to that effect.

(b) The agreement provides that it is enforceable or binding or words to that effect.

(c) All parties to the agreement expressly agree in writing, or orally in accordance with Section 1118, to its disclosure.

(d) The agreement is used to show fraud, duress, or illegality that is relevant to an issue in dispute.

§ 1124. ADMISSIBILITY OR DISCLOSURE OF ORAL AGREEMENT

An oral agreement made in the course of, or pursuant to, a mediation is not made inadmissible, or protected from disclosure, by the provisions of this chapter if any of the following conditions are satisfied:

(a) The agreement is in accordance with Section 1118.

(b) The agreement is in accordance with subdivisions (a), (b), and (d) of Section 1118, and all parties to the agreement expressly agree, in writing or orally in accordance with Section 1118, to disclosure of the agreement.

(c) The agreement is in accordance with subdivisions (a), (b), and (d) of Section 1118, and the agreement is used to show fraud, duress, or illegality that is relevant to an issue in dispute.

§ 1125. CONDITIONS CONSTITUTING END OF MEDIATION

(a) For purposes of confidentiality under this chapter, a mediation ends when any one of the following conditions is satisfied:

(1) The parties execute a written settlement agreement that fully resolves the dispute.

(2) An oral agreement that fully resolves the dispute is reached in accordance with Section 1118.

(3) The mediator provides the mediation participants with a writing signed by the mediator that states that the mediation is terminated, or words to that effect, which shall be consistent with Section 1121.

(4) A party provides the mediator and the other mediation participants with a writing stating that the mediation is terminated, or words to that effect, which shall be consistent with Section 1121. In a mediation involving more than two parties, the mediation may continue as to the remaining parties or be terminated in accordance with this section.

(5) For 10 calendar days, there is no communication between the mediator and any of the parties to the mediation relating to the dispute. The mediator and the parties may shorten or extend this time by agreement.

(b) For purposes of confidentiality under this chapter, if a mediation partially resolves a dispute, mediation ends when either of the following conditions is satisfied:

(1) The parties execute a written settlement agreement that partially resolves the dispute.

(2) An oral agreement that partially resolves the dispute is reached in accordance with Section 1118.

(c) This section does not preclude a party from ending a mediation without reaching an agreement. This section does not otherwise affect the extent to which a party may terminate a mediation.

§ 1126. CONFIDENTIALITY AFTER END OF MEDIATION

Anything said, any admission made, or any writing that is inadmissible, protected from disclosure, and confidential under this chapter before a mediation ends, shall remain inadmissible, protected from disclosure, and confidential to the same extent after the mediation ends.

§ 1127. ATTORNEY FEES FOR COMPELLING MEDIATOR TO TESTIFY OR PRODUCE WRITING

If a person subpoenas or otherwise seeks to compel a mediator to testify or produce a writing, as defined in Section 250, and the court or other adjudicative body determines that the testimony or writing is inadmissible under this chapter, or protected from disclosure under this chapter, the court or adjudicative body making the determination shall award reasonable attorney's fees and costs to the mediator against the person seeking the testimony or writing.

§ 1128. REFERENCE TO MEDIATION DURING SUBSEQUENT PROCEEDINGS

Any reference to a mediation during any subsequent trial is an irregularity in the proceedings of the trial for the purposes of Section 657 of the Code of Civil Procedure. Any reference to a mediation during any other subsequent noncriminal proceeding is grounds for vacating or modifying the decision in that proceeding, in whole or in part, and granting a new or further hearing on all or part of the issues, if the reference materially affected the substantial rights of the party requesting relief.

§ 1129. PRINTED DISCLOSURE AND ACKNOWLEDGEMENT REQUIREMENTS

(a) Except in the case of a class or representative action, an attorney representing a client participating in a mediation or a mediation consultation shall, as soon as reasonably possible before the client agrees to participate in the mediation or mediation consultation, provide that client with a printed disclosure containing the confidentiality restrictions described in Section 1119 and obtain a printed acknowledgment signed by that client stating that he or she has read and understands the confidentiality restrictions.

(b) An attorney who is retained after an individual agrees to participate in the mediation or mediation consultation shall, as soon as reasonably possible after being retained, comply with the printed disclosure and acknowledgment requirements described in subdivision (a).

(c) The printed disclosure required by subdivision (a) shall:

(1) Be printed in the preferred language of the client in at least 12-point font.

(2) Be printed on a single page that is not attached to any other document provided to the client.

(3) Include the names of the attorney and the client and be signed and dated by the attorney and the client.

(d) If the requirements in subdivision (c) are met, the following disclosure shall be deemed to comply with the requirements of subdivision (a):

Mediation Disclosure Notification and Acknowledgment

To promote communication in mediation, California law generally makes mediation a confidential process. California's mediation confidentiality laws are laid out in Sections 703.5 and 1115 to 1129, inclusive, of the Evidence Code. Those laws establish the confidentiality of mediation and limit the disclosure, admissibility, and a court's consideration of communications, writings, and conduct in connection with a mediation. In general, those laws mean the following:

- All communications, negotiations, or settlement offers in the course of a mediation must remain confidential.
- Statements made and writings prepared in connection with a mediation are not admissible or subject to discovery or compelled disclosure in noncriminal proceedings.
- A mediator's report, opinion, recommendation, or finding about what occurred in a mediation may not be submitted to or considered by a court or another adjudicative body.
- A mediator cannot testify in any subsequent civil proceeding about any communication or conduct occurring at, or in connection with, a mediation.

This means that all communications between you and your attorney made in preparation for a mediation, or during a mediation, are confidential and cannot be disclosed or used (except in extremely limited circumstances), even if you later decide to sue your attorney for malpractice because of something that happens during the mediation.

I, ____________ [Name of Client], understand that, unless all participants agree otherwise, no oral or written communication made during a mediation, or in preparation for a mediation, including communications between me and my attorney, can be used as evidence in any subsequent noncriminal legal action including an action against my attorney for malpractice or an ethical violation.

NOTE: This disclosure and signed acknowledgment does not limit your attorney's potential liability to you for professional malpractice, or prevent you from (1) reporting any professional misconduct by your attorney to the State Bar of California or (2) cooperating with any disciplinary investigation or criminal prosecution of your attorney.

[Name of Client] [Date signed]

[Name of Attorney] [Date signed]

(e) Failure of an attorney to comply with this section is not a basis to set aside an agreement prepared in the course of, or pursuant to, a mediation.

Chapter 3: Other Evidence Affected or Excluded by Extrinsic Policies

§ 1150. EVIDENCE TO TEST A VERDICT

(a) Upon an inquiry as to the validity of a verdict, any otherwise admissible evidence may be received as to statements made, or conduct, conditions, or events occurring, either within or without the jury room, of such a character as is likely to have influenced the verdict improperly. No evidence is admissible to show the effect of such statement, conduct, condition, or event upon a juror either in influencing him to assent to or dissent from the verdict or concerning the mental processes by which it was determined.

(b) Nothing in this code affects the law relating to the competence of a juror to give evidence to impeach or support a verdict.

§ 1151. SUBSEQUENT REMEDIAL CONDUCT

When, after the occurrence of an event, remedial or precautionary measures are taken, which, if taken previously, would have tended to make the event less likely to occur, evidence of such subsequent measures is inadmissible to prove negligence or culpable conduct in connection with the event.

§ 1152. ADMISSIBILITY OF EVIDENCE OF OFFER TO COMPROMISE

(a) Evidence that a person has, in compromise or from humanitarian motives, furnished or offered or promised to furnish money or any other thing, act, or service to another who has sustained or will sustain or claims that he or she has sustained or will sustain loss or damage, as well as any conduct or statements made in negotiation thereof, is inadmissible to prove his or her liability for the loss or damage or any part of it.

(b) In the event that evidence of an offer to compromise is admitted in an action for breach of the covenant of good faith and fair dealing or violation of subdivision (h) of Section 790.03 of the Insurance Code, then at the request of the party against whom the evidence is admitted, or at the request of the party who made the offer to compromise that was admitted, evidence relating to any other offer or counteroffer to compromise the same or substantially the same claimed loss or damage shall also be admissible for the same purpose as the initial evidence regarding settlement. Other than as may be admitted in an action for breach of the covenant of good faith and fair dealing or violation of subdivision (h) of Section 790.03 of the Insurance Code, evidence of settlement offers shall not be admitted in a motion for a new trial, in any proceeding involving an additur or remittitur, or on appeal.

(c) This section does not affect the admissibility of evidence of any of the following:

(1) Partial satisfaction of an asserted claim or demand without questioning its validity when such evidence is offered to prove the validity of the claim.

(2) A debtor's payment or promise to pay all or a part of his or her preexisting debt when such evidence is offered to prove the creation of a new duty on his or her part or a revival of his or her preexisting duty.

§ 1153. OFFER TO PLEAD GUILTY OR WITHDRAW PLEA OF GUILTY BY CRIMINAL DEFENDANT

Evidence of a plea of guilty, later withdrawn, or of an offer to plead guilty to the crime charged or to any other crime, made by the defendant in a criminal action is inadmissible in any action or in any proceeding of any nature, including proceedings before agencies, commissions, boards, and tribunals.

§ 1154. OFFER TO DISCOUNT A CLAIM

Evidence that a person has accepted or offered or promised to accept a sum of money or any other thing, act, or service in satisfaction of a claim, as well as any conduct or statements made in negotiation thereof, is inadmissible to prove the invalidity of the claim or any part of it.

§ 1155. LIABILITY INSURANCE

Evidence that a person was, at the time a harm was suffered by another, insured wholly or partially against loss arising from liability for that harm is inadmissible to prove negligence or other wrongdoing.

§ 1156. RECORDS OF MEDICAL OR DENTAL STUDY OF IN-HOSPITAL STAFF COMMITTEE

(a) In-hospital medical or medical-dental staff committees of a licensed hospital may engage in research and medical or dental study for the purpose of reducing morbidity or mortality, and may make findings and recommendations relating to such purpose. Except as provided in subdivision (b), the written records of interviews, reports, statements, or memoranda of such in-hospital medical or medical-dental staff committees relating to such medical or dental studies are subject to Title 4 (commencing with Section 2016.010) of Part 4 of the Code of Civil Procedure (relating to discovery proceedings) but, subject to subdivisions (c) and (d), shall not be admitted as evidence in any action or before any administrative body, agency, or person.

(b) The disclosure, with or without the consent of the patient, of information concerning him to such in-hospital medical or medical-dental staff committee does not make unprivileged any information that would otherwise be privileged under Section 994 or 1014; but, notwithstanding Sections 994 and 1014, such information is subject to discovery under subdivision (a) except that the identity of any patient may not be discovered under subdivision (a) unless the patient consents to such disclosure.

(c) This section does not affect the admissibility in evidence of the original medical or dental records of any patient.

(d) This section does not exclude evidence which is relevant evidence in a criminal action.

§ 1157. EXEMPTION FROM DISCOVERY OF PROCEEDINGS AND RECORDS OF SPECIFIED COMMITTEES AND BODIES

(a) Neither the proceedings nor the records of organized committees of medical, medical-dental, podiatric, registered dietitian, psychological, marriage and family therapist, licensed clinical social worker, professional clinical counselor, pharmacist, prehospital emergency medical care person or personnel, or veterinary staffs, or of a peer review body, as defined in Section 805 of the Business and Professions Code, having the responsibility of evaluation and improvement of the quality of care rendered in the hospital, or for that peer review body, or medical or dental review or dental hygienist review or chiropractic review or podiatric review or registered dietitian review or pharmacist review or veterinary review or acupuncturist review or licensed midwife review or prehospital emergency medical care person or personnel review committees of local medical, dental, dental hygienist, podiatric, dietetic, pharmacist, veterinary, acupuncture, chiropractic, or prehospital emergency medical care person or personnel societies, marriage and family therapist, licensed clinical social worker, professional clinical counselor, or psychological review committees of state or local marriage and family therapist, state or local licensed clinical social worker, state or local licensed professional clinical counselor, or state or local psychological associations or societies or licensed midwife associations or societies having the responsibility of evaluation and improvement of the quality of care, shall be subject to discovery.

(b) Except as hereinafter provided, a person in attendance at a meeting of any of the committees described in subdivision (a) shall not be required to testify as to what transpired at that meeting.

(c) The prohibition relating to discovery or testimony does not apply to the statements made by a person in attendance at a meeting of any of the committees described in subdivision (a) if that person is a party to an action or proceeding the subject matter of which was reviewed at that meeting, to a person requesting hospital staff privileges, or in an action against an insurance carrier alleging bad faith by the carrier in refusing to accept a settlement offer within the policy limits.

(d) The prohibitions in this section do not apply to medical, dental, dental hygienist, podiatric, dietetic, psychological, marriage and family therapist, licensed clinical social worker, professional clinical counselor, pharmacist, veterinary, acupuncture, midwifery, chiropractic, or prehospital emergency medical care person or personnel society committees that exceed 10 percent of the membership of the society, nor to any of those committees if a person serves upon the committee when his or her own conduct or practice is being reviewed.

(e) The amendments made to this section by Chapter 1081 of the Statutes of 1983, or at the 1985 portion of the 1985–86 Regular Session of the Legislature, at the 1990 portion of the 1989–90 Regular Session of the Legislature, at the 2000 portion of the 1999–2000 Regular Session of the Legislature, at the 2011 portion of the 2011–12 Regular Session of the Legislature, at the 2015 portion of the 2015–16 Regular Session of the Legislature, or at the 2024 portion of the 2023–24 Regular Session of the Legislature, do not exclude the discovery or use of relevant evidence in a criminal action.

(f) For purposes of this section, "prehospital emergency medical care person or personnel" has the same meaning as defined in paragraph (1) of subdivision (a) of Section 1797.188 of the Health and Safety Code.

§ 1160. STATEMENT OF BENEVOLENCE

(a) The portion of statements, writings, or benevolent gestures expressing sympathy or a general sense of benevolence relating to the pain, suffering, or death of a person involved in an accident and made to that person or to the family of that person shall be inadmissible as evidence of an admission of liability in a civil action. A statement of fault, however, which is part of, or in addition to, any of the above shall not be inadmissible pursuant to this section.

(b) For purposes of this section:

(1) "Accident" means an occurrence resulting in injury or death to one or more persons which is not the result of willful action by a party.

(2) "Benevolent gestures" means actions which convey a sense of compassion or commiseration emanating from humane impulses.

(3) "Family" means the spouse, parent, grandparent, stepmother, stepfather, child, grandchild, brother, sister, half brother, half sister, adopted children of parent, or spouse's parents of an injured party.

DIVISION 10: HEARSAY EVIDENCE

Chapter 1: General Provisions

§ 1200. THE HEARSAY RULE

(a) "Hearsay evidence" is evidence of a statement that was made other than by a witness while testifying at the hearing and that is offered to prove the truth of the matter stated.

(b) Except as provided by law, hearsay evidence is inadmissible.

(c) This section shall be known and may be cited as the hearsay rule.

§ 1201. MULTIPLE HEARSAY

A statement within the scope of an exception to the hearsay rule is not inadmissible on the ground that the evidence of such statement is hearsay evidence if such hearsay evidence consists of one or more statements each of which meets the requirements of an exception to the hearsay rule.

§ 1202. CREDIBILITY OF HEARSAY DECLARANT

Evidence of a statement or other conduct by a declarant that is inconsistent with a statement by such declarant received in evidence as hearsay evidence is not inadmissible for the purpose of attacking the credibility of the declarant though he is not given and has not had an opportunity to explain or to deny such inconsistent statement or other conduct. Any other evidence offered to attack or support the credibility of the declarant is admissible if it would have been admissible had the declarant been a witness at the hearing. For the purposes of this section, the deponent of a deposition taken in the action in which it is offered shall be deemed to be a hearsay declarant.

§ 1203. CROSS-EXAMINATION OF HEARSAY DECLARANT

(a) The declarant of a statement that is admitted as hearsay evidence may be called and examined by any adverse party as if under cross-examination concerning the statement.

(b) This section is not applicable if the declarant is (1) a party, (2) a person identified with a party within the meaning of subdivision (d) of Section 776, or (3) a witness who has testified in the action concerning the subject matter of the statement.

(c) This section is not applicable if the statement is one described in Article 1 (commencing with Section 1220), Article 3 (commencing with Section 1235), or Article 10 (commencing with Section 1300) of Chapter 2 of this division.

(d) A statement that is otherwise admissible as hearsay evidence is not made inadmissible by this section because the declarant who made the statement is unavailable for examination pursuant to this section.

§ 1203.1. HEARSAY STATEMENTS ADMISSIBLE AT PRELIMINARY HEARING

Section 1203 is not applicable if the hearsay statement is offered at a preliminary examination, as provided in Section 872 of the Penal Code.

§ 1204. HEARSAY STATEMENT OFFERED AGAINST CRIMINAL DEFENDANT

A statement that is otherwise admissible as hearsay evidence is inadmissible against the defendant in a criminal action if the statement was made, either by the defendant or by another, under such circumstances that it is inadmissible against the defendant under the Constitution of the United States or the State of California.

§ 1205. NO IMPLIED REPEAL

Nothing in this division shall be construed to repeal by implication any other statute relating to hearsay evidence.

Chapter 2: Exceptions to the Hearsay Rule

Article 1: Confessions and Admissions

§ 1220. ADMISSION OF PARTY

Evidence of a statement is not made inadmissible by the hearsay rule when offered against the declarant in an action to which he is a party in either his individual or representative capacity, regardless of whether the statement was made in his individual or representative capacity.

§ 1221. ADOPTIVE ADMISSION

Evidence of a statement offered against a party is not made inadmissible by the hearsay rule if the statement is one of which the party, with knowledge of the content thereof, has by words or other conduct manifested his adoption or his belief in its truth.

§ 1222. AUTHORIZED ADMISSION

Evidence of a statement offered against a party is not made inadmissible by the hearsay rule if:

(a) The statement was made by a person authorized by the party to make a statement or statements for him concerning the subject matter of the statement; and

(b) The evidence is offered either after admission of evidence sufficient to sustain a finding of such authority or, in the court's discretion as to the order of proof, subject to the admission of such evidence.

§ 1223. ADMISSION OF CO-CONSPIRATOR

Evidence of a statement offered against a party is not made inadmissible by the hearsay rule if:

(a) The statement was made by the declarant while participating in a conspiracy to commit a crime or civil wrong and in furtherance of the objective of that conspiracy;

(b) The statement was made prior to or during the time that the party was participating in that conspiracy; and

(c) The evidence is offered either after admission of evidence sufficient to sustain a finding of the facts specified in subdivisions (a) and (b) or, in the court's discretion as to the order of proof, subject to the admission of such evidence.

§ 1224. STATEMENT OF DECLARANT WHOSE LIABILITY OR BREACH OF DUTY IS IN ISSUE

When the liability obligation, or duty of a party to a civil action is based in whole or in part upon the liability, obligation, or duty of the declarant, or when the claim or right asserted by a party to a civil action is barred or diminished by a breach of duty by the declarant, evidence of a statement made by the declarant is as admissible against the party as it would be if offered against the declarant in an action involving that liability, obligation, duty, or breach of duty.

§ 1225. STATEMENT OF DECLARANT WHOSE RIGHT OR TITLE IS IN ISSUE

When a right, title, or interest in any property or claim asserted by a party to a civil action requires a determination that a right, title, or interest exists or existed in the declarant, evidence of a statement made by the declarant during the time the party now claims the declarant was the holder of the right, title, or interest is as admissible against the party as it would be if offered against the declarant in an action involving that right, title, or interest.

§ 1226. STATEMENT OF MINOR CHILD IN PARENT'S ACTION FOR CHILD'S INJURY

Evidence of a statement by a minor child is not made inadmissible by the hearsay rule if offered against the plaintiff in an action brought under Section 376 of the Code of Civil Procedure for injury to such minor child.

§ 1227. WRONGFUL DEATH ACTION – STATEMENTS BY DECEASED

Evidence of a statement by the deceased is not made inadmissible by the hearsay rule if offered against the plaintiff in an action for wrongful death brought under Article 6 (commencing with Section 377.60) of Chapter 4 of Title 3 of Part 2 of the Code of Civil Procedure.

§ 1228. STATEMENT OF MINOR CHILD AS VICTIM OF SEXUAL ABUSE

Notwithstanding any other provision of law, for the purpose of establishing the elements of the crime in order to admit as evidence the confession of a person accused of violating Section 261, 264.1, 285, 286, 287, 288, 289, or 647a of, or former Section 288a of, the Penal Code, a court, in its discretion, may determine that a statement of the complaining witness is not made inadmissible by the hearsay rule if it finds all of the following:

(a) The statement was made by a minor child under the age of 12, and the contents of the statement were included in a written report of a law enforcement official or an employee of a county welfare department.

(b) The statement describes the minor child as a victim of sexual abuse.

(c) The statement was made prior to the defendant's confession. The court shall view with caution the testimony of a person recounting hearsay where there is evidence of personal bias or prejudice.

(d) There are no circumstances, such as significant inconsistencies between the confession and the statement concerning material facts establishing any element of the crime or the identification of the defendant, that would render the statement unreliable.

(e) The minor child is found to be unavailable pursuant to paragraph (2) or (3) of subdivision (a) of Section 240 or refuses to testify.

(f) The confession was memorialized in a trustworthy fashion by a law enforcement official.

If the prosecution intends to offer a statement of the complaining witness pursuant to this section, the prosecution shall serve a written notice upon the defendant at least 10 days prior to the hearing or trial at which the prosecution intends to offer the statement.

If the statement is offered during trial, the court's determination shall be made out of the presence of the jury. If the statement is found to be admissible pursuant to this section, it shall be admitted out of the presence of the jury and solely for the purpose of determining the admissibility of the confession of the defendant.

Article 2: Declaration Against Interest

§ 1230. DECLARATION AGAINST INTEREST

Evidence of a statement by a declarant having sufficient knowledge of the subject is not made inadmissible by the hearsay rule if the declarant is unavailable as a witness and the statement, when made, was so far contrary to the declarant's pecuniary or proprietary interest, or so far subjected him to the risk of civil or criminal liability, or so far tended to render invalid a claim by him against another, or created such a risk of making him an object of hatred, ridicule, or social disgrace in the community, that a reasonable man in his position would not have made the statement unless he believed it to be true.

Article 2.5: Sworn Statements Regarding Gang-Related Crimes

§ 1231. EXCEPTION TO HEARSAY RULE

Evidence of a prior statement made by a declarant is not made inadmissible by the hearsay rule if the declarant is deceased and the proponent of introducing the statement establishes each of the following:

(a) The statement relates to acts or events relevant to a criminal prosecution under provisions of the California Street Terrorism Enforcement and Prevention Act (Chapter 11 (commencing with Section 186.20) of Title 7 of Part 1 of the Penal Code).

(b) A verbatim transcript, copy, or record of the statement exists. A record may include a statement preserved by means of an audio or video recording or equivalent technology.

(c) The statement relates to acts or events within the personal knowledge of the declarant.

(d) The statement was made under oath or affirmation in an affidavit; or was made at a deposition, preliminary hearing, grand jury hearing, or other proceeding in compliance with law, and was made under penalty of perjury.

(e) The declarant died from other than natural causes.

(f) The statement was made under circumstances that would indicate its trustworthiness and render the declarant's statement particularly worthy of belief. For purposes of this subdivision, circumstances relevant to the issue of trustworthiness include, but are not limited to, all of the following:

(1) Whether the statement was made in contemplation of a pending or anticipated criminal or civil matter, in which the declarant had an interest, other than as a witness.

(2) Whether the declarant had a bias or motive for fabricating the statement, and the extent of any bias or motive.

(3) Whether the statement is corroborated by evidence other than statements that are admissible only pursuant to this section.

(4) Whether the statement was a statement against the declarant's interest.

Article 3: Prior Statements of Witnesses

§ 1235. INCONSISTENT STATEMENT

Evidence of a statement made by a witness is not made inadmissible by the hearsay rule if the statement is inconsistent with his testimony at the hearing and is offered in compliance with Section 770.

§ 1236. PRIOR CONSISTENT STATEMENT

Evidence of a statement previously made by a witness is not made inadmissible by the hearsay rule if the statement is consistent with his testimony at the hearing and is offered in compliance with Section 791.

§ 1237. PAST RECOLLECTION RECORDED

(a) Evidence of a statement previously made by a witness is not made inadmissible by the hearsay rule if the statement would have been admissible if made by him while testifying, the statement concerns a matter as to which the witness has insufficient present recollection to enable him to testify fully and accurately, and the statement is contained in a writing which:

(1) Was made at a time when the fact recorded in the writing actually occurred or was fresh in the witness' memory;

(2) Was made (i) by the witness himself or under his direction or (ii) by some other person for the purpose of recording the witness' statement at the time it was made;

(3) Is offered after the witness testifies that the statement he made was a true statement of such fact; and

(4) Is offered after the writing is authenticated as an accurate record of the statement.

(b) The writing may be read into evidence, but the writing itself may not be received in evidence unless offered by an adverse party.

§ 1238. PRIOR IDENTIFICATION

Evidence of a statement previously made by a witness is not made inadmissible by the hearsay rule if the statement would have been admissible if made by him while testifying and:

(a) The statement is an identification of a party or another as a person who participated in a crime or other occurrence;

(b) The statement was made at a time when the crime or other occurrence was fresh in the witness' memory; and

(c) The evidence of the statement is offered after the witness testifies that he made the identification and that it was a true reflection of his opinion at that time.

Article 4: Spontaneous, Contemporaneous, and Dying Declarations

§ 1240. SPONTANEOUS STATEMENT

Evidence of a statement is not made inadmissible by the hearsay rule if the statement:

(a) Purports to narrate, describe, or explain an act, condition, or event perceived by the declarant; and

(b) Was made spontaneously while the declarant was under the stress of excitement caused by such perception.

§ 1241. CONTEMPORANEOUS STATEMENT

Evidence of a statement is not made inadmissible by the hearsay rule if the statement:

(a) Is offered to explain, qualify, or make understandable conduct of the declarant; and

(b) Was made while the declarant was engaged in such conduct.

§ 1242. DYING DECLARATION

Evidence of a statement made by a dying person respecting the cause and circumstances of his death is not made inadmissible by the hearsay rule if the statement was made upon his personal knowledge and under a sense of immediately impending death.

Article 5: Statements of Mental or Physical State

§ 1250. STATEMENT OF DECLARANT'S THEN EXISTING MENTAL OR PHYSICAL STATE

(a) Subject to Section 1252, evidence of a statement of the declarant's then existing state of mind, emotion, or physical sensation (including a statement of intent, plan, motive, design, mental feeling, pain, or bodily health) is not made inadmissible by the hearsay rule when:

(1) The evidence is offered to prove the declarant's state of mind, emotion, or physical sensation at that time or at any other time when it is itself an issue in the action; or

(2) The evidence is offered to prove or explain acts or conduct of the declarant.

(b) This section does not make admissible evidence of a statement of memory or belief to prove the fact remembered or believed.

§ 1251. STATEMENT OF DECLARANT'S PREVIOUSLY EXISTING MENTAL OR PHYSICAL STATE

Subject to Section 1252, evidence of a statement of the declarant's state of mind, emotion, or physical sensation (including a statement of intent, plan, motive, design, mental feeling, pain, or bodily health) at a time prior to the statement is not made inadmissible by the hearsay rule if:

(a) The declarant is unavailable as a witness; and

(b) The evidence is offered to prove such prior state of mind, emotion, or physical sensation when it is itself an issue in the action and the evidence is not offered to prove any fact other than such state of mind, emotion, or physical sensation.

§ 1252. LIMITATION ON ADMISSIBILITY OF STATEMENT OF MENTAL OR PHYSICAL STATE

Evidence of a statement is inadmissible under this article if the statement was made under circumstances such as to indicate its lack of trustworthiness.

§ 1253. STATEMENT DESCRIBING MEDICAL HISTORY, SYMPTOMS, OR PAIN, MADE FOR PURPOSES OF MEDICAL DIAGNOSIS OR TREATMENT

Subject to Section 1252, evidence of a statement is not made inadmissible by the hearsay rule if the statement was made for purposes of medical diagnosis or treatment and describes medical history, or past or present symptoms, pain, or sensations, or the inception or general character of the cause or external source thereof insofar as reasonably pertinent to diagnosis or treatment. This section applies only to a statement made by a victim who is a minor at the time of the proceedings, provided the statement was made when the victim was under the age of 12 describing any act, or attempted act, of child abuse or neglect. "Child abuse" and "child neglect," for purposes of this section, have the meanings provided in subdivision (c) of Section 1360. In addition, "child abuse" means any act proscribed by Chapter 5 (commencing with Section 281) of Title 9 of Part 1 of the Penal Code committed against a minor.

Article 6: Statements Relating to Wills and to Claims Against Estates

§ 1260. STATEMENT CONCERNING DECLARANT'S WILL OR REVOCABLE TRUST; TRUSTWORTHINESS OF STATEMENT

(a) Except as provided in subdivision (b), evidence of any of the following statements made by a declarant who is unavailable as a witness is not made inadmissible by the hearsay rule:

(1) That the declarant has or has not made a will or established or amended a revocable trust.

(2) That the declarant has or has not revoked his or her will, revocable trust, or an amendment to a revocable trust.

(3) That identifies the declarant's will, revocable trust, or an amendment to a revocable trust.

(b) Evidence of a statement is inadmissible under this section if the statement was made under circumstances that indicate its lack of trustworthiness.

§ 1261. STATEMENT OF DECEDENT OFFERED IN ACTION AGAINST ESTATE

(a) Evidence of a statement is not made inadmissible by the hearsay rule when offered in an action upon a claim or demand against the estate of the declarant if the statement was made upon the personal knowledge of the declarant at a time when the matter had been recently perceived by him and while his recollection was clear.

(b) Evidence of a statement is inadmissible under this section if the statement was made under circumstances such as to indicate its lack of trustworthiness.

Article 7: Business Records

§ 1270. "A BUSINESS"

As used in this article, "a business" includes every kind of business, governmental activity, profession, occupation, calling, or operation of institutions, whether carried on for profit or not.

§ 1271. BUSINESS RECORD

Evidence of a writing made as a record of an act, condition, or event is not made inadmissible by the hearsay rule when offered to prove the act, condition, or event if:

(a) The writing was made in the regular course of a business;

(b) The writing was made at or near the time of the act, condition, or event;

(c) The custodian or other qualified witness testifies to its identity and the mode of its preparation; and

(d) The sources of information and method and time of preparation were such as to indicate its trustworthiness.

§ 1272. ABSENCE OF ENTRY IN BUSINESS RECORDS

Evidence of the absence from the records of a business of a record of an asserted act, condition, or event is not made inadmissible by the hearsay rule when offered to prove the nonoccurrence of the act or event, or the nonexistence of the condition, if:

(a) It was the regular course of that business to make records of all such acts, conditions, or events at or near the time of the act, condition, or event and to preserve them; and

(b) The sources of information and method and time of preparation of the records of that business were such that the absence of a record of an act, condition, or event is a trustworthy indication that the act or event did not occur or the condition did not exist.

Article 8: Official Records and Other Official Writings

§ 1280. RECORD BY PUBLIC EMPLOYEE

Evidence of a writing made as a record of an act, condition, or event is not made inadmissible by the hearsay rule when offered in any civil or criminal proceeding to prove the act, condition, or event if all of the following applies:

(a) The writing was made by and within the scope of duty of a public employee.

(b) The writing was made at or near the time of the act, condition, or event.

(c) The sources of information and method and time of preparation were such as to indicate its trustworthiness.

§ 1281. RECORD OF VITAL STATISTIC

Evidence of a writing made as a record of a birth, fetal death, death, or marriage is not made inadmissible by the hearsay rule if the maker was required by law to file the writing in a designated public office and the writing was made and filed as required by law.

§ 1282. FINDING OF PRESUMED DEATH BY AUTHORIZED FEDERAL EMPLOYEE

A written finding of presumed death made by an employee of the United States authorized to make such finding pursuant to the Federal Missing Persons Act (56 Stats. 143, 1092, and P.L. 408, Ch. 371, 2d Sess. 78th Cong.; 50 U.S.C. App. 1001–1016), as enacted or as heretofore or hereafter amended, shall be received in any court, office, or other place in this state as evidence of the death of the person therein found to be dead and of the date, circumstances, and place of his disappearance.

§ 1283. RECORD BY FEDERAL EMPLOYEE THAT PERSON IS MISSING, CAPTURED, OR THE LIKE

An official written report or record that a person is missing, missing in action, interned in a foreign country, captured by a hostile force, beleaguered by a hostile force, besieged by a hostile force, or detained in a foreign country against his will, or is dead or is alive, made by an employee of the United States authorized by any law of the United States to make such report or record shall be received in any court, office, or other place in this state as evidence that such person is missing, missing in action, interned in a foreign country, captured by a hostile force, beleaguered by a hostile force, besieged by a hostile force, or detained in a foreign country against his will, or is dead or is alive.

§ 1284. STATEMENT OF ABSENCE OF PUBLIC RECORD

Evidence of a writing made by the public employee who is the official custodian of the records in a public office, reciting diligent search and failure to find a record, is not made inadmissible by the hearsay rule when offered to prove the absence of a record in that office.

§ 1285. STATEMENTS AT CIVIL HEARING FOR PERSON CONVICTED OF SEXUAL OFFENSE

Within an official written report or record of a law enforcement officer regarding a sexual offense that resulted in a person's conviction, the following statements are not made inadmissible by the hearsay rule at the civil hearing described in Section 6602 of the Welfare and Institutions Code when offered to prove the truth of the matter stated:

(a) A statement from a victim of the sexual offense.

(b) A statement from an eyewitness to the sexual offense.

(c) A statement from a sexual assault medical examiner who examined a victim of the sexual offense.

Article 9: Former Testimony

§ 1290. "FORMER TESTIMONY"

As used in this article, "former testimony" means testimony given under oath in:

(a) Another action or in a former hearing or trial of the same action;

(b) A proceeding to determine a controversy conducted by or under the supervision of an agency that has the power to determine such a controversy and is an agency of the United States or a public entity in the United States;

(c) A deposition taken in compliance with law in another action; or

(d) An arbitration proceeding if the evidence of such former testimony is a verbatim transcript thereof.

§ 1291. FORMER TESTIMONY OFFERED AGAINST PARTY TO FORMER PROCEEDING

(a) Evidence of former testimony is not made inadmissible by the hearsay rule if the declarant is unavailable as a witness and:

(1) The former testimony is offered against a person who offered it in evidence in his own behalf on the former occasion or against the successor in interest of such person; or

(2) The party against whom the former testimony is offered was a party to the action or proceeding in which the testimony was given and had the right and opportunity to cross- examine the declarant with an interest and motive similar to that which he has at the hearing.

(b) The admissibility of former testimony under this section is subject to the same limitations and objections as though the declarant were testifying at the hearing, except that former testimony offered under this section is not subject to:

(1) Objections to the form of the question which were not made at the time the former testimony was given.

(2) Objections based on competency or privilege which did not exist at the time the former testimony was given.

§ 1292. FORMER TESTIMONY OFFERED AGAINST PERSON NOT A PARTY TO FORMER PROCEEDING

(a) Evidence of former testimony is not made inadmissible by the hearsay rule if:

(1) The declarant is unavailable as a witness;

(2) The former testimony is offered in a civil action; and

(3) The issue is such that the party to the action or proceeding in which the former testimony was given had the right and opportunity to cross-examine the declarant with an interest and motive similar to that which the party against whom the testimony is offered has at the hearing.

(b) The admissibility of former testimony under this section is subject to the same limitations and objections as though the declarant were testifying at the hearing, except that former testimony offered under this section is not subject to objections based on competency or privilege which did not exist at the time the former testimony was given.

§ 1293. FORMER TESTIMONY OF MINOR AGAINST PARENT OR GUARDIAN AS EXCEPTION TO HEARSAY RULE; CHALLENGE TO TESTIMONY

(a) Evidence of former testimony made at a preliminary examination by a minor child who was the complaining witness is not made inadmissible by the hearsay rule if:

(1) The former testimony is offered in a proceeding to declare the minor a dependent child of the court pursuant to Section 300 of the Welfare and Institutions Code.

(2) The issues are such that a defendant in the preliminary examination in which the former testimony was given had the right and opportunity to cross-examine the minor child with an interest and motive similar to that which the parent or guardian against whom the testimony is offered has at the proceeding to declare the minor a dependent child of the court.

(b) The admissibility of former testimony under this section is subject to the same limitations and objections as though the minor child were testifying at the proceeding to declare him or her a dependent child of the court.

(c) The attorney for the parent or guardian against whom the former testimony is offered or, if none, the parent or guardian may make a motion to challenge the admissibility of the former testimony upon a showing that new substantially different issues are present in the proceeding to declare the minor a dependent child than were present in the preliminary examination.

(d) As used in this section, "complaining witness" means the alleged victim of the crime for which a preliminary examination was held.

(e) This section shall apply only to testimony made at a preliminary examination on and after January 1, 1990.

§ 1294. INCONSISTENT STATEMENT HEARSAY EXCEPTION

(a) The following evidence of prior inconsistent statements of a witness properly admitted in a conditional examination, preliminary hearing, or trial of the same criminal matter pursuant to Section 1235 is not made inadmissible by the hearsay rule if the witness is unavailable and former testimony of the witness is admitted pursuant to Section 1291:

(1) A video or audio recorded statement introduced at a conditional examination, preliminary hearing, or prior proceeding concerning the same criminal matter.

(2) A transcript, containing the statements, of the conditional examination, preliminary hearing, or prior proceeding concerning the same criminal matter.

(b) The party against whom the prior inconsistent statements are offered, at his or her option, may examine or cross-examine any person who testified at the conditional examination, preliminary hearing, or prior proceeding, as to the prior inconsistent statements of the witness.

(c) As used in this section, "conditional examination" has the same meaning as in Chapter 4 (commencing with Section 1335) of Title 10 of Part 2 of the Penal Code.

Article 10: Judgments

§ 1300. JUDGMENT OF CONVICTION OF CRIME PUNISHABLE AS FELONY

Evidence of a final judgment adjudging a person guilty of a crime punishable as a felony is not made inadmissible by the hearsay rule when offered in a civil action to prove any fact essential to the judgment whether or not the judgment was based on a plea of nolo contendere.

§ 1301. JUDGMENT AGAINST PERSON ENTITLED TO INDEMNITY

Evidence of a final judgment is not made inadmissible by the hearsay rule when offered by the judgment debtor to prove any fact which was essential to the judgment in an action in which he seeks to:

(a) Recover partial or total indemnity or exoneration for money paid or liability incurred because of the judgment;

(b) Enforce a warranty to protect the judgment debtor against the liability determined by the judgment; or

(c) Recover damages for breach of warranty substantially the same as the warranty determined by the judgment to have been breached.

§ 1302. JUDGMENT DETERMINING LIABILITY OF THIRD PERSON

When the liability, obligation, or duty of a third person is in issue in a civil action, evidence of a final judgment against that person is not made inadmissible by the hearsay rule when offered to prove such liability, obligation, or duty.

Article 11: Family History

§ 1310. STATEMENT CONCERNING DECLARANT'S OWN FAMILY HISTORY

(a) Subject to subdivision (b), evidence of a statement by a declarant who is unavailable as a witness concerning his own birth, marriage, divorce, a parent and child relationship, relationship by blood or marriage, race, ancestry, or other similar fact of his family history is not made inadmissible by the hearsay rule, even though the declarant had no means of acquiring personal knowledge of the matter declared.

(b) Evidence of a statement is inadmissible under this section if the statement was made under circumstances such as to indicate its lack of trustworthiness.

§ 1311. STATEMENT CONCERNING FAMILY HISTORY OF ANOTHER

(a) Subject to subdivision (b), evidence of a statement concerning the birth, marriage, divorce, death, parent and child relationship, race, ancestry, relationship by blood or marriage, or other similar fact of the family history of a person other than the declarant is not made inadmissible by the hearsay rule if the declarant is unavailable as a witness and:

(1) The declarant was related to the other by blood or marriage; or

(2) The declarant was otherwise so intimately associated with the other's family as to be likely to have had accurate information concerning the matter declared and made the statement (i) upon information received from the other or from a person related by blood or marriage to the other or (ii) upon repute in the other's family.

(b) Evidence of a statement is inadmissible under this section if the statement was made under circumstances such as to indicate its lack of trustworthiness.

§ 1312. ENTRIES IN FAMILY RECORDS AND THE LIKE

Evidence of entries in family Bibles or other family books or charts, engravings on rings, family portraits, engravings on urns, crypts, or tombstones, and the like, is not made inadmissible by the hearsay rule when offered to prove the birth, marriage, divorce, death, parent and child relationship, race, ancestry, relationship by blood or marriage, or other similar fact of the family history of a member of the family by blood or marriage.

§ 1313. REPUTATION IN FAMILY CONCERNING FAMILY HISTORY

Evidence of reputation among members of a family is not made inadmissible by the hearsay rule if the reputation concerns the birth, marriage, divorce, death, parent and child relationship, race, ancestry, relationship by blood or marriage, or other similar fact of the family history of a member of the family by blood or marriage.

§ 1314. REPUTATION IN COMMUNITY CONCERNING FAMILY HISTORY

Evidence of reputation in a community concerning the date or fact of birth, marriage, divorce, or death of a person resident in the community at the time of the reputation is not made inadmissible by the hearsay rule.

§ 1315. CHURCH RECORDS CONCERNING FAMILY HISTORY

Evidence of a statement concerning a person's birth, marriage, divorce, death, parent and child relationship, race, ancestry, relationship by blood or marriage, or other similar fact of family history which is contained in a writing made as a record of a church, religious denomination, or religious society is not made inadmissible by the hearsay rule if:

(a) The statement is contained in a writing made as a record of an act, condition, or event that would be admissible as evidence of such act, condition, or event under Section 1271; and

(b) The statement is of a kind customarily recorded in connection with the act, condition, or event recorded in the writing.

§ 1316. MARRIAGE, BAPTISMAL, AND SIMILAR CERTIFICATES

Evidence of a statement concerning a person's birth, marriage, divorce, death, parent and child relationship, race, ancestry, relationship by blood or marriage, or other similar fact of family history is not made inadmissible by the hearsay rule if the statement is contained in a certificate that the maker thereof performed a marriage or other ceremony or administered a sacrament and:

(a) The maker was a clergyman, civil officer, or other person authorized to perform the acts reported in the certificate by law or by the rules, regulations, or requirements of a church, religious denomination, or religious society; and

(b) The certificate was issued by the maker at the time and place of the ceremony or sacrament or within a reasonable time thereafter.

Article 12: Reputation and Statements Concerning Community History, Property Interests, and Character

§ 1320. REPUTATION CONCERNING COMMUNITY HISTORY

Evidence of reputation in a community is not made inadmissible by the hearsay rule if the reputation concerns an event of general history of the community or of the state or nation of which the community is a part and the event was of importance to the community.

§ 1321. REPUTATION CONCERNING PUBLIC INTEREST IN PROPERTY

Evidence of reputation in a community is not made inadmissible by the hearsay rule if the reputation concerns the interest of the public in property in the community and the reputation arose before controversy.

§ 1322. REPUTATION CONCERNING BOUNDARY OR CUSTOM AFFECTING LAND

Evidence of reputation in a community is not made inadmissible by the hearsay rule if the reputation concerns boundaries of, or customs affecting, land in the community and the reputation arose before controversy.

§ 1323. STATEMENT CONCERNING BOUNDARY

Evidence of a statement concerning the boundary of land is not made inadmissible by the hearsay rule if the declarant is unavailable as a witness and had sufficient knowledge of the subject, but evidence of a statement is not admissible under this section if the statement was made under circumstances such as to indicate its lack of trustworthiness.

§ 1324. REPUTATION CONCERNING CHARACTER

Evidence of a person's general reputation with reference to his character or a trait of his character at a relevant time in the community in which he then resided or in a group with which he then habitually associated is not made inadmissible by the hearsay rule.

Article 13: Dispositive Instruments and Ancient Writings

§ 1330. RECITALS IN WRITINGS AFFECTING PROPERTY

Evidence of a statement contained in a deed of conveyance or a will or other writing purporting to affect an interest in real or personal property is not made inadmissible by the hearsay rule if:

(a) The matter stated was relevant to the purpose of the writing;

(b) The matter stated would be relevant to an issue as to an interest in the property; and

(c) The dealings with the property since the statement was made have not been inconsistent with the truth of the statement.

§ 1331. RECITALS IN ANCIENT WRITINGS

Evidence of a statement is not made inadmissible by the hearsay rule if the statement is contained in a writing more than 30 years old and the statement has been since generally acted upon as true by persons having an interest in the matter.

Article 14: Commercial, Scientific, and Similar Publications

§ 1340. COMMERCIAL LISTS AND THE LIKE

Evidence of a statement, other than an opinion, contained in a tabulation, list, directory, register, or other published compilation is not made inadmissible by the hearsay rule if the compilation is generally used and relied upon as accurate in the course of a business as defined in Section 1270.

§ 1341. PUBLICATIONS CONCERNING FACTS OF GENERAL NOTORIETY AND INTEREST

Historical works, books of science or art, and published maps or charts, made by persons indifferent between the parties, are not made inadmissible by the hearsay rule when offered to prove facts of general notoriety and interest.

Article 15: Declarant Unavailable as Witness

§ 1350. ADMISSIBILITY OF STATEMENT IN SERIOUS FELONY PROSECUTIONS

(a) In a criminal proceeding charging a serious felony, evidence of a statement made by a declarant is not made inadmissible by the hearsay rule if the declarant is unavailable as a witness, and all of the following are true:

(1) There is clear and convincing evidence that the declarant's unavailability was knowingly caused by, aided by, or solicited by the party against whom the statement is offered for the purpose of preventing the arrest or prosecution of the party and is the result of the death by homicide or the kidnapping of the declarant.

(2) There is no evidence that the unavailability of the declarant was caused by, aided by, solicited by, or procured on behalf of, the party who is offering the statement.

(3) The statement has been memorialized in a tape recording made by a law enforcement official, or in a written statement prepared by a law enforcement official and signed by the declarant and notarized in the presence of the law enforcement official, prior to the death or kidnapping of the declarant.

(4) The statement was made under circumstances which indicate its trustworthiness and was not the result of promise, inducement, threat, or coercion.

(5) The statement is relevant to the issues to be tried.

(6) The statement is corroborated by other evidence which tends to connect the party against whom the statement is offered with the commission of the serious felony with which the party is charged. The corroboration is not sufficient if it merely shows the commission of the offense or the circumstances thereof.

(b) If the prosecution intends to offer a statement pursuant to this section, the prosecution shall serve a written notice upon the defendant at least 10 days prior to the hearing or trial at which the prosecution intends to offer the statement, unless the prosecution shows good cause for the failure to provide that notice. In the event that good cause is shown, the defendant shall be entitled to a reasonable continuance of the hearing or trial.

(c) If the statement is offered during trial, the court's determination shall be made out of the presence of the jury. If the defendant elects to testify at the hearing on a motion brought pursuant to this section, the court shall exclude from the examination every person except the clerk, the court reporter, the bailiff, the prosecutor, the investigating officer, the defendant and his or her counsel, an investigator for the defendant, and the officer having custody of the defendant. Notwithstanding any other provision of law, the defendant's testimony at the hearing shall not be admissible in any other proceeding except the hearing brought on the motion pursuant to this section. If a transcript is made of the defendant's testimony, it shall be sealed and transmitted to the clerk of the court in which the action is pending.

(d) As used in this section, "serious felony" means any of the felonies listed in subdivision (c) of Section 1192.7 of the Penal Code or any violation of Section 11351, 11352, 11378, or 11379 of the Health and Safety Code.

(e) If a statement to be admitted pursuant to this section includes hearsay statements made by anyone other than the declarant who is unavailable pursuant to subdivision (a), those hearsay statements are inadmissible unless they meet the requirements of an exception to the hearsay rule.

Article 16: Statements by Children Under the Age of 12 in Child Neglect and Abuse Proceedings

§ 1360. STATEMENT DESCRIBING CHILD ABUSE OR NEGLECT MADE BY CHILD UNDER AGE OF 12

(a) In a criminal prosecution where the victim is a minor, a statement made by the victim when under the age of 12 describing any act of child abuse or neglect performed with or on the child by another, or describing any attempted act of child abuse or neglect with or on the child by another, is not made inadmissible by the hearsay rule if all of the following apply:

(1) The statement is not otherwise admissible by statute or court rule.

(2) The court finds, in a hearing conducted outside the presence of the jury, that the time, content, and circumstances of the statement provide sufficient indicia of reliability.

(3) The child either:

(A) Testifies at the proceedings.

(B) Is unavailable as a witness, in which case the statement may be admitted only if there is evidence of the child abuse or neglect that corroborates the statement made by the child.

(b) A statement may not be admitted under this section unless the proponent of the statement makes known to the adverse party the intention to offer the statement and the particulars of the statement sufficiently in advance of the proceedings in order to provide the adverse party with a fair opportunity to prepare to meet the statement.

(c) For purposes of this section, "child abuse" means an act proscribed by Section 273a, 273d, or 288.5 of the Penal Code, or any of the acts described in Section 11165.1 of the Penal Code, and "child neglect" means any of the acts described in Section 11165.2 of the Penal Code.

Article 17: Physical abuse

§ 1370. HEARSAY EXCEPTION

(a) Evidence of a statement by a declarant is not made inadmissible by the hearsay rule if all of the following conditions are met:

(1) The statement purports to narrate, describe, or explain the infliction or threat of physical injury upon the declarant.

(2) The declarant is unavailable as a witness pursuant to Section 240.

(3) The statement was made at or near the time of the infliction or threat of physical injury. Evidence of statements made more than five years before the filing of the current action or proceeding shall be inadmissible under this section.

(4) The statement was made under circumstances that would indicate its trustworthiness.

(5) The statement was made in writing, was electronically recorded, or made to a physician, nurse, paramedic, or to a law enforcement official.

(b) For purposes of paragraph (4) of subdivision (a), circumstances relevant to the issue of trustworthiness include, but are not limited to, the following:

(1) Whether the statement was made in contemplation of pending or anticipated litigation in which the declarant was interested.

(2) Whether the declarant has a bias or motive for fabricating the statement, and the extent of any bias or motive.

(3) Whether the statement is corroborated by evidence other than statements that are admissible only pursuant to this section.

(c) A statement is admissible pursuant to this section only if the proponent of the statement makes known to the adverse party the intention to offer the statement and the particulars of the statement sufficiently in advance of the proceedings in order to provide the adverse party with a fair opportunity to prepare to meet the statement.

§ 1380. EFFECT OF HEARSAY RULE

(a) In a criminal proceeding charging a violation, or attempted violation, of Section 368 of the Penal Code, evidence of a statement made by a declarant is not made inadmissible by the hearsay rule if the declarant is unavailable as a witness, as defined in subdivisions (a) and (b) of Section 240, and all of the following are true:

(1) The party offering the statement has made a showing of particularized guarantees of trustworthiness regarding the statement, the statement was made under circumstances which indicate its trustworthiness, and the statement was not the result of promise, inducement, threat, or coercion. In making its determination, the court may consider only the circumstances that surround the making of the statement and that render the declarant particularly worthy of belief.

(2) There is no evidence that the unavailability of the declarant was caused by, aided by, solicited by, or procured on behalf of, the party who is offering the statement.

(3) The entire statement has been memorialized in a videotape recording made by a law enforcement official, prior to the death or disabling of the declarant.

(4) The statement was made by the victim of the alleged violation.

(5) The statement is supported by corroborative evidence.

(6) The victim of the alleged violation is an individual who meets both of the following requirements:

(A) Was 65 years of age or older or was a dependent adult when the alleged violation or attempted violation occurred.

(B) At the time of any criminal proceeding, including, but not limited to, a preliminary hearing or trial, regarding the alleged violation or attempted violation, is either deceased or suffers from the infirmities of aging as manifested by advanced age or organic brain damage, or other physical, mental, or emotional dysfunction, to the extent that the ability of the person to provide adequately for the person's own care or protection is impaired.

(b) If the prosecution intends to offer a statement pursuant to this section, the prosecution shall serve a written notice upon the defendant at least 10 days prior to the hearing or trial at which the prosecution intends to offer the statement, unless the prosecution shows good cause for the failure to provide that notice. In the event that good cause is shown, the defendant shall be entitled to a reasonable continuance of the hearing or trial.

(c) If the statement is offered during trial, the court's determination as to the availability of the victim as a witness shall be made out of the presence of the jury. If the defendant elects to testify at the hearing on a motion brought pursuant to this section, the court shall exclude from the examination every person except the clerk, the court reporter, the bailiff, the prosecutor, the investigating officer, the defendant and his or her counsel, an investigator for the defendant, and the officer having custody of the defendant. Notwithstanding any other provision of law, the defendant's testimony at the hearing shall not be admissible in any other proceeding except the hearing brought on the motion pursuant to this section. If a transcript is made of the defendant's testimony, it shall be sealed and transmitted to the clerk of the court in which the action is pending.

§ 1390. EVIDENCE OF STATEMENT; ELEMENTS; CONDUCT OF FOUNDATIONAL HEARING; CONSIDERATIONS; APPLICABILITY; EFFECT OF REPEAL

(a) Evidence of a statement is not made inadmissible by the hearsay rule if the statement is offered against a party that has engaged, or aided and abetted, in the wrongdoing that was intended to, and did, procure the unavailability of the declarant as a witness.

(b)

(1) The party seeking to introduce a statement pursuant to subdivision (a) shall establish, by a preponderance of the evidence, that the elements of subdivision (a) have been met at a foundational hearing.

(2) The hearsay evidence that is the subject of the foundational hearing is admissible at the foundational hearing. However, a finding that the elements of subdivision (a) have been met shall not be based solely on the unconfronted hearsay statement of the unavailable declarant, and shall be supported by independent corroborative evidence.

(3) The foundational hearing shall be conducted outside the presence of the jury. However, if the hearing is conducted after a jury trial has begun, the judge presiding at the hearing may consider evidence already presented to the jury in deciding whether the elements of subdivision (a) have been met.

(4) In deciding whether or not to admit the statement, the judge may take into account whether it is trustworthy and reliable.

(c) This section shall apply to any civil, criminal, or juvenile case or proceeding initiated or pending as of January 1, 2011.

DIVISION 11: WRITINGS

Chapter 1: Authentication and Proof of Writings

Article 1: Requirement of Authentication

§ 1400. AUTHENTICATION DEFINED

Authentication of a writing means (a) the introduction of evidence sufficient to sustain a finding that it is the writing that the proponent of the evidence claims it is or (b) the establishment of such facts by any other means provided by law.

§ 1401. AUTHENTICATION REQUIRED

(a) Authentication of a writing is required before it may be received in evidence.

(b) Authentication of a writing is required before secondary evidence of its content may be received in evidence.

§ 1402. AUTHENTICATION OF ALTERED WRITING

The party producing a writing as genuine which has been altered, or appears to have been altered, after its execution, in a part material to the question in dispute, must account for the alteration or appearance thereof. He may show that the alteration was made by another, without his concurrence, or was made with the consent of the parties affected by it, or otherwise properly or innocently made, or that the alteration did not change the meaning or language of the instrument. If he does that, he may give the writing in evidence, but not otherwise.

Article 2: Means of Authenticating and Proving Writings

§ 1410. ARTICLE NOT EXCLUSIVE

Nothing in this article shall be construed to limit the means by which a writing may be authenticated or proved.

§ 1410.5. VANDALISM; EVIDENCE OF GRAFFITI

(a) For purposes of this chapter, a writing shall include any graffiti consisting of written words, insignia, symbols, or any other markings which convey a particular meaning.

(b) Any writing described in subdivision (a), or any photograph thereof, may be admitted into evidence in an action for vandalism, for the purpose of proving that the writing was made by the defendant.

(c) The admissibility of any fact offered to prove that the writing was made by the defendant shall, upon motion of the defendant, be ruled upon outside the presence of the jury, and is subject to the requirements of Sections 1416, 1417, and 1418.

§ 1411. SUBSCRIBING WITNESS' TESTIMONY UNNECESSARY

Except as provided by statute, the testimony of a subscribing witness is not required to authenticate a writing.

§ 1412. USE OF OTHER EVIDENCE WHEN SUBSCRIBING WITNESS' TESTIMONY REQUIRED

If the testimony of a subscribing witness is required by statute to authenticate a writing and the subscribing witness denies or does not recollect the execution of the writing, the writing may be authenticated by other evidence.

§ 1413. WITNESS TO THE EXECUTION OF A WRITING

A writing may be authenticated by anyone who saw the writing made or executed, including a subscribing witness.

§ 1414. AUTHENTICATION BY ADMISSION

A writing may be authenticated by evidence that:

(a) The party against whom it is offered has at any time admitted its authenticity; or

(b) The writing has been acted upon as authentic by the party against whom it is offered.

§ 1415. AUTHENTICATION BY HANDWRITING EVIDENCE

A writing may be authenticated by evidence of the genuineness of the handwriting of the maker.

§ 1416. PROOF OF HANDWRITING BY PERSON FAMILIAR THEREWITH

A witness who is not otherwise qualified to testify as an expert may state his opinion whether a writing is in the handwriting of a supposed writer if the court finds that he has personal knowledge of the handwriting of the supposed writer. Such personal knowledge may be acquired from:

(a) Having seen the supposed writer write;

(b) Having seen a writing purporting to be in the handwriting of the supposed writer and upon which the supposed writer has acted or been charged;

(c) Having received letters in the due course of mail purporting to be from the supposed writer in response to letters duly addressed and mailed by him to the supposed writer; or

(d) Any other means of obtaining personal knowledge of the handwriting of the supposed writer.

§ 1417. COMPARISON OF HANDWRITING BY TRIER OF FACT

The genuineness of handwriting, or the lack thereof, may be proved by a comparison made by the trier of fact with handwriting (a) which the court finds was admitted or treated as genuine by the party against whom the evidence is offered or (b) otherwise proved to be genuine to the satisfaction of the court.

§ 1418. COMPARISON OF WRITING BY EXPERT WITNESS

The genuineness of writing, or the lack thereof, may be proved by a comparison made by an expert witness with writing (a) which the court finds was admitted or treated as genuine by the party against whom the evidence is offered or (b) otherwise proved to be genuine to the satisfaction of the court.

§ 1419. EXEMPLARS WHEN WRITING IS 30 YEARS OLD

Where a writing whose genuineness is sought to be proved is more than 30 years old, the comparison under Section 1417 or 1418 may be made with writing purporting to be genuine, and generally respected and acted upon as such, by persons having an interest in knowing whether it is genuine.

§ 1420. AUTHENTICATION BY EVIDENCE OF REPLY

A writing may be authenticated by evidence that the writing was received in response to a communication sent to the person who is claimed by the proponent of the evidence to be the author of the writing.

§ 1421. AUTHENTICATION BY CONTENT

A writing may be authenticated by evidence that the writing refers to or states matters that are unlikely to be known to anyone other than the person who is claimed by the proponent of the evidence to be the author of the writing.

Article 3: Presumptions Affecting Acknowledged Writings and Official Writings

§ 1450. CLASSIFICATION OF PRESUMPTION IN ARTICLE

The presumptions established by this article are presumptions affecting the burden of producing evidence.

§ 1451. ACKNOWLEDGED WRITINGS

A certificate of the acknowledgment of a writing other than a will, or a certificate of the proof of such a writing, is prima facie evidence of the facts recited in the certificate and the genuineness of the signature of each person by whom the writing purports to have been signed if the certificate meets the requirements of Article 3 (commencing with Section 1180) of Chapter 4, Title 4, Part 4, Division 2 of the Civil Code.

§ 1452. OFFICIAL SEALS

A seal is presumed to be genuine and its use authorized if it purports to be the seal of:

(a) The United States or a department, agency, or public employee of the United States.

(b) A public entity in the United States or a department, agency, or public employee of such public entity.

(c) A nation recognized by the executive power of the United States or a department, agency, or officer of such nation.

(d) A public entity in a nation recognized by the executive power of the United States or a department, agency, or officer of such public entity.

(e) A court of admiralty or maritime jurisdiction.

(f) A notary public within any state of the United States.

§ 1453. DOMESTIC OFFICIAL SIGNATURES

A signature is presumed to be genuine and authorized if it purports to be the signature, affixed in his official capacity, of:

(a) A public employee of the United States.

(b) A public employee of any public entity in the United States.

(c) A notary public within any state of the United States.

§ 1454. FOREIGN OFFICIAL SIGNATURES

A signature is presumed to be genuine and authorized if it purports to be the signature, affixed in his official capacity, of an officer, or deputy of an officer, of a nation or public entity in a nation recognized by the executive power of the United States and the writing to which the signature is affixed is accompanied by a final statement certifying the genuineness of the signature and the official position of (a) the person who executed the writing or (b) any foreign official who has certified either the genuineness of the signature and official position of the person executing the writing or the genuineness of the signature and official position of another foreign official who has executed a similar certificate in a chain of such certificates beginning with a certificate of the genuineness of the signature and official position of the person executing the writing. The final statement may be made only by a secretary of an embassy or legation, consul general, consul, vice consul, consular agent, or other officer in the foreign service of the United States stationed in the nation, authenticated by the seal of his office.

Chapter 2: Secondary Evidence of Writings

Article 1: Proof of the Content of a Writing

§ 1520. PROOF BY ORIGINAL

The content of a writing may be proved by an otherwise admissible original.

§ 1521. SECONDARY EVIDENCE RULE

(a) The content of a writing may be proved by otherwise admissible secondary evidence. The court shall exclude secondary evidence of the content of writing if the court determines either of the following:

(1) A genuine dispute exists concerning material terms of the writing and justice requires the exclusion.

(2) Admission of the secondary evidence would be unfair.

(b) Nothing in this section makes admissible oral testimony to prove the content of a writing if the testimony is inadmissible under Section 1523 (oral testimony of the content of a writing).

(c) Nothing in this section excuses compliance with Section 1401 (authentication).

(d) This section shall be known as the "Secondary Evidence Rule."

§ 1522. ADDITIONAL GROUNDS FOR EXCLUSION IN CRIMINAL ACTIONS; REQUEST TO EXCLUDE SECONDARY EVIDENCE

(a) In addition to the grounds for exclusion authorized by Section 1521, in a criminal action the court shall exclude secondary evidence of the content of a writing if the court determines that the original is in the proponent's possession, custody, or control, and the proponent has not made the original reasonably available for inspection at or before trial. This section does not apply to any of the following:

(1) A duplicate as defined in Section 260.

(2) A writing that is not closely related to the controlling issues in the action.

(3) A copy of a writing in the custody of a public entity.

(4) A copy of a writing that is recorded in the public records, if the record or a certified copy of it is made evidence of the writing by statute.

(b) In a criminal action, a request to exclude secondary evidence of the content of a writing, under this section or any other law, shall not be made in the presence of the jury.

§ 1523. USE OF ORAL TESTIMONY

(a) Except as otherwise provided by statute, oral testimony is not admissible to prove the content of a writing.

(b) Oral testimony of the content of a writing is not made inadmissible by subdivision (a) if the proponent does not have possession or control of a copy of the writing and the original is lost or has been destroyed without fraudulent intent on the part of the proponent of the evidence.

(c) Oral testimony of the content of a writing is not made inadmissible by subdivision (a) if the proponent does not have possession or control of the original or a copy of the writing and either of the following conditions is satisfied:

(1) Neither the writing nor a copy of the writing was reasonably procurable by the proponent by use of the court's process or by other available means.

(2) The writing is not closely related to the controlling issues and it would be inexpedient to require its production.

(d) Oral testimony of the content of a writing is not made inadmissible by subdivision (a) if the writing consists of numerous accounts or other writings that cannot be examined in court without great loss of time, and the evidence sought from them is only the general result of the whole.

Article 2: Official Writings and Recorded Writings

§ 1530. COPY OF WRITING IN OFFICIAL CUSTODY

(a) A purported copy of a writing in the custody of a public entity, or of an entry in such a writing, is prima facie evidence of the existence and content of such writing or entry if:

(1) The copy purports to be published by the authority of the nation or state, or public entity therein in which the writing is kept;

(2) The office in which the writing is kept is within the United States or within the Panama Canal Zone, the Trust Territory of the Pacific Islands, or the Ryukyu Islands, and the copy is attested or certified as a correct copy of the writing or entry by a public employee, or a deputy of a public employee, having the legal custody of the writing; or

(3) The office in which the writing is kept is not within the United States or any other place described in paragraph (2) and the copy is attested as a correct copy of the writing or entry by a person having authority to make attestation. The attestation must be accompanied by a final statement certifying the genuineness of the signature and the official position of (i) the person who attested the copy as a correct copy or (ii) any foreign official who has certified either the genuineness of the signature and official position of the person attesting the copy or the genuineness of the signature and official position of another foreign official who has executed a similar certificate in a chain of such certificates beginning with a certificate of the genuineness of the signature and official position of the person attesting the copy. Except as provided in the next sentence, the final statement may be made only by a secretary of an embassy or legation, consul general, consul, vice consul, or consular agent of the United States, or a diplomatic or consular official of the foreign country assigned or accredited to the United States. Prior to January 1, 1971, the final statement may also be made by a secretary of an embassy or legation, consul general, consul, vice consul, consular agent, or other officer in the foreign service of the United States stationed in the nation in which the writing is kept, authenticated by the seal of his office. If reasonable opportunity has been given to all parties to investigate the authenticity and accuracy of the documents, the court may, for good cause shown, (i) admit an attested copy without the final statement or (ii) permit the writing or entry in foreign custody to be evidenced by an attested summary with or without a final statement.

(b) The presumptions established by this section are presumptions affecting the burden of producing evidence.

§ 1531. CERTIFICATION OF COPY FOR EVIDENCE

For the purpose of evidence, whenever a copy of a writing is attested or certified, the attestation or certificate must state in substance that the copy is a correct copy of the original, or of a specified part thereof, as the case may be.

§ 1532. OFFICIAL RECORD OF RECORDED WRITING

(a) The official record of a writing is prima facie evidence of the existence and content of the original recorded writing if:

(1) The record is in fact a record of an office of a public entity; and

(2) A statute authorized such a writing to be recorded in that office.

(b) The presumption established by this section is a presumption affecting the burden of producing evidence.

Article 3: Photographic Copies and Printed Representations of Writings

§ 1550. PHOTOGRAPHIC COPIES MADE AS BUSINESS RECORDS [FIRST OF TWO; OPERATIVE TERM CONTINGENT]

A nonerasable optical image reproduction provided that additions, deletions, or changes to the original document are not permitted by the technology, a photostatic, microfilm, microcard, miniature photographic, or other photographic copy or reproduction, or an enlargement thereof, of a writing is as admissible as the writing itself if the copy or reproduction was made and preserved as a part of the records of a business (as defined by Section 1270) in the regular course of that business. The introduction of the copy, reproduction, or enlargement does not preclude admission of the original writing if it is still in existence. A court may require the introduction of a hard copy printout of the document.

§ 1550. PHOTOGRAPHIC COPIES MADE AS BUSINESS RECORDS [SECOND OF TWO; OPERATIVE DATE CONTINGENT]

(a) If made and preserved as a part of the records of a business, as defined in Section 1270, in the regular course of that business, the following types of evidence of a writing are as admissible as the writing itself:

(1) A nonerasable optical image reproduction or any other reproduction of a public record by a trusted system, as defined in Section 12168.7 of the Government Code, if additions, deletions, or changes to the original document are not permitted by the technology.

(2) A photostatic copy or reproduction.

(3) A microfilm, microcard, or miniature photographic copy, reprint, or enlargement.

(4) Any other photographic copy or reproduction, or an enlargement thereof.

(b) The introduction of evidence of a writing pursuant to subdivision (a) does not preclude admission of the original writing if it is still in existence. A court may require the introduction of a hard copy printout of the document.

§ 1550.1. ADMISSIBILITY OF REPRODUCED FILES, RECORDS, WRITINGS, PHOTOGRAPHS, FINGERPRINTS OR OTHER INSTRUMENTS

Reproductions of files, records, writings, photographs, fingerprints or other instruments in the official custody of a criminal justice agency that were microphotographed or otherwise reproduced in a manner that conforms with the provisions of Section 11106.1, 11106.2, or 11106.3 of the Penal Code shall be admissible to the same extent and under the same circumstances as the original file, record, writing or other instrument would be admissible.

§ 1551. PHOTOGRAPHIC COPIES WHERE ORIGINAL DESTROYED OR LOST

A print, whether enlarged or not, from a photographic film (including a photographic plate, microphotographic film, photostatic negative, or similar reproduction) of an original writing destroyed or lost after such film was taken or a reproduction from an electronic recording of video images on magnetic surfaces is admissible as the original writing itself if, at the time of the taking of such film or electronic recording, the person under whose direction and control it was taken attached thereto, or to the sealed container in which it was placed and has been kept, or incorporated in the film or electronic recording, a certification complying with the provisions of Section 1531 and stating the date on which, and the fact that, it was so taken under his direction and control.

§ 1552. PRINTED REPRESENTATION OF COMPUTER INFORMATION OR COMPUTER PROGRAM

(a) A printed representation of computer information or a computer program is presumed to be an accurate representation of the computer information or computer program that it purports to represent. This presumption is a presumption affecting the burden of producing evidence. If a party to an action introduces evidence that a printed representation of computer information or computer program is inaccurate or unreliable, the party introducing the printed representation into evidence has the burden of proving, by a preponderance of evidence, that the printed representation is an accurate representation of the existence and content of the computer information or computer program that it purports to represent.

(b) Subdivision (a) applies to the printed representation of computer-generated information stored by an automated traffic enforcement system.

(c) Subdivision (a) shall not apply to computer-generated official records certified in accordance with Section 452.5 or 1530.

§ 1553. PRINTED REPRESENTATIONS OF IMAGES STORED ON VIDEO OR DIGITAL MEDIUM

(a) A printed representation of images stored on a video or digital medium is presumed to be an accurate representation of the images it purports to represent. This presumption is a presumption affecting the burden of producing evidence. If a party to an action introduces evidence that a printed representation of images stored on a video or digital medium is inaccurate or unreliable, the party introducing the printed representation into evidence has the burden of proving, by a preponderance of evidence, that the printed representation is an accurate representation of the existence and content of the images that it purports to represent.

(b) Subdivision (a) applies to the printed representation of video or photographic images stored by an automated traffic enforcement system.

Article 4: Production of Business Records

§ 1560. COMPLIANCE WITH SUBPOENA DUCES TECUM FOR BUSINESS RECORDS; ALTERNATIVE PROCEDURE IN CIVIL ACTIONS; SUFFICIENCY OF COMPLIANCE BY NONPARTY BUSINESS

(a) As used in this article:

(1) "Business" includes every kind of business described in Section 1270.

(2) "Record" includes every kind of record maintained by a business.

(b) Except as provided in Section 1564, when a subpoena duces tecum is served upon the custodian of records or other qualified witness of a business in an action in which the business is neither a party nor the place where any cause of action is alleged to have arisen, and the subpoena requires the production of all or any part of the records of the business, it is sufficient compliance therewith if the custodian or other qualified witness delivers by mail or otherwise a true, legible, and durable copy of all of the records described in the subpoena to the clerk of the court or to another person described in subdivision (d) of Section 2026.010 of the Code of Civil Procedure, together with the affidavit described in Section 1561, within one of the following time periods:

(1) In any criminal action, five days after the receipt of the subpoena.

(2) In any civil action, within 15 days after the receipt of the subpoena.

(3) Within the time agreed upon by the party who served the subpoena and the custodian or other qualified witness.

(c) The copy of the records shall be separately enclosed in an inner envelope or wrapper, sealed, with the title and number of the action, name of witness, and date of subpoena clearly inscribed thereon; the sealed envelope or wrapper shall then be enclosed in an outer envelope or wrapper, sealed, and directed as follows:

(1) If the subpoena directs attendance in court, to the clerk of the court.

(2) If the subpoena directs attendance at a deposition, to the officer before whom the deposition is to be taken, at the place designated in the subpoena for the taking of the deposition or at the officer's place of business.

(3) In other cases, to the officer, body, or tribunal conducting the hearing, at a like address.

(d) Unless the parties to the proceeding otherwise agree, or unless the sealed envelope or wrapper is returned to a witness who is to appear personally, the copy of the records shall remain sealed and shall be opened only at the time of trial, deposition, or other hearing, upon the direction of the judge, officer, body, or tribunal conducting the proceeding, in the presence of all parties who have appeared in person or by counsel at the trial, deposition, or hearing. Records that are original documents and that are not introduced in evidence or required as part of the record shall be returned to the person or entity from whom received. Records that are copies may be destroyed.

(e) As an alternative to the procedures described in subdivisions (b), (c), and (d), the subpoenaing party in a civil action may direct the witness to make the records available for inspection or copying by the party's attorney, the attorney's representative, or deposition officer as described in Section 2020.420 of the Code of Civil Procedure, at the witness' business address under reasonable conditions during normal business hours. Normal business hours, as used in this subdivision, means those hours that the business of the witness is normally open for business to the public. When provided with at least five business days' advance notice by the party's attorney, attorney's representative, or deposition officer, the witness shall designate a time period of not less than six continuous hours on a date certain for copying of records subject to the subpoena by the party's attorney, attorney's representative, or deposition officer. It shall be the responsibility of the attorney's representative to deliver any copy of the records as directed in the subpoena. Disobedience to the deposition subpoena issued pursuant to this subdivision is punishable as provided in Section 2020.240 of the Code of Civil Procedure.

(f) If a search warrant for business records is served upon the custodian of records or other qualified witness of a business in compliance with Section 1524 of the Penal Code regarding a criminal investigation in which the business is neither a party nor the place where any crime is alleged to have occurred, and the search warrant provides that the warrant will be deemed executed if the business causes the delivery of records described in the warrant to the law enforcement agency ordered to execute the warrant, it is sufficient compliance therewith if the custodian or other qualified witness delivers by mail or otherwise a true, legible, and durable copy of all of the records described in the search warrant to the law enforcement agency ordered to execute the search warrant, together with the affidavit described in Section 1561, within five days after the receipt of the search warrant or within such other time as is set forth in the warrant. This subdivision does not abridge or limit the scope of search warrant procedures set forth in Chapter 3 (commencing with Section 1523) of Title 12 of Part 2 of the Penal Code or invalidate otherwise duly executed search warrants.

§ 1561. AFFIDAVIT ACCOMPANYING RECORDS

(a) The records shall be accompanied by the affidavit of the custodian or other qualified witness, stating in substance each of the following:

(1) The affiant is the duly authorized custodian of the records or other qualified witness and has authority to certify the records.

(2) The copy is a true copy of all the records described in the subpoena duces tecum or search warrant, or pursuant to subdivision (e) of Section 1560, the records were delivered to the attorney, the attorney's representative, or deposition officer for copying at the custodian's or witness' place of business, as the case may be.

(3) The records were prepared by the personnel of the business in the ordinary course of business at or near the time of the act, condition, or event.

(4) The identity of the records.

(5) A description of the mode of preparation of the records.

(b) If the business has none of the records described, or only part thereof, the custodian or other qualified witness shall so state in the affidavit, and deliver the affidavit and those records that are available in one of the manners provided in Section 1560.

(c) If the records described in the subpoena were delivered to the attorney or his or her representative or deposition officer for copying at the custodian's or witness' place of business, in addition to the affidavit required by subdivision (a), the records shall be accompanied by an affidavit by the attorney or his or her representative or deposition officer stating that the copy is a true copy of all the records delivered to the attorney or his or her representative or deposition officer for copying.

§ 1562. ADMISSIBILITY OF AFFIDAVIT AND COPY OF RECORDS

If the original records would be admissible in evidence if the custodian or other qualified witness had been present and testified to the matters stated in the affidavit, and if the requirements of Section 1271 have been met, the copy of the records is admissible in evidence. The affidavit is admissible as evidence of the matters stated therein pursuant to Section 1561 and the matters so stated are presumed true. When more than one person has knowledge of the facts, more than one affidavit may be made. The presumption established by this section is a presumption affecting the burden of producing evidence.

Chapter 3: Official Writings Affecting Property

§ 1600. OFFICIAL RECORD OF DOCUMENT AFFECTING PROPERTY INTEREST

(a) The record of an instrument or other document purporting to establish or affect an interest in property is prima facie evidence of the existence and content of the original recorded document and its execution and delivery by each person by whom it purports to have been executed if:

(1) The record is in fact a record of an office of a public entity; and

(2) A statute authorized such a document to be recorded in that office.

(b) The presumption established by this section is a presumption affecting the burden of proof.

§ 1601. PROOF OF CONTENT OF LOST OFFICIAL RECORD AFFECTING PROPERTY

(a) Subject to subdivisions (b) and (c), when in any action it is desired to prove the contents of the official record of any writing lost or destroyed by conflagration or other public calamity, after proof of such loss or destruction, the following may, without further proof, be admitted in evidence to prove the contents of such record:

(1) Any abstract of title made and issued and certified as correct prior to such loss or destruction, and purporting to have been prepared and made in the ordinary course of business by any person engaged in the business of preparing and making abstracts of title prior to such loss or destruction; or

(2) Any abstract of title, or of any instrument affecting title, made, issued, and certified as correct by any person engaged in the business of insuring titles or issuing abstracts of title to real estate, whether the same was made, issued, or certified before or after such loss or destruction and whether the same was made from the original records or from abstract and notes, or either, taken from such records in the preparation and upkeeping of its plant in the ordinary course of its business.

(b) No proof of the loss of the original writing is required other than the fact that the original is not known to the party desiring to prove its contents to be in existence.

(c) Any party desiring to use evidence admissible under this section shall give reasonable notice in writing to all other parties to the action who have appeared therein, of his intention to use such evidence at the trial of the action, and shall give all such other parties a reasonable opportunity to inspect the evidence, and also the abstracts, memoranda, or notes from which it was compiled, and to take copies thereof.

§ 1603. DEED BY OFFICER IN PURSUANCE OF COURT PROCESS

A deed of conveyance of real property, purporting to have been executed by a proper officer in pursuance of legal process of any of the courts of record of this state, acknowledged and recorded in the office of the recorder of the county wherein the real property therein described is situated, or the record of such deed, or a certified copy of such record, is prima facie evidence that the property or interest therein described was thereby conveyed to the grantee named in such deed. The presumption established by this section is a presumption affecting the burden of proof.

§ 1605. AUTHENTICATED SPANISH TITLE RECORDS

Duplicate copies and authenticated translations of original Spanish title papers relating to land claims in this state, derived from the Spanish or Mexican governments, prepared under the supervision of the Keeper of Archives, authenticated by the Surveyor-General or his successor and by the Keeper of Archives, and filed with a county recorder, in accordance with Chapter 281 of the Statutes of 1865–66, are admissible as evidence with like force and effect as the originals and without proving the execution of such originals.

Part 3

EXCERPTS FROM UNIFORM RULES OF EVIDENCE (1999)

ARTICLE V. PRIVILEGES

RULE 501. PRIVILEGES RECOGNIZED ONLY AS PROVIDED

Except as otherwise provided by constitution or statute or by these or other rules promulgated by [the Supreme Court of this State], no person has a privilege to:

(1) refuse to be a witness;

(2) refuse to disclose any matter;

(3) refuse to produce any object or record; or

(4) prevent another from being a witness or disclosing any matter or producing any object or record.

RULE 502. LAWYER-CLIENT PRIVILEGE

(a) Definitions. In this rule:

(1) "Client" means a person for whom a lawyer renders professional legal services or who consults a lawyer with a view to obtaining professional legal services from the lawyer.

(2) A communication is "confidential" if it is not intended to be disclosed to third persons other than those to whom disclosure is made in furtherance of the rendition of professional legal services to the client or those reasonably necessary for the transmission of the communication.

(3) "Lawyer" means a person authorized, or reasonably believed by the client to be authorized, to engage in the practice of law in any State or country.

(4) "Representative of the client" means a person having authority to obtain professional legal services, or to act on legal advice rendered, on behalf of the client or a person who, for the purpose of effectuating legal representation for a client, makes or receives a confidential communication while acting in the scope of employment for the client.

(5) "Representative of the lawyer" means a person employed, or reasonably believed by the client to be employed, by the lawyer to assist the lawyer in rendering professional legal services.

(b) General rule of privilege. A client has a privilege to disclose and to prevent any other person from disclosing a confidential communication made for the purpose of facilitating the rendition of professional legal services to the client:

(1) between the client or a representative of the client and the client's lawyer or a representative of the lawyer;

(2) between the lawyer and a representative of the lawyer;

(3) by the client or a representative of the client or the client's lawyer or a representative of the lawyer to a lawyer or a representative of a lawyer representing another party in a pending action and concerning a matter of common interest therein;

(4) between representatives of the client or between the client and a representative of the client; or

(5) among lawyers and their representatives representing the same client.

(c) Who may claim privilege. The privilege under this rule may be claimed by the client, the client's guardian or conservator, the personal representative of a deceased client, or the successor, trustee, or similar representative of a corporation, association, or other organization, whether or not in existence. A person who was the lawyer or the lawyer's representative at the time of the communication is presumed to have authority to claim the privilege, but only on behalf of the client.

(d) Exceptions. There is no privilege under this rule:

(1) if the services of the lawyer were sought or obtained to enable or aid anyone to commit or plan to commit what the client knew or reasonably should have known was a crime or fraud;

(2) as to a communication relevant to an issue between parties who claim through the same deceased client, regardless of whether the claims are by testate or intestate succession or by transaction inter vivos;

(3) as to a communication relevant to an issue of breach of duty by a lawyer to the client or by a client to the lawyer;

(4) as to a communication necessary for a lawyer to defend in a legal proceeding an accusation that the lawyer assisted the client in criminal or fraudulent conduct;

(5) Documents attested by a lawyer. as to a communication relevant to an issue concerning an attested document to which the lawyer is an attesting witness;

(6) Joint Clients. As to a communication relevant to a matter of common interest between or among two or more clients if the communication was made by any of them to a lawyer retained or consulted in common, when offered in an action between or among any of the clients; or

(7) as to a communication between public officer or agency and its lawyers unless the communication concerns a pending investigation, claim, or action and the court determines that disclosure will seriously impair the ability of the public officer or agency to act upon the claim or conduct a pending investigation, litigation, or proceeding in the public interest.

RULE 503. PHYSICIAN AND MENTAL-HEALTH PROVIDER PATIENT PRIVILEGE

(a) Definitions. As used in this rule:

(1) A communication is "confidential" if it is not intended to be disclosed to third persons, except those present to further the interest of the patient in the consultation, examination, or interview, those reasonably necessary for the transmission of the communication, and persons who are participating in the diagnosis and treatment of the patient under the direction of a [psychotherapist] [physician or psychotherapist] [physician or mental-health provider; [mental-health provider], including members of the patient's family.

(2) "Mental-health provider" means a person authorized, in any State or country, or reasonably believed by the patient to be authorized, to engage in the diagnosis or treatment of a mental or emotional condition, including addiction to alcohol or drugs.

(3) "Patient" means an individual who consults or is examined or interviewed by a [psychotherapist] [physician or psychotherapist] [physician or mental-health provider].

(4) "Physician" means a person authorized in any State or country, or reasonably believed by the patient so to be authorized to practice medicine.]

(5) "Psychotherapist" means a person authorized in any State or country, or reasonably believed by the patient to be authorized, to practice medicine, while engaged in the diagnosis or treatment of a mental or emotional condition, addiction to alcohol or drugs, or a person licensed or certified under the laws of any State or country, or reasonably believed by the patient to be licensed or certified, as a psychologist, while similarly engaged.

(b) General rule of privilege. A patient has a privilege to refuse to disclose and to prevent any other person from disclosing confidential communications made for the purpose of diagnosis or treatment of the patient's [physical,] mental[,] or emotional condition, including addiction to alcohol or drugs, among the patient, the patient's [psychotherapist] [physician or psychotherapist] [physician or mental health provider] [mental-health provider] and persons, including members of the patient's family, who are participating in the diagnosis or treatment under the direction of the [psychotherapist] [physician or psychotherapist] [physician or mental-health provider] [mental-health provider.]

(c) Who may claim the privilege. The privilege under this rule may be claimed by the patient, the patient's guardian or conservator, or the personal representative of a deceased patient. The person who was the [psychotherapist] [physician or psychotherapist] [physician or mental-health provider] [mental health provider] at the time of the communication is presumed to have authority to claim the privilege, but only on behalf of the patient.

(d) Exceptions. There is no privilege under this rule for a communication:

(1) Proceedings for hospitalization. There is no privilege under this rule for communications relevant to an issue in proceedings to hospitalize the patient for mental illness, if the [psychotherapist] [physician or psychotherapist] [physician or mental-health provider] [mental-health provider], in the course of diagnosis or treatment, has determined that the patient is in need of hospitalization.

(2) made in the course of a court-ordered investigation or examination of the [physical,] mental[,] or emotional condition of a the patient, whether a party or a witness, with respect to the particular purpose for which the examination is ordered, unless the court orders otherwise;

(3) relevant to an issue of the [physical,] mental[,] or emotional condition of the patient in any proceeding in which the patient relies upon the condition as an element of the patient's claim or defense or, after the patient's death, in any proceeding in which any party relies upon the condition as an element of the party's claim or defense;

(4) if the services of the [psychotherapist] [physician or psychotherapist] [physician or mental-health provider] [mental-health provider] were sought or obtained to enable or aid anyone to commit or plan to commit what the patient knew, or reasonably should have known, was a crime or fraud or mental or physical injury to the patient or another individual;

(5) in which the patient has expressed an intent to engage in conduct likely to result in imminent death or serious bodily injury to the patient or another individual;

(6) relevant to an issue in a proceeding challenging the competency of the [psychotherapist] [physician or psychotherapist] [physician or mental-health provider] [mental-health provider];

(7) relevant to a breach of duty by the [psychotherapist] [physician or psychotherapist] [physician or mental-health provider] [mental-health provider]; or

(8) that is subject to a duty to disclose under [statutory law].

RULE 504. SPOUSAL PRIVILEGE

(a) Confidential communication. A communication is confidential if it is made privately by an individual to the individual's spouse and is not intended for disclosure to any other person.

(b) Marital communications. An individual has a privilege to refuse to testify and to prevent the individual's spouse or former spouse from testifying as to any confidential communication made by the individual to the spouse during their marriage. The privilege may be waived only by the individual holding the privilege or by the holder's guardian, or conservator, or the individual's personal representative if the individual is deceased.

(c) Spousal testimony in criminal proceeding. The spouse of an accused in a criminal proceeding has a privilege to refuse to testify against the accused spouse.

(d) Exceptions. There is no privilege under this rule:

(1) in any civil proceeding in which the spouses are adverse parties;

(2) in any criminal proceeding in which a prima facie and unrefuted showing is made that the spouses acted jointly in the commission of the crime charged,

(3) in any proceeding in which one spouse is charged with a crime or tort against the person or property of the other, a minor child of either, an individual residing in the household of either, or a third person if the crime or tort is committed in the course of committing a crime or tort against the other spouse, a minor child of either spouse, or an individual residing in the household of either spouse; or

(4) in any other proceeding, in the discretion of the court, if the interests of a minor child of either spouse may be adversely affected by invocation of the privilege.

RULE 505. RELIGIOUS PRIVILEGE

(a) Definitions. In this rule:

(1) "Cleric" means a minister, priest, rabbi, accredited Christian Science Practitioner, or other similar functionary of a religious organization, or an individual reasonably believed so to be by the individual consulting the cleric.

(2) A communication is "confidential" if it is made privately and not intended for further disclosure except to other persons present in furtherance of the purpose of the communication.

(b) General rule of privilege. An individual has a privilege to refuse to disclose and to prevent another from disclosing in a confidential communication by the individual to a cleric in the cleric's professional capacity as a spiritual adviser.

(c) Who may claim the privilege. The privilege under this rule may be claimed by an individual or the individual's guardian or conservator, or the individual's personal representative if the individual is deceased. The individual who was the cleric at the time of the communication is presumed to have authority to claim the privilege but only on behalf of the communicant.

RULE 506. POLITICAL VOTE

(a) General rule of privilege. An individual has a privilege to refuse to disclose the tenor of the individual's vote at a political election conducted by secret ballot.

(b) Exceptions. The privilege under subdivision (a) does not apply if the court finds that the vote was cast illegally or determines that disclosure should be compelled pursuant to [the election laws of the State].

RULE 507. TRADE SECRETS

A person has privilege, which may be claimed by the person or the person's agent or employee, to refuse to disclose and to prevent other persons from disclosing a trade secret owned by the person, if the allowance of the privilege will not tend to conceal fraud or otherwise work injustice. If disclosure is directed, the court shall take such protective measures as the interest of the holder of the privilege and of the parties and the interests of justice require.

RULE 508. SECRETS OF STATE AND OTHER OFFICIAL INFORMATION; GOVERNMENTAL PRIVILEGES

(a) Claim of privilege under law of United States. If the law of the United States creates a governmental privilege that the courts of this State must recognize under the Constitution of the United States, the privilege may be claimed as provided by the law of the United States.

(b) Privileges created by laws of State. No governmental privilege is recognized except as provided in subdivision (a) or created by the constitution, statutes, or rules of this State.

(c) Effect of sustaining claim. If a claim of governmental privilege is sustained and it appears that a party is thereby deprived of material evidence, the court shall make any further orders the interests of justice require, including striking the testimony of a witness, declaring a mistrial, finding upon an issue as to which the evidence is relevant, or dismissing the action.

RULE 509. IDENTITY OF INFORMER

(a) Rule of privilege. The United States of a State has a privilege to refuse to disclose the identity of an individual who has furnished information relating to or assisted in an investigation of a possible violation of a law to a law enforcement officer or member of a legislative committee or its staff conducting an investigation.

(b) Who may claim. The privilege under this rule may be claimed by an appropriate representative of the government to which the information was furnished.

(c) Exceptions. There is no privilege under this rule if the identity of the informer or the informer's interest in the subject matter of the informer's communication has been disclosed by a holder of the privilege or by the informer's own action to persons who would have cause to resent the communication or if the informer appears as a witness for the government.

(d) Procedures. If it appears that an informer may be able to give testimony relevant to an issue in a criminal case, or to a fair determination of a material issue on the merits in a civil case to which the government is a party, and the informed government invokes the privilege, the court shall give the government an opportunity to show in chambers facts relevant to whether the informer can, in fact, supply the testimony. The showing ordinarily will be by affidavit, but the court may direct that testimony be taken if it finds that the matter cannot be resolved satisfactorily upon affidavit. If the court finds there is a reasonable probability that the informer can give the testimony, and the government elects not to disclose the informer's identity, in criminal cases the court on motion of the defendant or on its own motion shall grant appropriate relief, which may include one or more of the following: requiring the prosecuting attorney to comply, granting the defendant additional time or a continuance, relieving the defendant from making disclosures otherwise required of the defendant, prohibiting the prosecuting attorney from introducing specified evidence, and dismissing charges. In civil cases, the court may issue any order the interests of justice require. Evidence submitted to the court must be sealed and preserved to be made available to the appellate court in the event of an appeal, and the contents may not otherwise be revealed without consent of the informed government. All counsel and parties may be present at every stage of a proceeding under this subdivision except a showing in chambers, if the court has determined that no counsel or party may be present.

RULE 510. WAIVER OF PRIVILEGE

(a) Voluntary disclosure. A person upon whom these rules confer a privilege against disclosure waives the privilege if the person or the person's predecessor, while holder of the privilege, voluntarily discloses or consents to disclosure of any significant part of the privileged matter. This rule does not apply if the disclosure itself is privileged.

(b) Involuntary disclosure. A claim of privilege is not waived by a disclosure that was compelled erroneously or made without an opportunity to claim the privilege.

RULE 511. COMMENT UPON OR INFERENCE FROM CLAIM OF PRIVILEGE; INSTRUCTION

(a) Comment or inference not permitted. A claim of a privilege, whether in the present proceeding or upon a previousoccasion, is not a proper subject of comment by judge or counsel. No inference may be drawn from the claim.

(b) Claiming privilege without knowledge of jury. In jury cases, proceedings must be conducted, to the extent practicable, so as to facilitate the making of claims of privilege without the knowledge of the jury.

(c) Jury instruction. Upon request, any party against whom the jury might draw an adverse inference from a claim of privilege is entitled to an instruction that no inference may be drawn therefrom.

Part 4 CROSS-REFERENCE CHARTS

The cross-reference charts delineate how each Federal Rule of Evidence correlates with the California Evidence Code section (in the first chart), and how each California Evidence Code section correlates with the Federal Rule of Evidence (in the second chart). The charts also describe the "general topic" of each Federal Rule of Evidence and each of the pertinent sections of the California Evidence Code. Areas that are shaded indicate that there is a substantive difference between the pertinent Federal Rule of Evidence and pertinent California Evidence Code section (either by their text or by precedent interpreting their text).

Federal Rules of Evidence to California Evidence Code:

FRE	**CEC**	**General Topic**
101	300 (scope) 120, 130, 200 (definitions with equivalent in FRE 101) 7, 100, 105, 110, 115, 125, 135, 140, 145, 150, 160, 165, 170, 175, 177, 180, 185, 190, 195, 205, 210, 215, 220, 225, 230, 235, 240, 250, 255, 260 (other definitions)	Scope/definitions
102	2	Purpose/construction

FRE	CEC	General Topic
103(a), (b)	353, 354	Preserving claims of error
104	400, 401, 402, 403, 404, 405, 406	Preliminary questions
105	355	Limiting instructions
106	356	Rule of completeness
107	No CEC equivalent	Illustrative aids
201	450, 451, 452, 453, 454, 455, 457, 458, 459	Judicial notice
301	500, 550, 604, 606; see also 110 (defining "burden of producing evidence"), 115 (defining "burden of proof"), 190 (defining "proof")	Presumptions in civil cases
302	602	Choice of law for presumptions
401	350, 210 (defining "relevant evidence")	Test for relevance
402	351	Admissibility of relevant evidence
403	352, 352.1 (special rule for victim's address and phone number), 352.2 (special rule for creative expression)	Balancing of probative value against danger of unfair prejudice
404(a)(1)		General prohibition of character evidence
404(a)(2)(A)	790, 1102	Exception when a defendant's character is admissible in criminal cases
404(a)(2)(B), (a)(2)(C)	1103	Exceptions when a victim's character is admissible in criminal cases
404(a)(3)	786	Exception for character for truthfulness
404(b)	1101(b)	"Other acts" evidence

FRE	CEC	General Topic
405	787, 1100	Methods of proving character evidence
406	1105	Habit evidence
407	1151	Subsequent remedial measures
408	1119, 1152, 1154	Compromise offers and negotiations
409	1152	Offers to pay medical and similar expenses
410	1153	Pleas, statements during plea discussion
411	1155	Liability insurance
412	782, 783, 1103, 1106	Further limitations on character evidence (rape shield law)
413	1108	Character evidence in sexual assault cases
414	1108	Character evidence in child molestation cases
415	No equivalent in CEC	Sex and molestation-related character evidence in civil cases
501	910, 950-1070	Privileges
502	912	Claw back provisions for attorney-related materials
601	700	Witness competency
602	702, 170 (defining "perceive")	Requirement of personal knowledge
603	710, 165 (defining "oath")	Oath requirement
604	751	Interpreters
605	703, 703.5	Judge's competency as a witness
606(a)	704	Competency of jurors to testify at trial

FRE	CEC	General Topic
606(b)	1150	Competency of jurors to impeach verdicts
607	785	Who may impeach witnesses
608	780, 786, 790	Character for truth and veracity
609	788, 452.5 (admissibility of misdemeanor convictions under hearsay rule)	Impeachment by criminal conviction
610	789	Religious beliefs or opinions to impeach
611	320, 765, 767, 772, 773, 776, 778	Mode and order of examining witnesses and presenting evidence
612	768, 771	Using writings to refresh recollection
613	769, 770	Witness's prior statements to impeach
614	775	Power to court to call/ examine witnesses
615	320 (regulating order of proof), 777	Excluding witnesses
701	800, 804	Lay opinion testimony
702	720, 801	Expert opinion testimony
703	801, 804	Bases of expert opinion testimony
704	805	Opinions on the ultimate issue
705	721, 802	Disclosing facts underlying report's opinion
706	722, 730, 731, 732, 733	Court appointed expert witnesses
801(a), (b), (c)	150 ("hearsay evidence"), 135 ("declarant"), 175 ("person"), 225 ("statement"), 1200 ("hearsay evidence")	Hearsay defined

FRE	CEC	General Topic
801(d)(1)(A)[1]	1235, 1294	Prior inconsistent statements
801(d)(1)(B)	791, 1236	Prior consistent statements
801(d)(1)(C)	1238	Prior identifications
801(d)(2)(A)	1220	Adverse party admissions
801(d)(2)(B)	1221	Adopted admissions
801(d)(2)(C)	1222	Authorized admissions
801(d)(2)(D)	1224	Admissions by agents or employees
801(d)(2)(E)	1223	Co-conspirator's statements
802	1200	Rule against hearsay
803(1)	1240, 1241	Present sense impression exception
803(2)	1240, 1241	Excited utterance exception
803(3)	1250, 1260	State of mind exception
803(4)	1253	Exception for statements for medical diagnosis
803(5)	1237	Recorded recollection exception
803(6)	1271	Business records exception
803(7)	1272	Absence of business records exception
803(8)	1280	Public records exception
803(9)	1281	Vital statistics exception
803(10)	1284	Absence of public records exception

[1]The substantive difference between the FRE and CEC will no longer exist if the proposed amendment to FRE 801(d)(1)(A) takes effect on December 1, 2026.

FRE	CEC	General Topic
803(11)	1315	Religious records exception
803(12)	1316	Exception for certificates of marriage, baptism and other ceremonies
803(13)	1312	Family records exception
803(14)	No CEC equivalent	Exception for documents affecting interests in property
803(15)	1330	Exception for statements in property-related documents
803(16)	1331	Ancient documents exception
803(17)	1340	Exception for market reports and commercial publications
803(18)	721(b), 1341	Exception for statements in learned treatises
803(19)	1313, 1314	Exception for reputation concerning personal or family history
803(20)	1320, 1322, 1323	Exception for reputation concerning boundaries or general history
803(21)	1324	Exception for reputation concerning character
803(22)	1300	Exception for judgments of prior convictions
803(23)	No CEC equivalent	Exception for judgments involving personal, family or general history, or boundaries
804(a)	240 (defining "unavailable as a witness")	"Unavailability" defined

FRE	CEC	General Topic
804(b)(1)	1290, 1291, 1292	Former testimony exception
804(b)(2)	1242	Dying declaration exception
804(b)(3)	1230	Declaration against interest exception
804(b)(4)	1310, 1311	Exception for statements of personal or family history
804(b)(6)	1350, 1390	Forfeiture by wrongdoing exception
805	1201	Hearsay within hearsay
806	1202, 1203	Attacking/supporting credibility of hearsay declarants
807	No CEC equivalent	Residual exception
901(a)	1400, 1401	General authentication requirement
901(b)(1)	1413	Authentication, by testimony of a witness with knowledge
901(b)(2), (3)	1415, 1416, 1417, 1418	Authentication, by handwriting comparisons
901(b)(4)	1421	Authentication, by distinctive characteristics
901(b)(5)	No CEC equivalent	Authentication of voice recordings
901(b)(6)	No CEC equivalent	Authentication of telephone conversations
901(b)(7)	1600, 1603	Authentication of public records
901(b)(8)	1419	Authentication of ancient documents and data compilations

FRE	CEC	General Topic
901(b)(9)	No CEC equivalent	Authentication of a process or system
901(b)(10)	1410	Authentication through statutorily provided means
902	1451, 1452, 1453, 1454, 1603	Documents that self-authenticate
903	1411	Necessity of subscribing witness's testimony to authenticate
1001	250 (defining "writing"), 255 (defining "original"), 260 (defining "duplicate")	Definitions applicable to best evidence rule
1002	1520, 1521, 1523	Requirement of original writing
1003	1531, 1550, 1550.1, 1551, 1552, 1553	Admissibility of duplicates
1004(a)	1523(b), 1601 (lost official record affecting property)	Exception for lost originals
1004(b)	1523(c)(1)	Exception for writings beyond judicial process
1004(c)	No CEC equivalent	Exception for documents introduced against a party in possession of original
1004(d)	1523(c)(2)	Exception for collateral writings
1005	1530, 1532	Copies of public records
1006	1521	Summaries of writings
1007	No CEC equivalent	Exception when content of writing is admitted by adverse party
1008	310, 312	When court or jurors decides best evidence questions

Part 4. Cross-Reference Charts

FRE	CEC	General Topic
1101	300	Applicability of FREs
1102	No CEC equivalent	Process for amendment
1103	1	Title of Rules

California Evidence Code to Federal Rules of Evidence:

CEC	FRE	General Topic
100	101	Application of definitions
105	No FRE equivalent	Definition of "action"
110	No FRE equivalent	Definition of "burden of producing evidence"
115	No FRE equivalent	Definition of "burden of proof"
120	101(b)(1) ("civil case")	Definition of "civil action"
125	No FRE equivalent	Definition of "conduct"
130	101(b)(2) ("criminal case")	Definition of "criminal action"
135	801(b)	Definition of "declarant"
140	No FRE equivalent	Definition of "evidence"
145	No FRE equivalent	Definition of "the hearing"
150	801(c)	Definition of "hearsay evidence"
160	No FRE equivalent	Definition of "law"
165	No FRE equivalent	Definition of "oath"
170	No FRE equivalent	Definition of "perceive"
175	No FRE equivalent	Definition of "person"
177	No FRE equivalent	Definition of "dependent person"
180	No FRE equivalent	Definition of "personal property"
185	No FRE equivalent	Definition of "property"
190	No FRE equivalent	Definition of "proof"
195	No FRE equivalent	Definition of "public employee"
200	101(b)(3) ("public office")	Definition of "public entity"

CEC	FRE	General Topic
205	No FRE equivalent	Definition of "real property"
210	401	Definition of "relevant evidence"
215	No FRE equivalent	Definition of "spouse"
220	No FRE equivalent	Definition of "state"
225	801(a)	Definition of "statement"
230	No FRE equivalent	Definition of "statute"
235	No FRE equivalent	Definition of "trier of fact"
240	804(a)	Definition of "unavailable as witness"
250	1001(a)	Definition of "writing"
255	1001(d)	Definition of "original"
260	1001(e)	Definition of "duplicate"
300	1101	Applicability of CEC
310	1008	Questions of law to be decided by court
311	No FRE equivalent	Procedure where foreign or sister-state law cannot be determined
312	1008	Jury as trier of fact
320	611	Power of court to regulate order of proof
350	401, 402	Irrelevant evidence inadmissible
351	401, 402	All relevant evidence admissible
351.1	No FRE equivalent	Polygraph results inadmissible
351.2	No FRE equivalent	Immigration status inadmissible in civil action for personal injury or wrongful death
351.3	No FRE equivalent	Disclosure of immigration status in civil action
351.4	No FRE equivalent	Disclosure of immigration status in criminal action
352	403	Balancing of probative value against danger of undue prejudice

CEC	FRE	General Topic
352.1	No FRE equivalent	Address and telephone number of victim of criminal sex act
352.2	No FRE equivalent	Admission of creative expressions
353	103	Effect of erroneous admission of evidence
354	103	Effect of erroneous exclusion of evidence
355	105	Admissibility for limited purpose
356	106	Rule of completeness
400	No FRE equivalent	Definition of "preliminary fact" and "the admissibility or inadmissibility of evidence"
401	No FRE equivalent	Definition of "proffered evidence"
402	104	Determination of preliminary fact
403	104	Determination of preliminary fact (relevance, personal knowledge or authenticity)
404	No FRE equivalent	Determination of whether proffered evidence is incriminatory
405	104	Determination of preliminary fact
406	104(e)	Evidence affecting weight or credibility
410	No FRE equivalent	Definition of "direct evidence"
411	No FRE equivalent	Direct evidence of one witness sufficient
412	No FRE equivalent	Party having power to produce better evidence
413	No FRE equivalent	Party's failure to explain or deny evidence
450	201	Judicial notice
451	201	Mandatory judicial notice
452	201	Permissive judicial notice

CEC	FRE	General Topic
452.5	No FRE equivalent	Judicial notice of computer-generated records
453	201(c)(2)	Compulsory judicial notice upon request
454	201	Information that may be used in taking judicial notice
455	201(e)	Opportunity to present information to court
456	No FRE equivalent	Noting for record denial of request to take judicial notice
457	201(f)	Instructing jury on matter judicially noticed
458	No FRE equivalent	Judicial notice by trial court in subsequent proceedings
459	No FRE equivalent	Judicial notice by reviewing court
460	No FRE equivalent	Appointment of expert for advice in taking judicial notice
500	301	Party who has burden of proof
501	No FRE equivalent	Burden of proof in criminal action
502	No FRE equivalent	Instructions on burden of proof
520	No FRE equivalent	Burden of proving person guilty of crime
521	No FRE equivalent	Burden of proving person did not exercise care
522	No FRE equivalent	Burden of proving person is insane
550	301	Burden of producing evidence
600	No FRE equivalent	Presumption and inference defined
601	No FRE equivalent	Conclusive versus rebuttable presumption
602	302	Statute making one fact prima facie evidence of another fact
603	No FRE equivalent	Definition of presumption affecting the burden of producing evidence

CEC	FRE	General Topic
604	301	Effect of presumption affecting burden of producing evidence
605	No FRE equivalent	Definition of presumption affecting the burden of proof
606	301	Effect of presumption affecting burden of proof
607	No FRE equivalent	Effect of certain presumption in criminal action
620	No FRE equivalent	Conclusive presumptions
622	No FRE equivalent	Facts recited in written instrument conclusively presumed to be true
623	No FRE equivalent	Estoppel by own statement or conduct
624	No FRE equivalent	Estoppel of tenant to deny title of landlord
630	No FRE equivalent	Presumptions in this article are presumptions affecting burden of producing evidence
631	No FRE equivalent	Money delivered by one to another presumed to have been due to latter
632	No FRE equivalent	Thing delivered by one to another presumed to have belonged to latter
633	No FRE equivalent	Obligation delivered up to the debtor presumed to have been paid
634	No FRE equivalent	Person in possession of order on himself is presumed to have paid the money or delivered the thing accordingly
635	No FRE equivalent	Obligation possessed by creditor presumed not to have been paid
636	No FRE equivalent	Payment of earlier rent or installments presumed from receipt for later rent or installments
637	No FRE equivalent	Things which a person possesses presumed to be owned by him

CEC	FRE	General Topic
638	No FRE equivalent	Person who exercises acts of ownership over property presumed to be owner
639	No FRE equivalent	Judgment presumed to correctly determine rights of parties
640	No FRE equivalent	Writing presumed to be truly dated
641	No FRE equivalent	Letter correctly addressed and mailed presumed to have been received
642	No FRE equivalent	Person having duty to convey real property presumed to have conveyed it
643	No FRE equivalent	Authenticity of ancient document presumed
644	No FRE equivalent	Book purporting to be published by public authority presumed to have been
645	No FRE equivalent	Book purporting to contain reports of cases presumed correct
645.1	No FRE equivalent	Printed materials purporting to be particular newspaper or periodical presumed to be that newspaper or periodical
646	No FRE equivalent	Res ipsa loquitur
647	No FRE equivalent	Facts in return of registered process server presumed true
660	No FRE equivalent	Presumptions in this article are presumptions affecting burden of proof
662	No FRE equivalent	Owner of legal title to property presumed to be owner of full beneficial title
663	No FRE equivalent	Ceremonial marriage presumed valid
664	No FRE equivalent	Official duty presumed to have been regularly performed

CEC	FRE	General Topic
665	No FRE equivalent	Person presumed to intend ordinary consequence of voluntary act
666	No FRE equivalent	Court presumed to have acted in lawful exercise of its jurisdiction
667	No FRE equivalent	Person not heard from in five years presumed dead
668	No FRE equivalent	Unlawful intent presumed from unlawful act
669	No FRE equivalent	Failure to exercise due care presumed (per se negligence)
669.1	No FRE equivalent	Rule, policy, manual or guideline of state or local government not basis for per se negligence
670	No FRE equivalent	Check presumed to be paid from bank statement
700	601	Competency
701	No FRE equivalent	Disqualification of witness
702	602	Personal knowledge
703	605	Judge as witness
703.5	605	Judge as witness in subsequent proceeding
704	606(a)	Juror as witness
710	603	Oath required
711	No FRE equivalent	Confrontation
720	702	Qualification of expert witness
721	705	Cross-examination of expert witness
722	706(d)	Credibility of expert witness (disclosure to jury of expert witness appointment and compensation)
723	No FRE equivalent	Limit on number of expert witnesses
730	706(a)	Appointment by court of expert witness

CEC	FRE	General Topic
731	706(c)	Payment of court-appointed expert witness
732	706(b)	Calling and examining court-appointed expert
733	706(e)	Right to produce other expert evidence
750	No FRE equivalent	Rules relating to witnesses apply to interpreters and translators
751	604	Oath required of interpreters and translators
752	No FRE equivalent	Interpreters for witnesses
753	No FRE equivalent	Translators of writings
754	No FRE equivalent	Interpreters for deaf or hard of hearing
756	No FRE equivalent	Reimbursement to courts for court interpreter services
760	No FRE equivalent	Definition of "direct examination"
761	No FRE equivalent	Definition of "cross examination"
762	No FRE equivalent	Definition of "redirect examination"
763	No FRE equivalent	Definition of "recross-examination"
764	No FRE equivalent	Definition of "leading question"
765	611(a)	Court to control mode of interrogation
766	No FRE equivalent	Witness must give responsive answers
767	611(c)	Leading questions
768	612	Examining witness re: writings
769	613(a)	Inconsistent statement or conduct
770	613(b)	Evidence of inconsistent statement of witness
771	612	Production of writing used to refresh memory
772	611	Order of examination

CEC	FRE	General Topic
773	611(b)	Cross-examination
774	No FRE equivalent	Reexamination
775	614	Court may call witness
776	611(c)	Examination of adverse party or witness
777	615	Exclusion of witnesses
778	611(a)	Recall of witness
780	608	Credibility
782	412	Evidence of sexual conduct of complaining witness to attack credibility in criminal cases
783	412	Evidence of sexual conduct to attack credibility of plaintiff in civil sexual harassment suit
785	607	Any party may attack or support witness's credibility
786	608, 404(a)(3)	Character evidence
787	405(b)	Specific incidents of conduct to prove character
788	609	Prior felony conviction
789	610	Religious belief
790	608 (evidence of truthfulness), 404(a)(2) (criminal cases)	Opening door for evidence of good character
791	801(d)(1)(B) (hearsay exception)	Prior consistent statement to support credibility
795	No FRE equivalent	Hypnosis
800	701	Opinion testimony by lay witness
801	702, 703	Opinion testimony by expert witness
801.1	No FRE equivalent	Expert testimony regarding medical causation
802	705 (expert witnesses)	Statement of basis of opinion

CEC	FRE	General Topic
803	No FRE equivalent	Opinion based on improper matter
804	701, 703	Opinion based on opinion or statement of another
805	704	Opinion on ultimate issue
870	No FRE equivalent	Opinion as to sanity
900	No FRE equivalent	Definitions of this chapter govern construction of only this division
901	No FRE equivalent	Definition of "proceeding"
902	No FRE equivalent	Definition of "civil proceeding"
903	No FRE equivalent	Definition of "criminal proceeding"
905	No FRE equivalent	Definition of "presiding officer"
910	501	Applicability of privilege rules
911	No FRE equivalent	No privilege to refuse to testify or produce evidence unless otherwise provided by law
912	502	Waiver of privilege
913	No FRE equivalent	Commenting on/drawing inferences from exercise of privilege
914	No FRE equivalent	Determining claim of privilege/ limitation on punishment for contempt
915	No FRE equivalent	Disclosure of privileged information in ruling on claim of privilege
916	No FRE equivalent	Exclusion of privileged information where persons authorized to claim privilege not present
917	No FRE equivalent	Presumptions that certain communications are confidential
918	No FRE equivalent	Effect of error in overruling claim of privilege
919	No FRE equivalent	Admissibility of privileged information where disclosure erroneously compelled

CEC	FRE	General Topic
920	No FRE equivalent	No implied repeal of any other statute relating to privileges
930	No FRE equivalent	Criminal defendant's privilege not to be called as a witness
940	No FRE equivalent	Privilege against self-incrimination
950	No FRE equivalent	Definition of "lawyer"
951	No FRE equivalent	Definition of "client"
952	No FRE equivalent	Definition of "confidential communication between lawyer and client"
953	No FRE equivalent	Definition of "holder of the privilege"
954	502(g)(1)	Lawyer-client privilege
955	No FRE equivalent	When lawyer is required to claim privilege
956	No FRE equivalent	Crime or fraud exception to lawyer-client privilege
956.5	No FRE equivalent	No lawyer-client privilege where disclosure necessary to prevent criminal act likely to result in death or bodily harm
957	No FRE equivalent	No lawyer-client privilege where parties claiming through deceased client
958	No FRE equivalent	No lawyer-client privilege as to issue of breach of duty arising out of lawyer-client relationship
959	No FRE equivalent	No lawyer-client privilege where lawyer as attesting witness
960	No FRE equivalent	No lawyer-client privilege as to intention of deceased client concerning writing affecting property interest

CEC	FRE	General Topic
961	No FRE equivalent	No lawyer-client privilege as to validity of writing executed by deceased client affecting property interest
962	No FRE equivalent	No lawyer-client privilege in action between joint clients
965	No FRE equivalent	Definitions re: lawyer referral service-client privilege
966	No FRE equivalent	Lawyer referral service-client privilege
967	No FRE equivalent	When lawyer referral service must claim privilege
968	No FRE equivalent	Crime or fraud exception to lawyer referral service-client privilege
970	No FRE equivalent	Privilege not to testify against a spouse
971	No FRE equivalent	Privilege not to be called as witness against spouse
972	No FRE equivalent	When spousal privilege not applicable
973	No FRE equivalent	Waiver of spousal privilege
980	No FRE equivalent	Privilege for confidential marital communications
981	No FRE equivalent	Crime or fraud exception to marital communications privilege
982	No FRE equivalent	No marital communications privilege in commitment or similar proceeding
983	No FRE equivalent	No marital communications privilege in proceeding to establish competence
984	No FRE equivalent	No marital communications privilege in proceeding between spouses
985	No FRE equivalent	No marital communications privilege in certain criminal proceedings

CEC	FRE	General Topic
986	No FRE equivalent	No marital communications privilege in juvenile court proceedings
987	No FRE equivalent	No marital communications privilege in communication offered by spouse who is criminal defendant
990	No FRE equivalent	Definition of "physician"
991	No FRE equivalent	Definition of "patient"
992	No FRE equivalent	Definition of "confidential communication between patient and physician"
993	No FRE equivalent	Definition of "holder of the privilege"
994	No FRE equivalent	Physician-patient privilege
995	No FRE equivalent	When physician required to claim privilege
996	No FRE equivalent	No physician-patient privilege concerning condition of patient where raised by patient as litigant
997	No FRE equivalent	Crime or tort exception to physician-patient privilege
998	No FRE equivalent	No physician-patient privilege in criminal proceeding
999	No FRE equivalent	No physician-patient privilege in proceeding to recover damages on account of conduct of patient
1000	No FRE equivalent	No physician-patient privilege where parties claiming through deceased patient
1001	No FRE equivalent	No physician-patient privilege as to issue of breach of duty arising out of physician-patient relationship
1002	No FRE equivalent	No physician-patient privilege re: intention of deceased patient concerning writing affecting property interest

CEC	FRE	General Topic
1003	No FRE equivalent	No physician-patient privilege re: validity of writing executed by deceased patient affecting property interest
1004	No FRE equivalent	No physician-patient privilege in commitment or similar proceeding
1005	No FRE equivalent	No physician-patient privilege in proceeding to establish competence
1006	No FRE equivalent	No physician-patient privilege as to information physician or patient is required to report
1007	No FRE equivalent	No physician-patient privilege in proceeding to terminate right, license, or privilege
1010	No FRE equivalent	Definition of "psychotherapist"
1010.5	No FRE equivalent	Patient-educational therapist privilege
1011	No FRE equivalent	Definition of "patient"
1012	No FRE equivalent	Definition of "confidential communication between patient and psychotherapist"
1013	No FRE equivalent	Definition of "holder of the privilege"
1014	No FRE equivalent	Psychotherapist-patient privilege
1015	No FRE equivalent	When psychotherapist is required to claim privilege
1016	No FRE equivalent	No psychotherapist-patient privilege concerning mental or emotional condition of patient where raised as patient as litigant
1017	No FRE equivalent	No psychotherapist-patient privilege where psychotherapist is appointed by court or Board of Prison Terms
1018	No FRE equivalent	Crime or tort exception to psychotherapist-patient privilege

CEC	FRE	General Topic
1019	No FRE equivalent	No psychotherapist-patient privilege for parties claiming through deceased patient
1020	No FRE equivalent	No psychotherapist-patient privilege as to issue of breach of duty arising out of psychotherapist-patient relationship
1021	No FRE equivalent	No psychotherapist-patient privilege re: intention of deceased patient concerning writing affecting property interest
1022	No FRE equivalent	No psychotherapist-patient privilege re: validity of writing by deceased patient affecting property interest
1023	No FRE equivalent	No psychotherapist-patient privilege in proceeding to determine sanity of criminal defendant
1024	No FRE equivalent	No psychotherapist-patient privilege where patient dangerous to self or others
1025	No FRE equivalent	No psychotherapist-patient privilege in proceeding to establish competence
1026	No FRE equivalent	No psychotherapist-patient privilege as to information psychotherapist or patient is required to report
1027	No FRE equivalent	No psychotherapist-patient privilege for patient under 16 who is victim of crime
1030	No FRE equivalent	Definition of "member of the clergy"
1031	No FRE equivalent	Definition of "penitent"
1032	No FRE equivalent	Definition of "penitential communication"
1033	No FRE equivalent	Privilege of penitent
1034	No FRE equivalent	Privilege of clergy member

CEC	FRE	General Topic
1035	No FRE equivalent	Definition of "victim" (sexual assault counselor-victim privilege)
1035.2	No FRE equivalent	Definition of "sexual assault counselor"
1035.4	No FRE equivalent	Definition of "confidential communication between the sexual assault counselor and the victim"
1035.6	No FRE equivalent	Definition of "holder of the privilege"
1035.8	No FRE equivalent	Victim of sexual assault's privilege
1036	No FRE equivalent	Sexual assault counselor's privilege
1036.2	No FRE equivalent	Definition of "sexual assault"
1037	No FRE equivalent	Definition of "victim" (domestic violence counselor-victim privilege)
1037.1	No FRE equivalent	Definitions of "domestic violence counselor" and "domestic violence victim service organization"
1037.2	No FRE equivalent	Definition of "confidential communication" and when court may compel disclosure (domestic violence counselor-victim privilege)
1037.3	No FRE equivalent	Effect of domestic violence counselor-victim privilege on obligation to report child abuse
1037.4	No FRE equivalent	Definition of "holder of the privilege" (domestic violence counselor-victim privilege)
1037.5	No FRE equivalent	Who may claim domestic violence counselor-victim privilege
1037.6	No FRE equivalent	When domestic violence counselor must claim privilege
1037.7	No FRE equivalent	Definition of "domestic violence"
1037.8	No FRE equivalent	Informing victim on limitations on confidentiality of communications

CEC	FRE	General Topic
1038	No FRE equivalent	Human trafficking caseworker-victim privilege
1038.1	No FRE equivalent	When court may compel disclosure of human trafficking-caseworker-victim privileged information
1038.2	No FRE equivalent	Definitions (human trafficking caseworker-victim privilege)
1038.3	No FRE equivalent	Human trafficking caseworker-victim privilege does not limit obligation to report child abuse
1040	No FRE equivalent	Privilege for official information
1041	No FRE equivalent	Privilege for identify of informer
1042	No FRE equivalent	Adverse order or finding re: official information privilege in certain cases
1043	No FRE equivalent	Discovery or disclosure of peace or custodial officer's personnel records
1044	No FRE equivalent	Access to medical or psychological history
1045	No FRE equivalent	Access to records of complaints where investigations or discipline concern peace officer
1046	No FRE equivalent	Motion to include copy of police report in excessive force case
1047	No FRE equivalent	Police records not subject to disclosure; disclosure of supervisorial officer's records
1050	No FRE equivalent	Privilege to protect secrecy of vote
1060	No FRE equivalent	Privilege to protect trade secret
1061	No FRE equivalent	Definitions of "trade secret" and "article"; procedure for assertion of trade secret privilege
1062	No FRE equivalent	Exclusion of public from portion of criminal proceeding in which trade secret may be disclosed

CEC	FRE	General Topic
1063	No FRE equivalent	Provisions governing requests to seal articles protected by trade secret privilege
1070	No FRE equivalent	Newsman's refusal to disclose news source
1100	405	Manner of proof of character
1101	404	Character evidence inadmissible to prove conduct
1102	404(a)(2)(A)	Opinion and reputation evidence of character of criminal defendant
1103	404(a)(2)(B), 412	Evidence of character of victim of crime
1104	404	Character trait for care or skill
1105	406	Habit or custom to prove specific behavior
1106	412	Specific instances of plaintiff's sexual conduct in civil action alleging sexual harassment
1107	No FRE equivalent	Admissibility of expert evidence regarding intimate partner violence
1107.5	No FRE equivalent	Admissibility of expert testimony regarding human trafficking
1108	413, 414, 415	Evidence of another sexual offense
1109	No FRE equivalent	Evidence of other acts of domestic violence, abuse of elder or dependent person, and child abuse
1115	No FRE equivalent	Definitions of "mediation," "mediator," and "mediation consultation"
1116	No FRE equivalent	Effect of chapter (on mediation)
1117	No FRE equivalent	Applicability of chapter (on mediation)
1118	No FRE equivalent	Definition of "oral agreement"

CEC	FRE	General Topic
1119	408	Inadmissibility/confidentiality of mediation communications, negotiations, and settlement discussions
1120	No FRE equivalent	Exceptions to inadmissibility of mediation communications
1121	No FRE equivalent	Admissibility of mediation report
1122	No FRE equivalent	Conditions for admissibility of mediation communication or writing
1123	No FRE equivalent	Admissibility of disclosure of written settlement agreement
1124	No FRE equivalent	Admissibility of disclosure of oral agreement
1125	No FRE equivalent	Conditions constituting the end of the mediation
1126	No FRE equivalent	Confidentiality after end of mediation
1127	No FRE equivalent	Attorney fees for compelling mediator to testify or produce writing
1128	No FRE equivalent	Reference to mediation during subsequent proceedings
1129	No FRE equivalent	Printed disclosure and acknowledgment requirements for mediation
1150	606(b)	Evidence to test a verdict
1151	407	Subsequent remedial conduct
1152	408, 409	Admissibility of evidence of offer to compromise
1153	410	Offer to plead guilty or withdraw plea of guilty by criminal defendant
1154	408	Offer to discount a claim
1155	411	Evidence of liability insurance
1156	No FRE equivalent	Records of medical or dental study of in-hospital staff committee

CEC	FRE	General Topic
1157	No FRE equivalent	Exemption from discovery of proceedings and records of specified committees and bodies
1160	No FRE equivalent	Statement of benevolence
1200	801(c), 802	Hearsay rule/definition of hearsay
1201	805	Multiple hearsay
1202	806	Credibility of hearsay declarant
1203	806	Cross-examination of hearsay declarant
1203.1	1101(d)(3)	Hearsay statements admissible at preliminary hearing
1204	No FRE equivalent	Hearsay statement offered against criminal defendant (where inadmissible under Constitution)
1205	No FRE equivalent	No implied repeal of any other statute relating to hearsay evidence
1220	801(d)(2)(A)	Admission of party
1221	801(d)(2)(B)	Adoptive admission
1222	801(d)(2)(C)	Authorized admission
1223	801(d)(2)(E)	Admission of co-conspirator
1224	801(d)(2)(D)	Statement of declarant whose liability or breach of duty is in issue
1225	No FRE equivalent	Statement of declarant whose right or title is in issue
1226	No FRE equivalent	Statement of minor child in parent's action for child's injury
1227	No FRE equivalent	Statement by deceased in wrongful death action
1228	No FRE equivalent	Statement of minor child as victim of sexual abuse
1230	804(b)(3)	Declarations against interest
1231	No FRE equivalent	Sworn statements regarding gang-related crimes

CEC	FRE	General Topic
1235[2]	801(d)(1)(A)	Prior inconsistent statement
1236	801(d)(1)(B)	Prior consistent statement
1237	803(5)	Past recollection recorded
1238	801(d)(1)(C)	Prior identification
1240	803(1), 803(2)	Spontaneous statement
1241	803(1), 803(2)	Contemporaneous statement
1242	804(b)(2)	Dying declaration
1250	803(3)	Statement of declarant's then-existing mental or physical state
1251	No FRE equivalent	Statement of declarant's previously existing mental or physical state
1252	No FRE equivalent	Limitation on admissibility of statement of mental or physical state (trustworthiness)
1253	803(4)	Statement describing medical history, symptoms, or pain, made for purposes of medical diagnosis or treatment
1260	803(3)	Statement concerning declarant's will or revocable trust
1261	No FRE equivalent	Statement of decedent offered in action against estate
1270	No FRE equivalent	Definition of "a business"
1271	803(6)	Business record exception
1272	803(7)	Absence of entry in business records
1280	803(8)	Public records exception
1281	803(9)	Vital statistics exception
1282	No FRE equivalent	Finding of presumed death by authorized federal employee

[2]The substantive difference between the FRE and CEC will no longer exist if the proposed amendment to FRE 801(d)(1)(A) takes effect on December 1, 2026.

CEC	FRE	General Topic
1283	No FRE equivalent	Record by federal employee that person is missing, captured, or the like
1284	803(10)	Absence of public records exception
1285	No FRE equivalent	Statements at civil hearing for person convicted of sexual offense
1290	804(b)(1)	Definition of "former testimony"
1291	804(b)(1)	Former testimony offered against party to former proceeding
1292	804(b)(1)	Former testimony offered against person not a party to former proceeding
1293	No FRE equivalent	Former testimony of minor against parent or guardian
1294	801(d)(1)(A)	Prior inconsistent statement (former testimony)
1300	803(22)	Exception for judgment of conviction of felony
1301	No FRE equivalent	Exception for judgment against person entitled to indemnity
1302	No FRE equivalent	Exception for judgment determining liability of third person
1310	804(b)(4)(A)	Statement concerning declarant's own family history
1311	804(b)(4)(B)	Statement concerning family history of another
1312	803(13)	Exception for entries in family records
1313	803(19)	Exception for reputation in family concerning family history
1314	803(19)	Exception for reputation in community concerning family history
1315	803(11)	Exception for church records concerning family history

CEC	FRE	General Topic
1316	803(12)	Exception for marriage, baptismal, and similar certificates
1320	803(21)	Exception for reputation concerning community history
1321	No FRE equivalent	Exception for reputation concerning public interest in property
1322	803(21)	Exception for reputation concerning boundary or custom affecting land
1323	803(20)	Exception for statement concerning boundary
1324	803(21)	Exception for reputation concerning character
1330	803(15)	Exception for recitals in writing affecting property
1331	803(16)	Exception for recitals in ancient writings
1340	803(17)	Exception for commercial lists and the like
1341	803(18)	Exceptions for publications containing facts of general notoriety and interest
1350	804(b)(6)	Admissibility of statement in serious felony prosecutions where declarant unavailable as witness
1360	No FRE equivalent	Exception for statement regarding child abuse or neglect made by child under age of 12
1370	No FRE equivalent	Exception for physical abuse
1380	No FRE equivalent	Effect of exception for physical abuse
1390	804(b)(6)	Exception for statement offered against party who wrongfully procured unavailability of declarant
1400	901(a)	Authentication defined
1401	901(a)	Authentication requirement
1402	No FRE equivalent	Authentication of altered writing

CEC	FRE	General Topic
1410	901(b) (non-exhaustive list)	Nothing in this article limits means by which writing may be authenticated
1410.5	No FRE equivalent	Vandalism/graffiti
1411	903	Necessity of subscribing witness's testimony for authentication
1412	No FRE equivalent	Use of other evidence when subscribing witness's testimony required
1413	901(b)(1)	Authentication by witness to the execution of a writing
1414	No FRE equivalent	Authentication by admission
1415	901(b)(2), (3)	Authentication by handwriting evidence
1416	901(b)(2)	Authentication of handwriting through opinion by person familiar therewith
1417	901(b)(3)	Authentication of handwriting through comparison made by trier of fact
1418	901(b)(3)	Authentication of handwriting through comparison made by expert witness
1419	901(b)(8)	Authentication of writing by exemplars when writing is 30 years old
1420	No FRE equivalent	Authentication by evidence of reply
1421	901(b)(4)	Authentication by content
1450	No FRE equivalent	Presumptions in this article are presumptions affecting burden of producing evidence
1451	902(8)	Acknowledged writings presumed to be genuine
1452	902(1)	Official seals presumed to be genuine

CEC	FRE	General Topic
1453	902(2)	Domestic official signatures presumed to be genuine
1454	902(3)	Foreign official signatures presumed to be genuine
1520	1002	Original writing as proof of content of a writing
1521	1002, 1006	Secondary evidence rule
1522	No FRE equivalent	Grounds for exclusion of secondary evidence of content of writing in criminal actions
1523	1002, 1004	Use of oral testimony to establish contents of writing
1530	1005	Copy of writing in official custody is prima facie evidence of existence and content of such writing
1531	1003	Certification of copy of writing for evidence
1532	1005	Official record of a writing as prima facie evidence of existence and content of original recorded writing
1550	1003	Photographic copies made as business records
1550.1	1003	Admissibility of reproduced files, records, writings, photographs, fingerprints or other instruments
1551	1003	Photographic copies where original lost or destroyed
1552	1003	Printed representation of computer information or computer program
1553	1003	Printed representation of images stored on video or digital medium
1560	No FRE equivalent	Compliance with subpoena duces tecum for business records
1561	No FRE equivalent	Contents of affidavit accompanying records

CEC	FRE	General Topic
1562	No FRE equivalent	Admissibility of affidavit and copy of records
1600	901(b)(7)	Official record of document affecting property interest
1601	1004(a)	Proof of content of lost official record affecting property
1603	901(b)(7), 902(4)	Deed by officer in pursuance of court process prima facie evidence of conveyance
1605	No FRE equivalent	Authenticated Spanish title records

Table of Major Differences Between the Federal Rules of Evidence and California Evidence Code

This table covers the major differences between the Federal Rules of Evidence (FRE) and California Evidence Code (CEC), setting forth the topic, the pertinent Rule(s) and Code section(s), and summarizing the major differences between the two bodies of law (some of which may exist in case law interpreting the Rules, the Code or the pertinent constitutional provisions). This table does *not* purport to list *all* of the differences.

Topic	FRE	CEC	Difference
Judicial Notice	201	450-459	FRE applies to adjudicative facts only; California applies to legislative and legal facts as well; FRE allows a broader range of sources to be considered for judicial notice than CEC §452
Presumptions	301	500, 550, 602, 604, 606	FRE (unlike CEC) only employs presumptions that shift the burden of production unless state law provides the rule of decision

Topic	FRE	CEC	Difference
Relevance	401	350	FRE (unlike CEC) does not require the fact to be in dispute; it only needs to be of consequence
Discretion of court to exclude relevant evidence	403	352	None
Character Evidence	404(a)	1101(a)	None
Defendant's Character	404(a)(2)(A), FRE 405	1102	None
Victim's Character	404(a)(2)(B), (a)(2)(B), FRE 405	1103	(1) FRE allows character evidence of a victim through reputation and opinion testimony only; CEC allows specific acts as well (2) FRE allows introduction of *any* character trait of the victim after evidence of defendant's trait is admitted (but CEC limits it to trait for violence) (3) FRE (unlike CEC) allows prosecution to introduce evidence that victim had "peaceful" character if defendant introduces any evidence that the victim was the "first aggressor"

Topic	FRE	CEC	Difference
Character for Truth and Veracity	404(a)(3), 608	1100, 780, 786, 787, 790	(1) In FRE, specific instances of character for truth and veracity may be inquired into on cross examination; in CEC, that is only permitted in criminal cases due to the California Constitution (2) In FRE, extrinsic evidence may not be admitted to prove a specific instance of character for truth and veracity; in CEC, extrinsic evidence is permitted in criminal cases due to the California Constitution (3) In FRE (unlike CEC), the "bad before good" rule applies in all cases; in CEC, it only applies in civil cases due to the California Constitution (4) FRE permits inquiry into specific acts on cross-examination to attack truthfulness; California law does not
Other Crimes, Wrongs, Acts	404(b)	1101(b)	None
Subsequent Remedial Measures	407	1151	FRE (unlike CEC) prohibits admission of subsequent remedial measures in product defect or failure to warn cases based on strict liability
Humanitarian Gestures	409	1152, 1160	Under FRE, only the offer to pay medical expenses is barred; under CEC, both offer and accompanying statements of fault are barred

Topic	FRE	CEC	Difference
Criminal Pleas and Plea Negotiations	410	1153	FRE bars admission of failed guilty and nolo contendere pleas (CEC bars only admission of failed guilty pleas); FRE (unlike CEC) also bars admission of statements during plea discussion with an attorney for the prosecuting authority
Victim's Sexual Behavior	412	1103, 782, 1103, 1106	Both rules are "rape shield laws" that can apply in criminal and civil cases, although CEC is considered in conjunction with CEC 782 and 783 and may allow sexual history to challenge credibility
Propensity evidence in sexual assault and domestic violence cases	413-415	1108, 1109	FRC is strictly limited to prior sexual assaults and child molestations to prove propensity, while CEC also extends to prior acts of domestic violence, elder abuse, and child abuse
Privileges	501, 502	910, 912, 917, 950-1070	(1) FRE (unlike CEC) allows a court to examine privileged material to examine whether an exception to the privilege applies (2) The contours of many of the privileges under federal common law differ from those under CEC
Competency of Jurors to Impeach Verdict	606(b)	1150	FRE (unlike CEC) generally bars admission of what was said or done during jury deliberations to impeach a verdict

Topic	FRE	CEC	Difference
Prior Convictions to Impeach	609	788	FRE uses a series of differing balancing tests to assess which felony and dishonesty-related misdemeanor convictions may be used to impeach, while CEC entrusts courts to engage in a case-by-case balancing
Expert Opinion Testimony	702, 703	720, 801, 804	(1) FRE (unlike CEC) uses *Daubert* test; CEC uses *Frye* test for scientific expert testimony and a *Daubert*-like test for other expert testimony (2) FRE allows an expert to relay inadmissible evidence when explaining the basis of opinion as "non-hearsay" evidence, while CEC prohibits experts from relaying "case-specific facts" that form the basis for an expert opinion
Prior Inconsistent and Consistent Statements	801(d)(1)(A), 801(d)(1)(B)	1235, 1236, 1294, 1236	(1) Until possibly Dec 1, 2026 (when a change to FRE 801(d)(1)(A) may take effect), FRE (unlike CEC) requires prior inconsistent statements to be under oath (2) FRE (unlike CEC) only requires a prior consistent statement to come *before* a motive to fabricate when admitting it for its truth
Present Sense Impression Exception	803(1)	1241	CEC (unlike FRE) limits the exception to statements pertaining to the declarant's conduct

Topic	FRE	CEC	Difference
State of Mind Exception	803(3)	1250-1252	FRE (unlike CEC) only applies to present/then-existing state of mind or future intent or plan; CEC applies to past state of mind if the declarant is unavailable
Statements for Medical Diagnosis or Treatment Exception	803(4)	1253	FRE applies broadly to anyone's mental/physical state; CEC is limited exclusively to statements by minors in child abuse/neglect cases; otherwise, statements of past or present physical condition must satisfy the state of mind exception at CEC 1250-1252
Public Records Exception	803(8)	1280-1282	FRE (unlike CEC) has three specific categories of public records that fall within the exception; CEC's exception largely tracks its business records exception
Former Testimony Exception	804(b)(1)	1290-1292	CEC (but not FRE) permits former testimony to be admitted in civil cases against a non-party and in criminal cases if the former testimony was introduced by the party's "predecessor in interest"
Dying Declaration Exception	804(b)(2)	1242	(1) FRE restricts use to homicide cases or civil cases; CEC allows them in all cases (2) CEC only applies if the declarant actually dies
Ancient Document Exception	803(16)	1331	FRE requires document to be 20 years old; CEC requires 30 years old

Topic	**FRE**	**CEC**	**Difference**
Residual Hearsay Exception	807	No CEC equivalent	FRE (unlike CEC) has a residual hearsay exception
Best Evidence Rule	1001-1008	1520-1523, 1530-1532, 1550-1553	(1) FRE (unlike CEC) has exceptions to the best evidence rule when original writings are in the possession of the objecting party and when the content of the writing has been admitted by the objecting party (2) FRE (unlike CEC) has a different procedure for admitting "copies" of "official records"

www.ingramcontent.com/pod-product-compliance
Lightning Source LLC
LaVergne TN
LVHW080634011026
849160LV00014B/1209
* 9 7 9 8 8 9 9 6 3 9 2 7 2 *